330 Flynn
Flynn
Economics
WITHDRAWN
3rd edition.

W9-AQZ-605

$22.99
on1035015735

Economics

3rd Edition

by Sean Masaki Flynn, PhD

for dummies®

A Wiley Brand

Economics For Dummies®, 3rd Edition

Published by: **John Wiley & Sons, Inc.,** 111 River Street, Hoboken, NJ 07030-5774, www.wiley.com

Copyright © 2018 by John Wiley & Sons, Inc., Hoboken, New Jersey

Published simultaneously in Canada

No part of this publication may be reproduced, stored in a retrieval system or transmitted in any form or by any means, electronic, mechanical, photocopying, recording, scanning or otherwise, except as permitted under Sections 107 or 108 of the 1976 United States Copyright Act, without the prior written permission of the Publisher. Requests to the Publisher for permission should be addressed to the Permissions Department, John Wiley & Sons, Inc., 111 River Street, Hoboken, NJ 07030, (201) 748-6011, fax (201) 748-6008, or online at http://www.wiley.com/go/permissions.

Trademarks: Wiley, For Dummies, the Dummies Man logo, Dummies.com, Making Everything Easier, and related trade dress are trademarks or registered trademarks of John Wiley & Sons, Inc., and may not be used without written permission. All other trademarks are the property of their respective owners. John Wiley & Sons, Inc., is not associated with any product or vendor mentioned in this book.

LIMIT OF LIABILITY/DISCLAIMER OF WARRANTY: WHILE THE PUBLISHER AND AUTHOR HAVE USED THEIR BEST EFFORTS IN PREPARING THIS BOOK, THEY MAKE NO REPRESENTATIONS OR WARRANTIES WITH RESPECT TO THE ACCURACY OR COMPLETENESS OF THE CONTENTS OF THIS BOOK AND SPECIFICALLY DISCLAIM ANY IMPLIED WARRANTIES OF MERCHANTABILITY OR FITNESS FOR A PARTICULAR PURPOSE. NO WARRANTY MAY BE CREATED OR EXTENDED BY SALES REPRESENTATIVES OR WRITTEN SALES MATERIALS. THE ADVICE AND STRATEGIES CONTAINED HEREIN MAY NOT BE SUITABLE FOR YOUR SITUATION. YOU SHOULD CONSULT WITH A PROFESSIONAL WHERE APPROPRIATE. NEITHER THE PUBLISHER NOR THE AUTHOR SHALL BE LIABLE FOR DAMAGES ARISING HEREFROM.

For general information on our other products and services, please contact our Customer Care Department within the U.S. at 877-762-2974, outside the U.S. at 317-572-3993, or fax 317-572-4002. For technical support, please visit https://hub.wiley.com/community/support/dummies.

Wiley publishes in a variety of print and electronic formats and by print-on-demand. Some material included with standard print versions of this book may not be included in e-books or in print-on-demand. If this book refers to media such as a CD or DVD that is not included in the version you purchased, you may download this material at http://booksupport.wiley.com. For more information about Wiley products, visit www.wiley.com.

Library of Congress Control Number: 2018937401

ISBN 978-1-119-47638-2 (pbk); ISBN 978-1-119-47627-6 (ebk); ISBN 978-1-119-47632-0 (epdf)

Manufactured in the United States of America

10 9 8 7 6 5 4 3 2 1

Contents at a Glance

Introduction 1

Part 1: Economics: The Science of How People Deal with Scarcity 5
- CHAPTER 1: What Economics Is and Why You Should Care 7
- CHAPTER 2: Cookies or Ice Cream? Exploring Consumer Choices 21
- CHAPTER 3: Producing Stuff to Maximize Happiness 33

Part 2: Microeconomics: The Science of Consumer and Firm Behavior 55
- CHAPTER 4: Supply and Demand Made Easy 57
- CHAPTER 5: Introducing Homo Economicus, the Utility-Maximizing Consumer 83
- CHAPTER 6: The Core of Capitalism: The Profit-Maximizing Firm 101
- CHAPTER 7: Why Economists Love Free Markets and Competition 127
- CHAPTER 8: Monopolies: Bad Behavior without Competition 151
- CHAPTER 9: Oligopoly and Monopolistic Competition: Middle Grounds 173

Part 3: Applying the Theories of Microeconomics 191
- CHAPTER 10: Property Rights and Wrongs 193
- CHAPTER 11: Asymmetric Information and Public Goods 205
- CHAPTER 12: Health Economics and Healthcare Finance 221
- CHAPTER 13: Behavioral Economics: Investigating Irrationality 237

Part 4: Macroeconomics: The Science of Economic Growth and Stability 255
- CHAPTER 14: How Economists Measure the Macroeconomy 257
- CHAPTER 15: Inflation Frustration: Why More Money Isn't Always Good 277
- CHAPTER 16: Understanding Why Recessions Happen 297
- CHAPTER 17: Fighting Recessions with Monetary and Fiscal Policy 325
- CHAPTER 18: Grasping Origins and Effects of Financial Crises 353

Part 5: The Part of Tens 363
- CHAPTER 19: Ten Seductive Economic Fallacies 365
- CHAPTER 20: Ten Economic Ideas to Hold Dear 371
- CHAPTER 21: Ten (Or So) Famous Economists 375

Appendix: Glossary 383

Index 389

Table of Contents

INTRODUCTION 1
About This Book. 1
Foolish Assumptions. 3
Icons Used in This Book 3
Beyond the Book 4
Where to Go from Here 4

PART 1: ECONOMICS: THE SCIENCE OF HOW
PEOPLE DEAL WITH SCARCITY 5

CHAPTER 1: **What Economics Is and Why You Should Care** 7
Considering a Little Economic History 8
Pondering just how nasty, brutish, and short life used to be 8
Identifying the institutions that raise living standards. 9
Looking toward the future 10
Framing Economics as the Science of Scarcity 10
Sending Microeconomics and Macroeconomics to
Separate Corners. 11
Getting up close and personal: Microeconomics 11
Zooming out: Macroeconomics and the big picture 14
Understanding How Economists Use Models and Graphs 16
Introducing your first model: The demand curve. 17
Drawing your own demand curve. 20

CHAPTER 2: **Cookies or Ice Cream? Exploring Consumer
Choices** 21
Describing Human Behavior with a Choice Model. 22
Pursuing Personal Happiness 23
Using utility to measure happiness 23
Taking "selfless" actions into account. 23
Self-interest can promote the common good. 24
You Can't Have Everything: Examining Limitations 25
Resource constraints 25
Technology constraints. 25
Time constraints 26
Opportunity cost: The unavoidable cost 26
Making Your Choice: Deciding What and How Much You Want. 27
Exploring Violations and Limitations of the Economist's Choice
Model 29
Understanding uninformed decision-making. 29
Making sense of irrationality 30

CHAPTER 3: **Producing Stuff to Maximize Happiness** 33

Figuring Out What's Possible to Produce 34

Classifying resources 35

Clarifying human capital 35

Diminishing returns 36

Allocating resources 37

Graphing your production possibilities 38

Reaching new frontiers with better technology 41

Deciding What to Produce 42

Comparing market results and government interventions 43

Opting for a mixed economy 49

Promoting Technology and Innovation 52

PART 2: MICROECONOMICS: THE SCIENCE
OF CONSUMER AND FIRM BEHAVIOR 55

CHAPTER 4: **Supply and Demand Made Easy** 57

Deconstructing Demand 58

Prices and other stuff: Looking at what affects quantity
demanded 59

Graphing the demand curve 60

Opportunity costs: Setting the slope of the demand curve . . 62

Elasticity: Looking at extreme demand cases 63

Sorting Out Supply 65

Graphing the supply curve 65

Using elasticity to understand extreme supply cases 69

Bringing Supply and Demand Together 70

Market equilibrium: Seeking a balance 71

Demonstrating the stability of the market equilibrium 72

Adjusting to new market equilibriums when supply or
demand changes 74

Price Controls: Keeping Prices Away from Market Equilibrium 76

Setting upper limits with price ceilings 77

Propping up prices with price floors 79

CHAPTER 5: **Introducing Homo Economicus, the
Utility-Maximizing Consumer** 83

Choosing by Ranking 84

Getting Less from More: Diminishing Marginal Utility 85

Choosing Among Many Options When Facing a Limited Budget . . . 88

Trying to buy as much (marginal) utility as you can 88

Purchasing the best combination of two goods to
maximize total utility 91

Aiming for equal marginal utility per dollar 93

Deriving Demand Curves from Diminishing Marginal Utility 95

Seeing how price changes affect quantities demanded 96

Graphing the price and quantity changes to form
a demand curve. 97

CHAPTER 6: **The Core of Capitalism: The Profit-
Maximizing Firm** 101

A Firm's Goal: Maximizing Profits 102

Facing Competition 103

Listing the requirements for perfect competition 103

Taking prices but setting quantities 104

Distinguishing between accounting profits and
economic profits 106

Analyzing a Firm's Cost Structure 107

Focusing on costs per unit of output 108

Examining average variable costs. 110

Watching average fixed costs fall 111

Tracking the movement of average total costs. 111

Focusing on marginal costs 112

Noticing where marginal cost equals average cost 113

Comparing Marginal Revenues with Marginal Costs 115

Finding where marginal revenue equals marginal cost. 116

Visualizing profits 118

Visualizing losses. 120

Pulling the Plug: When Producing Nothing Is Your Best Bet. 121

Distinguishing between the short run and the long run
in microeconomics 122

The short-run shutdown condition: Variable costs
exceed total revenues. 123

The long-run shutdown condition: Total costs exceed
total revenues 125

CHAPTER 7: **Why Economists Love Free Markets and
Competition** 127

Ensuring That Benefits Exceed Costs: Competitive
Free Markets 128

Examining the traits of a properly functioning market 129

Analyzing the efficiency of free markets 130

Measuring everyone's gains with total surplus. 132

When Free Markets Lose Their Freedom: Dealing with
Deadweight Losses 138

Coming up short: The deadweight loss from a price ceiling. . . . 139

Death and taxes: Finding the deadweight loss of a tax 140

Hallmarks of Perfect Competition: Zero Profits and Lowest
Possible Costs 143

Understanding the causes and consequences of
perfect competition. 144
Peering into the process of perfect competition 145
Graphing how profits guide firm entry and exit 146

CHAPTER 8: **Monopolies: Bad Behavior without
Competition** 151
Examining Profit-Maximizing Monopolies. .152
Zeroing in on the problems monopolies cause 152
Identifying the source of the problem: Decreasing
marginal revenues. 153
Choosing an output level to maximize profits 158
Comparing Monopolies with Competitive Firms 161
Looking at output and price levels 162
Deadweight losses: Quantifying the harm caused
by monopolies. 163
Losing efficiency. 164
Considering Good Monopolies 165
Encouraging innovation and investment with patents 165
Reducing annoyingly redundant competitors. 165
Keeping costs low with natural monopolies 166
Regulating Monopolies. 167
Subsidizing a monopoly to increase output 167
Imposing minimum output requirements. 167
Regulating monopoly pricing. 168
Breaking up a monopoly into several competing firms. 171

CHAPTER 9: **Oligopoly and Monopolistic Competition:
Middle Grounds** 173
Oligopolies: Looking at the Allure of Joining Forces. 174
Sharing power over prices 174
Cartel behavior: Trying to imitate monopolists. 175
Considering the criteria for coordinating a cartel. 176
Understanding Incentives to Cheat the Cartel 176
Fleshing out the Prisoner's Dilemma 177
Enforcing the agreement: Resolving the dilemma
with credible threats. 180
Seeing that OPEC is trapped in a Prisoner's Dilemma 181
Using an enforcer to help OPEC members stick to quotas 182
Regulating Oligopolies 183
Breaking up dominant firms 184
Attempting to apply antitrust laws 184
Studying a Hybrid: Monopolistic Competition 185
Benefiting from product differentiation. 185
Facing profit limits. 186

PART 3: APPLYING THE THEORIES OF MICROECONOMICS 191

CHAPTER 10: **Property Rights and Wrongs** 193

Allowing Markets to Reach Socially Optimal Outcomes 194

Examining Externalities: The Costs and Benefits Others Feel from Your Actions 195

Noting the effects of negative externalities 196

Accepting positive amounts of negative externalities 198

Dealing with negative externalities 199

Calculating the consequences of positive externalities 200

Subsidizing things that provide positive externalities 201

Tragedy of the Commons: Overexploiting Commonly Owned Resources 202

Overgrazing on a commonly owned field 202

Extinctions and poor property rights 203

Avoiding the tragedy 204

CHAPTER 11: **Asymmetric Information and Public Goods** 205

Facing Up to Asymmetric Information 206

Realizing that asymmetric information limits trade 206

Souring on the lemons problem: The used car market 207

Issuing insurance when you can't tell individuals apart 211

Providing Public Goods 215

Taxing to provide public goods 216

Enlisting philanthropy to provide public goods 216

Providing a public good by selling a related private good 217

Ranking new technology as a public good 219

CHAPTER 12: **Health Economics and Healthcare Finance** 221

Defining Health Economics and Healthcare Finance 222

Noting the Limits of Health Insurance 222

Adverse selection: Looking at who buys insurance 223

Combating adverse selection 224

Comparing Healthcare Internationally 227

Inflated Demand: Suffering from "Free" and Reduced-Cost Healthcare 228

Diverting funds to lower-value uses 228

Rationing healthcare 229

Facing shortages and higher prices 230

Combatting inefficiency with bureaucracy 231

Investigating Singapore's Secrets 233

Exploring cost-saving features 233

Weighing costs and benefits of medical procedures 234

Supporting cost-cutting innovations 234

Trying to copy Singapore's success 235

CHAPTER 13: **Behavioral Economics: Investigating Irrationality** 237

Explaining the Need for Behavioral Economics 238
Complementing Neo-Classical Economics with Behavioral Economics. 239
Examining our Amazing, Efficient, and Error-Prone Brains. 240
Deciphering heuristics 240
Deconstructing brain modularity 242
Cogitating on cognitive biases. 242
Surveying Prospect Theory 244
Shrinking packages and loss aversion 245
Framing effects and advertising 245
Anchoring and credit card bills 246
Examining the endowment effect. 247
Stipulating status quo bias. 247
Countering Myopia and Time Inconsistency. 248
Focusing on myopia 249
Tattling on time inconsistency. 249
Beating self-control problems with precommitments. 250
Gauging Fairness and Self-Interest. 251
Defining fairness 251
Examining the experimental evidence for fairness 251
Digesting the experimental evidence on fairness 253

PART 4: MACROECONOMICS: THE SCIENCE OF ECONOMIC GROWTH AND STABILITY. 255

CHAPTER 14: **How Economists Measure the Macroeconomy**. . . . 257

Getting a Grip on the GDP (and Its Parts) 258
Leaving some things out of GDP. 259
Tallying up what counts in GDP. 259
Accounting for streams of incomes, and assets 260
Following the funds, around and around 262
Counting stuff when it's made, not when it's sold 263
Watching GDP rise with the good, the bad, and the ugly 264
Diving In to the GDP Equation. 265
"C" is for consumption (that's good enough for me!). 266
"I" is for investment in capital stock 268
The big "G" (government, that is). 269
Measuring foreign trade with "NX" 270
Making Sense of International Trade and Its Effect on the Economy. 271
"Trade deficit" ain't fightin' words 272
Considering assets — not just cash 273
Wielding a comparative advantage. 274

CHAPTER 15: **Inflation Frustration: Why More Money Isn't Always Good**..................277

Buying an Inflation: When Too Much Money Is a Bad Thing........279
  Balancing money supply and demand.......................279
  Giving in to the inflation temptation....................282
  Tallying up the effects of inflation....................286
Measuring Inflation...287
  Creating your very own market basket 288
  Calculating the inflation rate 289
  Setting up a price index 290
  Determining the real standard of living with the price index 291
  Identifying price index problems 292
Pricing the Future: Nominal and Real Interest Rates.............293
  Using the Fisher equation 294
  Realizing that predictions aren't perfect 294

CHAPTER 16: **Understanding Why Recessions Happen**...........297

Introducing the Business Cycle 298
Striving for Full-Employment Output 299
Returning to Y*: The Natural Result of Price Adjustments 300
Responding to Economic Shocks: Short-Run and Long-Run Effects 301
  Defining some critical terms 301
  The tao of P: Looking at price adjustments in the long run 303
  A shock to the system: Adjusting to a shift in aggregate demand 304
  Dealing with fixed prices in the short run 305
  Putting together the long and short of it..................308
Heading toward Recession: Getting Stuck with Sticky Prices 309
  Cutting wages or cutting workers 310
  Adding up the costs of wages and profits 310
  Returning to Y* with and without government intervention 311
Achieving Equilibrium with Sticky Prices: The Keynesian Model.....312
  Adjusting inventories instead of prices 314
  Boosting GDP in the Keynesian model.....................322

CHAPTER 17: **Fighting Recessions with Monetary and Fiscal Policy**..325

Stimulating Demand to End Recessions 326
  Aiming for full-employment output 326
  Back to work: Shifting the AD curve right 328

Generating Inflation: The Risk of Too Much Stimulation..........328
    Trying to increase output beyond Y*......................329
    Tracing the movement of real wages......................331
    Failing to stimulate: What happens when a stimulus
    is expected..333
Figuring Out Fiscal Policy..336
    Increasing government spending to help end recessions......337
    Dealing with deficits......................................338
Dissecting Monetary Policy..340
    Identifying the benefits of fiat money over the
    gold standard..341
    Realizing you can have too much money!....................342
    Getting the basics about bonds.............................344
    Seeing the link between bond prices and interest rates.......345
    Changing the money supply to change interest rates.........346
    Lowering interest rates to stimulate the economy 346
    Understanding how rational expectations can
    limit monetary policy 348
    Examining quantitative easing and the Great Recession 350

CHAPTER 18: **Grasping Origins and Effects of Financial Crises** 353
Understanding How Debt-Driven Bubbles Develop.............354
    Embracing borrowing in a booming economy 355
    Offering larger loans as collateral values rise 355
    Relaxing lending standards 356
    Borrowing more in hopes of profit..........................356
    Watching the process gain momentum......................357
Seeing the Bubble Burst...357
    Deleveraging: Trying to ditch debt as prices fall..............358
    Comprehending bank collapses caused by
    bursting bubbles...358
    Leading into a recession....................................359
After the Crisis: Looking at Recovery 360
    Enduring a broken banking system 360
    Struggling with structural mismatches......................361
    Noting the limits of government policy 362

PART 5: THE PART OF TENS.......................................363

CHAPTER 19: **Ten Seductive Economic Fallacies** 365
The Lump of Labor...365
The World Is Facing Overpopulation 366
Sequence Indicates Causation....................................366
Protectionism Is the Best Solution to Foreign Competition 367

The Fallacy of Composition 368
If It's Worth Doing, Do It 100 Percent 368
Free Markets Are Dangerously Unstable .369
Low Foreign Wages Mean That Rich Countries Can't Compete 369
Tax Rates Don't Affect Work Effort 370
Forgetting Unintended Consequences. 370

CHAPTER 20: Ten Economic Ideas to Hold Dear 371
Self-Interest Can Improve Society. 371
Free Markets Require Regulation 372
Economic Growth Relies on Innovation 372
Freedom and Democracy Make Us Richer. 372
Education Raises Living Standards 372
Intellectual Property Boosts Innovation. .373
Weak Property Rights Cause All Environmental Problems 373
International Trade Is a Good Thing. 373
Government Can Provide Public Goods. .374
Preventing Inflation Is Easy 374

CHAPTER 21: Ten (Or So) Famous Economists 375
Adam Smith 375
David Ricardo. 376
Karl Marx 376
Alfred Marshall. 377
John Maynard Keynes 378
Kenneth Arrow and Gerard Debreu 378
Milton Friedman 378
Paul Samuelson 379
Robert Solow 379
Gary Becker 380
Robert Lucas 380

APPENDIX: GLOSSARY 383

INDEX 389

Introduction

Economics is all about humanity's struggle to achieve happiness in a world full of constraints. There's never enough time or money to do everything people want, and things like curing cancer are still impossible because the necessary technologies haven't been developed yet. But people are clever. They tinker and invent, ponder and innovate. They look at what they have and what they can do with it and take steps to make sure that if they can't have everything, they'll at least have as much as possible.

Having to choose is a fundamental part of everyday life. The science that studies *how* people choose — economics — is indispensable if you really want to understand human beings both as individuals and as members of larger organizations. Sadly, though, economics has typically been explained so badly that people either dismiss it as impenetrable gobbledygook or stand falsely in awe of it — after all, if it's hard to understand, it must be important, right?

I wrote this book so you can quickly and easily understand economics for what it is — a serious science that studies a serious subject and has developed some seriously good ways of explaining human behavior out in the (very serious) real world. Economics touches on nearly everything, so the returns on reading this book are huge. You'll understand much more about people, the government, international relations, business, and even environmental issues.

About This Book

The Scottish historian Thomas Carlyle called economics the "dismal science," but I'm going to do my best to make sure that you don't come to agree with him. I've organized this book to try to get as much economics into you as quickly and effortlessly as possible. I've also done my best to keep it lively and fun.

In this book, you find the most important economic theories, hypotheses, and discoveries without a zillion obscure details, outdated examples, or complicated mathematical "proofs." Among the topics covered are

>> How the government fights recessions and unemployment

>> How and why international trade is good for both individuals and nations

>> Why poorly designed property rights are responsible for environmental problems such as global warming, pollution, and species extinctions

>> How profits guide businesses to produce the goods and services you take for granted

>> How economic incentives affect healthcare costs, prices, and efficiency

>> Why competitive firms are almost always better for society than monopolies

>> How the Federal Reserve controls the money supply, interest rates, and inflation all at the same time

>> Why government policies such as price controls and subsidies often cause much more harm than good

>> How the simple supply and demand model can explain the prices of everything from comic books to open-heart surgeries

You can read the chapters in any order, and you can immediately jump to what you need to know without having to read a bunch of stuff that you couldn't care less about.

Economists like competition, so you shouldn't be surprised that there are a lot of competing views. Indeed, it's only through vigorous debate and careful review of the evidence that the profession improves its understanding of how the world works. This book contains core ideas and concepts that economists agree are true and important — I try to steer clear of fads or ideas that foster a lot of disagreement. (If you want to be subjected to my opinions and pet theories, you'll have to buy me a drink.)

Note: Economics is full of two things you may not find very appealing: jargon and algebra. To minimize confusion, whenever I introduce a new term, I put it in *italics* and follow it closely with an easy-to-understand definition. Also, whenever I bring algebra into the discussion, I use those handy *italics* again to let you know that I'm referring to a mathematical variable. For instance, I is the abbreviation for investment, so you may see a sentence like this one: I think that I is too big.

I try to keep equations to a minimum, but sometimes they help make things clearer. In such instances, I sometimes have to use several equations one after another. To avoid confusion about which equation I'm referring to at any given time, I give each equation a number, which I put in parentheses. For example,

$$(1) \quad E = mc^2$$

$$(2) \quad MTV = ESPN + CNN^2$$

Foolish Assumptions

I wrote this book assuming some things about you:

» You're sharp, thoughtful, and interested in how the world works.

» You're a high school or college student trying to flesh out what you're learning in class, or you're a citizen of the world who realizes that a good grounding in economics will help you understand everything from business and politics to social issues like poverty and environmental degradation.

» You want to know some economics, but you're also busy leading a very full life. Consequently, although you want the crucial facts, you don't want to have to read through a bunch of minutiae to find them.

» You're not totally intimidated by numbers, facts, and figures. Indeed, you welcome them because you like to have things proven to you instead of taking them on faith because some pinhead with a PhD says so.

» You like learning *why* as well as *what*. That is, you want to know why things happen and how they work instead of just memorizing factoids.

Icons Used in This Book

To make this book easier to read and simpler to use, I include a few icons that can help you find and fathom key ideas and information.

REMEMBER

This icon alerts you that I'm explaining a fundamental economic concept or fact that you would do well to stash away in your memory for later. It saves you the time and effort of marking the book with a highlighter.

TECHNICAL STUFF

This icon tells you that the ideas and information that it accompanies are a bit more technical or mathematical than other sections of the book. This information can be interesting and informative, but I've designed the book so that you don't need to understand it to get the big picture about what's going on. Feel free to skip this stuff.

TIP

This icon points out time and energy savers. I place this icon next to suggestions for ways to do or think about things that can save you some effort.

This icon discusses any troublesome areas in economics you need to know. Keep an eye open for them to alert you of potential pitfalls.

WARNING

Beyond the Book

To view this book's Cheat Sheet, simply go to www.dummies.com and search for "Economics For Dummies Cheat Sheet" for a handy reference guide that answers common questions about economics.

To gain access to the additional tests and practice online, all you have to do is register. Just follow these simple steps:

1. **Find your PIN access code.**

   Print-book users: If you purchased a print copy of this book, turn to the inside front cover of the book to find your access code.

   E-book users: If you purchased this book as an e-book, you can get your access code by registering your e-book at www.dummies.com/go/getaccess. Go to that website and find your book. Click it and answer the security questions to verify your purchase. You'll receive an email with your access code.

2. **Go to Dummies.com and click Activate Now.**

3. **Find your product (*Economics For Dummies*, 3rd Edition) and then follow the on-screen prompts to activate your PIN.**

Now you're ready to go! You can come back to the program as often as you want — simply log in with the username and password you created during your initial login. No need to enter the access code a second time.

For Technical Support, please visit http://wiley.custhelp.com or call Wiley at 1-800-762-2974 (U.S.), +1-317-572-3994 (international).

Where to Go from Here

This book is set up so that you can understand what's going on even if you skip around. The book is also divided into independent parts so that you can, for instance, read all about microeconomics without having to read anything about macroeconomics. The table of contents and index can help you find specific topics easily. But, hey, if you don't know where to begin, just do the old-fashioned thing and start at the beginning.

1

Economics: The Science of How People Deal with Scarcity

IN THIS PART . . .

Find out what economics is, what economists do, and why these things are important.

Decipher how people decide what brings them the most happiness.

Understand how goods and services are produced, how resources are allocated, and the roles of government and the market.

» Observing how people cope with scarcity

» Separating macroeconomics and microeconomics

» Getting a grip on the graphs and models that economists love to use

Chapter **1**

What Economics Is and Why You Should Care

E conomics is the science that studies how people and societies make decisions that allow them to get the most out of their limited resources. And because every country, every business, and every person has to deal with constraints, economics is literally everywhere. For instance, you could be doing something else right now besides reading this book. You could be exercising, watching a movie, or talking with a friend. You should only be reading this book if doing so is the best possible use of your very limited time. In the same way, you should hope that the paper and ink used to make this book have been put to their best use and that every last tax dollar that your government spends is being used in the best way.

Economics gets to the heart of these issues, analyzing the behavior of individuals and firms, as well as social and political institutions, to see how well they convert humanity's limited resources into the goods and services that best satisfy human wants and desires.

Considering a Little Economic History

To better understand today's economic situation and what sort of policy and institutional changes may promote the greatest improvements, you have to look back on economic history to see how humanity got to where it is now. Stick with me: I make this discussion as painless as possible.

Pondering just how nasty, brutish, and short life used to be

For most of human history, people didn't manage to squeeze much out of their limited resources. Standards of living were quite low, and people lived poor, short, and rather painful lives. Consider the following facts, which didn't change until just a few centuries ago:

>> Life expectancy at birth was about 25 years.

>> More than 30 percent of newborns never made it to their fifth birthdays.

>> A woman had a one in ten chance of dying every time she gave birth.

>> Most people had experienced horrible diseases and/or starvation.

>> The standard of living was low and stayed low, generation after generation. Except for the nobles, everybody lived at or near subsistence, century after century.

In the last 250 years or so, however, everything changed. For the first time in history, people figured out how to use electricity, engines, complicated machines, computers, radio, television, biotechnology, scientific agriculture, antibiotics, aviation, and a host of other technologies. Each has allowed people to do much more with the limited amounts of air, water, soil, and sea they were given on planet Earth. The result has been an explosion in living standards, with life expectancy at birth now over 70 years worldwide and with many people able to afford much better housing, clothing, and food than was imaginable a few hundred years ago.

Of course, not everything is perfect. Grinding poverty is still a fact in a large fraction of the world, and even the richest nations have to cope with pressing economic problems like unemployment and how to transition workers from dying industries to growing industries. But the fact remains that overall, the modern world is a much richer place than its predecessor, and most nations now have sustained economic growth, which means that living standards rise year after year.

Identifying the institutions that raise living standards

The obvious reason for higher living standards, which continue to rise, is that human beings have recently figured out lots of new technologies, and people keep inventing more. But if you dig a little deeper, you have to wonder why a technologically innovative society didn't happen earlier.

The Ancient Greeks invented a simple steam engine and the coin-operated vending machine. They even developed the basic idea behind the programmable computer. But they never quite got around to having an industrial revolution and entering on a path of sustained economic growth.

And despite the fact that there have always been really smart people in every society on earth, it wasn't until the late 18th century, in England, that the Industrial Revolution actually got started and living standards in many nations rose substantially and kept on rising, year after year.

REMEMBER

So what factors combined in the late 18th century to so radically accelerate economic growth? The short answer is that the following institutions were in place:

>> **Democracy:** Because the common people outnumbered the nobles, the advent of democracy meant that for the first time, governments reflected the interests of a society at large. A major result was the creation of government policy that favored merchants and manufacturers rather than the nobility.

>> **The limited liability corporation:** Under this business structure, investors could lose only the amount of their investment and not be liable for any debts that the corporation couldn't pay. Limited liability greatly reduced the risks of investing in businesses and, consequently, led to much more investing.

>> **Patent rights to protect inventors:** Before patents, inventors usually saw their ideas stolen before they could make any money. By giving inventors the exclusive right to market and sell their inventions, patents gave a financial incentive to produce lots of inventions. Indeed, after patents came into existence, the world saw its first full-time inventors — people who made a living inventing things.

>> **Widespread literacy and education:** Without highly educated inventors, new technologies don't get invented. And without an educated workforce, they can't be mass-produced. Consequently, the decision that many nations made to make primary and then secondary education mandatory paved the way for rapid and sustained economic growth.

Institutions and policies like these have given people a world of growth and opportunity and an abundance so unprecedented in world history that the greatest public health problem in many countries today is obesity.

Looking toward the future

The challenge moving forward is to get even more of what people want out of the world's limited pool of resources. This challenge needs to be faced because problems like infant mortality, child labor, malnutrition, endemic disease, illiteracy, and unemployment are all alleviated by higher living standards and an increased ability to pay for solutions to such problems.

Along those lines, it's important to point out that many poverty-related problems can be cured by extending to poorer nations the institutions that have already been proven by already-rich countries to lead to rising living standards. In addition, developing nations can also learn from the mistakes that were made by already-rich countries back when they were in the process of figuring out how to raise living standards — mistakes related to promoting economic growth without causing massive amounts of pollution, numerous species extinctions, or widespread resource depletion.

TIP

Consequently, there are two related and very good reasons for you to read this book and get a firm grasp about economics:

>> **You can discover how modern economies function.** Doing so can give you an understanding not only of how they've so greatly raised living standards but also of where they need some improvement.

>> **By getting a thorough handle on fundamental economic principles, you can judge for yourself the economic policy proposals that politicians and others run around promoting.** After reading this book, you'll be much better able to sort the good from the bad.

Framing Economics as the Science of Scarcity

Scarcity is the fundamental and unavoidable phenomenon that creates a need for the science of economics: There isn't nearly enough time or stuff to satisfy all desires, so people have to make hard choices about what to produce and consume so that if they can't have everything, they at least have the best that was possible under the circumstances. Without scarcity of time, scarcity of resources, scarcity of information, scarcity of consumable goods, and scarcity of peace and goodwill on Earth, human beings would lack for nothing. Chapter 2 gets deep into scarcity and the tradeoffs that it forces people to make.

Economists analyze the decisions people make about how to best maximize human happiness in a world of scarcity. That process turns out to be intimately connected with a phenomenon known as *diminishing returns*, which describes the sad fact that each additional amount of a resource that's thrown at a production process brings forth successively smaller amounts of output.

Like scarcity, diminishing returns is unavoidable, and in Chapter 3, I explain how people very cleverly deal with this phenomenon in order to get the most out of humanity's limited pool of resources.

Sending Microeconomics and Macroeconomics to Separate Corners

The main organizing principle I use in this book is to divide economics into its two broad pieces, macroeconomics and microeconomics:

>> **Microeconomics** focuses on individual people and individual businesses. For individuals, it explains how they behave when faced with decisions about where to spend their money or how to invest their savings. For businesses, it explains how profit-maximizing firms behave individually, as well as when competing against each other in markets.

>> **Macroeconomics** looks at the economy as an organic whole, concentrating on factors such as interest rates, inflation, and unemployment. It also encompasses the study of economic growth and the methods governments use to try to moderate the harm caused by recessions.

Underlying both microeconomics and macroeconomics are some basic principles such as scarcity and diminishing returns. Consequently, I spend the rest of Part I explaining these fundamentals before diving in to microeconomics in Part II and macroeconomics in Part III. But first, this section gives you an overview of microeconomics and macroeconomics.

Getting up close and personal: Microeconomics

Microeconomics gets down to the nitty gritty, studying the most fundamental economic agents: individuals and firms. This section delves deeper into the micro side of economics, including info on supply and demand, competition, property rights, problems with markets, and the economics of healthcare.

Balancing supply and demand

In a modern economy, individuals and firms produce and consume everything that gets made. Supply and demand determine prices and output levels in competitive markets. Producers determine supply, consumers determine demand, and their interaction in markets determines what gets made and how much it costs. (See Chapter 4 for details.)

Individuals make economic decisions about how to get the most happiness out of their limited incomes. They do this by first assessing how much *utility*, or satisfaction, each possible course of action would give them. They then weigh costs and benefits to select the course of action that will yield the greatest amount of utility possible given their limited incomes. These decisions generate the demand curves that affect prices and output levels in markets. I cover these decisions and demand curves in Chapter 5.

In a similar way, the profit-maximizing decisions of firms generate the supply curves that affect markets. Every firm will decide what to produce and how much to produce by comparing costs and revenues. A unit of output will only be produced if doing so will increase its maker's profit. In particular, a firm will only produce a unit if the increase in revenue from selling it exceeds the unit's cost of production. This behavior underpins the upward slope of supply curves and how they affect prices and output levels in markets, as I discuss in Chapter 6.

Considering why competition is so great

You may not feel warm and fuzzy about profit-maximizing firms, but economists love them — just as long as they're stuck in competitive industries. The reason is that firms that are forced to compete end up satisfying two wonderful conditions:

>> They're *allocatively efficient,* which simply means that they produce the goods and services that consumers most greatly desire to consume.

>> They're *productively efficient,* which means that they produce these goods and services at the lowest possible cost.

REMEMBER

The allocative and productive efficiency of competitive firms are the basis of Adam Smith's famous *invisible hand* — the idea that when constrained by competition, each firm's greed ends up causing it to act in a socially optimal way, as if guided to do the right thing by an invisible hand. I discuss this idea, and much more about the benefits of competition, in Chapter 7.

Examining problems caused by lack of competition

Unfortunately, not every firm is constrained by competition. And when that happens, firms don't end up acting in socially optimal ways. The most extreme case is *monopoly*, a situation where there's only one firm in an industry — meaning that it has absolutely no competition. Monopolies behave very badly, restricting output in order to drive up prices and inflate profits. These actions hurt consumers and may go on indefinitely unless the government intervenes.

A less-extreme case of lack of competition is *oligopoly*, a situation in which only a few firms are in an industry. In such situations, firms often make deals not to compete against each other so that they can keep prices high and make bigger profits. However, these firms often have a hard time keeping their agreements with each other. This fact means that oligopoly firms often end up competing against each other despite their best efforts not to. Consequently, government regulation isn't always needed. You can read more about monopolies in Chapter 8 and oligopolies in Chapter 9.

Reforming property rights

REMEMBER

You can rely upon markets and competition to produce socially beneficial results only if society sets up a good system of property rights. A *property right* gives a person the exclusive authority to determine how a productive resource can be used. Thus, for example, a person who has the property right (ownership) over a piece of land can determine whether it will be used for farming, as an amusement park, or as a nature preserve. All pollution issues, as well as all cases of species loss, are the direct result of poorly designed property rights generating perverse incentives to do bad things. Economists take this problem seriously and have done their best to reform property rights in order to alleviate pollution and eliminate species loss. I discuss these issues in detail in Chapter 10.

Dealing with other common market failures

Monopolies, oligopolies, and poorly designed property rights all lead to what economists like to call *market failures* — situations in which markets don't deliver socially optimal outcomes. Two other common causes of market failure are asymmetric information and public goods:

>> **Asymmetric information:** Asymmetric information refers to situations in which either the buyer or the seller knows more about the quality of the good that he or she is negotiating over than does the other party. Because of the uneven playing field and the suspicions it creates, a lot of potentially beneficial economic transactions never get completed.

>> **Public goods:** Public goods are goods or services that are impossible to provide to just one person; if you provide them to one person, you have to provide them to everybody. (Think of an outdoor fireworks display, for example.) The problem is that most people try to get the benefit without paying for it.

I discuss both these situations, and ways to deal with them, in Chapter 11.

Diagnosing healthcare economics

Almost everyone is deeply concerned about access to affordable, high-quality medical care — medical care delivered through government-run national health systems, through employer-sponsored health insurance, or by direct payments made by consumers. Each system provides different incentives that can affect efficiency, usage, and cost — sometimes quite perversely. Chapter 12 gets you up to date on the incentives, regulations, and policies that determine how both coverage and affordability can be improved from an economics standpoint.

Understanding behavioral economics

People aren't always rational, and that matters because most of economics was developed by asking what a rational person would do in one situation or another. *Behavioral economics* fills in the gaps by looking at decision-making when people aren't being rational. Four billion years of evolution has left us with brains that are prone to errors, including being overconfident and too focused on the present, being easily confused by irrelevant information, and being unable to see the bigger picture when making financial decisions. I spend Chapter 13 rationally explaining all this irrational behavior. It's crazy fun.

Zooming out: Macroeconomics and the big picture

Macroeconomics treats the economy as a unified whole. Studying macroeconomics is useful because certain factors, such as interest rates and tax policy, have economy-wide effects and also because when the economy goes into a recession or a boom, every person and every business is affected. This section gives you an overview of macroeconomics.

Measuring the economy

Economists measure *gross domestic product* (GDP), the value of all goods and services produced in a nation's economy in a given period of time, usually a quarter or a year. Totaling up this number is vital because if you can't measure how the economy is doing, you can't tell whether government polices intended to improve the economy are helping or hurting. Chapter 14 explains GDP in more depth.

Inflation measures how prices in the economy increase over time. This topic, inflation, is the focus of Chapter 15, and it is crucial because high rates of inflation usually accompany huge economic problems, including deep recessions and countries defaulting on their debts.

It's also important to study inflation because poor government policy is the sole culprit behind high rates of inflation — meaning that governments are responsible when big inflations happen.

Looking at international trade

International trade occurs when consumers, firms, or governments purchase products or resources made in other countries. Because imported goods often compete with locally produced goods, international trade is the subject of endless political controversy and attempts to erect import duties or numerical quotas to keep foreign goods out and thereby make life easier for domestic producers.

Those disputes are intensified by concerns about whether foreign working conditions are humane, whether foreign producers are unfairly subsidized by their governments, and whether currency exchange rates are being manipulated by foreign governments to give their own firms a cost advantage over firms in other countries. Chapter 14 explains how economists analyze these and other globalization issues.

Understanding and fighting recessions

REMEMBER

A *recession* occurs when the total amount of goods and services produced in an economy declines. Recessions are very painful for two reasons:

>> Less output means less consumption.

>> Many workers lose their jobs because firms need fewer workers to produce the reduced amount of output.

Recessions linger because institutional factors in the economy make it very hard for prices in the economy to fall. If prices *could* fall quickly and easily, recessions would quickly resolve themselves. But because prices can't quickly and easily fall, economists have had to develop antirecessionary policies to help get economies out of recessions as quickly as possible.

The man most responsible for developing antirecessionary policies was the English economist John Maynard Keynes, who in 1936 wrote the first macroeconomics book about fighting recessions. Chapter 16 introduces you to his model of the economy and how it explicitly takes account of the fact that prices can't quickly and easily fall to get you out of recessions. It serves as the perfect vehicle for illustrating the two things that *can* help get you out of a recession.

REMEMBER

Chapter 17 discusses two things governments can use to fight a recession:

>> **Monetary policy:** Monetary policy uses changes in the money supply to change interest rates in order to stimulate economic activity. For instance, if the government causes interest rates to fall, consumers borrow more money to buy things like houses and cars, thereby stimulating economic activity and helping to get the economy moving faster.

>> **Fiscal policy:** Fiscal policy refers to using increased government spending or lower tax rates to help fight recessions. For instance, if the government buys more goods and services, economic activity increases. In a similar fashion, if the government cuts tax rates, consumers end up with higher after-tax incomes, which, when spent, increase economic activity.

In the first decades after Keynes's antirecessionary ideas were put into practice, they seemed to work really well. However, they didn't fare so well during the 1970s, and it became apparent that although monetary and fiscal policy were powerful antirecessionary tools, they had their limitations.

For this reason, Chapter 17 also covers how and why monetary and fiscal policy are constrained in their effectiveness. The key concept is called *rational expectations.* It explains how rational people very often change their behavior in response to policy changes in ways that limit the effectiveness of those changes. It's a concept that you need to understand if you're going to come up with informed opinions about current macroeconomic policy debates.

Financial crises are recessions triggered by the failure of important financial institutions to keep their financial promises. Such failures often happen after consumers or businesses take on too much debt and are unable to repay loans to banks. Sometimes they occur when a government takes on too much debt and cannot repay its bondholders. Chapter 18 discusses the causes and consequences of financial crises.

Understanding How Economists Use Models and Graphs

Economists like to be logical and precise, which is why they use a lot of algebra and other math. But they also like to present their ideas in easy-to-understand and highly intuitive ways, which is why they use so many graphs.

The graphs economists use are almost always visual representations of economic models. An *economic model* is a mathematical simplification of reality that allows you to focus on what's really important by ignoring lots of irrelevant details. For instance, the economist's model of consumer demand focuses on how prices affect the amounts of goods and services that people want to buy. Obviously, other things, such as changing styles and tastes, affect consumer demand as well, but price is key.

To avoid a graph-induced panic as you flip through the pages of this book, I spend a few pages helping you get acquainted with what you encounter in other chapters. Take a deep breath; I promise this won't hurt.

Introducing your first model: The demand curve

When economists look at demand, they simplify by concentrating on prices. Consider orange juice, for example. The price of orange juice is the major thing that affects how much orange juice people are going to buy. (I don't care which dietary trend is in vogue — if orange juice cost $50 a gallon, you'd probably find another diet.) Therefore, it's helpful to abstract from those other things and concentrate solely on how the price of orange juice affects the quantity of orange juice that people want to buy.

Suppose that economists go out and survey consumers, asking them how many gallons of orange juice they would buy each month at three hypothetical prices: $10 per gallon, $5 per gallon, and $1 per gallon. The results are summarized in the following table:

Gallons of Orange Juice That Consumers Want to Buy

Price	Gallons
$10	1
$5	6
$1	10

Economists refer to the quantities that people would be willing to purchase at various prices as the *quantity demanded* at those prices. What you find if you look at the data in the preceding table is that the price of orange juice and the quantity demanded of orange juice have an *inverse relationship* with each other — meaning that when one goes up, the other goes down.

REMEMBER

Because this inverse relationship between price and quantity demanded holds true for nearly all goods and services, economists refer to it as the *law of demand*. But quite frankly, the law of demand becomes much more immediate and interesting if you can *see* it rather than just think about it.

Creating a demand curve by plotting out the data

The best way to *see* the quantity demanded at various prices is to plot it out on a graph. In the standard demand graph, the horizontal axis represents quantity, and the vertical axis represents price.

In Figure 1-1, I've graphed the orange juice data in the preceding table and marked three points and labeled them *A*, *B*, and *C*. The horizontal axis of Figure 1-1 measures the number of gallons of orange juice that people demand each month at various prices per gallon. The vertical axis measures the prices.

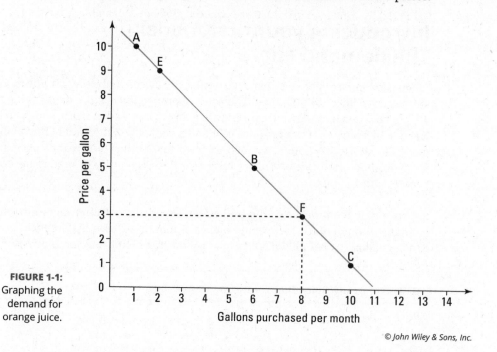

FIGURE 1-1:
Graphing the demand for orange juice.

© *John Wiley & Sons, Inc.*

Point *A* is the visual representation of the data in the top row of the preceding orange juice table. It tells you that at a price of $10 per gallon, people want to purchase only 1 gallon per month of orange juice. Similarly, Point *B* tells you that they demand 6 gallons per month at a price of $5, and Point *C* tells you that they demand 10 gallons per month at a price of $1 per gallon.

Notice that I've connected the Points *A*, *B*, and *C* with a line. I've done this to make up for the fact that the economists who conducted the survey asked about what people would do at only three prices. If they'd had a big enough budget to ask consumers about every possible price ($8.46 per gallon, $2.23 per gallon, and so on), there'd be an infinite number of dots on the graph. But because they didn't do that, I draw a straight line passing through the data points, which should do a pretty good job of estimating what people's demands are for prices that the economists didn't survey.

The straight line connecting the points in Figure 1-1 is a *demand curve*. I know it doesn't curve at all, but for simplicity, economists use the term *demand curve* to refer to all plotted relationships between price and quantity demanded, regardless of whether they're straight or curvy lines. (This is consistent with the fact that economists are both eggheads *and* squares.)

Straight or curvy, you can visualize the fact that price and quantity demanded have an *inverse relationship:* When price goes up, quantity demanded goes down. The inverse relationship implies that demand curves slope downward.

Generalizing a bit, you can also see that the slope of a demand curve gives quick intuition about the sensitivity of the inverse relationship between price and quantity demanded. If a demand curve is very steep, then you know that it would take a large change in price to cause a small change in quantity demanded. By contrast, a very flat demand curve tells you that a small change in price would result in a large change in quantity demanded.

Extending that reasoning even further, you can see that demand curves with changing slopes (that is, demand curves that aren't perfectly straight lines) tell you that the relationship between price and quantity demanded varies. On the steeper parts of such curves, a change in price causes a relatively small change in quantity demanded. On the flatter part of such curves, a change in price causes a relatively large change in quantity demanded.

Using the demand curve to make predictions

Graphing out a demand curve allows for a much greater ability to make quick predictions. For instance, you can use the straight line I've drawn in Figure 1-1 to estimate that at a price of $9 per gallon, people would want to buy about 2 gallons of orange juice per month. I've labeled this Point *E* on the graph.

Suppose that you can see only the data in the preceding orange juice table and can't look at Figure 1-1. Can you quickly estimate for me how many gallons per month people are likely to demand if the price of orange juice is $3 per gallon? Looking at the second and third rows of this table you have to conclude that people will demand somewhere between 6 and 10 gallons per month. But figuring out exactly how many gallons will be demanded would take some time and require some annoying calculations.

By contrast, if you look at Figure 1-1, it's easy to figure out how many gallons per month people would demand at $3 per gallon. You start at $3 on the vertical axis, move sideways to the right until you hit the demand curve at Point *F*, and drop down vertically until you get to the horizontal axis, where you discover that you're at 8 gallons per month. (To clarify, I've drawn in a dotted line that follows this path.) As you can see, using a figure rather than a table makes coming up with model-based predictions much, much simpler.

Drawing your own demand curve

Try a simple exercise that involves plotting some points and drawing lines between them. Imagine that the government came out with a research report showing that people who drink orange juice have lower blood pressure, fewer strokes, and a better sex life than people who don't drink orange juice. What do you think will happen to the demand for orange juice? Obviously, it should increase.

To verify this, our intrepid team of survey economists goes out again and asks people how much orange juice they would now like to buy each month at each of the three prices listed earlier in the "Introducing your first model: The demand curve" section: $10, $5, and $1. The new responses are here:

Gallons of OJ That Consumers Want to Buy After Reading New Government Report

Price	Gallons
$10	4
$5	9
$1	13

Your assignment, should you choose to accept it, is to plot these three points on Figure 1-1. After you've done that, connect them with a straight line. (Yes, you can write in the book!)

What you've just created is a new demand curve that reflects people's new preferences for orange juice in light of the government survey. Their increased demand is reflected in the fact that at any given price, they now demand a larger quantity of juice than they did before. For instance, whereas before they wanted only 1 gallon per month at a price of $10, they now would be willing to buy 4 gallons per month at that price.

There is still, of course, an inverse relationship between price and quantity demanded, meaning that even though the health benefits of orange juice make people demand more orange juice, people are still sensitive to higher orange juice prices. Higher prices still mean lower quantities demanded, and your new demand curve still slopes downward.

Use your new demand curve to figure out how many gallons per month people are now going to want to buy at a price of $7 and at a price of $2. Figuring these things out from the data in the preceding table would be hard, but figuring them out using your new demand curve should be easy.

» **Cataloguing the constraints that limit choice**

» **Modeling choice behavior like an economist**

» **Evaluating the limitations of the choice model**

Chapter **2**

Cookies or Ice Cream? Exploring Consumer Choices

E conomics is all about *how* groups and individuals make choices and *why* they choose the things that they do. Economists have spent a great deal of time analyzing how groups make choices, but because group choice behavior usually turns out to be very similar to individual choice behavior, my focus in this chapter is on individuals.

To keep things simple, my explanation of individual choice behavior focuses on *consumer behavior* because most of the choices people make on a day-to-day basis involve which goods and services to consume. Human beings are constantly forced to choose because their wants almost always exceed their means. Limited resources, or *scarcity*, is at the heart not only of economics but also of ecology and biology. Darwinian evolution is all about animals and plants competing over limited resources to produce the greatest number of offspring. Economics is about human beings choosing among limited options to maximize happiness.

Describing Human Behavior with a Choice Model

Human beings may be complicated creatures with sometimes mystifying behavior, but most people are usually fairly predictable and consistent and behave pretty much like other people. You can gain a lot by studying choice behavior because if you can understand the choices people made in the past, you stand a good chance of understanding the choices they'll make in the future.

Understanding (and even predicting) future choice behavior is very important because major shifts in the economic environment are typically the result of millions of small individual decisions that add up to a major trend. For instance, the circumstances under which millions of individuals choose to pursue work or school cumulate to major effects on the unemployment rate. And the choices these individuals make about how much of their paychecks to save or spend affect whether interest rates will be high or low and also whether gross domestic product (GDP) and overall economic output will increase or decrease. (I discuss GDP in Chapter 14.)

REMEMBER

In order to predict how self-interested individuals make their choices, economists have created a model of human behavior that assumes that people are rational and able to calculate subtle tradeoffs between possible choices. This model is a three-stage process:

1. Evaluate how happy each possible option can make you.

2. Look at the constraints and tradeoffs limiting your options.

3. Choose the option that will maximize your overall happiness.

Although not a complete description of human choice behavior, this model generally makes accurate predictions. However, many people question this explanation of human behavior. Here are three common objections:

>> Are people really so self-interested? Aren't people often motivated by what's best for others?

>> Are people really aware at all times of all their options? How are they supposed to rationally choose among new things that they've never tried before?

>> Are people really free to make decisions? Aren't they constrained by legal, moral, and social standards?

I spend the next few sections of this chapter expanding on the three-step economic choice model and addressing the objections to it.

Pursuing Personal Happiness

Economists like to think of human beings as free agents with free wills. To economists, people are usually rational and, thus, normally capable of making sensible decisions. But that begs the question of what motivates people and, in turn, of what sorts of things people will choose to do given their free wills.

In a nutshell, economists assume that the basic motivation driving most people most of the time is a desire to be happy. This assumption implies that people make choices on the basis of whether or not those choices will make them as happy as they can be given their circumstances. This section examines how the pursuit of happiness affects consumer behavior.

Using utility to measure happiness

If people make choices on the basis of which ones will bring them the most happiness, they need a way of comparing how much happiness each possible thing brings with it. Along these lines, economists assume that people get a sense of satisfaction or pleasure from the things life offers. Sunsets are nice. Eating ice cream is nice. Friendship is nice. And I happen to like driving fast.

REMEMBER

Economists suppose that you can compare all possible things that you may experience with a common measure of happiness or satisfaction that they call *utility*. Things you like a lot have high utility. Things that you like only a little have low utility. And things you hate (like toxic waste or foods that cause you to have allergic reactions) have negative utility. Utility acts as a common denominator that allows people to sensibly compare even radically different things.

The concept of utility is very broad. For a hedonist, utility may be the physical gratification of experiencing sensual pleasures. But for a morally conscientious person, utility may be the sense of moral satisfaction received when doing the right thing in a particular situation. The important idea for economists is that people are able to sort out and compare the utilities of various possible activities.

Taking "selfless" actions into account

Economists take it as a given that people make their choices in life in order to maximize their personal happiness. This viewpoint immediately raises objections because people are often willing to endure great personal suffering in order to help others.

However, an economist can view *altruism*, helping others at one's own expense, as a personal preference. The mother who doesn't eat in order to give what little food she has to her infant may be pursuing a goal (helping her child) that maximizes the *mother's* own happiness. The same can be said about people who donate to charities. Most people consider such generosity "selfless," but it's also consistent with assuming that people do things to make themselves happy. If people give because doing so makes them feel good, their selfless action is motivated by selfish intention.

REMEMBER

Because economists view human motivation as intrinsically self-interested economics is often accused of being immoral; however, economics is concerned with how people achieve their goals rather than with questioning the morality of those goals. For instance, some people like honey, but others do not. Economists make no distinction between these two groups regarding the rightness or wrongness of their preferences. Rather, what interests economists is how each group behaves given its preferences. Consequently, economics is *amoral* rather than immoral.

Economists are people, too, and they're very concerned with things like social justice, climate change, and poverty. They just tend to interpret the desire to pursue morality and equity as an individual goal that maximizes individual happiness rather than as a group goal that should be pursued in order to achieve some sort of collective good.

Self-interest can promote the common good

Adam Smith, one of the fathers of modern economics, believed that if society was set up correctly, people chasing after their individual happiness would provide for other people's happiness as well. As he famously pointed out in *An Inquiry into the Nature and Causes of the Wealth of Nations,* published in 1776, "It is not from the benevolence of the butcher, the brewer, or the baker, that we can expect our dinner, but from their regard to their own interest."

REMEMBER

Put differently, the butcher, the brewer, and the baker make stuff for you not because they like you but because they want your money. Yet because they want your money, they end up producing for you everything that you need to have a nice meal. When you trade them your money for their goods, everyone is happier. You think that not having to prepare all that food is worth more to you than keeping your money. And they think that getting your money is worth more to them than the toil involved in preparing all that food.

Adam Smith expanded on this notion by saying that a person pursing his own selfish interests may be "led by an invisible hand to promote an end which was no part of his intention." Because economists recognize this "invisible hand," they're less concerned with intent than with outcome and less concerned with what makes people happy than with how they pursue the things that make them happy.

You Can't Have Everything: Examining Limitations

Life is full of limitations. Time, for instance, is always in limited supply, as are natural resources. The second stage of the economic choice model looks at the constraints that force you to choose among your happy options.

For example, oil can be used to manufacture pharmaceuticals that can save many lives. But it can also be used to make gasoline, which can be used to drive ambulances, which also save lives. Both pharmaceuticals and gasoline are good uses for oil, so society has to come up with some way of deciding how much oil gets to each of these two good uses, knowing all the while that each gallon of oil that goes to one can't be used for the other.

This section outlines the various constraints, as well as the unavoidable cost — *opportunity cost* — of getting what you want. For more on how markets use supply and demand to allocate resources in the face of constraints, please see Chapter 4.

Resource constraints

The most obvious constraints on human happiness are the physical limitations of nature. Not only are the supplies of oil, water, and fish limited, but so are the radio frequencies on which to send signals and the hours of sunshine to drive solar-powered cars. There's simply not enough of most natural resources for everyone to have as much as they want.

The limited supply of natural resources is allocated in many different ways. In some cases, as with some endangered species, laws guarantee that nobody can have any of the resource. With the electromagnetic spectrum, national governments portion out the spectrum to broadcasters or mobile phone operators. But for the most part, private property and prices control the allocation of natural resources.

Under such a system, the use of the resource goes to the highest bidder. Although this system can discriminate against the poor because they don't have much to bid with, it does ensure that the limited supply of the resource at least goes to people who value it highly — in other words, to those who have chosen this resource to maximize their happiness.

Technology constraints

You have a much higher standard of living than your ancestors did. You have a cushier life because of improvements in the technology of converting raw resources into things people like to use. Yet technology improves less quickly than people would like, and as a result people's choices are limited at any given moment by how advanced technology is right then. Therefore, it's natural to think of technology as being a constraint that limits choices.

REMEMBER

As technology improves over time, people are able to produce more from the limited supply of resources on the planet. Or, put slightly differently, as technology improves, individuals have more and better choices. In the last 200 years, people have figured out how to immunize children against deadly diseases, how to use electricity to provide light and mechanical power, how to build a rocket capable of putting people on the moon, and how to dramatically increase farm yields to feed more people. In just the last 30 years, the Internet and cheap mobile phones have revolutionized everything from entertainment to how governments communicate with their citizens.

Time constraints

Time is a precious resource. Worse yet, time is a resource in fixed supply. Therefore, the best that technology can do for people is to allow them to produce more in the limited amount of time that they have or to grant them a few more years of life through better medical technology.

But even with a longer life span, you can only be in one place at a time so that you only have a finite amount of time to work with. This means you must choose how to allocate your limited amount of time between leisure and labor, and between taking time to do things you like and selling your time to employers so that you can earn wages to pay for things you like. This trade-off implies that time is a precious commodity about which people must make serious choices.

Opportunity cost: The unavoidable cost

The economic idea of *opportunity cost* is closely related to the idea of time constraints. You can do only one thing at a time, which means that, inevitably, you're always giving up a bunch of other things.

REMEMBER

The *opportunity cost* of any activity is the value of the best alternative thing you could've done instead. For instance, this morning, I could've chatted on the phone with a friend, watched TV, or worked hard writing this chapter. I chose to chat with my friend because that made me happiest. (Don't tell my editor!) Of the two things that I didn't choose, I consider working on the chapter to be better than watching TV. So the opportunity cost of chatting on the phone was not getting to spend the time working on this chapter.

TIP

Opportunity cost depends only on the value of the best alternative option because you can always reduce a complicated choice with many options down to a simple choice between two things: Option X versus the best alternative option out of all the other options you can choose from. It doesn't matter whether you have 3 alternative options or 3,000.

Simplifying a decision down to only two options makes choosing easy. You should go with option X (rather than the best alternative option) only if the pleasure you will receive from option X exceeds the opportunity cost of not getting to enjoy the best alternative option. And you should select the best alternative option only if the opportunity cost of forgoing it exceeds the pleasure you would get from consuming option X.

Suppose that you can choose only one item from a selection of desserts that includes pecan ice cream, donuts, chocolate chip cookies, and peach cobbler. Select one of these at random — say, pecan ice cream. Then, out of all the other desserts, identify the one that you like best out of that group. In my case, it'd be chocolate chip cookies.

My decision about which dessert to eat now comes down to simply comparing how I feel about pecan ice cream and chocolate chip cookies. To select the ice cream means enduring the opportunity cost of not eating the cookies. I'll do that only if the pleasure from eating the ice cream exceeds the opportunity cost of forgoing the chocolate chip cookies. And I'll opt for the chocolate chip cookies only if the opportunity cost of forgoing the chocolate chip cookies exceeds the pleasure I would get from eating the ice cream.

Making Your Choice: Deciding What and How Much You Want

At its most basic, the third stage of the economic choice model is nothing more than cost-benefit analysis. In the third stage, you simply choose the option for which the benefits outweigh the costs by the largest margin.

The cost-benefit model of how people make decisions is very powerful in that it seems to correctly describe how most decisions are made. But this version of cost-benefit analysis can tell you only *whether* people choose a given option. In other words, it's only good at describing all-or-nothing decisions like whether or not to eat ice cream. A much more powerful version of cost-benefit analysis uses the concept of *marginal utility* to tell you not just whether I'm going to eat ice cream but *how much* of it I will decide to eat.

To see how marginal utility works, recognize that the amount of utility that a given thing brings usually depends on how much of that given thing a person has already had. For instance, if you've been really hungry, the first slice of pizza that you eat brings you a lot of utility. The second slice is also pleasant but not quite as good as the first because you're no longer starving. The third, in turn, brings less utility than the second. And if you keep forcing yourself to eat, you may find that the 12th or 13th slice of pizza actually makes you sick and brings you negative utility.

Economists refer to this phenomenon as *diminishing marginal utility.* Each additional, or *marginal,* unit that is consumed brings less utility than the previous unit so that the extra utility, or *marginal utility,* brought by each successive unit diminishes as you consume more and more units. Here, each successive slice of pizza brings with it less additional, or marginal, utility than the previous slice.

To see how diminishing marginal utility predicts how people make decisions about how much of something to consume, consider having $10 to spend on $2 pizza slices or $2 baskets of fries. Economists presume that the goal of people faced with a limited budget is to adjust the quantities of each possible thing they can consume to maximize their *total utility.*

If I buy only four slices of pizza, then I free up $2 to spend on a basket of fries. And because it's my first basket of fries, eating it probably brings me lots of marginal utility. Indeed, if the marginal utility gained from that first basket of fries exceeds the marginal utility lost by giving up that fifth slice of pizza, I'll definitely make the switch. I'll keep adjusting the quantities of each food until I find the combination that maximizes how much total utility I can purchase using my $10.

Because different people have different preferences, the quantities of each good that will maximize each person's total utility are usually different. Someone who detests fries will spend all his $10 on pizza. A person who can't stand pizza will spend all her money on fries. And for people who choose to have some of each, the optimal quantities of each depend on their feelings about the two goods and how fast their marginal utilities decrease. Check out Chapter 5 for more detail on diminishing marginal utility and how it causes demand curves to slope downward.

Allowing for diminishing marginal utility makes this model of choice behavior very powerful. It tells you not only what people will choose but how much of each thing they will choose. It's not perfect, however. For example, it assumes that people have a clear sense of the utility of various things, a good idea of how fast marginal utilities diminish, and no trouble making comparisons. I discuss these substantial criticisms in the next section.

MARGINAL UTILITY IS FOR THE BIRDS!

Economists are very confident that cost-benefit analysis and diminishing marginal utility are good descriptions of decision-making because there's plenty of evidence that other species also behave in ways consistent with these concepts.

For instance, scientists can train birds to peck at one button in order to earn food and another button to earn time on a treadmill. If scientists increase the cost of one of the options by increasing the number of clicks required to get it, the birds respond rationally by not clicking so much on the button for that option. But even more interesting is that they also switch to clicking more on the button for the other option.

The birds seem to understand that they have only a limited number of clicks they can make before they get exhausted, and they allocate these clicks between the two options to maximize their total utility. Consequently, when the relative costs and benefits of the options change, they change their behavior quite rationally in response.

Most species also seem to be affected by diminishing marginal utility and become indifferent to marginal (that is, additional) units of something that they've recently enjoyed a lot of. So although economists' models of human behavior may seem to ignore some relevant factors, they do take into account some very fundamental and universal behaviors.

Exploring Violations and Limitations of the Economist's Choice Model

For simplicity, economists often assume that people are fully informed and totally rational when they make decisions. You may think that gives people way too much credit, but models based on those assumptions work surprisingly well much of the time.

However, in the real world, people aren't always informed about the decisions they need to make, and they aren't always as reasonable as economists assume. In this section, I note some of the limitations of the choice model and explain why they may not matter all that much in the long run.

Understanding uninformed decision-making

When economists apply the choice model, they assume a situation in which a person knows all the possible options, knows how much utility each will bring, and knows the opportunity costs of each one. But how do you evaluate whether it would be better to sit on top of Mount Everest for five minutes or hang-glide over the Amazon for ten minutes? Because you've never done either, you aren't well-informed about the constraints and costs of the choice and probably don't even know what the utilities of the two options are.

Politicians touting novel new programs often ask voters to make similarly uninformed choices. They make their proposals sound as good as possible, but in many cases, nobody really knows what they may be getting into.

Things are similarly murky with respect to choices involving luck or uncertainty. People buying lottery tickets in state lotteries have no idea about the eventual possible gain because the size of the prize depends on how many tickets are sold before the drawing is made. The people who choose to play lotteries also tend to have highly exaggerated "guesstimates" about their chances of winning.

Economists account for this reality by assuming that when faced with uninformed decisions, people make their best guesses about not only uncertain outcomes but also about how much they may like or dislike things with which they have no previous experience. Although this may seem like a fudge, because people in the real world are obviously making decisions in such situations (they do, in fact, buy a whole lot of lottery tickets), the people in those situations must be fudging a bit as well.

Whether people make good choices when they are uninformed is hard to say. Obviously, people would prefer to be better informed before choosing. And some people do shy away from less certain options. But overall, the economist's model of choice behavior seems quite capable of dealing with situations of incomplete information and uncertainty about random outcomes.

Making sense of irrationality

Even when people are fully informed about their options, they often make logical errors in evaluating costs and benefits. I go through three of the most common errors in the following subsections. Don't be alarmed if you find that you've made these errors yourself: After people have these choice errors explained to them, they typically stop making the errors and start behaving in a manner consistent with rationally weighing marginal benefits against marginal costs.

Sunk costs are sunk!

REMEMBER

Economists refer to costs that have already been incurred and which should therefore not affect your current and future decision-making as *sunk costs*. Rationally speaking, you should consider only the future, potential marginal costs and benefits of your current options.

Suppose you just spent $15 to get into an all-you-can-eat sushi restaurant. How much should you eat? More specifically, when deciding how much to eat, should you care about how much you paid to get into the restaurant? To an economist, the answer to the first question is "Eat exactly the amount of food that makes you most happy." And the answer to the second question is "How much it cost you to get in doesn't matter because whether you eat 1 piece of sushi or 80 pieces of sushi; the cost was the same."

Put differently, because the cost of getting into the restaurant is now in the past, it should be completely unrelated to your current decision of how much to eat. After all, if you were suddenly offered $1,000 to leave the sushi restaurant and eat next door at a competitor's, would you refuse simply because you felt you had to eat a lot at the sushi restaurant in order to get your money's worth out of the $15 you spent? Of course not.

Unfortunately, most people tend to let sunk costs affect their decision-making until an economist points out to them that sunk costs are irrelevant — or, as economists never tire of saying, "Sunk costs are sunk!" (On the other hand, non-economists quickly tire of hearing this phrase.)

Mistaking a big percentage for a big dollar amount

Costs and benefits are absolute, but people make the mistake of thinking of the costs and benefits as percentages or proportions. Instead, you should compare the total costs against the total benefits, because the benefit of, say, driving to the next town to get a discount is the absolute dollar amount you save, not the percentage you save.

Suppose you decide to save 10 percent on a mobile phone by making a one-hour round trip to a store in another town. You plan to buy the phone for only $90 instead of buying it at your local store for $100. Next, ask yourself whether you'd also be willing to drive one hour in order to buy a home theater system for $1,990 in the next town rather than for $2,000 at your local store. You do the math, and because you would save only 0.5 percent, you decide to buy the system for $2,000 at the local store. You may think you're being smart, but you've just behaved in a colossally inconsistent and irrational way. In the first case, you were willing to drive one hour to save $10. In the second, you were not.

Confusing marginal and average

Suppose your local government has recently built three bridges at a total cost of $30 million. That's an average cost of $10 million per bridge. A local economist does a study and estimates that the total benefits of the three bridges to the local economy add up to $36 million, or an average of $12 million per bridge.

A politician then starts trying to build a fourth bridge, arguing that because bridges on average cost $10 million but on average bring $12 million in benefits, it would be foolish not to build another bridge. Should you believe him? After all, if each bridge brings society a net gain of $2 million, you would want to keep building bridges forever.

REMEMBER

What really matter in this decision are *marginal* costs and *marginal* benefits, not *average* ones (see the earlier section "Making Your Choice: Deciding What and How Much You Want" to review marginal utility). Who cares what costs and benefits all the previous bridges brought with them? You have to compare the costs of that extra, marginal bridge with the benefits of that extra, marginal bridge. If the marginal benefits exceed the marginal costs, you should build the bridge. If the marginal costs exceed the marginal benefits, you should not.

For example, suppose that an independent watchdog group hires an engineer to estimate the cost of building one more bridge and an economist to estimate the benefits of building one more bridge. The engineer finds that because the three shortest river crossings have already been taken by the first three bridges, the fourth bridge will have to be much longer. In fact, the extra length will raise the construction cost to $15 million.

At the same time, the economist does a survey and finds that a fourth bridge isn't really all that necessary. At best, it will bring with it only $8 million in benefits. Consequently, this fourth bridge shouldn't be built because its marginal cost of $15 million exceeds its marginal benefit of $8 million. By telling voters only about the *average* costs and benefits of past bridges, the politician supporting the project is grossly misleading them. So watch out anytime somebody tries to sell you a bridge.

Chapter **3**

Producing Stuff to Maximize Happiness

lthough it's true that human beings face scarcity and can't have everything they want (as I discuss in Chapter 2), it's also true that they have a
lot of options. Productive technology is now so advanced that people can
convert the planet's limited supply of resources into an amazing variety of goods
and services, including cars, computers, airplanes, cancer treatments, video
games, and even totally awesome For Dummies books like this one.

In fact, thanks to advanced technologies, people are spoiled for choices. The huge
variety of goods and services that can be produced means that people must choose
wisely if they want to convert the planet's limited resources into the goods and
services that will provide the greatest possible happiness when consumed.

This chapter explains how economists analyze the process by which societies
choose exactly what to produce in order to maximize human happiness. For every
society, the process can be divided into two simple steps:

1. **Figure out all the possible combinations of goods and services that it
   could produce given its limited resources and the currently available
   technology.**

2. **Choose one of these output combinations — presumably, the combination that maximizes happiness.**

Economists view success in each of the two steps in terms of two particular types of efficiency:

>> **Productive efficiency:** Producing any given good or service using the fewest possible resources

>> **Allocative efficiency:** Allocating society's limited supply of resources to firms and industries so that they end up producing the products most wanted by consumers.

This chapter shows you how a society achieves both productive and allocative efficiency — that is, how a society can produce the things that people most want at the lowest possible cost. I give you the lowdown on diminishing returns, production possibilities frontier graphs (yeah, graphs!), and the interplay between markets and governments.

Figuring Out What's Possible to Produce

In determining what's possible to produce in an economy, economists list two major factors that affect both the maximum amounts and the types of output that will be produced:

>> **Limited resources:** The first factor is obvious. If resources were unlimited, goods and services would be as well.

>> **Diminishing returns:** The more you make of something, the more expensive it becomes to produce. Even with mass production, after some level of output the cost of producing additional units will begin to rise. Eventually, the increasing cost exceeds the benefit of producing additional units. That of course limits how much of the product in question you will want to produce, even if it's your favorite thing. In such situations, resources should be reallocated to producing units of other products for which the benefits still outweigh the costs.

A key result of diminishing returns is that societies are usually better off when they devote their limited resources to producing moderate amounts of many goods rather than producing a huge amount of just one thing.

This section gives you the lowdown on how limited resources and diminishing returns determine production possibilities. It also shows you how to represent these possibilities graphically.

Classifying resources

You can't get output without inputs of resources. Economists traditionally divide inputs, or factors of production, into four classes:

>> **Land:** Land isn't just real estate but all naturally occurring resources that can be used to produce things people want to consume. Land includes the weather, plant and animal life, geothermal energy, and the electromagnetic spectrum.

>> **Labor:** Labor is the work that people must do in order to produce things. A tree doesn't become a house without human intervention.

>> **Capital:** Capital is human-made machines, tools, and structures that aren't directly consumed but are used to produce other things that people do directly consume. For instance, a car that you drive for pleasure is a consumption good, but an identical car that you use to haul around bricks for your construction business is capital. Capital includes factories, roads, sewers, electrical grids, the Internet, and so on.

>> **Entrepreneurial ability:** The human resource, distinct from labor, that combines the other three factors of production (land, labor, and capital) to produce new products or make innovations in the production of existing products. The difference between labor and entrepreneurial ability is that labor is simply work at a known task, whereas entrepreneurial ability is the skill of improving how we make an existing product or the wherewithal to invent a completely new product. Without entrepreneurial ability, we'd be stuck making the same things the same way, forever.

Clarifying human capital

With respect to the factor of production known as labor, economists often speak of human capital, which is the knowledge and skills that people use to help them produce output. For instance, I have a lot of human capital with regard to teaching economics, but I have extremely low human capital with regard to painting and singing.

If you put a person to work at a job for which she has high human capital, she'll produce much better or much more output than a person with low human capital, even though they both supply the same amount of labor in terms of hours worked.

An important consequence is that skilled workers (high human capital) get paid more than unskilled workers (low human capital). Therefore, a good way for societies to become richer is to improve the skills of their workers through education and training. If societies can raise workers' human capital levels, not only can they produce more with the same inputs of limited land, labor, and capital, but their workers will also be paid more and enjoy higher standards of living.

However, building up human capital is costly, and at any given instant, you should think of the level of human capital in a society as being fixed. Combined with limitations on the amount of land, labor, capital, and entrepreneurial ability, the limitation on human capital means that the society will be able to produce only a limited amount of output. And along these same lines, the decisions about where to best allocate these limited resources become crucial because the resources must be used for production of the goods and services that will bring the greatest amount of happiness. (For more on limited resources and production possibilities, see the upcoming section "A little here, a little there: Allocating resources.")

Diminishing returns

REMEMBER

Diminishing returns is probably the most important economic factor in determining exactly what to produce out of all the things that could possibly be produced, given the limited supply of resources. For virtually everything people make, the amount of additional output you get from each additional unit of input decreases as you use more and more of the input.

Diminishing returns is sometimes referred to as the low-hanging fruit principle. Imagine being sent into an apple orchard at harvest time to pick apples. During the first hour, you pick a lot of apples because you go for the low-hanging ones that are the easiest to reach. In the second hour, however, you can't pick as many because you have to start reaching awkwardly for fruit that is higher up. During the third hour you pick even fewer apples; you now have to jump off the ground every time you try to pick an apple because the only ones left are even farther away. Table 3-1 demonstrates how your productivity — your output for a given amount of input — diminishes with each additional hour you work.

TABLE 3-1 **Diminishing Returns to Apple Picking**

Hour Worked	Apples Picked	Labor Cost per Apple
First	300	2 cents
Second	200	3 cents
Third	120	5 cents

Another way to see the effect of diminishing returns is to note the increasing costs for producing output. If you pay workers $6 per hour to pick apples, your cost to have 300 apples picked in the first hour is two cents per apple (Table 3-1). The second hour yields only 200 apples, costing you three cents per apple (because you still have to pay the worker $6 for that hour's work). Only 120 get picked in the third hour, so the labor cost per apple rises to five cents. Eventually, the effects of diminishing returns drive prices so high that you stop devoting further labor resources to picking additional apples.

Virtually all production processes show diminishing returns and not just for labor. Additional amounts of any particular input usually result in smaller and smaller increments of output, holding all other inputs constant.

Allocating resources

Because diminishing returns guarantees that a production process will eventually become too costly, a society normally allocates its limited resources widely, to many different production processes.

Imagine that you can allocate workers to either picking apples or picking oranges. You can sell both apples and oranges for $1 each, but the production of both fruits involves diminishing returns so that additional workers acting as fruit pickers yield successively smaller increments of output, no matter which fruit they're picking.

Allocating all your workers to picking oranges, for example, is unproductive because the output you'll get from the last worker picking oranges will be much less than the output you'd get from the first worker picking oranges. The smart thing to do is to take a worker away from picking oranges and reassign him to picking apples. As the last worker picking oranges, he didn't produce much. But as the first worker picking apples, he'll pick a lot of them. Because you pay him the same wage regardless of which fruit he's picking, you use your labor more intelligently by having him pick apples, because one apple sells for as much money as one orange.

You may also want to reassign a second worker, and perhaps a third or a fourth. But because diminishing returns applies just as much to picking apples as it does to picking oranges, you don't want to reassign all the workers. Each additional worker assigned to picking apples produces less than the previous worker picking apples. At some point, moving additional workers from picking oranges to picking apples no longer benefits you, and you've reached what economists refer to as an optimal allocation of your labor resource. As soon as you've found this sweet spot, you have no further incentive to move workers from picking one fruit to picking the other because no additional moving of workers will increase total fruit picking. At this point, you've maximized your fruit-picking potential.

Graphing your production possibilities

Economists have a handy graph called the production possibilities frontier (PPF) that lets you visualize the effect of diminishing returns and view the trade-offs you make when you reallocate inputs from producing one thing to producing another. The Production Possibilities Frontier, which is sometimes referred to as the production possibilities curve, also shows how limited resources constrain your ability to produce output. Figure 3-1 shows a PPF graph that corresponds to the data in Table 3-2.

TABLE 3-2   ## Outputs of Apples and Oranges as the Labor Allocation Changes

	Combo 1	Combo 2	Combo 3	Combo 4	Combo 5	Combo 6
Workers picking oranges	0	1	2	3	4	5
Workers picking apples	5	4	3	2	1	0
Output of oranges	0	300	500	620	680	700
Output of apples	700	680	620	500	300	0

Table 3-2 shows how the total output of apples and oranges changes as you make different allocations of five available workers to picking apples or oranges. For instance, if you put all five people to work picking only apples for one whole day, you get 700 apples picked and zero oranges picked. If you move one worker to oranges (so four workers are picking apples and one worker is picking oranges), you get 680 apples picked and 300 oranges picked. Because of diminishing returns, taking one worker away from apples reduces apple output by only 20. But moving that worker to oranges increases orange production by 300 because that worker is the first one picking oranges and can get the low-hanging fruit.

Graphing the combinations

You can graph your production possibilities by plotting on a graph the various combinations of two output goods that can be produced as you vary the amount of a resource that is allocated between them. Figure 3-1 plots the six output combinations that result from varying the allocation of workers in Table 3-2, thereby graphing all your production possibilities. Point A corresponds to putting all your workers to work picking apples. Point B corresponds to the output you get from four workers picking apples and one worker picking oranges, and so on.

Note that each of the six points is attainable in the sense that you can actually produce the corresponding quantities of each fruit through some allocation of the five workers' labor. On the other hand, a point like C is not attainable. You can't allocate your five workers in any way to produce that many apples and oranges. Perhaps if you had more workers you could produce such an output combination, but you're limited to only five workers.

Imagine that instead of allocating labor by worker, you allocate it by time. The five workers each work for one day, so you have 5 worker-days of labor to allocate. You can now allocate, for instance, 3.2 worker-days to apple-picking and 1.8 worker-days to orange-picking. This arrangement allows you to fill in the graph and draw a line connecting the six points that correspond to the output combinations that you get when allocating labor by worker.

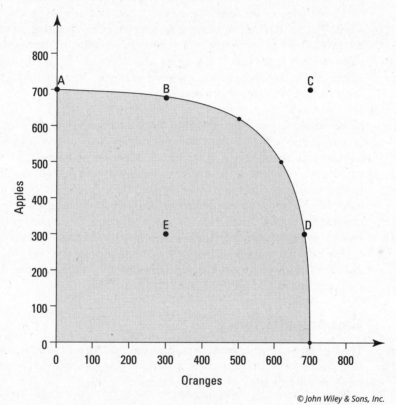

© John Wiley & Sons, Inc.

FIGURE 3-1:
The production possibilities frontier (PPF) for the data in Table 3-2.

A line passing through the points that represent various output combinations is called the production possibilities frontier, or PPF, because it divides the area of the graph into two parts: The combinations of output that are possible to produce given your limited supply of labor are under the line in the shaded area, and those that are not possible to produce are above it in the unshaded area. In this way, the PPF graph captures the effect of scarce resources on production. Some output combinations are just not producible given the limited supply of labor.

REMEMBER

The PPF is a simplification of the real world, derived by allocating one input between just two outputs. The real world is, of course, more complicated, with many different resources allocated among many different outputs. But the principles of limited resources and diminishing returns that show up so clearly on the PPF graph also apply to the much greater variety of both inputs and outputs in the real world.

Interpreting the shape of the graph

The bowed-out curvature of the PPF graph illustrates the effects of diminishing returns. In Figure 3-1, the changing slope as you move along the frontier shows that the trade-off between apple production and orange production depends on where you start. If you're at Point A, where you're allocating all your resources to the production of apples, then you can, by reallocating resources, produce a lot more oranges at the cost of giving up only a few apples. But if you start at Point D, where you're already producing a lot of oranges, then you have to give up a lot of apples to get just a few more oranges.

In economic jargon, the changing slope of the PPF in the face of diminishing returns is due to the fact that the opportunity costs of production vary depending on your current allocation of resources. (Check out Chapter 2 for more on opportunity cost, which is equal to the value of the best option you didn't choose.) If you're already producing a lot of apples, the opportunity costs of devoting even more labor to more apple production are very high because you're giving up a lot of potential orange production. On the other hand, the opportunity costs of devoting that labor to orange production are very low because you have to give up producing only a few apples. Clearly, you should devote the labor to picking the fruit that has the lower opportunity costs because, in this example, both fruits bring the same benefit: $1 per fruit sold.

Gauging efficiency

TIP

The PPF is very handy because any points that lie on the PPF itself (on the frontier) clearly show the output combinations you get when you're productively efficient, or wasting none of your resources.

In the example, you can't increase the production of apples without reducing the production of oranges, and vice versa. For instance, if you start at Point B, the only way to increase apple production is to slide up along the frontier, which implies reducing orange production. You have to make this tradeoff because you don't have any wasted labor lying around with which you could get more apples without reducing the amount of labor already devoted to orange picking.

All the points below the line are productively inefficient. Consider Point E in Figure 3-1, which corresponds to producing 300 apples and 300 oranges. You produce at a point like E only if you're being productively inefficient. In fact, you can see from Table 3-2 that you can produce these numbers by sending only one worker to pick apples and another worker to pick oranges. You're using just two of your five workers; the labor of the other three workers is either being wasted or not used at all.

In the real world, you end up at points like E because of inefficient production technology or poor management. For one reason or another, the resources that are available aren't being used to produce as much output as they could. Any manager who has five workers to allocate but produces only output combination E should be fired!

REMEMBER

Efficient economies should always be producing at some point on their frontiers, because if they're inside, they're wasting their limited resources and aren't maximizing the happiness that could be gotten from them.

Reaching new frontiers with better technology

One simplification of the PPF is that other than the particular input you are allocating, you are implicitly holding constant all other productive inputs, including technology. But humanity's level of technological sophistication is constantly increasing, allowing people to produce much more from a given set of resources than before.

Economists represent this increase in productivity by shifting the PPF outward. In Figure 3-2, the shaded area represents new combinations of output that, thanks to better technology, can now be produced using the same amount of resources as before. The PPF is still curved because better technologies don't get rid of diminishing returns. Even with a better technology, if you start increasing the amount of a particular input, you get successively smaller additional increases in output.

In Figure 3-2, the new technology shift is balanced in the sense that it increases your ability to produce more of both goods. An example of a balanced technological change would be improvements in fertilizers or pesticides that increase crop yields of both apples and oranges.

But most technological innovations are biased. For instance, suppose that you're considering a PPF where the two output goods are wheat and steel. An improvement in steel-making technology obviously allows you to make more steel from your limited resources but has no effect at all on your ability to make wheat. Consequently, as Figure 3-3 shows, the PPF does not shift out evenly. Rather, it shifts out at the end where all your particular input (say, labor) is devoted to steel, but remains fixed at the end where all your particular input is devoted to wheat production.

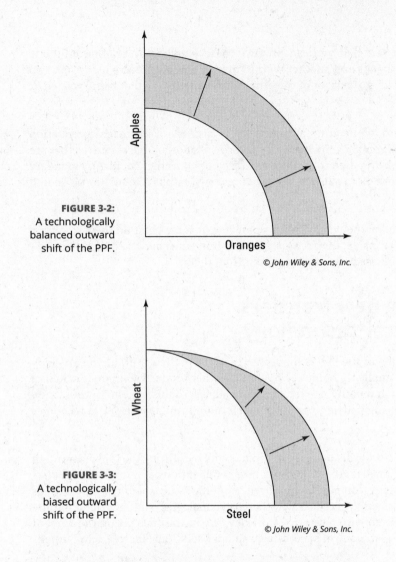

© John Wiley & Sons, Inc.

FIGURE 3-2:
A technologically balanced outward shift of the PPF.

FIGURE 3-3:
A technologically biased outward shift of the PPF.

Deciding What to Produce

After a society locates the frontier of efficient output combinations (see the preceding sections), the next step is choosing the point along the frontier that produces the combination of goods and services that makes people most happy. Choosing only from among frontier combinations guarantees productive efficiency. Choosing the single frontier combination that maximizes happiness assures allocative efficiency.

Because determining where the frontier lies is mostly a matter of engineering and applying current technology to available resources, it creates little controversy.

But deciding which particular combination of outputs a society as a whole should choose is much more complicated. People have preferences both as individuals and as groups about which products make them happiest. An individual choosing a point along his own personal PPF encounters no conflict; he just determines what combination of outputs makes him happiest and then he produces and consumes it. The decision-making process becomes vastly more complicated when you consider an entire society's PPF, in which case you're sure to have vigorous disagreement about which combination of outputs to produce with the society's limited resources.

For instance, your neighbor may not mind all the pollution produced by the fact that he likes driving his SUV day and night. If he were living in his own world, the pollution wouldn't matter, but because you live near him, you're affected by the pollution and object. Perhaps you'll seek government intervention that will limit what your neighbor is doing. Similarly, the government argues over what it should produce with its limited resources: Some people favor farm subsidies while others favor defense spending or programs to aid the poor.

Because of competing priorities, some sort of decision-making process must be established to determine what will actually get produced and to (try to) make sure that it pleases most of the people most of the time. In most modern economies, this process is the result of both private and public decisions acting through a combination of free markets and government action. The process is not always smooth, but it has delivered the highest standards of living in world history.

In this section, I discuss the pros and cons of free markets and government interventions and why it is that most nations have opted for mixtures of the two rather than attempting to rely exclusively on one or the other.

Comparing market results and government interventions

When analyzing the ways in which modern economies and societies select a combination of goods and services to produce, realize that current laws and institutions are the result of conflicting pressures to either

>> Leave markets to their own devices when turning resources into output.

>> Use the power of government to intervene in markets in order to secure a different set of outcomes.

Keep the following three factors in mind when considering the fight between leaving the markets alone and intervening:

>> **Complexity:** Modern economies are hugely complicated, with literally millions of goods and services produced using limited supplies of land, labor, capital, and entrepreneurial ability. Markets handle this complexity easily, but government interventions usually don't — meaning that they often risk substantial reductions in productive and allocative efficiency.

>> **Side effects:** Some goods and services, such as cocaine and coal-burning power plants, have negative consequences that often fall on "third parties" who weren't directly involved in either the production or the consumption of those products. These negative consequences bring forth substantial pressure for government intervention in the economy because markets, if left alone, will produce a lot of these goods and services and, consequently, a lot of negative consequences for third parties.

>> **Inequality:** Some people end up consuming a very large proportion of the goods and services produced, and others end up with very little. Such unequal distribution also brings forth a great deal of pressure for government intervention in the economy in order to equalize living standards.

These factors are both a consequence and a cause of the fact that modern economies are largely a mix of market production and government intervention. For the most part, what to produce, how much of it to produce, and who gets it are decided by voluntary transactions made by individuals and businesses. But sometimes, the government uses its powers to achieve outcomes that wouldn't happen if individuals and businesses were left to their own devices.

In both cases, a huge apparatus of law and tradition governing economic transactions helps society produce a combination of output that is, hopefully, both productively efficient (so resources are not wasted) and allocatively efficient (so the economy is producing the things that people want most). Next, I outline the benefits and the drawbacks that both markets and governments bring to the economic table.

The magic of markets: Directing resources automatically

Market economies are simply collections of billions of small, face-to-face transactions between buyers and sellers. Economists use the term market production to capture what happens when one individual offers to make or sell something to another individual at a price agreeable to both.

REMEMBER

In markets, the allocation of resources is facilitated by the fact that each resource has a price, and whoever is willing to pay the price gets the resource. In fact, market economies are often called price systems because prices serve as the signals that direct resources. Holding supply constant, products in high demand have high prices, and products in low demand have low prices. Because businesses like to make money, they follow the price signals and produce more of what has a high price and less of what has a low price. In this way, markets tend to take limited resources and use them to produce what people most want — or at least, what people are most willing to pay for.

For instance, the guy who sells you a TV at the local store has no idea about the total demand for TVs in the world, how many tons of steel or plastic are needed to produce them, or how many other things weren't produced because the steel and plastic needed to make the TVs was used for TVs rather than other things. All he knows is that you're willing to pay him for a TV. And if he's making a profit selling TVs, he orders more TVs from the factory. The factory, in turn, increases production, taking resources away from the production of other things.

Markets have the benefit of figuring out, automatically, the things that people want. To grasp why this is so amazing, consider that you live in a world of more than 7 billion people. It would be very hard for any single person to gather enough information to figure out what each of them most wants to buy. It would take several lifetimes to speak with each of them, even just to find out what they want for dinner, let alone all the other things they would most like to purchase on a typical day. But because production and distribution in modern economies aren't centrally controlled (by a small number of government officials working together in a single place), nobody needs to know the big picture.

COMMUNISM, LONG LINES, AND TOILET PAPER

In a *command economy*, all economic activity is done on the orders of the government. Until the fall of the Berlin Wall and the subsequent collapse of communism in the late 1980s and early 1990s, a large part of the world's population lived in countries that had command economies. Sadly, they didn't live very well.

Shortages of everything from sugar to clothing to toilet paper were constant. More seriously, doctors often lacked hypodermic needles and medicines for their patients, and food was often in short supply.

(continued)

(continued)

Goods and services weren't allocated using a price system whereby output went to those willing and able to pay for it. Rather, because everyone in a communist country is ideologically equal, the government attempted to give everyone an equal share of the goods and services made. The result, though, wasn't an equal division; instead, there were long lines, with those able to stand in line the longest getting more than their fair share. The lines were so long that people often stood in line for an entire day just to get one roll of toilet paper. If you saw a line forming, you got in it as fast as you could, even if you didn't know what people were standing in line for. Because everything was in short supply, it was almost certainly something you'd want.

What caused this mess? Centralization. In Moscow, government officials called *central planners* attempted to determine the correct amounts to produce for 24 million different items. It was an impossible task! To see why, consider toilet paper. First, you estimate how many millions of rolls of toilet paper are needed. Then you have to figure out how many trees to cut down to make that much paper and how many railcars you need to carry those trees to paper mills and how many workers it takes to run those mills. At the same time, you have to try to balance the production of toilet paper against the other zillion things that also require trees, railcars, and workers.

The entire problem is far too complex and requires far too much information to be solved. The result was that resources were constantly being misdirected and wasted. For instance, food often rotted at farms because no railcars had been scheduled to take it to cities; the officials hadn't accounted for an early harvest, and the railcars were busy elsewhere. In a price system, the farmers would have simply paid to bid the railcars away from other uses. This solution wasn't possible in a centralized economy in which prices weren't used to allocate resources.

In a competitive market, many sellers compete against each other to attract customers. Here are some of the advantages of competition:

>> **Using resources efficiently and keeping prices low:** A competitive market tends to guarantee productive efficiency because the best way for sellers to keep prices low is to make sure that they're using all their resources efficiently, with nothing going to waste. Because competition is ongoing, the pressure to be productively efficient is constant.

>> Sellers also have a big incentive to improve efficiency in order to undersell their rivals and steal their customers. Because every firm has this incentive, prices tend to be driven so low that the businesses can just barely make a profit.

>> **Encouraging improvements in technology:** In terms of the PPF (which I discuss in the earlier section "Graphing your production possibilities"), market

production with a lot of competition tends to ensure not only that economies produce along the frontier, but also that they have frontiers that are constantly being pushed outward as firms improve productive efficiency thanks to the efforts of *entrepreneurs* who supply the entrepreneurial ability that generates innovation and invention.

The misdeeds of markets: Ignoring morals and fairness

Markets aren't perfect. In particular, they suffer from two major problems:

>> Markets produce whatever people are willing to pay for, even if these things aren't good for the people or the environment. As long as profits are to be made, you can be pretty certain that a supply will arise to satisfy any demand. The fact that illegal drugs are widely and cheaply available — despite vigorous government programs to stop their production and distribution — is probably the best example of the robustness of markets. But although it's nice that markets are so hell-bent on giving people what they're willing to pay for, illegal drugs are an excellent example of the fact that markets will deliver things without caring about their social value or negative consequences such as drug addiction, broken families, and increased crime.

Along the same lines, producers sometimes utilize production methods that consumers don't like. Child labor and sweatshop labor are primary examples. Often the government must intervene to change these practices when the price system doesn't provide enough incentive for producers to reform such objectionable practices.

>> Markets don't in any way guarantee fairness or equity. The other big problem with markets is that they cater to those who have money to spend. The price system gives an incentive to produce only the things that people are willing and able to pay for. If someone is very poor, he can't give producers an incentive to provide him with even basic necessities such as medicine and food.

A related problem with markets is income and wealth inequality. Because market systems reward those who are best able to provide goods and services that people want to buy, some sellers end up becoming very rich because they're better at providing what people want. This invariably leads to large inequalities in wealth that many people find offensive.

The case for government intervention

Many societies use their governments to intervene and address the problems that markets create or cannot fix. Government interventions in the economy usually take one of three forms:

>> **Penalties or bans on producing or consuming goods or services considered dangerous or immoral:** These bans often work only partially because the market still has large incentives to provide such goods and services. For example, governments may ban drugs or impose "sin taxes" on things like alcohol and tobacco, which, though legal, are thought to be products whose use should be discouraged.

>> **Subsidies to encourage the production of goods and services considered desirable:** For instance, most governments heavily subsidize the education of children and the provision of medical care. They do so because of the fear that insufficient education and inadequate medical care will be provided without the subsidies. Education and medical care also often provide large spill-over benefits to the wider public. Consider immunizations. They not only protect those who are immunized but also those who aren't because immunization eliminates the possibility of the immunized infecting the non-immunized.

>> **Taxes on the well-off to provide goods and services to the less fortunate and to reduce inequalities in income and wealth:** These taxes are put toward things like good parks, clean air, and art, as well as goods and services for the poor. Governments tax individuals and businesses in order to raise the money to provide such things.

In terms of the PPF graph, each of these government interventions causes the economy to produce and allocate an output combination different from the one that society would have ended up with if the markets had made all the production and allocation decisions.

Depending on the situation, the output combination produced by a government intervention may be better or worse than the market combination in terms of productive efficiency, allocative efficiency, or both. Which combination is, in fact, better depends on the specifics of each case.

The case against government intervention

Government intervention is a powerful force for redirecting economic activity, but it doesn't necessarily make the economy better. In fact, there are at least three good reasons to worry that government intervention will make things worse:

>> **Special interests:** Government programs are often the result of special interest lobbying that persuades the legislature to put the interests of a small group ahead of the interests of the general public.

>> **Inefficiency:** Even when pursuing the common good, government programs often deliver poor service because they have no competition to create incentives to produce government goods and services efficiently.

MO' MONEY FOR MOHAIR

Mohair is extremely warm wool that grows on a special variety of goat. During World War II, the U.S. government decided that it needed mohair for the warm jackets worn by bomber pilots in their unheated cockpits. As a result, the government started giving a large subsidy to encourage the production of mohair. But planes have now been heated for nearly 70 years, and bomber jackets are nowadays made of synthetics. Yet the mohair subsidy remains, and mohair producers receive millions of dollars every year. Why? Because the mohair producers lobby the U.S. government very hard each year to renew the subsidy. For each producer, the subsidy is worth a lot of money. And because only a fraction of one cent of the average tax bill goes to the mohair subsidy, no one protests it. Consequently, the mohair subsidy survives not because it does society any good but because lobbying pays off in a democracy. Many other government programs are similarly deficient of widespread social benefits.

>> **Inflexibility:** Government interventions usually lack the flexibility of the price system, which is able to constantly redirect resources to accommodate people's changing willingness to pay for one good rather than another. Government policies take years to pass, and laws are usually written in a very precise manner that doesn't allow for changing circumstances and rapid innovation — things that the price system handles with ease.

Although markets sometimes fail to deliver everything that society wants, government intervention isn't a cure-all. Markets are very good at delivering the vast majority of things that people want and can usually do so at the lowest possible cost. Consequently, government intervention should be well thought out lest it make things worse rather than better.

Opting for a mixed economy

In the real world, few societies opt for an extreme type of economy, such as one that is totally market-based or one that features constant and pervasive government intervention. Instead, most societies opt for some mixture of markets, government intervention, and what economists refer to as traditional production. In their purest forms, these three types of economy can be defined as follows:

>> **Market:** A market economy is one in which almost all economic activity happens in markets with little or no interference by the government. Because of the lack of government intervention, this system is also often referred to as *laissez faire,* which is French for "to allow to do" or "to leave alone."

>> **Command:** A command economy is one in which all economic activity is directed by the government.

>> **Traditional:** A traditional economy is one in which production and distribution are handled along the lines of longstanding cultural traditions. For instance, until the caste system was abolished in India during the last century, the production of nearly every good and service could be done only by someone born into the appropriate caste. Similarly, in medieval Europe, you couldn't typically be part of the government or attain high military rank unless you were born a noble.

Because nearly every modern economy is a mixture of these three pure forms, most modern economies fall into the very inclusive category called mixed economies. With the exception of a few isolated traditional societies, however, the traditional economy part of the mixture has tended to decline in significance because most production has shifted to markets and because traditional economic restrictions with regard to age and gender have become less important (and more illegal).

REMEMBER

Mixed economies today are a mixture of the command economy and the market economy. The mixtures that you find in most countries typically feature governments that mostly allow markets to determine what's produced but that also mix in limited interventions in an attempt to make improvements over what the market would do if left to its own devices.

The precise nature of the mixture depends on the country, with the United States and the United Kingdom featuring more emphasis on markets and France and Germany, for instance, featuring more emphasis on government intervention. On the other hand, a few totalitarian states like North Korea still persist in running pure command economies as part of their all-encompassing authoritarian regimes.

Noting the failure of command and the absence of laissez faire

Command economies have historically been dismal failures (see the sidebar "Communism, long lines, and toilet paper" for details). Even well-intentioned governments can't gather enough information about production and distribution to do a good job allocating resources. In fact, they do a much worse job than price systems do.

Consequently, the opposite extreme, absolutely no government intervention, can seem like an attractive option. Such laissez-faire systems were first suggested by French economists several hundred years ago in response to the habit of governments of that era to intervene very heavily in economic activity. However, no pure laissez-faire economy has ever existed or probably could ever exist. The simple fact is that properly functioning market economies that use price mechanisms to allocate resources require a huge amount of government support.

REMEMBER

Among other things, market economies need governments to

>> Enforce property rights so people don't steal

>> Provide legal systems to write and enforce contracts so people can make purchases and sales of goods and services

>> Enforce standardized systems of weights and measures so people know they aren't being cheated

>> Provide a stable money supply that's safe from counterfeiters

>> Enforce patents and copyrights to encourage innovation and creativity

Notice that all these things must be in place in order for markets to function. Consequently, a more moderate, more modern version of laissez faire says that government should provide the institutional framework necessary for market economies to function, and then it should get out of the way and let people make and sell whatever is demanded.

Deciding on the amount of government intervention

Because command economies don't work very well and laissez-faire economies can't really exist, most societies have opted for one form or another of mixed economy in which governments and markets share economic responsibilities. The precise nature of that mix varies from country to country but all such mixtures feature some instances of direct governmental command and control of economic activity interacting with markets that use a price system to allocate resources.

The vast majority of people want governments to do more than just set up the institutions necessary for markets to function. They want governments to stop the production and sale of things like drugs or to subsidize the production of things that the market economy may not provide a lot of, like housing for the poor. They often also want to tax well-off citizens to pay for government programs.

Many government programs are so commonplace that you don't even think of them as being government interventions. For instance, free public schools, safety features on cars, warning labels on medicine bottles, taxes on alcohol and tobacco, and mandatory contributions to retirement systems are all government interventions in the economy.

The government interventions needed to implement such programs are, in many cases, not efficient. But many people would argue that there's quite a bit more to life than efficiency and that the inefficiencies caused by many government interventions are well worth the benefits that they produce. For such people, the government interventions in question increase overall happiness despite the fact that they are, strictly speaking, inefficient.

REMEMBER

At the end of the day, all government interventions — both good and bad — are the result of a political process. In democracies, the amount of government intervention is, broadly speaking, a reflection of the will of the people. Nations in which people have more trust in markets, like the United States and the United Kingdom, tend to feature mixed economies with less government intervention than nations in which people are more suspicious of corporations and impersonal market forces, like France and Germany.

Promoting Technology and Innovation

Technology is, in many ways, like any other good that can be provided by a market. If there's a profit incentive to inventing a new technology, businesspeople will figure out a way to invent it, just as they figure out ways to deliver all the other things that people are willing to pay for. However, unless government sets up the right set of laws and property rights, firms won't find it profitable to innovate.

Thus, one of the most important jobs of government is helping to promote the invention of new technologies so that people can enjoy higher living standards. Here are several ways in which government supports technology:

>> **Funding research:** Governments provide a good deal of direct support through research grants and university subsidies.

>> **Protecting intellectual property rights:** A crucial thing to understand about innovation is the indirect role that governments play not by subsidizing new technology but by guarding it. In particular, the patents granted by governments provide a huge economic incentive for both individuals and businesses to innovate. A patent guarantees inventors of new products or business methods the exclusive right to profit from their innovations, usually for about 20 years in most countries.

REMEMBER

It's not a coincidence that economic growth in the United States and Western Europe took off 200 years ago, right after patents became widely enforced. For the first time in world history, there was a secure financial incentive to use your brain to innovate. Before that time, innovating was extremely risky because after all your hard work, others would simply copy your invention and sell it without your permission.

Copyrights for literary, musical, and cinematic works serve a similar purpose. A great deal more art is produced when artists know that they can make a living. Along these lines, the easy duplication and distribution of digital media on the Internet is a troubling development because it has weakened artists' ability to charge for the art that they work so hard to produce.

>> **Encouraging education:** You shouldn't be surprised that every rich country in the world has a policy of universal primary and secondary education as well as strong universities. Smart new technologies require well-educated researchers from good educational systems.

Advanced economies also require smart, well-educated workers to implement the new technologies. Consequently, it's very important that education be available to everyone if an economy is to utilize the constant flow of innovative new processes and tools that researchers develop.

POLITICAL SYSTEMS VERSUS ECONOMIC SYSTEMS

The three categories used by economists to distinguish economic systems — market, command, and traditional — are only meant to convey information about a nation's economic system. By contrast, terms like communism, capitalism, democracy, and socialism tend to either focus exclusively on a nation's political system or on how a nation's political system is interwoven with its economic system.

Consider the word democracy. It refers to a political system in which a nation's government is controlled by its citizens. Whether they direct the government to institute an economic system that is market, command, or traditional isn't specified by that fact that the country is run democratically. The fact that a country is a democracy also says nothing by itself about whether the government favors private ownership or government control of businesses.

In contrast, communist and socialist systems are supposed to feature democratic governments owning and operating all the businesses in an economy on behalf of the people. That is, both systems are by definition supposed to encompass both a nation's political system as well as its economic system.

(continued)

(continued)

Please note, however, that actual communist and socialist governments have tended to fail in achieving their democratic political aspirations. Instead, communist and socialist nations like the old Soviet Union, North Korea, Cuba, and, recently, Venezuela, tend to feature non-democratic totalitarian governments that use their almost total control over commerce as yet another tool for suppressing their citizens.

Finally, understand that the term *capitalism* has many conflicting definitions. For some, it refers to economies featuring private property and free markets. To others, it's defined by industrialization and the use of large amounts of capital equipment in the production process. Yet another group uses it to describe a political-economic system in which the rich owners of large businesses use their power and influence over both commerce and the government to exploit the poor. Because of these many conflicting (and controversial!) definitions, economists tend to avoid the term *capitalism* in favor of more precise descriptive terms like *market-based economy*.

2

Microeconomics: The Science of Consumer and Firm Behavior

IN THIS PART . . .

Discover the relationships among prices, quantity supplied, and quantity demanded and how changes in supply or demand affect market equilibrium.

Understand how people maximize their happiness by navigating marginal utility, weighing alternatives, and choosing just the right amounts given their limited budgets.

Know how and why firms set output levels to maximize profits and what they do when they lose money.

Check out the social benefits of markets, how they can maximize total surplus, and what taxes and price controls do in a market setting.

Find out what monopolies are and how they behave.

Examine what collusion is and why some collusive oligopolies work while others don't.

or demanded

» **Focusing on market equilibrium**

» **Understanding how shifts in demand or supply affect market equilibrium**

» **Identifying policies that prevent market equilibrium**

Chapter 4

Supply and Demand Made Easy

I n the modern economy, most economic activity takes place in *markets*, places where buyers and sellers come together to trade money for a good or service. A market doesn't have to be an actual place, and many markets nowadays exist only in cyberspace. But no matter what sort of institutional arrangement markets have, they all tend to behave in the same way.

REMEMBER

A very simple model called *supply and demand* does an excellent job of describing how markets work, regardless of which good or service is being bought and sold. This model very reasonably separates buyers from sellers and then summarizes each group's behavior with a single line on a graph. The buyers' behavior is captured by the *demand curve*, and the sellers' behavior is captured by the *supply curve.* By putting these two curves on the same graph, economists can show how buyers and sellers interact to determine how much of any particular item will be sold, as well as the price at which it will be sold.

The supply and demand model of markets is the economics profession's most famous contribution to human understanding. It's useful in so many areas, shedding light on exactly how markets set prices and allocate resources, as well as giving accurate predictions about how government policies will affect the behavior of markets. For instance, this model can tell you why the price of gas goes up during the summer and why the price of wheat goes down after a good harvest. It can also predict — correctly — that agricultural price supports will cause an overproduction of food and that rent control will lead to a shortage of housing.

I begin this chapter by explaining demand and supply separately and showing you how to draw and manipulate supply curves and demand curves; the demand curves capture the behavior of buyers, and the supply curves capture the behavior of suppliers. The next step is to watch the curves interact to see how markets function both when left to their own devices and when subject to government regulation or intervention. After reading this chapter, you should have new insights on virtually everything you read about commerce, business, and politics.

Deconstructing Demand

People want to buy things, and economists refer to that desire as *demand.* When they say *demand,* economists aren't referring to pie-in-the-sky dreams or to mere wishful thinking along the lines of, "I want a billion jillion scoops of ice cream!" Rather, when they say *demand,* economists mean how much of something people are both *willing and able* to pay for. So although I may want a billion jillion scoops of ice cream (butter pecan, please!), that's not my demand in the sense that economists use it. Rather, my demand is three scoops, because that's how much I'm willing and able to buy at the price that my local ice cream shop charges.

To be precise, what I've actually just described is my *quantity demanded,* which refers to how much I demand at a specific price, holding constant everything else in the world, including my income, my preferences, and the prices of other goods and services. By contrast, when an economist uses the word *demand,* he means the whole range of quantities that a person will demand while holding constant all other possible influencing factors.

In this section, I look at how a product's own price determines a demand curve's slope and how changes in any other factor — including preferences and the prices of other products — can shift the position of the demand curve.

Prices and other stuff: Looking at what affects quantity demanded

Economists divide everything that can possibly affect the quantity demanded into two groups: the price and everything else. Here's what "everything else" includes:

>> **Tastes and preferences:** Chief among the non-price things that affect quantity demanded are tastes and preferences. For instance, no matter how low the price gets, I won't buy even a single container of cherry-and-chocolate ice cream, because I think it's gross. At the same time, however, lots of people love cherry-and-chocolate ice cream so much that even if the price got very high, they'd still be willing to buy quite a bit of it. No matter how much a container of a certain flavor costs, the people who love it will always have a higher quantity demanded than I will. Because this is true for every possible price, you can say that they have a *higher demand* than I do.

>> **Other prices:** People's demand for product X is affected not only by the price of product X, but also by the prices of everything else they can possibly buy. If, for example, the price of movie tickets rise, people are likely to not only go to the movies less often but to spend the money they save by not going to the movies so often on other entertainment activities, such as going to concerts. Thus, a change in the price of *movie* tickets will affect their quantity demanded of *concert* tickets — even when the price of concert tickets hasn't changed.

>> **Income:** As you get richer, you increase your quantity demanded of certain goods that you've always liked and can now afford to buy more of. These are called *normal goods.* On the other hand, you decrease your quantity demanded of things that you were buying only because you were too poor to get what you really wanted. These are called *inferior goods.* For example, new cars are normal goods, and really old, poorly running used cars are inferior goods. Similarly, freshly made organic salads are normal goods, and three-day-old, discounted bread is an inferior good.

Given the complexity of variables such as preferences and income, why do economists insist on dividing everything that could influence your quantity demanded into only two groups, the price and everything else? First, they want to concentrate on prices. Second, when you translate the concept of demand into a graph and create a demand curve, prices have a very different effect than do the other variables. Price changes move you along a given demand curve, while the other variables determine where the curve is placed and how it's shaped.

Graphing the demand curve

Prices have an *inverse relationship* with the quantity demanded. In other words, the higher the price, the less quantity people demand (if all the other things that could possibly affect the quantity demanded are held constant). That's why a demand curve slopes downward.

I've drawn a demand curve in Figure 4-1. Say that this demand curve represents the demand for cabbages. On the vertical axis is the price of cabbages, measured in dollars. The horizontal axis is the number, or quantity, of cabbages that are demanded at any given price.

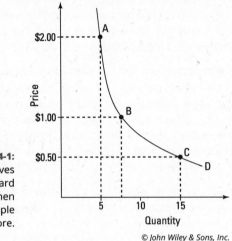

FIGURE 4-1:
Demand curves slope downward because when prices fall, people buy more.

© John Wiley & Sons, Inc.

As you can see, the demand curve slopes downward, reflecting the fact that there's an inverse relationship between the price of cabbages and the number of cabbages people want to buy. For instance, consider Point *A* on the demand curve. At that point, people demand five cabbages at a price of $2 per cabbage. However, as you can see by looking at Point *B*, if the price drops to $1 per cabbage, people demand eight cabbages. And if the price drops to only $0.50 per cabbage, they demand 15 cabbages.

Here's how changes in price and other factors are reflected in the demand curve:

>> Increases or decreases in price simply move you *along* the demand curve.

>> Nonprice factors (such as changes in people's income or wealth and changes in their tastes or preferences) determine where the demand curve is located and how it's shaped, so if any of these factors changes, the demand curve *shifts* its location.

For instance, suppose that a government health study comes out saying that cabbages make people really attractive to members of the opposite sex. Naturally, this is going to increase the demand for cabbages. Geometrically, the effect is to shift the demand curve to the right. I've illustrated this effect in Figure 4-2, where the demand curve before the study is announced is labeled D, and the demand curve after the study is announced is labeled D'.

Whenever a demand curve moves, economists say that there has been a *shift in demand.* In this case, demand has increased, whereas if the curve had shifted to the left, you would say that demand decreased. Implicit in this way of describing the movements is the fact that the quantities demanded either increase or decrease *while holding prices constant.*

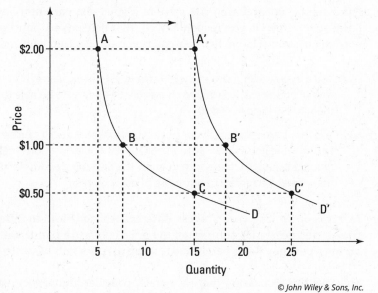

FIGURE 4-2:
An increase in demand causes the demand curve to shift right from D to D'.

© John Wiley & Sons, Inc.

WARNING

You have to distinguish between changes in quantities demanded that occur because the price changes (these are movements along a given curve) and changes in quantities demanded that occur because something besides the price changes (these are shifts of the entire curve). Anything besides the price that affects the quantity demanded shifts the demand curve left or right.

To see the difference, compare Point A and Point A'. Both points share the same price of $2 per cabbage, but thanks to the recently released government study, people now demand 15 cabbages at that price (at Point A') rather than 5 cabbages at that price (at Point A). Because the price is the same for the two points, you *know* that the change in the quantity demanded was caused by something other than price. Similarly, you can look at what happens to the quantity demanded while holding the price constant at $1: It increases from 8 before the study to 18 after, moving from Point *B* to Point *B'*.

Opportunity costs: Setting the slope of the demand curve

A product's price is a measure of sacrifice, of the quantity of other goods and services that must be given up to obtain one unit of the product in question. The *slopes of demand curves* indicate how people react to changes in prices — and, consequently, to changes in how much of other goods and services must be sacrificed to obtain one unit of the product in question.

For instance, imagine that the price of a good you currently buy falls from $10 down to $9. How do you respond? Well, that depends on how you feel about the good in question relative to other goods you could spend your money on:

>> You may buy a lot more of the good in question because extra units bring you a lot of happiness, and you're consequently grateful to be able to purchase them for $9 instead of $10.

>> You may barely increase your buying because although it's nice that you can now buy the good for $9 instead of $10, extra units just don't make you all that much happier. In such a situation, the best thing about the price cut is that it frees up money to buy more of other things.

In terms of demand curves, these different reactions lead to different slopes. The person who buys a lot more when the price falls has a flat demand curve, and the person whose purchases barely budge when the price falls has a steep demand curve.

To make this discussion more concrete, consider Figure 4-3, where I've drawn two separate demand curves on two separate graphs. The one on the left is my demand for pecans. The one on the right is my sister's demand for pecans.

Notice that my demand curve has a very steep slope, whereas my sister's demand curve is very flat. The difference is completely the result of differences in how we react to price changes. You can see this by comparing my quantity demanded at Point *A* with my quantity demanded at Point *B*. Even though the price doubles from $1 per bag of pecans to $2 per bag of pecans, my quantity demanded falls only from six bags to five bags. By contrast, when the price doubles from $1 per bag to $2 per bag, my sister's quantity demanded falls greatly, from 15 bags to only 5 bags.

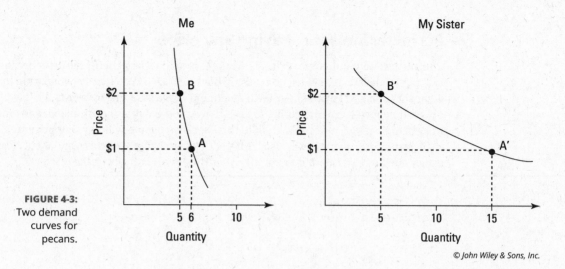

FIGURE 4-3:
Two demand curves for pecans.

© John Wiley & Sons, Inc.

Loosely speaking, this means that my sister is much less attached to pecans than I am. When I see the price double, it barely reduces my quantity demanded, meaning that I'm willing to give up a lot of other things that I could've spent the money on in order to keep buying almost as many pecans as before.

My sister, on the other hand, reacts very differently. Although she initially buys more pecans than I do when the price is only a dollar, doubling the price causes her to cut her pecan-buying by ten bags. What this says is that when the price doubles, she decides that she would be better off cutting back sharply on pecan purchases in order to spend her money on other things. In plain English, she's not nearly as attached to pecans as I am. (Pecan pie, pecan peanut butter cookies, butter pecan ice cream . . . mmmmmm!)

Elasticity: Looking at extreme demand cases

Economists have borrowed the word *elasticity* to describe how changes in one variable affect another variable. If they say *demand elasticity,* they're referring to how much the quantity demanded changes when the price changes. If the same change in price causes my quantity demanded to fall much less than my sister's quantity demanded (as in Figure 4-3), then my demand curve has a lot less demand elasticity than does my sister's.

Extreme cases of demand elasticity are illustrated in Figure 4-4 using two demand curves, the first being perfectly vertical and the second being perfectly horizontal.

Perfectly inelastic: Paying any price

The vertical demand curve, *D* in Figure 4-4, is said to be *perfectly inelastic*, because exactly *Q* units are demanded no matter what the price is. You may be wondering just what sort of a good would have such a demand curve, and the answer is life-saving drugs. If you need exactly *Q* units to keep living, you'll pay any price asked. Ransoms in kidnappings are also probably like this, because people will pay any price to get their family members back. Also, drug addicts probably feel this way about their drugs; they're so desperate to get high that they don't care about the price.

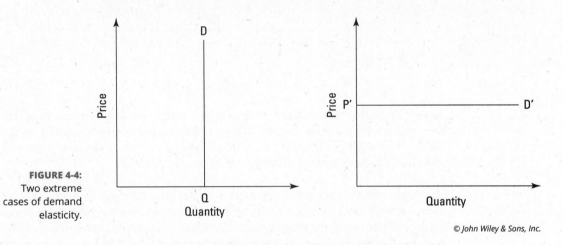

FIGURE 4-4:
Two extreme cases of demand elasticity.

© John Wiley & Sons, Inc.

Perfectly elastic: Buying all or nothing

The horizontal demand curve, *D'* in Figure 4-4, is said to be *perfectly elastic.* To understand this name, try to imagine a very gradually sloping demand curve that's almost — but not quite — horizontal. On such a very shallowly sloped demand curve, even a small change in price causes a big change in the quantity demanded. Indeed, the flatter a demand curve becomes, the greater the change in the quantity demanded for any given price change. For instance, look at Figure 4-3 and compare how a $1 change in the price of pecans causes a much bigger change in my sister's quantity demanded on her flatter demand curve than it does on my steeper demand curve.

You can think of a perfectly horizontal demand curve as being the most extreme case of this phenomenon, so that even the tiniest change in price brings forth an infinite change in quantity demanded. That is, if prices are above *P'* in the right-hand graph in Figure 4-4, you buy nothing, and if prices are at *P'* or just a penny less, you buy a whole lot. (*Infinite* is a whole lot.)

A concrete example of such a situation would be if you worked for a large restaurant chain and had to buy tons of ketchup. Your choices are brand X and brand Y, but because they taste exactly the same, the only thing that matters is the price. Consequently, if the price of brand X is even the slightest bit lower than brand Y, you'll buy tons of brand X and none of brand Y. If the price of X is even slightly higher than that of brand Y, you'll buy tons of Y and none of X.

Please realize that demand curves that are perfectly elastic or perfectly inelastic are not normal. Nearly all demand curves slope downward, meaning that moderate changes in prices bring forth moderate changes in quantities demanded. In Chapter 5, I explain why this is so by looking at how consumers make trade-offs between different goods in order to maximize the happiness that they can get from spending their limited budgets.

Sorting Out Supply

In the economist's view of the *supply* of goods and services, the key concept is that supplying things is costly, and you have to pay people to supply the things you want. Even more interesting, though, is the fact that the more you want them to supply, the higher their costs of supplying each additional unit. In other words, the first units tend to be relatively inexpensive to produce, while later units become more and more costly to produce. (In Chapter 6, I explain why this holds true.) If you want producers to make more and more, you have to pay them more and more.

In this section, I explain how rising costs cause supply curves to slope upward and how entire supply curves can shift when the costs of inputs change.

Graphing the supply curve

A *supply curve* shows the minimum prices at which someone is willing to sell various amounts of a good or service. Because production costs rise as people make more of something, suppliers insist on more money for larger quantities. That's why supply curves slope upward.

Imagine that a farmer named Babbage likes to grow cabbage. In Figure 4-5, I graph Mr. Babbage's supply of cabbages and label it S. (I was tempted to label it B^S, for *Babbage's Supply*, but I didn't want you telling your friends that my book was full of B^S.)

The horizontal axis gives the number of cabbages supplied, while the vertical axis gives the price per cabbage that you have to pay to get Mr. Babbage to supply you any given number of cabbages. Thus, Point *A* says that you have to pay Mr. Babbage 50 cents per cabbage if you want him to supply you with five cabbages.

Because Mr. Babbage's production costs rise as he tries to grow more and more cabbages, you have to pay him $1 per cabbage if you want him to grow you ten cabbages, as shown by Point *B*. And you have to pay $1.50 per cabbage if you want 15 cabbages, as shown by Point *C*.

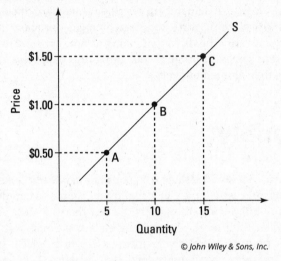

© John Wiley & Sons, Inc.

FIGURE 4-5:
Supply curves have an upward slope because of increasing production costs.

REMEMBER

Keep in mind that the points on the supply curve don't represent the prices that Mr. Babbage *wants* to receive for any given amount of cabbages — obviously, he wants to receive a gazillion dollars for each one. Rather, what each dollar amount on a supply curve represents is the minimum that you could pay him and still get him to produce the desired amount. At Point *A*, you can get him to produce five cabbages if you pay him 50 cents per cabbage; if you offer him 49 cents per cabbage, he won't do it. Why not? Because he has costs, and he can cover them at 50 cents per cabbage but not at 49 cents per cabbage.

Separating sales price and production cost

Economists split all the things that can affect the quantity supplied into two groups: the price and everything else. The things that go into *everything else* all relate to production costs — the costs of supplying the good in question.

TIP

When you see a particular supply curve, imagine that it derives from a particular production technology used by the supplier. Because each possible technology creates its own unique relationship between output levels and costs, some technologies give rise to steeply sloped supply curves, while others generate fairly flat supply curves. (See Chapter 6 for all the details on firms' supply curves.)

Regardless of exactly how the curve is sloped or where it's positioned, the fact that costs increase as output increases means that you need to offer a higher and higher price to the supplier if you want to obtain more units. And that's basically why prices move you along supply curves.

Price changes: Moving along the supply curve

Varying the price of an item moves you along a given supply curve because the supply curve represents the minimum payment you need to give the supplier in order for him to supply the amount of output you want.

REMEMBER

Suppliers look at whatever price is being offered and make as many units as are profitable but no more. Because costs rise with each additional unit produced, the only way to get suppliers to produce more is to offer them higher prices. Therefore, raising or lowering prices moves you *along* the supply curve as the suppliers' quantities supplied respond to changing prices.

To see how this works, consider what happens if you offer to pay Mr. Babbage $1 per cabbage, and then you let him choose how many cabbages he wants to produce. Given his supply curve in Figure 4-5, he's going to want to produce exactly ten cabbages and no more. That's because for cabbage number one through cabbage number nine, the cost of production is less than what you're paying him. For example, consider Point *A* from Figure 4-5. At Point *A*, his production costs are 50 cents per cabbage. That means that if you're going to pay him $1 per cabbage, he'll be making a nice profit. Similarly, because his cost per cabbage for producing six cabbages is also less than $1 per cabbage, he'll also want to make number six. The same is true of cabbages seven, eight, and nine.

At ten cabbages, Mr. Babbage is indifferent, because his cost per cabbage is $1 and you're offering him $1. In such cases, economists assume that he'll produce the tenth just to keep the buyer happy. But notice that Mr. Babbage would not produce at Point *C* if you were offering him $1 per cabbage. That's because his cost of production is $1.50 per cabbage, and he would lose money.

Cost changes: Shifting the supply curve

Because a supplier's production costs determine where his supply curve is located and how it's sloped, changes in production costs cause changes in the supply curve. Things that make production more costly will shift the supply curve up, and things that lower costs will shift the supply curve down.

Suppose Mr. Babbage's production costs increase because the government imposes a new organic farming law under which he's required to grow cabbages without using pesticides. In response, he has to hire lots of extra workers to kill pests with tweezers instead of simply spraying cheap chemicals.

Figure 4-6 shows the change in the supply curve. Because Mr. Babbage's production costs have increased, the minimum you have to pay him to produce any given level of output also goes up. Consequently, his supply curve can be thought of as shifting upward vertically from S_0 to S_1.

I've drawn the shift to show that Mr. Babbage's cost of production is 50 cents higher for each cabbage, no matter how many cabbages are produced. Compare Points A and A'. Before the new environmental regulation, Mr. Babbage was willing to produce five cabbages if you paid him 50 cents per cabbage. After the policy change, you have to pay him $1.00 per cabbage if you want him to grow you five cabbages.

Similarly, Points B and B' show that before the regulation, he would grow you ten cabbages if you offered him $1 per cabbage. Now, you have to offer him $1.50 per cabbage if you want him to grow ten.

TIP

It's perfectly kosher to think of supply curves as moving left and right when cost structures shift. That is, you can say that the supply curve shifts *left* when costs increase, and you can quickly extrapolate that a decrease in costs would shift the supply curve to the *right*.

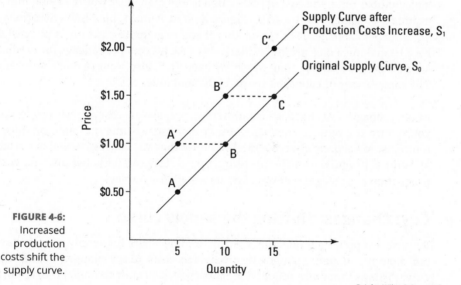

© John Wiley & Sons, Inc.

FIGURE 4-6:
Increased production costs shift the supply curve.

For instance, consider the quantity supplied at a price of $1.00 both before and after the cost increase. Before the cost increase, Mr. Babbage is willing to supply you ten cabbages for $1.00, putting you at Point B on the original supply curve. But after the cost increase, he's willing to supply you only five cabbages for $1.00, putting you at Point A' on the shifted supply curve. Similarly, at a price of $1.50, Mr. Babbage was previously willing to supply you with 15 cabbages (Point C), whereas after the cost increase he's willing to supply only ten cabbages at that price (Point B').

Having two ways to interpret supply curve shifts is actually rather handy. In some situations it's easier to think of the shifts as either right or left, while in others it's easier to think of them as up or down.

Using elasticity to understand extreme supply cases

Two extreme supply curves help to illustrate how production costs and prices combine to determine the quantity that will be supplied at any particular price. I've illustrated these two cases in Figure 4-7. The graph on the left shows a vertical supply curve and illustrates what economists call *perfectly inelastic supply.* The graph on the right with a horizontal supply curve illustrates what economists call *perfectly elastic supply.*

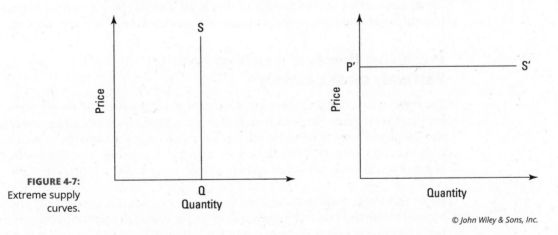

FIGURE 4-7:
Extreme supply curves.

© John Wiley & Sons, Inc.

Being unable to make more: Perfectly inelastic supply

The left graph of Figure 4-7 illustrates a situation in which the price has no effect on the quantity supplied. As you can see in the graph, no matter how low or how high the price, the quantity Q is supplied. Because the quantity supplied is completely unresponsive to the price, it is said to be *perfectly inelastic,* and supply situations that look like this are usually referred to as situations of *perfectly inelastic supply.*

I expect you're curious about what things have perfectly inelastic supply curves. The answer is unique things that cannot be reproduced. Examples include:

>> **The Hope Diamond:** Because it's one of a kind — there'd still be only one Hope Diamond, no matter how much anyone wanted to pay — its supply curve is vertical.

>> **Land:** As comedian Will Rogers said back in the early 20th century, "Buy land. They ain't making more of it."

>> **The electromagnetic spectrum:** There's only one set of radio frequencies, and everyone has to share because there's no way to make more.

An interesting thing about such situations is that there are no production costs. Because of this, offering the owner a price is not an incentive in the way it is when you pay a producer enough to make something for you. Rather, the price serves solely to transfer the right of ownership and usage from one person to another.

Historically, the fact that the quantity of land supplied has nothing to do with production costs has been the justification for property taxes. The way governments see it, they can tax land as harshly as they want because there's no need to worry that the amount of land — and, consequently, the tax base — will ever decrease.

Producing however much you want: Perfectly elastic supply

The right-hand graph in Figure 4-7 illustrates the case where the supply curve is perfectly horizontal. The idea here is that the supplier is producing something that has nonincreasing costs. No matter how many units you want her to produce, it always costs her only P' dollars to make a unit. Consequently, whether you want one unit produced or one jillion units produced, you pay her P' dollars per unit.

In the real world, there probably aren't any supply curves that are perfectly elastic because production costs typically rise with output levels (as I explain in Chapter 6). But a few supply curves do come close. For instance, the supply curve for pencils looks nearly perfectly elastic because pencil companies seem to be able to increase production levels by millions of units with only very small increases in costs.

Bringing Supply and Demand Together

Now it's time to bring supply and demand curves together so they can interact. First up is the market equilibrium point, where the supply and demand curves cross — in that discussion, I show you how markets determine the amounts, as well as the prices, of goods and services sold. Then I explain how markets find new equilibrium points when demand or supply curves shift.

Market equilibrium: Seeking a balance

Supply and demand curves are especially useful when you graph them on the same axes. In Figure 4-8, I've drawn a demand curve and a supply curve and labeled them *D* and *S*, respectively.

REMEMBER

The point where the supply and demand curves cross marks how much the good or service in question costs and how much of it gets sold. Just remember: X marks the spot! This price and quantity are known as the *market price* and the *market quantity.*

In Figure 4-8, I label the market price and market quantity as P^* and Q^*, respectively. What makes this price and this quantity special is that at price P^*, the quantity that buyers demand is equal to the quantity that producers want to supply.

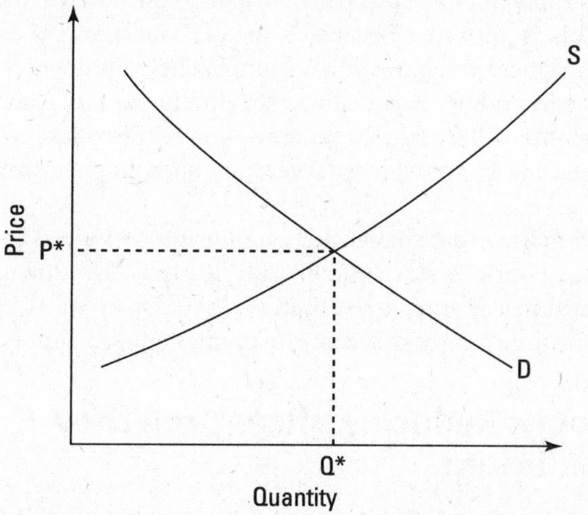

© John Wiley & Sons, Inc.

FIGURE 4-8: The market equilibrium price and quantity happen where the demand curve crosses the supply curve.

Start at price P^* and move to the right along the dashed line. You can see that buyers demand Q^* at that price and sellers supply Q^* at that price. Because quantity demanded equals quantity supplied, both producers and consumers are content. The consumers get exactly the quantity that they want to buy at price P^*, and the producers sell exactly the quantity that they want to sell at price P^*. With everyone getting what they want, nobody is going to cause any changes.

Economists use the word *equilibrium* to describe situations like this one, in which all of the involved parties are happy with the status quo and thus have no reason to change their current behavior. By contrast, situations in which one or more of the parties have an incentive to change their behavior are referred to as *disequilibrium* situations.

REMEMBER

A wonderful thing about the model of demand and supply is that at any price besides the market price, P^*, there is always some sort of pressure from either buyers or sellers to bring the model back to the equilibrium price and quantity. Consequently, no matter where the market starts, it always ends back at equilibrium — market forces will always push the price and quantity back to these values. Consequently, the market price and market quantity are also called the *equilibrium price* and the *equilibrium quantity*.

Demonstrating the stability of the market equilibrium

The market equilibrium is called a *stable equilibrium* because no matter where the demand and supply model starts off, it always gravitates back to the market equilibrium. This is very nice because it means that markets are self-correcting, and if you know where the demand and supply curves are, you know where prices and quantities will end up. Especially gratifying is the fact that the actions of the market participants — buyers and sellers — move the market toward equilibrium without the need for any outside intervention, such as government regulations.

In this section, I show that the market equilibrium is indeed stable. First, I focus on the fact that if prices start higher than P^*, they fall down to P^*. After that, I show you that if prices start lower than P^*, they rise up to P^*. The fact that prices always move toward P^* indicates that the market equilibrium is stable.

Excess supply: Reducing prices until they reach equilibrium

In Figure 4-9, you can see what happens when you have a price like P^H that starts out higher than the market equilibrium price, P^*. At price P^H, the quantity demanded by buyers, Q^D, is less than the quantity supplied by sellers, Q^S. (I use dashed lines to show where P^H intersects the demand and supply curves.) Economists refer to such a situation as an *excess supply* or a *surplus*. A situation of excess supply can't be an equilibrium because sellers aren't able to sell everything they want to sell at price P^H.

In fact, of the total amount that sellers want to sell, Q^S, only the amount Q^D is sold, meaning that the remaining amount, $Q^S - Q^D$, remains unsold unless something is done. Well, something *is* done. Sellers see the huge pile of unsold goods and do what any store does when it can't sell something at current prices: They have a sale.

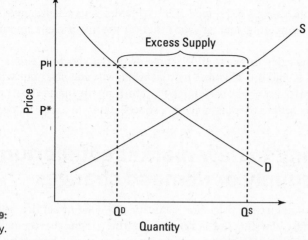

FIGURE 4-9:
Excess supply.

© John Wiley & Sons, Inc.

Sellers lower the price and keep lowering it until supply no longer exceeds demand. You can see in Figure 4-9 that this means sellers keep lowering the price until it falls all the way down to P^*, because that's the only price at which the quantity demanded by buyers equals the quantity that sellers want to supply.

Excess demand: Raising prices until they reach equilibrium

Figure 4-10 shows a situation in which the initial price, P^L, is lower than the market equilibrium price, P^*. You can see that in this case, the problem is not excess supply but rather *excess demand* because at price P^L, the amount that buyers want to buy, Q^D, exceeds the amount that suppliers want to sell, Q^S.

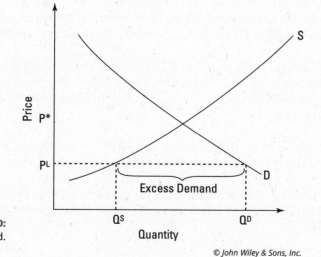

FIGURE 4-10:
Excess demand.

© John Wiley & Sons, Inc.

In other words, there is a *shortage* of $Q^D - Q^S$ units. As a result, buyers start bidding the price up, competing against each other for the insufficient amount of the good.

As long as the price is less than P^*, some degree of shortage exists, and the price continues to be bid up. This means that whenever you start out with a price less than P^*, the price is pushed back up to P^*, returning the market to its equilibrium — the only place where there is neither a shortage nor an excess supply.

Adjusting to new market equilibriums when supply or demand changes

Market forces adjust the price and quantity of a good or service until they correspond to where the demand curve crosses the supply curve (see the preceding section for details). After the price and quantity reach that point — the *market equilibrium* — they don't change. They stay right there as long as the demand and supply curves don't move.

In this section, I show you how prices and quantities *do* adjust if the demand and supply curves change. I illustrate by first showing you a demand curve shift, followed by a supply curve shift.

Reacting to an increase in demand

If demand increases and supply stays the same, the equilibrium price and the equilibrium quantity both increase. Take a close look at Figure 4-11, which shows what happens if the demand curve shifts to the right from D_0 to D_1 while the supply curve S stays the same. Before the shift, the market equilibrium price is P^*_0, and the market equilibrium quantity is Q^*_0. When the demand curve shifts to the right to D_1, the price momentarily stays the same at P^*_0. But this price can't last because with the new demand curve, there is now an excess demand. That is, at price P^*_0, the quantity demanded, Q^D_1, exceeds the quantity supplied, Q^*_0.

Any such shortage causes buyers to bid up the price (see the earlier section "Excess demand: Raising prices until they reach equilibrium"). The result is that the price rises and continues to rise until it reaches P^*_1, the price where demand curve D_1 crosses supply curve S.

Note that when moving from the first equilibrium to the second, the equilibrium quantity increases from Q^*_0 to Q^*_1. This result makes good sense because if demand increases and buyers are willing to pay more for something, you would expect more of it to be supplied. Also, the price goes up from one equilibrium to the other because to get suppliers to supply more in a world of rising costs, you have to pay them more.

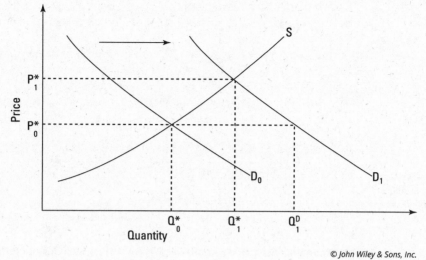

© John Wiley & Sons, Inc.

FIGURE 4-11:
A rightward shift
of the demand
curve.

A much more subtle thing to realize, however, is that the slope of the supply curve *interacts* with the demand curve to determine how big the changes in price and quantity will be. Think of a vertical (perfectly inelastic) supply curve, such as the one in the left-hand graph of Figure 4-7. For such a supply curve, any increase in demand increases *only* the price because the quantity can't increase. On the other hand, if you are dealing with a horizontal (perfectly elastic) supply curve, as in the right-hand graph of Figure 4-7, a rightward shift in demand increases *only* the quantity, because the price is fixed at P'.

When you consider these two extreme cases, it hammers home the point that in a situation like Figure 4-11, neither demand nor supply is in complete control. Their interaction jointly determines equilibrium prices and quantities and how they change if the demand curve or the supply curve shifts.

Reacting to a decrease in supply

If supply decreases and demand stays the same, the equilibrium price increases, but the equilibrium quantity decreases. Consider Figure 4-12, in which the supply curve shifts from S_0 to S_1 because of an increase in production costs. (As I discuss in the earlier section "Cost changes: Shifting the supply curve," this increase in costs can be considered to shift the supply curve either up or to the left. In Figure 4-12, I've drawn a vertical arrow to indicate a vertical shift, but I could've just as correctly put in a left arrow to indicate a leftward shift.)

The shift in supply causes the market equilibrium to adjust. The original equilibrium is at price P^*_0 and quantity Q^*_0, which is the point where the demand curve D and the original supply curve S_0 cross. When production costs increase, the supply curve shifts to S_1.

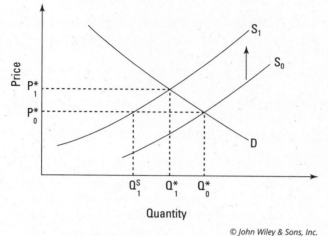

FIGURE 4-12:
A vertical shift of
the supply curve.

Quantity

© John Wiley & Sons, Inc.

For a moment, the price remains at P^*_0. But this price cannot continue because the quantity demanded at this price, Q^*_0, exceeds the quantity supplied, Q^s_1. This situation of excess demand causes the price to be bid up until reaching the new equilibrium price of P^*_1, at which price the quantity demanded equals the quantity supplied at Q^*_1.

If you compare this situation of increasing costs with the situation of increasing demand in the preceding section, you notice that in both cases, the equilibrium price rises. However, be sure to note that the equilibrium quantities go in opposite directions. An increase in demand causes an increase in equilibrium quantity, but an increase in costs causes a reduction in equilibrium quantity.

REMEMBER

The equilibrium quantity falls when supply decreases because the increase in production costs doesn't just affect the producer. In order to stay in business, the producer has to pass along the cost increase. But when he passes the increase along, it has a tendency to discourage buyers. The result is that the equilibrium quantity falls because some buyers are not willing to pay the higher prices. Those who still want to buy are willing to pay the higher prices — a fact that is reflected in the increased market price.

Price Controls: Keeping Prices Away from Market Equilibrium

Left to its own devices, a market always adjusts until the price and quantity are determined by where the demand and supply curves cross. The market equilibrium price has the very nice property that everyone who wants to buy at that price can do so, and everyone who wants to sell at that price can also do so. In other words, the quantity demanded equals the quantity supplied.

However, the market price is not always the politically expedient price, and governments sometimes interfere in markets to prevent the market equilibrium from being reached. Such interventions happen because politically influential buyers think the market price is too high or because politically influential sellers think the market price is too low.

Unfortunately, government intervention creates a whole new set of problems related to the misallocation of resources. In some cases, government intervention even hurts those whom the intervention is designed to help. In this section, I explain the effects of two kinds of government intervention: price ceilings and price floors. Price ceilings prevent prices from rising to the market equilibrium, whereas price floors keep prices from falling to the market equilibrium. (Obviously, you use only one or the other!)

Setting upper limits with price ceilings

Sometimes the government intervenes in a market to ensure that the price stays below the market equilibrium price, P^*. Such policies are called *price ceilings* because they prevent the price from rising as high as it would if left alone. Prices hit the ceiling and then go no higher.

You may have heard about price ceilings on apartment rent. For instance, in an attempt to provide low-cost housing for the poor, city governments may place price ceilings on how much a landlord can charge. The problem is that with prices artificially low, the quantity demanded is greater than the quantity supplied, creating a shortage.

To see how this works, look at Figure 4-13, in which the price ceiling P^c lies below the market equilibrium price of P^*. To make clear that you have a ceiling that the price can't rise above, I've drawn a solid horizontal line starting from P^c and extending right.

However, at the ceiling price, the quantity demanded, Q^D, far exceeds the quantity supplied, Q^S. This may not seem like such a big problem, but the shortage has to be dealt with somehow. You have to figure out a way to allocate the insufficient supply among all the people who want it. What often happens is that people end up waiting in lines, or *queues*, to get the limited supply.

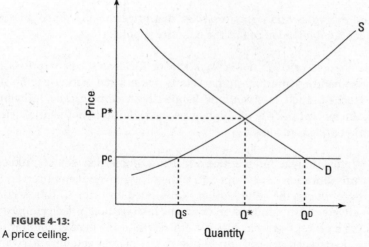

FIGURE 4-13:
A price ceiling.

© John Wiley & Sons, Inc.

During my grad school days at Berkeley, there were price ceilings for how much rent a landlord could charge — a policy euphemistically referred to as *rent control.* Because rents were kept far below their market equilibrium value, there were always many more people who wanted to rent apartments than there were apartments available. The result was that any time an apartment became available, you stood in line with — literally — 200 people to fill out a rental application. With so many potential renters vying for one apartment, the landlord could take his pick — hence, rental applications were often five to ten pages long and asked you *everything.* If you weren't picked, you had to go get in the next line for the next apartment that happened to come on the market.

It didn't matter if you had enough money to pay higher rent. It didn't matter if you were much more desperate than other potential renters. Because the government had created an excess demand, you had to wait in line and hope and pray that you'd get an apartment.

The main result of the policy was that thousands of people wasted tens of thousands of hours each year waiting in line — and some of them still didn't get apartments! Even worse was the fact that the policy actually reduced the total number of apartments available in the city of Berkeley. You can see this by the fact that $Q^S < Q^*$ in Figure 4-13. The quantity supplied of apartments falls from Q^* to Q^S because the rent-control price is not high enough to compensate many property owners for the costs of making their apartments available for rent. Those with the highest costs cease providing apartments when the price of rentals is forced down from P^* to P^C.

FIRST WORLD SUPPORTS, THIRD WORLD SUFFERING

A perverse result of agricultural price supports in rich countries like the United States and the nations of the European Union is the great damage they inflict on developing nations. For instance, the U.S. price of sugar is substantially higher than the world price because the United States restricts imports of cheaper foreign sugar in order to help U.S. food production giants sell corn-based sweeteners. The result is that thousands of poor Third World farmers who could otherwise make a living selling sugar to Americans are left without a livelihood.

Even worse is what the United States does with some of the many tons of excess agricultural products that pile up due to its agricultural price supports. Not wanting to sell the excess in the United States and thereby depress U.S. prices, the government often sends the stuff free to developing countries as food aid. That sounds nice and friendly, but when all that free wheat hits Nigeria, it puts Nigerian farmers out of business. That in turn ends up making Nigeria dependent on foreign food because it no longer has enough local farmers to produce sufficient quantities of wheat to feed its own people.

Even worse, many of the newly bankrupted farmers move from the countryside to cities in search of employment, worsening urban-overcrowding problems and themselves becoming dependent on free foreign wheat to survive when most of them can't find employment. Thus, the U.S. government's attempt to make its relatively very wealthy farmers a bit richer ends up causing catastrophic harm to the truly very poor farmers of developing nations.

To avoid these problems, economists recommend that food aid from rich countries only be sent to poor countries during times of famine or drought when local farmers are unable to produce enough to feed their country. Food aid should be withdrawn as soon as a crisis ends so that it doesn't permanently undercut local food prices and the ability of local farmers to make a living.

Propping up prices with price floors

With a *price floor*, the government keeps the price of a product above its market equilibrium value in order to raise the incomes of those producing the product. Figure 4-14 shows an example where the floor price, P^F, is greater than the market equilibrium price, P^*. To clarify that prices can't fall below P^F, I've drawn a solid horizontal line at that price.

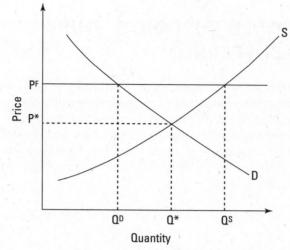

© John Wiley & Sons, Inc.

FIGURE 4-14:
A price floor.

The problem here is that at price P^F, the quantity supplied, Q^S, is much bigger than the quantity demanded, Q^D. The normal response to such a situation of excess supply would be for the price to fall. The way the government prevents this and keeps the price propped up is by stepping in and buying the excess supply.

In other words, of the total amount Q^S that's supplied at price P^F, regular consumers demand and purchase Q^D. The remainder, $Q^S - Q^D$, must be purchased by the government. That doesn't sound so bad until you read about price floors in agriculture, which are usually referred to euphemistically as *price supports* (as in, "You poor thing! All you need is a little *support!*").

Price supports generate huge piles of surplus farm output that nobody wants to buy. Consider the price support system for milk that the U.S. Department of Agriculture ran in the 1980s and 1990s. Each year, the Department of Agriculture had to buy up hundreds of thousands of gallons of milk that nobody wanted to buy at the high price the government was maintaining to help dairy farmers. What did the department do with all of that milk? It turned it into cheese that it couldn't sell (because it was also supporting the price of cheese) and stored that surplus cheese in huge refrigerated warehouses — indefinitely! And yes, this was all done at the taxpayer's expense.

Because many people have protested this sort of wastefulness, the government switched policies for some crops. The government now pays many farmers *not* to farm. That way, the farmers still get paid, but there's no worry about an excess supply that has to be destroyed or given away (for concerns about food aid, go back to the earlier sidebar "First World supports, Third Word suffering"). In terms of Figure 4-14, the goal of these policies is to shift the supply curve left until it intersects the demand curve directly over quantity Q^D. If that can be done, there will be no excess supply at price P^F.

For both price ceilings and price floors, the message you should take away is that interfering with markets typically causes great mischief. (Yet, deep inside, I'm actually hoping that the government decides to support the salaries of academic economists. I'd love to end up getting paid *not* to teach.)

» Taking account of diminishing
  marginal utility

» Watching how people weigh
  alternatives

» Choosing exactly the right amounts
  within a limited budget

Chapter **5**

Introducing Homo Economicus, the Utility-Maximizing Consumer

This chapter gets behind the demand curve (which I introduce in Chapter 4) by showing you how people come to choose the things they choose. This decision-making process is very important because human wants are what drive the economy. Firms don't randomly produce goods and services; they produce the things that people want to buy and are spending money on.

The thing that makes studying this process hard is the fact that people have so many different things they can spend their money on. If an economist was asked to research how you would spend $100 in a store that sold only blueberry muffins, his job wouldn't be so hard. What's impressive is that economists have come up with a way to explain how you would spend $100 in a store that has hundreds or even thousands of items for sale.

Even more impressive is the fact that an economist can explain not only which items you would buy but also how many of each you would buy. In other words, economic theory can explain not just *what* you demand but also the *quantities* you demand, which is where demand curves come from.

I start the chapter by discussing *utility*, which is how economists measure human happiness. Economists assume that people act in ways that maximize their happiness, but human actions are constrained, especially by limited budgets. I explain how people navigate these constraints to get the most happiness possible given the limits involved. Finally, I show how these decisions underlie and explain the slope and position of demand curves.

People must make choices because their means for satisfying their wants are limited. There's never enough money or time to do everything that you desire. Consequently, you need to choose wisely to get the most happiness out of the limited resources that you do have.

Economists and engineers refer to problems of this sort as *constrained optimization problems* because people are trying to optimize their happiness given the fact that they're constrained by their limited resources. The rest of this chapter shows you how economists model the way that people go about solving their everyday constrained optimization problem: deciding how to best spend their limited incomes on available goods and services — choosing not only which things to buy but also how much of each.

Choosing by Ranking

In order for people to choose between the exceedingly different goods and services available in the economy, they must have a way of comparing them. Comparing costs is pretty easy; you just compare prices. But how do you compare the benefits of various goods and services? How do you assess whether it's better to spend $20 on Swiss chocolate bars or on a new plaid shirt? In what ways are chocolate and shirts even comparable?

REMEMBER

Obviously, people do manage to make a comparison and rank the two choices. The way economists imagine that people do this is by assigning a common measure of happiness to each possible thing they could buy and use. Economists call this common measure of happiness *utility*, and they imagine that if they could some-how get inside your brain and measure utility, they could do so using a unit that they very uncreatively refer to as a *util*.

Given those assumptions, economists have come up with two alternative ways of thinking about how people make comparisons and choices:

>> **Cardinal utility:** Decision making under this system is based on assigning specific numbers of utils to different things — for instance, 25 utils to the pleasure associated with eating a brownie or 75 utils to the pleasure associated with watching a sunset. Making such specific assignments is called *cardinal utility* (like cardinal numbers: 1, 2, 3 . . .). Some people object to cardinal utility because it's not clear that people make such assessments — after all, how many utils do you think you receive from a sunny day or an infant's smile?

>> **Ordinal utility:** A much less objectionable thing to do is to think in terms of *ordinal utility,* a system in which you simply rank things. For instance, instead of saying that the sunset has a utility of 75, which makes it preferred over the brownie with a utility of 25, you can simply say that you prefer sunsets to brownies. This system has a much more intuitive feeling for most people and eliminates the need to try to measure things using the imaginary unit called the util.

It's been proven mathematically that you can describe the same human choice behavior using ordinal utility that you can using cardinal utility, which means that economists don't *have* to use cardinal utility. But I'm going to anyway! Why? Because explaining the crucial concept of diminishing marginal utility using the cardinal utility system is much easier. You can also explain diminishing marginal utility using the ordinal system, but the math is so hard that it's normally taught only to PhD students. So please forgive me if the cardinal utility system seems a bit unrealistic, but it's really the best way to convey this incredibly important idea.

Getting Less from More: Diminishing Marginal Utility

People get bored even with things they like; they get tired of repetition and sameness. Economists have to take account of this when studying how people choose to spend their money.

For instance, if I haven't had any pizza in a long time, I'll get a huge amount of utility from eating a slice. The melted cheese, the basil and garlic in the sauce, and the warmth in my mouth all make me very, very happy. But the thrill of pizza is dampened by eating that first slice so that if I eat a second slice, it's still very good, but not as good as the first. And if I have a third slice, it's not as good as the second. And if I keep eating and eating and eating, the additional slices of pizza will soon get sickening and produce pain instead of pleasure if I eat them.

This phenomenon isn't limited to pizza; it applies to nearly everything. Unless you're addicted to something, you get tired of it as you have more of it, and each additional unit brings you less happiness than the previous unit. To make this phenomenon clearer, look at Figure 5-1, which shows my cumulative, total utility as I eat more and more slices of pizza. For instance, my total utility after eating one slice of pizza is 24 utils. After eating two slices, it's 36 utils. And after three slices, it's 46 utils.

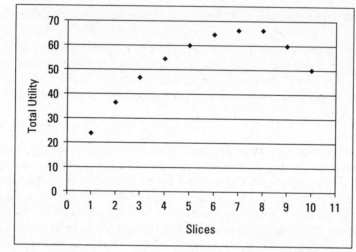

© John Wiley & Sons, Inc.

FIGURE 5-1:
My total utility as I eat more and more slices of pizza.

Notice that the amount of total utility changes with each successive slice of pizza. These incremental changes in total utility are known as *marginal utility*. As you further consider the numbers, you should notice that the extra, or marginal, utility associated with each slice is decreasing:

>> **First slice:** My total utility increases by 24 utils, from 0 to 24 utils. So the marginal utility of my first slice is 24 utils.

>> **Second slice:** My total utility increases from 24 to 36 utils, so that the marginal utility for my second slice is 12 utils.

>> **Third slice:** My marginal utility for the third slice is 10 utils because my total utility increases from 36 to 46 utils.

REMEMBER

Economists refer to this phenomenon as *diminishing marginal utility* because the extra utility, or *marginal utility*, that each successive slice brings with it decreases relative to the marginal utility brought by the previous slice. Diminishing marginal utility is simply a reflection of the fact that people get fed up or bored with things. Or, in the case of food and drink, their appetite decreases with each unit they consume.

Look at what happens in Figure 5-1 after slice number eight. My total utility actually goes down, because slice number nine is making me a little sick. And if I have slice number ten, I'm even sicker, so total utility falls again. What this decrease in total utility implies is that marginal utility must be negative for slices nine and ten. The data in Figure 5-1 shows that although my total utility increases for slices one through seven, it stalls at slice number eight and falls for slices nine and ten.

In Figure 5-2, I plot the marginal utility that I get for each slice of pizza. I feel diminishing marginal utility as I eat more and more slices of pizza, because the marginal utility that comes with each additional slice is always less than that of the previous slice. Specifically, although my marginal utility is 24 utils for the first slice, it falls to 0 utils for slice eight and then actually becomes negative for slices nine and ten because eating them makes me ill. You can see quite clearly from the downward slope of the points that my marginal utility diminishes as I eat more and more slices of pizza.

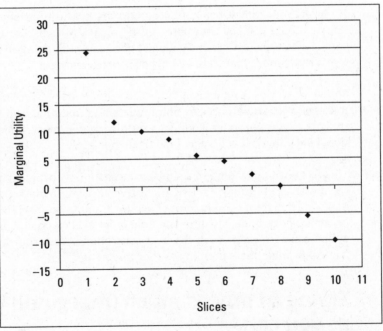

FIGURE 5-2:
The marginal utility I derive from each slice of pizza.

© John Wiley & Sons, Inc.

TIP

You have to be careful not to confuse diminishing marginal utility with *negative* marginal utility. As you see in Figure 5-2, there is diminishing marginal utility for all slices of pizza starting with the second, because each successive slice has a smaller marginal utility than the previous one. But the marginal utilities are still positive for all slices up to slice seven, and they become negative only for slices nine and ten.

That fact implies that you enjoy eating every slice up to and including the seventh slice because doing so brings you an increase in utility (happiness). So don't think that just because marginal utility is diminishing for a particular slice, you wouldn't want to eat it. Marginal utility can be diminishing but still positive. The only slices you'll outright want to avoid are the ninth and tenth.

Choosing Among Many Options When Facing a Limited Budget

The phenomenon of diminishing marginal utility makes studying human choices very interesting because preferences can't be determined in the abstract. Rather, they depend on what you've already had.

If I haven't had any ice cream for months and you ask me whether I want chocolate or vanilla, I'll say chocolate. But if you ask me whether I want chocolate or vanilla after I've just eaten a gallon of chocolate, I'm going to say vanilla because I've already more than satisfied my chocolate cravings.

So the answer to the question "Chocolate or vanilla?" isn't as straightforward as it seems. Your preferences exhibit diminishing marginal utility, and even something that you normally like a lot won't bring you much marginal utility (additional happiness) if you've just indulged in it a lot.

This fact ends up leading to a simple rule about how people make decisions when faced with limited budgets. Essentially, people want to maximize their total utility in buying a certain combination of goods — and to do that, the marginal utilities per dollar have to be equal for the final units of each good. I explain this process with a concrete example in the next subsection before showing you the mathematical formula that summarizes the simple rule.

Trying to buy as much (marginal) utility as you can

A person interested in maximizing her utility will want to figure out how to best allocate any limited budget so as to purchase the combination of goods and services that will bring her the largest possible amount of utility. But in doing so, she has to take account of the fact that each product is subject to diminishing marginal utility, so that each successive unit purchased and consumed brings less additional, or marginal, utility than the previous unit.

Suppose that I have $10 to spend and, because I'm going to the local student bar, the only two things I can spend it on are pints of beer and slices of pizza. It becomes clear to me that the intelligent thing to do is to think in terms of buying up as much utility as I can with my limited budget. Both beer and pizza make me happy, but my goal isn't just to be happy; it's to be as happy as possible given my limited budget. So I want to make sure that every dollar buys me the maximum possible amount of utility.

I don't care where utility comes from. One util from beer makes me just as happy as one util from pizza; all I care about is buying up as many utils as possible. To do that, the key concept turns out to be the price of utility. Beer and pizza have prices measured in dollars, but what is the price of a util?

Well, it depends. The first three columns in Table 5-1 repeat the data from Figure 5-1 that gave my total and marginal utilities for ten slices of pizza. But the final two columns include new data (*MU* stands for *marginal utility.*)

TABLE 5-1 **Determining the Price of Utility for Pizza**

Slice	Total Utility	Marginal Utility	MU per Dollar at $1 per Slice	MU per Dollar at $2 per Slice
1	24	24	24	12
2	36	12	12	6
3	46	10	10	5
4	54	8	8	4
5	60	6	6	3
6	64	4	4	2
7	66	2	2	1
8	66	0	0	0
9	60	–6	–6	–3
10	50	–10	–10	–5

What I've done in these last two columns is to calculate how much it costs to get some additional happiness (marginal utility) if the way you're getting it is by buying slices of pizza. Consider the fourth column, which assumes that each slice of pizza costs $1. If you buy one slice, it brings you a marginal utility of 24 utils at a cost of $1. So the MU per dollar of the first slice is 24.

But now consider spending a second dollar to buy a second slice of pizza. Because that second slice brings a marginal utility of only 12 utils, the MU per dollar spent here is only 12. And because diminishing marginal utility continues to decrease the marginal utility of each additional slice of pizza, each additional dollar buys you less additional utility than the previous dollar.

The final column of Table 5-1 shows you that the MU per dollar that you get from pizza depends on how much each slice of pizza costs. If pizza costs $2 per slice, each dollar spent brings you only half as much marginal utility as when pizza costs $1 per slice. For instance, because each slice now costs $2, when you buy the first slice and it brings you 24 utils, you're getting only 12 utils per dollar spent. Similarly, while the second slice still brings you 12 additional utils of happiness, because it now costs you $2 to get those utils, your MU per dollar is only 6 utils.

In Table 5-2, I give you the same sort of information as in Table 5-1, but this time it's for my total utility, marginal utility, and MU per dollar when I'm drinking beer that costs $2 per pint. As you can see from the third column, I exhibit diminishing marginal utility with regard to beer, as my MU for each beer falls from 22 utils for the first pint down to −12 utils for the tenth pint. As a result, my MU per dollar spent in the fourth column falls from 11 per dollar for the first pint down to −6 per dollar for the last pint.

TABLE 5-2

Determining the Price of Utility for Beer

Pint	Total Utility	Marginal Utility	MU per Dollar at $2 per Pint
1	22	22	11
2	40	18	9
3	56	16	8
4	70	14	7
5	80	10	5
6	86	6	3
7	88	2	1
8	88	0	0
9	82	−6	−3
10	70	−12	−6

Purchasing the best combination of two goods to maximize total utility

When facing a limited budget, the trick is to see how to allocate purchases to get the most total utility. Tables 5-1 and 5-2 show you how much utility I can get by spending money on either pizza or beer. I have $10 to spend. As a first attempt, consider the two most extreme options: blowing all the money on pizza, or blowing all the money on beer. (Pizza costs $1 per slice, and beer costs $2 per pint.)

If I spend all $10 on pizza, I can buy 10 slices of pizza, which would give me a total utility of 50 utils. On the other hand, if I spend all $10 on beer, I can buy 5 pints at $2 each and thereby get 80 total utils. If these were my only two options, I would clearly prefer to spend all my money on beer because it brings me more utils than does buying only pizza.

However, there's a much better thing to do. I can get even more total utility if I wisely mix up my consumption a bit and spend some of my money on beer and some of it on pizza.

REMEMBER

The way I get the most utility possible out of my $10 is simple: I take each of the ten dollars in turn and spend it on whichever good brings more utility. I don't think of my task as buying slices of pizza or pints of beer. Rather, my job is buying utility. For every dollar spent, I want to buy as much utility as possible, and I don't care whether that utility comes from beer or pizza.

The only thing complicating this process of spending each dollar on whichever good will bring the most utility is the fact that I have diminishing marginal utility for both beer and pizza, meaning that the amount of utility I'll be able to buy with each extra dollar spent will depend on how much beer or pizza I've already bought. But given the information in Tables 5-1 and 5-2, I can figure out the best thing I should do with each dollar:

>> **Dollar 1:** What should I do with the first dollar? From the fourth column of Table 5-1, you can see that if I spend that dollar on pizza, I can buy 24 utils of utility. On the other hand, the fourth column of Table 5-2 tells you that if I spend that first dollar on beer (along with a second dollar because pints cost $2), I'll get only 11 utils of utility. So, the obvious thing to do with the first dollar is to buy pizza rather than beer.

>> **Dollar 2:** If I use my second dollar to buy a second slice of pizza, I'll get 12 utils of utility. If I buy beer with that second dollar (along with a third dollar because the price of a pint is $2), I'll get only 11 utils for that second dollar because it will be spent on buying the first pint. So, it's better to spend the second dollar on pizza rather than beer.

>> **Dollars 3 and 4:** At dollar number three, everything changes. That's because if I spend a third dollar on pizza, it will bring 10 utils. But if I spend that third dollar (along with a fourth dollar since each pint costs $2) on a pint, I get an MU per dollar of 11 utils (for each dollar). So I should spend dollars three and four on buying the first pint of beer.

>> **Dollar 5:** I'll want to spend the fifth dollar on pizza rather than beer, because I'll get 10 utils of marginal utility if I use this dollar to buy the third slice of pizza but only 9 utils of marginal utility if I use this dollar (along with a sixth dollar since pints cost $2 each) to purchase a second pint of beer.

>> **Dollars 6 and 7:** I should spend dollars six and seven on beer, because I'll get an MU per dollar of 9 utils for my second pint, whereas I'll get only 8 utils if I spend the sixth dollar on a fourth slice of pizza.

>> **Dollars 8, 9, and 10:** For dollar number eight, the MUs per dollar are tied. If I use this dollar to buy a fourth slice of pizza, I get 8 utils. I'll get the same by spending that eighth dollar (plus the ninth dollar, because pints cost $2 each) on a third pint of beer. So I should spend my last three dollars buying a fourth slice of pizza and a third pint of beer.

In Table 5-3, I list where I should spend each of my ten dollars. Notice that the total utility I can purchase with my $10 is 110 utils. That's much better than the 50 utils I would get spending all the money on pizza or the 80 utils I would get spending it all on beer. By spending each dollar in sequence on whichever good brings the most utility, I've done much better than I could by spending the money on only one good or the other.

TABLE 5-3

How I Optimally Spend Each Dollar in My Budget

Dollar	Good Chosen	MU per Dollar
1	Pizza	24
2	Pizza	12
3	Beer	11
4	Beer	11
5	Pizza	10
6	Beer	9
7	Beer	9
8	Pizza	8
9	Beer	8
10	Beer	8
Total utils		**110**

Also notice that I end up buying four slices of pizza and three pints of beer. Given this budget and these prices, my quantity demanded of pizza is four slices and my quantity demanded of beer is three pints. The process of maximizing utility is also the basis of demand curves and the relationship between quantity demanded and price. (I discuss demand curves in Chapter 4 and return to them later in this chapter, in the section "Deriving Demand Curves from Diminishing Marginal Utility.") In the next section, I present the magic formula for choosing where to spend your money in any situation.

Aiming for equal marginal utility per dollar

In this section, I explain a simple formula that guides people to maximize the total utility they can get out of spending any budget — no matter how many goods there are to choose from or how much they each cost.

To keep things simple, I begin by showing you the version of the formula that applies to deciding how to best spend your budget when there are only two goods or services to choose from. When you get the hang of the two-good version, the multigood version is effortless.

Call the two goods X and Y, and say that their respective prices are P_x dollars for each unit of X and P_y dollars for each unit of Y. Also, their respective marginal utilities are MU_x and MU_y. The formula looks like this:

$$(1) \quad \frac{MU_x}{P_x} = \frac{MU_y}{P_y}$$

REMEMBER

What the formula means is that if a person has allocated her limited budget optimally between the two goods, then at the optimal quantities of X and Y, the marginal utilities per dollar of X and Y will be equal.

This relationship holds true in the example in the preceding section. Look back at Table 5-3. When I optimally spend my $10 on beer and pizza, the optimal amounts of each are four slices of pizza and three pints of beer. From the third column of Table 5-4, you can see that marginal utilities per dollar for the fourth slice of pizza and the third pint of beer are indeed equal at 8 utils per dollar, just as the formula in Equation (1) dictates.

Seeing why the marginal utilities per dollar must be equal

If marginal utilities per dollar aren't equal, you'll want to keep rearranging your purchases until they are. In this section, I demonstrate *why* marginal utilities per dollar have to be equal if you want to maximize your utility when spending a limited budget.

HOW INFLATION AFFECTS PURCHASING COMBINATIONS

An interesting thing to notice when you stare at Equation (1) or Equation (3) in this chapter is that if all the prices in the denominators were to suddenly go up by the same multiple, all the equalities would remain intact, meaning that people would still choose to buy the same amounts of every good. For example, if there were suddenly an inflation that exactly doubled all prices, people would still choose to buy exactly the same quantities of everything as they did before.

The idea behind this result is that if my income doubles at the same time that the prices of everything I buy double, nothing has really changed. I can still purchase exactly the same quantities of goods and services as I used to purchase before the inflation. And because those quantities were the ones that were maximizing my utility before, they'll still be maximizing my utility now. As a result, you may mistakenly conclude that inflation doesn't matter.

But in Chapter 15, I tell you about the great horrors of inflation. These horrors are caused by the fact that you never, in real life, see a *perfect* inflation like the one I just described in which the prices of all goods and services go up by exactly the same amount at exactly the same time.

Instead, what happens is that the prices of different goods and services go up at different rates, so the fractions in Equations (1) and (3) are thrown completely out of whack because their denominators change at different rates. When that happens, people start drastically changing their quantities demanded in an attempt to reestablish equality between all their marginal utilities per dollar. As they do this, chaos results; some firms find demand suddenly falling for their products, while others find it suddenly rising. So don't let Equations (1) or (3) make you think that inflation doesn't matter in the real world. It does.

First, imagine that I choose some other quantities of each good, so that for the final unit of X and the final unit of Y that I purchase,

$$(2) \quad \frac{MU_x}{P_x} > \frac{MU_y}{P_y}$$

Let pizza be X and beer be Y. From Tables 5-2 and 5-3, you can see that if I purchase four pints of beer and two slices of pizza, the MU per dollar for the fourth pint of beer is 7, and the MU per dollar for the second slice of pizza is 16. Clearly, the MU per dollar of pizza is much bigger than the MU per dollar of beer if I spend my limited budget in this way.

But this way of spending my budget isn't optimal. The reason is that the money I'm spending on what is currently the final unit of X (pizza) buys more marginal utility than the money I'm currently spending on the final unit of Y (beer). If I can get more utility by spending a dollar on X than I can on Y, I should take money away from spending on Y in order to spend it on X. And as long as the inequality in Equation (2) holds true, I should continue to take money away from Y in order to increase spending on X.

Applying the formula to multiple goods and services

To maximize total utility, you should rearrange your purchases so that for the final units of each good, the marginal utilities per dollar are equal. If that isn't true, one of the goods offers you a higher amount of happiness for each dollar spent, meaning that you want to rearrange your purchases to spend more on that good. Only when Equation (1) (from earlier) holds will you not want to rearrange any more, because neither good offers you more happiness per dollar than the other.

Also realize that Equation (1) can be generalized to apply to many goods. For example, in the case of three goods, you would arrange your buying so that for the last unit of each of the three goods X, Y, and Z:

(3) $$\frac{MU_x}{P_x} = \frac{MU_y}{P_y} = \frac{MU_z}{P_z}$$

If any of the three goods has a higher marginal utility per dollar than the others, you'll rearrange your purchases to buy less of the others and more of that good. And you keep rearranging until Equation (3) holds true.

Deriving Demand Curves from Diminishing Marginal Utility

Diminishing marginal utility is one reason demand curves slope downward. You can get a hint of this from Figure 5-1, where you see that the marginal utility that comes with each successive slice of pizza decreases. If your goal is to use your money to buy up as much utility as possible in order to make yourself as happy as possible, you'd be willing to pay less and less for each successive slice of pizza, because each successive slice of pizza brings with it less utility than the previous slice.

However, Figure 5-1 is not a demand curve, for two reasons:

>> **Price:** It doesn't take into account the effect prices have on the quantity demanded.

>> **Other goods:** It looks at only one good in isolation, whereas the quantity demanded of a good is determined by finding the solution to the more general problem of allocating a limited budget across all available goods in order to maximize total utility. In other words, you can't look at each good in isolation. How much of it you want to buy depends not only on its price but also on the prices of everything else and how their marginal utilities vary as you buy more or less of them.

This section builds up demand curves from first principles, showing you how changes in a good's own price will cause movements along that good's demand curve if you hold all other possible influencing factors constant. It also shows you how changes in any of those other possible influencing factors — including the prices of other goods as well as changes in preferences — can shift the entire demand curve to a new position.

Seeing how price changes affect quantities demanded

Price changes affect the quantity demanded of each good. As the prices of different goods vary with respect to each other, so will the quantity demanded of each good to obtain as much utility as possible given the new prices.

In the example I've been using in this chapter, I've had to decide how to best spend $10 when my choices are slices of pizza or pints of beer. I want to make one change to that example: Say that pizza now costs $2 per slice rather than $1 per slice. What I want to show you is how this price change affects the quantity demanded of both pizza and beer.

The changes in quantities demanded result from the fact that the new, higher price of pizza reduces the marginal utility per dollar of pizza. Doubling the price of pizza means that the marginal utility per dollar generated by each slice of pizza is exactly half of what it was before. You can see this by comparing the fourth and fifth columns of Table 5-2. Because the increase in price lowers the marginal utility that each dollar spent on pizza buys, it's naturally going to affect where I spend my limited budget of $10.

As you may expect, a higher price of pizza will lead me to eat less pizza and drink more beer. You can prove this by spending, in order, each of my dollars so that I buy whichever good has the higher marginal utility. (The earlier section "Purchasing the best combination of two goods to maximize total utility" walks you through the process.) The results are summarized in Table 5-4.

TABLE 5-4 **How I Optimally Spend My Budget When the Price of Pizza is $2**

Dollar	Good Chosen	MU per Dollar
1	Pizza	12
2	Pizza	12
3	Beer	11
4	Beer	11
5	Beer	9
6	Beer	9
7	Beer	8
8	Beer	8
9	Beer	7
10	Beer	7
Total utils		**94**

By comparing Table 5-4 with Table 5-3, you can see that raising the price of pizza from $1 to $2 has affected not only my quantity demanded of pizza but also my quantity demanded of beer. For pizza, my quantity demanded has fallen from four slices down to only one. For beer, my quantity demanded has increased from three pints to four pints.

The increase in the price of pizza has also made me poorer in the only sense that really matters: I'm less happy. Due to the price increase, the total number of utils that I can purchase with my $10 budget has fallen from 110 down to only 94. Despite rearranging my quantities consumed of beer and pizza to make the most of the new situation, the price increase still hurts me overall.

Graphing the price and quantity changes to form a demand curve

You can use information about how quantity demanded changes when price goes up to plot out points on a demand curve. For instance, in the pizza example, you can plot these two points: four slices demanded at a price of $1, and one slice demanded at a price of $2. Figure 5-3 plots these two points and sketches in the rest of the demand curve. Keep in mind two things:

>> The downward slope of the pizza demand curve derives in part from the diminishing marginal utility of pizza.

>> As the price of pizza changes, the quantity demanded of pizza does not change in isolation; it changes as the result of rearranging the quantity demanded of both beer and pizza in order to maximize total utility.

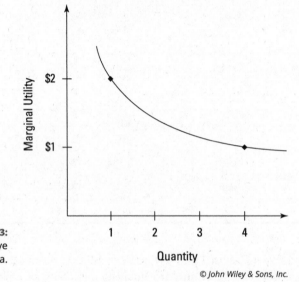

FIGURE 5-3:
My demand curve
for slices of pizza.

© John Wiley & Sons, Inc.

REMEMBER

Demand curves for individual goods aren't made in isolation. Certainly, a relationship exists between a good's price and its quantity demanded. However, when the good's price changes, that change affects the entire budgeting decision — not just for that good, but for *every* good. The resulting change in the good's quantity demanded is just part of the overall rearrangement of spending that strives to keep maximizing total utility given the new price.

Consider how the increase in the price of pizza affects the demand curve for beer. My quantity demanded of beer went from three pints to four pints when the price of pizza increased from $1 to $2. But the price of beer was unchanged. What this means is that the demand curve for beer must have shifted (which I explain in Chapter 4). I illustrate this shift in Figure 5-4. Point A on demand curve D shifts over to become Point A' on demand curve D'.

REMEMBER

Events where changes in the price of one good affect the quantity demanded of another good are called *cross-price effects*. By contrast, when a change in a good's own price affects its own quantity demanded, you have *own-price effects*. Please note that although cross-price effects cause demand curves to shift, own-price effects cause movements along given demand curves.

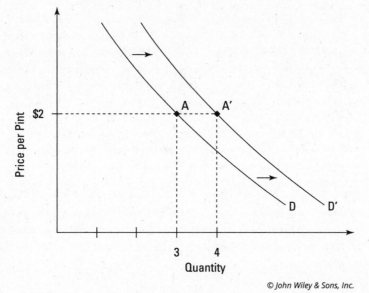

© John Wiley & Sons, Inc.

FIGURE 5-4:
My demand curve for beer shifts to the right when the price of pizza increases.

TIP

The direction of a cross-price effect depends on the situation. In this chapter, I allow consumers to purchase only two goods: beer and pizza. The result is that when the price of pizza goes up, consumers switch some of their purchasing power over to buying beer — or, as economists say, they *substitute* from one good to the other (see the sidebar "Examining complementary and substitute goods"). That's why when the price of pizza goes up, the demand curve for beer in Figure 5-4 shifts to the right.

But in the real world, where many other consumption goods are available, the demand curve could very well shift the other direction. For instance, some people like drinking beer only when they eat pizza. For them, an increase in the price of pizza may decrease *both* the amount of pizza eaten and the amount of beer drunk.

Such people think of beer and pizza as a bundle. An increase in the price of one member of the bundle increases the price of the entire bundle. These people would buy less of each member of the bundle in order to free up money to spend on the many other consumption goods available. For consumers with these preferences and with the option of buying goods besides beer and pizza, when the price of pizza goes up, the demand curve for beer would shift left.

EXAMINING COMPLEMENTARY AND SUBSTITUTE GOODS

Some things just go together. Hot dogs and hot dog buns. Hamburgers and ketchup. Shoes and shoelaces. In each of these pairs, the goods in question are more useful or more pleasing when consumed along with the other member of the pair.

Because such goods complement each other, economists refer to them as *complementary goods.* An interesting thing about complementary goods is that changes in the price of one complement affect the other complement. For instance, if hot dogs go on sale, not only do people buy more hot dogs; they also buy more hot dog buns. And more mustard is sold, too.

By contrast, consider *substitute goods* — goods that serve similar functions so that if the price of one goes up, people switch to the other one. For instance, if the price of train travel goes up, more people drive cars. And if the cost of postal mail goes up, more people use e-mail.

Both complementary goods and substitute goods are the result of cross-price effects. An increase in the price of a complement causes the quantity demanded of its pair to fall, while an increase in the price of a substitute causes the quantity demanded of its pair to rise.

As you look around the economy, make sure you think of it as one great big organic whole, where things don't happen in isolation. When the price of one good changes, it affects not just that good but also many other goods that are either substitutes or complements. And if the prices of the substitutes or complements change, too, as a result of the initial price change, then all their substitutes and complements are also affected. It's like a gigantic ripple effect.

maximize profits

» **Deconstructing a firm's cost structure**

» **Determining a firm's profit-maximizing output level**

» **Seeing how costs determine a firm's supply curve**

» **Understanding how firms react to losing money**

Chapter **6**

The Core of Capitalism: The Profit-Maximizing Firm

In modern market economies like the one you live in, nearly everything you eat, drink, wear, drive, ride, fly, or use is made by some sort of business enterprise. So, naturally, economists devote a huge amount of effort to studying how businesses behave.

In this chapter, I show you how economists model a firm that's a member of a competitive industry, meaning a firm that's just one of many firms competing against each other for your business. It's important to understand how firms behave in competitive industries for two reasons:

» Most firms in the real world face a lot of competition because they're either members of perfectly competitive industries (which I talk about in this chapter) or monopolistically competitive industries (which I discuss in Chapter 9).

>> All firms — even those that don't face much competition — behave in remarkably similar ways.

Above all, firms like to maximize profits. And even more importantly, all firms go about maximizing profits in the same way: by producing exactly the level of output at which the cost of producing one more unit just equals the increase in revenue that the firm gets from selling that unit.

In this chapter, I show you why firms behave this way. When you know that, you'll have a strong understanding of how *all* firms work, whether they face strong competition from rivals or have no rivals at all.

A Firm's Goal: Maximizing Profits

Firms are brought into existence by people in order to produce things. That statement should make you want to ask a fundamental question: *Why* do people bother creating firms to make things? One reason could be altruism. Another could be that making things is fun. Another could be that the people who start a firm are bored doing other things. But economists think the answer is much simpler.

REMEMBER

Economists assume that the overriding goal of all corporations is to make as big a profit as possible. Economists make this assumption for two reasons:

>> If you ask around, profit maximization is near the top of every firm's to-do list.

>> No matter what other goals a firm may have, it still wants to maximize profits after taking steps to achieve those other goals.

For instance, a firm that wants to have a factory that emits no greenhouse gases still, after it builds such a factory, wants to make as much money as possible. After all, after it's taken the steps necessary to protect the environment, why not make a nice big profit?

When the ice cream company Ben & Jerry's started, it donated a large percentage of its profits to charity. Given such a policy, the best way to help worthy causes was for Ben & Jerry's to make as big a profit as possible.

Many noneconomists object to people's earning profits, but profits ensure that firms receive crucial inputs of entrepreneurial ability and risk-taking. Think of someone who has the opportunity to start her own business. She could keep working for someone else and receive a steady wage. What is her incentive to strike out on her own and risk starting a business that may fail? The incentive is that she will receive the profits if the business does well. Without potential profits, no one would risk leaving a safe job in order to innovate, and consumers as a whole would be hurt because the supply of great new products and services would come to a halt. (In Chapter 14, I explain in detail how entrepreneurial ability receives profits in exchange for assuming the financial risks associated with innovation and invention.)

Facing Competition

Firms may or may not face a lot of competition from other firms. At one extreme lies *monopoly*, in which a firm faces no competition because it's the only firm in its industry. At the other extreme lies what economists call *perfect competition*, a situation in which a firm competes against many other firms in an industry in which they all produce an identical good. And in between the extremes lie two situations: *oligopoly*, where there are two, three, or (at most) a few firms in an industry; and *imperfect (monopolistic) competition*, in which there are many competitors, but each produces a slightly unique good. (See Chapters 8 and 9 for details on monopolies, oligopolies, and monopolistic competition.)

In this chapter, you find out how firms behave under perfect competition, because in addition to explaining how important markets such as the stock market behave, this situation is also the simplest case to understand. It's simple because when there are many competitors in an industry in which every firm is producing identical products, none of them has any control over the prices they charge.

Listing the requirements for perfect competition

To see why firms engaging in perfect competition have no control over the prices they charge, you have to understand that perfect competition assumes three things about the firms in an industry:

>> There are many of them.

>> Each of them represents a very small part of the industry.

>> They all sell identical or nearly identical products.

Wheat farming is an example of an industry that satisfies each of the three criteria of perfect competition. There are literally tens of thousands of wheat farmers in the United States. None of them produces more than a small percentage of the total wheat produced each year, and all their wheat is basically identical.

To see why these things together mean that individual farmers have no control over the price of wheat, start with the fact that the farmers are producing a nearly identical product. Because the wheat from one farm looks like the wheat from any other farm, the only way a Kansas wheat farmer can entice me to buy from him rather than from a Texas wheat farmer is to offer me a lower price. Because all the wheat is identical, all I care about is price, meaning that farmers have to compete on price and price alone.

With price jumping to the fore as the key factor in the wheat market, you can use supply and demand analysis to figure out what the price will be. The price is determined by where the *market demand curve* for wheat crosses the *market supply curve* for wheat (see Chapter 4 for details). How are these curves determined?

>> **Market demand curve:** Determined by adding up the individual demand curves of all the people who want to buy wheat

>> **Market supply curve:** Comes from adding up the individual supply curves of all the individual wheat farmers

This is where the first two assumptions of perfect competition come into play: Because there are so many wheat farmers, and because each of them produces such a very small part of the total supply of wheat, the market supply curve for wheat is unaffected by the presence or absence of any individual supply curve of any particular farmer. If a billion bushels of wheat are sold every year, the market price is unaffected by whether a small farmer with only 1,000 bushels to sell bothers showing up to the market or not. He's just too small a player to cause the market price to change.

If every player is too small to cause the market price to change, then each one has to take as a given whatever price is generated by market demand interacting with market supply.

Taking prices but setting quantities

If the three assumptions of perfect competition are met, they produce a situation in which individual firms have no control over the prices they can charge. In fact, under perfect competition, economists refer to firms as *price takers* because they have to take the price as given and deal with it.

REMEMBER

When you come right down to it, even the most powerful firm can hope to control only two things: how much of its product to make and what price to charge. Because firms have no control over their prices under perfect competition, that narrows the list to one: The only thing that price-taking firms can control is how much to produce.

Firms choose to make whatever quantity maximizes their profits. This fact is mathematically convenient because the quantity of output that a firm chooses to produce controls each of the two things that determine profits: total revenues and total costs.

REMEMBER

To see this fact more clearly, you have to know that a firm's profit is simply defined as its total revenue minus its total costs. Put into math, you get the following equation, where *TR* stands for total revenue and *TC* stands for total costs:

(1) $\text{Profit} = TR - TC$

For a competitive firm, its total revenue, *TR*, is simply the quantity, *q*, of its output that it chooses to sell times the market price, *p*, that it can get for each unit:

(2) $TR = pq$

For instance, if I can sell apples for $1 each and I sell 37 apples, my total revenue is $37 ($1 per apple × 37 apples = $37).

But notice that because the price at which I can sell *(p)* is out of my hands if I'm a price taker, the only way I can control my total revenue is by deciding how many apples to sell. So a firm can determine its total revenue by its decision about how big or small to make *q*.

Much of the rest of this chapter is devoted to showing you that the firm's total costs, *TC*, are also determined by how big or small *q* is. But the interesting thing here is that although each extra unit of *q* sold brings in a revenue of *p* dollars, the cost of each unit of *q* manufactured depends on how many units of *q* have already been made. Costs tend to increase as firms produce more and more, so each successive unit costs more than the previous unit. This fact ends up limiting the number of units that a firm wants to produce.

Suppose that I can sell as many apples as I want for $1 each. The first apple costs 10 cents to produce, the second one costs 20 cents, the third one costs 30 cents, and so on. In such a case, I'm willing to produce no more than ten apples. Why? Because for each of the first nine apples, I'll make a profit, but for apple ten (which costs $1 to produce), I'll break even. If I produce any more apples, I'll sustain a loss. (Apple number 11, for instance, would cost $1.10 to produce, but I'd get only $1 for selling it.)

Consequently, you can see that both the *TR* and *TC* terms in profit equation (1) are determined by the firm's choice of *q*. The only thing left to figure out is exactly how big to make *q* in order to maximize profits. It turns out that there's a ridiculously simple formula that gives the solution. Pay attention, because you just may, uh, profit from reading this chapter.

Distinguishing between accounting profits and economic profits

To an economist, the terms *profit* and *loss* refer to whether the revenue from selling a firm's output is bigger or smaller than the costs that must be incurred to produce that output. If the revenue exceeds the costs, the firm is *running a profit*, whereas if the costs exceed the revenue, the firm is *running a loss.* If the two are equal, the firm is *breaking even.*

Consider a business that sells lemonade. Both the accountant and the economist agree that the firm's revenue is simply how much money the firm makes from selling its product. However, they differ on what to count as costs when calculating profit:

>> **Accounting profit:** The accountant considers costs to be only actual monies spent in running the business: how much the firm pays its workers, how much it pays to buy supplies, and so on. Consider a business that sells lemonade. If the firm has revenues of $10,000 and it spends $9,000 to make those revenues, the accountant concludes that the firm has a profit of $1,000. This number is the firm's *accounting profit* — the type of profit that is reported every day in financial statements and newspaper articles.

REMEMBER

>> **Economic profit:** Economic profit takes into account not just the money costs directly incurred by running a business but also the opportunity costs incurred. Think about the entrepreneur who starts this lemonade business. After paying for his materials and for his employees' wages, his accounting profits are $1,000. But is that really a good deal?

Suppose that this person left a job as a computer programmer to open the lemonade business, and in the same amount of time that it took the lemonade business to turn a $1,000 profit, he would have made $10,000 in wages if he had stayed at his old job. That is, he gave up the opportunity to earn $10,000 in wages to open up a business that makes him only a $1,000 accounting profit. He actually sustains an *economic loss* of $9,000. When you know this fact, his decision to switch careers doesn't seem like such a good idea.

Economists like to concentrate on economic profits and losses rather than accounting profits or losses because the economic profits and losses are what motivate people. By taking into account economic profits and losses, you get directly at what motivates firms to produce not only the types of goods they choose to produce but the quantities of those goods as well. In this example, you can imagine that when other computer programmers see what happened to this guy when he switched careers, they're not going to follow him.

For the rest of the chapter, whenever you see any costs listed, assume that they are *economic costs*; that is, they include not only money directly spent operating a business but also the costs of other opportunities forgone in order to operate the business. Likewise, whenever you see a profit or a loss, assume that it's an economic profit or an economic loss — the factor that motivates entrepreneurs to want to do something or to avoid doing it.

The most important application of this concept is to determine how much output a firm should produce. If producing the 12th unit of a product produces an economic profit, obviously the firm wants to produce it. But if increasing production to a 13th unit would result in an economic loss, obviously the firm doesn't want to produce it.

Analyzing a Firm's Cost Structure

To see how costs and revenues interact to determine economic profits or losses, economists like to break up a firm's total costs into two subcategories:

>> **Fixed costs:** Fixed costs are costs that have to be paid even if the firm isn't producing anything. For instance, after a rent contract is signed for the firm's headquarters, that rent must be paid whether the firm produces anything or not. Similarly, if the firm has taken out a loan, it's legally required to make its debt payments whether it's producing zero units of output or a billion.

>> **Variable costs:** Variable costs are costs that vary with the amount of output produced. For instance, if you are in the lemonade-making business and you choose to produce nothing, you obviously don't have to buy any lemons. But the more lemonade you do produce, the more you spend buying lemons. Similarly, producing more lemonade requires more workers, so your labor costs also vary with the amount of output you produce.

Fixed costs can be represented as *FC* and variable costs as *VC*. Together, they sum up to a firm's total costs, or *TC*:

(3) $TC = FC + VC$

TIP

As you look at Equation (3), keep in mind that it deals with the economic costs facing the firm and therefore captures the opportunity costs of the firm's expenditures on both fixed costs and variable costs. (All expenditures, whether they're fixed costs or variable costs, involve opportunity costs — the other things you gave up buying in order to spend the money you spent on your fixed and variable costs.)

Focusing on costs per unit of output

The reason economists distinguish between fixed and variable costs is that they have very different effects on a firm's decision regarding how much to produce. Take a look at Table 6-1, which gives data on LemonAid Corporation, a lemonade producer.

TABLE 6-1 ## The Cost Structure of LemonAid Corporation

Workers	Output	Fixed Costs	Average Fixed Costs	Variable Costs	Average Variable Costs	Total Costs	Average Total Costs	Marginal Costs
0	0	100	—	0	—	100	—	—
1	50	100	2.00	80	1.60	180	3.60	1.60
2	140	100	0.71	160	1.14	260	1.86	0.89
3	220	100	0.45	240	1.09	340	1.55	1.00
4	290	100	0.34	320	1.10	420	1.45	1.14
5	350	100	0.29	400	1.14	500	1.43	1.33
6	400	100	0.25	480	1.20	580	1.45	1.60
7	440	100	0.23	560	1.27	660	1.50	2.00
8	470	100	0.21	640	1.36	740	1.57	2.67

When LemonAid Corporation gets started, it buys a juicer machine for $100, which gives it fixed costs of $100. It then has to decide how much to produce, which in turn determines how many workers it needs to hire. In the first column, the number of workers varies from zero to eight. If the firm hires no workers, you can see in the top entry of the second column that no output is produced. But if it hires workers, output increases as you move down the second column. More workers mean more output.

Studying increasing and decreasing returns

Pay attention to the fact that the amount of additional, or marginal, output produced by each additional worker is not constant. In the LemonAid Corporation example, if you go from no workers to one worker, output increases from nothing to 50 bottles of lemonade. However, as you go from one worker to two workers, output increases from 50 bottles to 140 bottles. Put into economic jargon, the second worker's *marginal output* is 90 bottles, whereas the first worker's marginal output is only 50 bottles. (*Note:* Economists sometimes refer to a firm's output as its *product*, so a worker's marginal output can also be referred to as her *marginal product.*)

Now look at these facts in terms of costs and benefits. If you have to pay each worker the same wage of $80 per day ($10 per hour for 8 hours of work), you're going to like the fact that although the first worker produces 50 bottles for his $80 pay, the second worker produces 90 bottles for her $80 pay.

REMEMBER

When the amount of return you get for a given amount of input (one more worker) increases as you add successive units of input, economists refer to the situation as *increasing returns.* Increasing returns occur when a piece of productive capital is initially undermanned. Consider a sailboat that works optimally with a crew of ten. Could one person run the ship? Yes, but his productivity would be very low as he would have to be running from one job to the next and trying to do everything himself — raising sails, weighing anchor, calculating drift, steering the vessel, and so on. In such situations, efficiency is improved and increasing returns per worker result by increasing the number of workers toward the optimal number of workers for that particular piece of productive capital.

Increasing returns only happen, though, when a piece of productive capital is undermanned. Thus, if you scan down the second column of Table 6-1, you find that increasing returns don't last forever. Indeed, in the case of LemonAid Corporation, increasing returns end almost immediately. Consider what happens to output when you add a third worker. Output does increase but only by 80 units, from 140 bottles to 220 bottles. And things get successively worse with each additional worker. Adding a fourth worker increases output by only 70 bottles. Adding a fifth increases output by only 60 bottles.

REMEMBER

When each successive unit of an input, like labor, brings with it a smaller increase in output than the previous unit of input, economists call the situation *diminishing returns.*

Determining the cause of diminishing returns

I go into detail about what causes diminishing returns in Chapter 3, but I briefly explain here. What's going on is that LemonAid Corporation bought only one juicer machine for squeezing the juice out of lemons.

The first worker can use the machine to squeeze enough juice for 50 bottles by carrying lemons to the machine and then operating the machine. But it turns out that two workers together can do even better by dividing up the work: One brings lemons to the machine, and the other operates it. Working together, they can produce a total of 140 bottles — more than double the 50 bottles that one worker could produce working alone.

However, a third worker doesn't increase output nearly as much as a second because the two major tasks — carrying and operating — have already been taken care of. At best, he can just help the first two workers do these tasks a little faster. The same holds true for all successive workers: Having them is helpful, but each one adds less to output than the previous one because things start getting crowded and there really isn't much room left for improvement.

Examining average variable costs

Variable costs are affected by the fact that additional workers first bring increasing returns (when the firm's capital is undermanned) but then decreasing returns (when the capital is overmanned). In the case of the LemonAid Corporation example in Table 6-1, the variable costs are all labor costs, with each worker having to be paid $80 per day. You can see these variable costs increase as you move down the fifth column.

REMEMBER

What's much more interesting than looking at variable costs is looking at *average variable costs* (*AVC*), which are defined as variable costs divided by quantity (*VC/q*). For instance, because one worker produces 50 bottles of output at a variable cost of $80, the average variable cost is $80 / 50 = $1.60 per bottle. When two workers together cost $160 in variable costs but produce 140 bottles, the average variable cost for two workers is only $160 / $140 = $1.14 per bottle.

The decrease in average variable costs is the result of increasing returns: The fact that when moving from one worker to two workers, variable costs double (from $80 to $160), but output more than doubles (from 50 bottles to 140 bottles).

When diminishing returns set in, average variable costs start to rise, which you can see as you move down the sixth column of Table 6-1. This happens because although each additional worker costs an extra $80, each additional worker after the second worker brings a smaller increase in output than his predecessor. Each successive $80 wage payment brings with it fewer and fewer additional bottles produced, so the average variable cost per bottle must rise.

LemonAid Corporation's average variable costs show up as a subtle U shape when you plot them on a graph, which I do in Figure 6-1. (I also show the company's average fixed costs and average total costs.) Keep this average variable cost curve in mind because it has a huge effect on how many bottles the firm's managers want to produce in order to maximize firm profits.

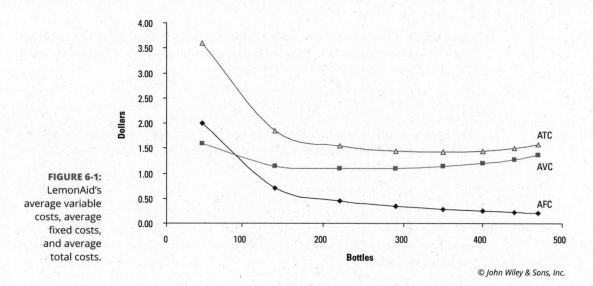

REMEMBER

FIGURE 6-1:
LemonAid's average variable costs, average fixed costs, and average total costs.

© John Wiley & Sons, Inc.

Watching average fixed costs fall

Average fixed costs (AFC) are defined as fixed costs divided by quantity (*FC/q*). Average fixed costs always decline, because the same fixed cost gets divided up over a greater and greater number of units of output as output increases.

The fixed costs of LemonAid Corporation are always the $100 it paid for the juicer machine, no matter what amount of output it produces. As a result, the more lemonade it produces, the less average fixed costs are. That's why *AFC* falls (see the fourth column of Table 6-1) from a value of $2.00 per bottle when 50 bottles are produced using one worker down to only $0.21 per bottle when 470 bottles are produced using eight workers. When you plot out average fixed costs per bottle, as in Figure 6-1, you get a downward sloping *AFC* curve. Keep this fact in mind because it helps explain the shape of the average total costs (*ATC*) curve, as I explain in the next section.

Tracking the movement of average total costs

Average fixed costs always decline as output increases, while average variable costs first fall (due to increasing returns) and then rise (due to diminishing returns) — see the preceding sections for details. Because total costs are the sum of fixed costs and variable costs, *average total costs* obviously depend on how average fixed costs and average variable costs sum up.

Average total costs (ATC) are defined as total costs divided by quantity (TC/q). Now, take a look back at Equation (3) earlier in the chapter. If you divide every term in Equation (3) by q, you get the following:

(4) $$\frac{TC}{q} = \frac{FC}{q} + \frac{VC}{q}$$

You can simplify this equation by realizing that average costs equal the various costs divided by the quantity, q. In other words, $ATC = TC/q$, $AFC = FC/q$, and $AVC = VC/q$. What you get is

(5) $$ATC = AFC + AVC$$

You can see clearly from this equation that average total costs depend on how average fixed costs and average variable costs interact. There are two key points to understand here:

>> **Average total costs _(ATC)_ must always be greater than average variable costs _(AVC)_, because you have to add in average fixed costs _(AFC)_.** Look at Figure 6-1, which shows that the _ATC_ curve is above the _AVC_ curve. The vertical distance between them at any particular level of output is equal to the _AFC_ at that output level. As you move from lower output levels to higher output levels, the _ATC_ and _AVC_ curves converge because _AFC_ becomes smaller and smaller. (In other words, the vertical distance between the _ATC_ and _AVC_ curves also gets smaller and smaller.)

>> **Average total costs _(ATC)_ will reach a minimum value at a higher level of output than average variable costs _(AVC)_.** For instance, Table 6-1 shows that average variable costs reach their minimum value of $1.09 when three workers are hired and 220 bottles are produced. Average total costs, however, reach their minimum of $1.43 when five workers are hired and 350 bottles are produced.

The reason this happens is that average fixed costs are always falling, meaning that in Equation (5), the _AFC_ part on the right-hand side of the equation is always getting smaller and smaller. This constant decline helps to temporarily offset the increases in average variable costs that happen when diminishing returns set in. Consequently, although average variable costs bottom out at three workers, average total costs don't bottom out and start increasing until the fifth worker.

Focusing on marginal costs

The preceding sections demonstrate how the manager of a firm can use her data on total costs, fixed costs, and variable costs to calculate, respectively, average total costs, average fixed costs, and average variable costs. But what she really wants to know is what quantity, q, of output she should produce in order to maximize profits. To solve this problem, she needs one more cost concept: marginal cost.

REMEMBER

Marginal cost is how much total costs increase when you produce one more unit of output. Crucially, the marginal cost of one more unit of output depends on how much output has already been produced.

To see this, examine the total costs column of Table 6-1. Notice that total costs increase from $100 in the first row to $180 in the second row as output increases from 0 bottles to 50 bottles when the firm hires the first worker. In other words, costs go up $80 while output goes up 50 bottles. So each of these extra, or *marginal*, 50 bottles on average increases costs by $80 / 50 = $1.60 each. The marginal cost per bottle, MC, is defined as follows:

(6) $\quad MC = \dfrac{\text{change in } TC}{\text{change in } q}$

As you move down the marginal costs column of Table 6-1, you can see that marginal costs first fall and then rise. This is yet another reflection of the fact that LemonAid Corporation's production process exhibits increasing returns followed by diminishing returns. Because the second worker produces much more than the first worker but costs the same, the marginal cost falls when the second worker is added. For successive workers, costs keep increasing but marginal output keeps declining, which means marginal costs must rise.

Noticing where marginal cost equals average cost

REMEMBER

Here's a fun fact that economists love: If you plot out marginal costs to create a marginal cost (*MC*) curve, that curve will cross both the average variable cost (*AVC*) curve and average total cost (*ATC*) curve at their minimum points — that is, at the bottom of their respective U shapes. (What, you don't see the cause for celebration?)

Look at Figure 6-2, where I plot the *AVC*, *ATC*, and *MC* curves you get by plotting out the data in Table 6-1. The *MC* curve goes through the minimum points of both the *AVC* and *ATC* curves. This happens because the marginal cost at each unit determines whether the *AVC* and *ATC* curves are increasing or decreasing.

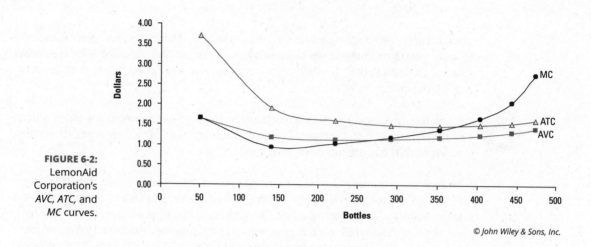

FIGURE 6-2:
LemonAid
Corporation's
AVC, ATC, and
MC curves.

© John Wiley & Sons, Inc.

If that doesn't make sense, consider another example. Instead of thinking about costs, think about heights. Suppose you have a room with ten people in it, and you determine that the average height of the people in the room is 5'6". Now think about what's going to happen to that average if another person walks into the room:

>> If the 11th person is taller than 5'6", the average will rise.

>> If the 11th person is shorter than average, the average will fall.

>> If the 11th person is exactly 5'6" tall, the average will stay the same.

The same sort of reasoning applies to marginal costs and average costs. After *q* units of output, you can compute *AVC* and *ATC*, just like you can compute the average height after the first ten people enter the room. After that, *AVC* and *ATC* either rise or fall depending on the *MC* of the next unit of output, just as the average height of the people in the room increases, decreases, or stays the same depending on the height of the next person entering the room.

TIP

Here's how the marginal cost of next unit of output can change the average variable and total costs:

>> If the *MC* is less than the previous average costs, the averages fall.

>> If the *MC* is greater than the previous average costs, the averages rise.

>> If the *MC* is exactly the same as the previous average costs, the averages stay the same.

You can see these effects graphically by looking at various parts of Figure 6-2. First, look at the output level of 140 bottles. At that output level, the *MC* of producing one more bottle is less than both *ATC* and *AVC*, meaning that *ATC* and *AVC* will decrease if output is increased by one more bottle. That's why the *AVC* curve and the *ATC* curve are downward sloping at that output level. The average curves are being pulled down by the low value of *MC*.

Next, look at the output level of 440 bottles. You can see that the *MC* at that output level is higher than the *ATC* and the *AVC*. Consequently, both *AVC* and *ATC* must be increasing. This increase is reflected geometrically by the upward slopes of both the *AVC* curve and the *ATC* curve. The curves slope upward because the high value for *MC* is pulling them up.

Now, put some pieces together. Notice that the *MC* curve causes both the *AVC* curve and the *ATC* curve to be U-shaped (albeit subtly). On the left side of Figure 6-2, the fact that *MC* is less than the average curves means that the average curves slope downward. On the figure's right side, the fact that *MC* is greater than the average curves means the average curves slope upward.

So you've come full circle to the fact that the *MC* curve has to cross the two average curves at their respective minimum points — at the bottoms of their respective U shapes. To the left of such a crossing point, the average must be falling because *MC* is less than the average. And to the right, the average must be rising because *MC* is larger than the average. But where the curves cross, the average curve is neither rising nor falling because the *MC* of that unit of output is equal to the current average. (In other words, a 5'6" person has walked into a room that already has a 5'6" average height, so the average doesn't budge.)

Economists love to go on and on about this fact, but it's really just a reflection of the effect that increasing and then decreasing returns have on cost curves. Costs first fall and then rise. And there's some point in the middle at which they momentarily stay the same, frozen for an instant while transitioning from falling to rising. That point must be where marginal cost equals average cost, because only when *MC* equals average cost can average cost be stationary.

Comparing Marginal Revenues with Marginal Costs

Here's a sad but true fact to keep in mind: Firms can't always make a profit. That's because a firm in a perfectly competitive industry can't control the price at which its output sells, and sometimes that price is too low for the firm to make a profit no matter what quantity it produces. When that happens, the best the firm can do is to minimize its losses and hope for the price to change. If the price drops low enough, the best thing to do may be to shut down production immediately, because that way the firm will lose only its fixed costs. (I discuss the difference between fixed and variable costs in the earlier section "Analyzing a Firm's Cost Structure.")

Later in the chapter, I discuss this sad situation in more detail. But first, I focus on a happier situation — one in which the market price is high enough that a firm wants to produce a positive amount of output. This may or may not mean that a firm is making a profit, but even if it isn't, its losses aren't great enough to halt production.

Finding where marginal revenue equals marginal cost

In the typical case where market prices are high enough that a firm wants to make a positive amount of output, a ridiculously simple formula is used to determine the optimal quantity of output, q, that the firm should produce. The firm wants to produce at the level of output where marginal revenue equals marginal cost ($MR = MC$).

Producing where $MR = MC$ does two things:

>> It minimizes the firm's loss if it has to take a loss due to a low selling price for its output.

>> It maximizes the firm's profit if it's able to make a profit because the selling price is high enough.

REMEMBER

The idea behind $MR = MC$ basically comes down to a cost–benefit analysis. If producing and selling a bottle brings in more revenue than it costs to make the bottle, then make it. If not, then don't make it. Easy, right?

Imagine that LemonAid Corporation can sell each bottle of lemonade that it produces for \$2. Economists like to say that the marginal revenue of each bottle is \$2, because each and every bottle when sold brings in an extra \$2. In terms of algebra, you can say that $p = MR$, where p is the market price that this competitive firm must charge for each unit of output.

What the firm's managers must do is decide how much to produce based on whether any given bottle will cost more or less than the \$2 marginal revenue that the firm would get by selling it.

TIP

Be very careful at this point. You have to remember that the relevant cost that the managers look at is an individual bottle's marginal cost, MC. That's because if they're deciding on making that particular bottle, they need to isolate that bottle's production cost from the costs of all previously produced bottles in order to compare it to the revenue that the bottle will bring if it's produced and sold. MC does just that by ignoring all previous bottles and focusing on what the next bottle will cost to make.

If the *MC* of that bottle is less than $2, obviously there is a gain to be made by making it, and the managers will choose to make it. On the other hand, if the *MC* is bigger than $2, producing the bottle would cause a loss, and the managers would choose not to produce it.

By looking at the *MC* of every possible bottle (the 1st, the 5th, the 97th, and so on) and comparing it with marginal revenue that the firm could get by selling it, the managers can determine exactly how many bottles to produce. The necessary comparisons can be done by looking at a table of costs, such as Table 6-1, but it's even easier to make the comparisons graphically.

In Figure 6-3, I've drawn in the marginal cost *(MC)*, average variable cost *(AVC)*, and average total cost *(ATC)* curves for LemonAid Corporation. I've also drawn in a horizontal line at $2, which is the marginal revenue for selling any and all bottles that the firm may choose to produce. I've labeled the line $p = MR = \$2$ to indicate the fact that the selling price of the bottle is $2, which is also the marginal revenue.

Look at the quantity q^*, which corresponds to where the horizontal $p = MR = \$2$ line crosses the *MC* curve. As you can see, $q^* = 440$ bottles. This is the level of output that the firm will choose to produce in order to maximize profits.

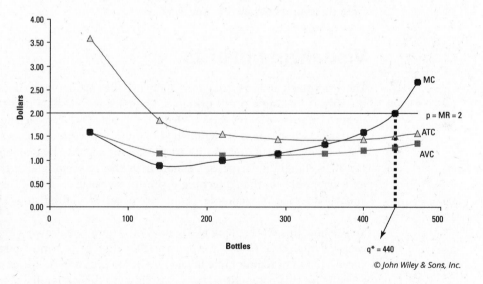

FIGURE 6-3:
The firm's optimal output level, q^*, happens where *MC* and *MR* cross.

© *John Wiley & Sons, Inc.*

To understand why adhering to $MR = MC$ maximizes profits, look at Table 6-1 and consider each unit of output, q, for which $q < 440$. For all those units, the marginal revenue is greater than the marginal cost $(MR > MC)$, meaning that producing and selling each of those bottles brings in more money than it costs to make. For instance, look at bottle number 140. It has a marginal cost of only $0.89 but can be sold for $2.00. Clearly, LemonAid Corporation should make that bottle because the firm makes more selling it than it costs to produce. The same is true for all the bottles for which $q < 440$; the firm should produce all of them because they all bring in more money than they cost to make.

On the other hand, for all units above the q^* level of output ($q > 440$), the situation is reversed: The marginal revenue is less than the marginal cost ($MR < MC$). The firm would lose money if it produced and sold those bottles. For instance, at an output level of 470 bottles, the MC is \$2.67, but the MR is only \$2.00. If the firm produced at that output level, it would lose 67 cents on bottle number 470. Clearly, the company doesn't want to do this.

By comparing the marginal revenues and marginal costs at all output levels, you can see that the managers of LemonAid Corporation want to produce exactly $q^* = 440$ units, the number of units where the MR and MC lines cross.

REMEMBER

Producing where $MR = MC$ doesn't guarantee you a profit, but it does at least make sure that you produce only units that bring in more money than they cost to make. The reason this formula by itself can't guarantee a profit is that it doesn't take account of the fixed costs you have to pay no matter what level of output you're producing. Even though you produce only units for which marginal revenue is at least as great as marginal cost, you still may not make enough of a gain from those units to pay off your fixed costs.

Visualizing profits

There's a quick and easy way to visually use the cost curves to determine whether the firm is making a profit or a loss. The trick is to realize that the two components of profits, total revenue *(TR)* and total costs *(TC)*, can each be represented by rectangles whose areas are equivalent to their respective sizes. As a result, you can immediately tell whether profits are positive or negative by looking to see whether the *TR* rectangle is larger or smaller than the *TC* rectangle. If the *TR* rectangle exceeds the size of the *TC* rectangle, profits are positive. And if the *TR* rectangle is smaller than the *TC* rectangle, profits are negative — the firm is running a loss.

To see how this works, look at Figure 6-4, where I've drawn a generalized set of average total cost *(ATC)*, average variable cost *(AVC)*, and marginal cost *(MC)* curves, plus a horizontal line labeled $p = MR$ to indicate that price equals marginal revenue for this competitive firm. Switching to this generalized set of curves will (I hope!) convince you that the geometric way of determining the size of a firm's profits holds true for *any* set of cost curves.

REMEMBER

The big trick behind expressing total revenue as a rectangular area is to remember that a firm's total revenue when it's producing the profit-maximizing output level, q^*, is simply price times that quantity, or $TR = pq^*$. Just as you can define the area of a rectangular room as length times width, you can define total revenue on a graph as a rectangle determined by price times quantity. In Figure 6-4, total revenue *(TR)* is a rectangle of height p and width q^*. Its four corners are located at the origin, at p, at the point where the $p = MR$ line crosses the MC curve, and at q^*.

You can also use a rectangle to represent the total costs that the firm incurs when producing q^* units of output. To figure out where to draw this rectangle, you have to use a little math trick to convert the information that the average total cost *(ATC)* curve gives you into what you want to graph, total costs *(TC)*. To see how to apply this math trick, first look at Point B in Figure 6-4. It shows the average total cost *(ATC) per unit* when the firm is producing output level q^*. The reason the trick is handy is because it shows that the rectangle whose width is q^* and whose height is given by the ATC at output level q^* is actually equal to the firm's total costs. That is, TC is equal to the area of the rectangle whose four corners are the origin, the point I've labeled A, the point I've labeled B, and q^*.

TIP

The heart of the math trick is realizing that when the firm is producing at q^*, $ATC = TC / q^*$. If you multiply both sides of this equation by q^*, you find that $ATC \times q^* = TC$. This equation tells you that TC (total cost) is indeed equal to the product of ATC (the average per-unit cost) and q^* (the number of items), or to the area of a rectangle of height ATC and width q^* — exactly the rectangle that I just showed you!

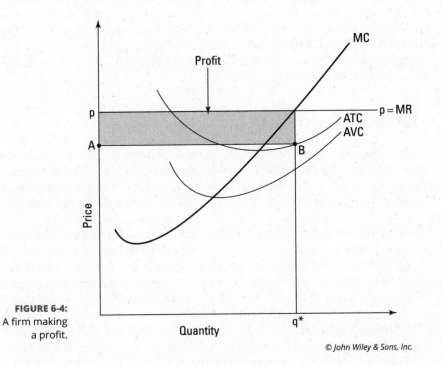

FIGURE 6-4:
A firm making
a profit.

© *John Wiley & Sons, Inc.*

The firm's profits, which are by definition equal to $TR - TC$, can also be represented by the area of a specific rectangle. In fact, the profit is equal to the area of the shaded rectangle in Figure 6-4. That's because profits are simply the difference between TR and TC. Because the TR rectangle is larger than the TC rectangle in this case, the firm is making a profit whose size is equivalent to the area of the shaded rectangle that's defined by the area of the larger TR rectangle minus the area of the smaller TC rectangle.

Imagine what would happen if the price, p, increased. First, notice that the optimal output, q^*, would increase because the place where the horizontal $p = MR$ line crosses the MC curve would move up and to the right. Simultaneously, the total revenue rectangle would increase in size, as would the total cost rectangle. But which one grows faster? Do profits rise or fall?

Go ahead and draw in some lines to convince yourself that profits will in fact increase — that is, the shaded profit rectangle will grow in size as the price increases. As you'll discover, a rising price increases the firm's profits.

You can prove that a rising price increases profits by noting that as q^* shifts right with increases in p, both the width and the height of the profit rectangle get bigger. The width of the profit rectangle gets bigger with each increase in q^* because the width of the profit rectangle is by definition exactly equal to q^*. The height also increases because as you move farther to the right, the distance between the MC curve and the ATC curve increases due to the fact that the slope of the MC curve is steeper than the slope of the ATC curve. Thus, with both the width and the height of the profit rectangle increasing simultaneously, the area of the profit rectangle must be increasing as well.

Visualizing losses

So what happens if the price falls? This section explains how profits can go negative if the price falls far enough. Consider the situation illustrated in Figure 6-5, where the cost curves are the same as in Figure 6-4 but the price (and therefore the marginal revenue [MR]) at which the firm can sell its product is much lower.

Following the $MR = MC$ rule for selecting the optimal output level, the firm will choose to produce at the output level q^*_2 where the new lower $p = MR$ line crosses the MC curve. But because of the low price at which the firm is forced to sell its output, it will not be able to make a profit. (I've labeled the optimal output level for the firm in Figure 6-5 as q^*_2 to clarify that the optimal output level in this case, where the price is lower, is different from the optimal output level q^* in Figure 6-4, where the price is higher.)

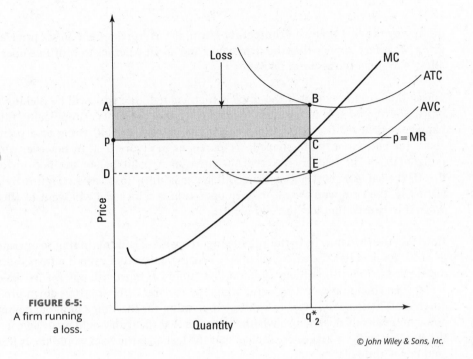

FIGURE 6-5:
A firm running
a loss.

© John Wiley & Sons, Inc.

You can see the size of the loss geometrically by comparing the *TR* and the *TC* rectangles that occur in this situation. Because $TR = pq^*_2$, total revenue is equal to the area of a rectangle of height p and width q^*_2. Consequently, the *TR* is equal to the area of the rectangle whose four corners lie at the origin, at p, at C, and at q^*_2. It's smaller than the *TC* rectangle defined by the origin, Point *A*, Point *B*, and q^*_2. Because the area of the total cost rectangle exceeds the area of the total revenue rectangle, the firm is running a loss equivalent to the size of the shaded area in Figure 6-5.

Pulling the Plug: When Producing Nothing Is Your Best Bet

You may wonder why a firm would stay in business if it's running a loss rather than a profit. The usual answer is that it hopes that things will turn around soon. Either it expects the price at which it can sell its products to rise, or it expects that it can somehow reduce its costs of production.

Notice that those hopes are based upon outcomes that aren't necessarily under the firm's control. Indeed, you can best see the firm's general lack of control over its destiny by the fact that as a competitive firm, it has to take the market price as given. That fact implies that the firm's decision about whether to continue operating is in some sense out of its hands.

To see this, first note that if the price is high enough, the firm will be making a profit and should stay in business to keep collecting the profit. Graphically, this happens whenever the horizontal $p = MR$ line crosses the MC curve at a point above the bottom of the U-shaped ATC curve, as in Figure 6-4. If, however, the horizontal $p = MR$ line crosses the MC curve at a point below the bottom of the U-shaped ATC curve, the firm will be making a loss, as in Figure 6-5. Naturally, the firm won't want to keep operating at a loss and will want to shut down if it expects that low price to persist.

However, the firm may be better off staying in business and continuing to operate at a loss for a while. The existence of fixed costs implies that even if a firm shuts down production, it'll still operate at a loss (the firm must still pay for its fixed costs, even though it won't be generating any revenue after shutting down production). Whether it's better to continue operating for the time being or to shut down immediately depends on whether the loss that the firm would incur by continuing to operate is bigger or smaller that the loss that the firm would incur if it shut down immediately.

This section explains how the size of a firm's fixed costs are the key to understanding whether a loss-making firm will want to shut down immediately or continue operating until those fixed-cost commitments expire.

Distinguishing between the short run and the long run in microeconomics

REMEMBER

In microeconomics, the *short run* is the period of time between the present and when a firm's fixed-cost contracts expire. It's the period during which the continuing existence of fixed-cost commitments prevents the firm from being able to terminate its purchases of productive inputs.

For example, consider a firm that has signed a rent contract for one year. Even if the firm is losing money and decides to fire all its employees and sell all its inventory, the firm will still have to pay rent until the contract expires.

Thus, the existence of fixed-cost commitments implies that a loss-making firm can't completely halt all its operations and exit its line of business until all its fixed-cost contracts have expired. Because the particular length of those fixed-cost commitments varies from firm to firm, there's no set definition of how long the "short run" will last. For any particular firm, it lasts *until* the firm's fixed-cost commitments expire.

Extending that logic, the *long run* begins as soon as the short run ends. The start of the long run is important because it marks the moment when the firm's fixed-cost commitments are completed and the firm is fully able to end all business operations and exit its industry.

The short-run shutdown condition: Variable costs exceed total revenues

REMEMBER

A loss-making firm chooses to shut down production immediately if the size of the loss that it'd make by shutting down immediately is less than the size of the loss that it'd make by continuing in operation and producing output until its fixed-cost contracts expire. Economists call this situation the *short-run shutdown condition*.

Suppose you're in charge of a firm that has a fixed-cost commitment consisting of a monthly rent of $1,000. That rent commitment implies that even if you produce nothing, you'd sustain a loss of $1,000 per month until the short run ends and you can get out of your rent commitment. But that potential loss doesn't mean that you should *definitely* start producing stuff in order to try to make back some of the rent expenditure. You should choose to produce only if doing so results in either an outright profit or a loss of less than the $1,000 you stand to lose by doing nothing.

Consider Figure 6-6, where the price at which the firm can sell its output is so low that the marginal revenue ($p = MR$) line and the marginal cost *(MC)* curve intersect at a point *below* the average variable cost *(AVC)* curve. What does this mean? Put simply, the total revenues in this case are actually *less than* variable costs. (Total revenues are represented by the rectangle whose four corners are at the origin and Points p, B, and q^*_3, where q^*_3 represents the optimal output level at this price. Variable costs are represented by the rectangle whose four corners are the origin and Points C, D, and q^*_3.)

What this means is that by producing q^*_3 units, the firm doesn't even bring in enough total revenue to cover the variable costs associated with producing that many units. Not only is the firm going to lose its fixed costs, but it's also losing even more money by not being able to cover the variable costs associated with producing q^*_3. The logical thing to do in such a situation is to shut down production immediately and produce nothing. By producing zero units, you lose only your fixed costs. By producing q^*_3, you lose even more money because you can't even cover your variable costs.

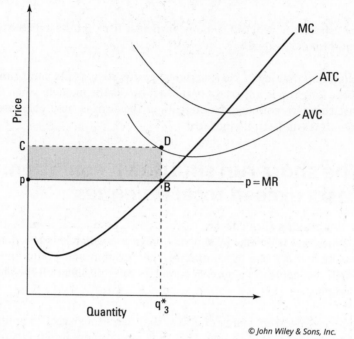

© John Wiley & Sons, Inc.

FIGURE 6-6:
A firm running
such a huge
loss that it can't
even cover its
variable costs.

As a more concrete example, suppose that fixed costs are $1,000 and that by producing q^*_3 units the firm makes total revenues of $400 and incurs variable costs of $500. Because total revenues cover only $400 of the $500 in variable costs, the firm loses $100 in variable costs by producing. Add to that the $1,000 of fixed costs the firm will incur no matter how much it produces, and the firm will lose a total of $1,100 by producing q^*_3 units of output. By contrast, if it shuts down and produces nothing, it loses only the $1,000 in fixed costs. Clearly, the firm should choose to shut down production immediately (in the short run) instead of waiting until the long run when its fixed-cost commitment expires.

REMEMBER

For the general case, the short-run shutdown condition works as follows. If a firm's total revenues at q^*_3 are less than variable costs, it's better to shut down immediately (that is, in the short run). Graphically, this happens anytime the horizontal $p = MR$ (marginal revenue) line intersects the MC (marginal cost) curve at a point below the U-shaped AVC (average variable cost) curve. In all such situations, total revenues will be less than variable costs — implying that it's better to shut down immediately than to continue to produce until the firm's fixed-cost commitments have expired in the long run.

The long-run shutdown condition: Total costs exceed total revenues

REMEMBER

The *long-run shutdown condition* occurs when a loss-making firm is better off waiting until its fixed-cost commitments have expired before shutting down production. It's better off waiting until the long run to shut down production if the firm's total revenues currently exceed its variable costs but are less than its total costs. Graphically, this happens in any situation where the horizontal $p = MR$ (marginal revenue) line intersects the MC (marginal costs) curve at any point on the segment of the MC curve that lies above the bottom of the U-shaped AVC (average variable costs) curve but below the bottom of the U-shaped ATC (average total costs) curve, as in Figure 6-5.

In such a situation, the firm is guaranteed to lose money. But as long as the firm is stuck with its current set of fixed cost commitments, the firm is better off producing rather than shutting down immediately. If it produces, its total revenue will exceed its variable costs, meaning that it can use the excess to pay off at least part of its fixed costs. On the other hand, if it shuts down and produces nothing, it'll lose all of its fixed costs and thereby do worse.

Look at Figure 6-5. In this case, the firm is more than covering its variable costs because total revenues (represented by the box whose four corners are the origin and Points P, C, and q^*_2) exceed variable costs (represented by the box whose four corners are the origin and Points D, E, and q^*_2). Although this firm is losing money, it's better off producing q^*_2 rather than $q = 0$ because total revenues exceed variable costs. The firm can take the extra money left over after paying variable costs and use it to pay off some of its fixed costs.

As a more concrete example, suppose that the firm's fixed costs are $1,000 and that when producing output level q^*_2, it has a total revenue of $800 and variable costs of $700. The first $700 of the $800 in total revenues can go to paying off the variable costs, leaving $100 to pay off a portion of the $1,000 in fixed costs. The result is an overall loss of $900, rather than a $1,000 loss if the firm produces nothing. Thus, this firm should continue operating in the short run and wait until the long run — when its fixed-cost commitments have ended — before shutting down production and exiting its industry.

» **Demonstrating that free markets maximize total surplus**

» **Reducing total surplus with taxes and price controls**

» **Producing at the lowest possible cost to society**

» **Adjusting to changes in supply and demand**

Chapter **7**

Why Economists Love Free Markets and Competition

Economists love *competitive free markets* — markets in which numerous buyers freely interact with numerous competitive firms. Indeed, economists firmly believe that when competitive free markets work properly, they're the very best way to convert society's limited resources into the goods and services that people want to buy. (Please note that for brevity, I sometimes just say "free markets" or "markets" in this chapter rather than writing "competitive free markets" each time. I'm trying to maximize my resources here.)

Why do economists place such great confidence in competitive free markets? Because the interaction of supply and demand (which I discuss in Chapter 4) leads to an outcome in which every unit of output that's produced satisfies two excellent conditions:

>> It's produced at the minimum cost possible, meaning that there's no waste or inefficiency.

>> Its benefits are always at least as big as its costs. That is, competitive free markets produce only output that makes the world better off or at least no worse off.

Economists also love competitive free markets because they provide a gold standard against which all other economic institutions can be judged. In fact, economists refer to many economic problems as *market failures* precisely because they are instances where if markets could function properly, the problems would quickly go away.

In this chapter, I show you that competitive free markets ensure that benefits exceed costs for all the output produced. I also show you that competitive free markets produce the *socially optimal quantity* of output — the level that maximizes the benefits that society can get from its limited supply of resources. Finally, I show you how competitive industries adjust to changes in supply and demand to ensure that everything that's being produced is produced at the lowest possible cost to society.

Ensuring That Benefits Exceed Costs: Competitive Free Markets

Society has only a limited amount of land, labor, and capital out of which to make things. Consequently, society must be very attentive when figuring out how to best convert its limited resources into the goods and services that people most greatly desire.

REMEMBER

Economists love competitive free markets because, if they are operating properly, they make sure that resources are allocated optimally. In particular, such markets assure that resources go toward producing only output for which the benefits exceed the costs.

This point can be easily demonstrated using nothing more complicated than a supply and demand graph (such as the type I introduce in Chapter 4). But first, this section explains the conditions under which competitive free markets can function properly and thereby deliver such nice results.

Examining the traits of a properly functioning market

REMEMBER

Free markets guarantee optimal outcomes only if these conditions are met:

» **Buyers and sellers all have access to the same full and complete information about the good or service in question.** This guarantees that both parties will be willing to negotiate without having to worry that the other guy has some secret information. (In Chapter 11, I explain how markets break down if one side or the other has more information.)

» **Property rights are set up so that the only way buyers can get the good or service in question is by paying sellers for it.** This ensures that sellers have an incentive to produce output. As a counterexample, consider trying to sell tickets to an outdoor fireworks display: Because everyone knows that they can see the display for free, nobody wants to pay for a ticket. And with nobody willing to pay for a ticket, producers have no incentive to put on a display. (In Chapter 11, I discuss situations like these and how society must deal with them given that markets can't.)

» **Supply curves capture all the production costs associated with making the good or service in question.** This requirement helps ensure that markets can make the proper cost-benefit calculations. For instance, if a steel factory can pollute for free, there's no way that the price of steel will incorporate the damage that the factory's pollution does to the environment. On the other hand, if the government forces the factory to continuously pay for cleanup costs, these costs will be reflected in the market price, thereby allowing society to properly weigh the costs and benefits of the company's output. (Chapter 10 deals with ways to help markets along if supply and demand curves don't reflect all costs and benefits.)

» **Demand curves capture all the benefits derived from the good or service in question.** This requirement also ensures proper cost-benefit analysis. If these first four conditions for free markets are met, market forces can reach a social optimum — but only if they're free from interference. Hence the need for two more conditions: one that limits buyers and sellers, and another that constrains government intervention.

» **There are both numerous buyers and numerous sellers, such that nobody is big enough to affect the market price.** This is often called the *price-taking assumption* because everybody just has to take prices as given. This requirement eliminates problems such as monopolies, in which individual buyers or sellers are so powerful that they can manipulate the market price in their own favor.

» **The market price is completely free to adjust to equalize supply and demand for the good or service in question.** The sixth requirement stipulates that supply and demand must be allowed to freely determine the market price and market quantity unimpeded by government-imposed price ceilings or floors. (In Chapter 4, I explain the problems with price ceilings and floors and discuss how they hurt society.)

Basically, these six points accomplish two broad goals: They guarantee that people will want to buy and sell in a market environment, and they ensure that markets will take into account all the costs and all the benefits of producing and then consuming a given amount of output.

Analyzing the efficiency of free markets

Economists use supply and demand curves to demonstrate that free markets produce socially optimal levels of output. But the simple insight behind this result is that a unit of output can be socially beneficial to produce and consume only if the benefits that people derive from consuming it exceed the costs of producing it.

This simple idea is, in fact, why demand curves and supply curves are so useful in analyzing the social optimum. Demand curves quantify the benefits that people get from consumption by showing what they'd be willing to pay to consume each and every particular unit of output (see Chapter 4 for details). Similarly, supply curves quantify the cost of producing each and every particular unit of output (see Chapter 6).

Using supply and demand to compare costs and benefits

By drawing the demand and supply curves for a good or service on the same graph, you can easily compare the benefits and costs of producing each and every unit of output. To see how this is done, take a look at Figure 7-1, on which I've drawn a demand curve, D, and a supply curve, S.

To start, look at one unit of output on the horizontal axis. At that output level, go up to the demand curve and see that people are willing to pay $8 for one unit of output. At the same time, by going up to the supply curve, you can see that firms are willing to supply one unit at a cost of $2.

Putting these facts together, you can see that it's socially beneficial to produce this first unit of output because it's worth more to buyers ($8) than it costs sellers to produce ($2). Put slightly differently, although the resources that it takes to make that unit of output cost society only $2, they bring $8 in benefits when they're converted into this particular good or service. Because the benefits exceed the costs, this is a unit of output that *should be* produced.

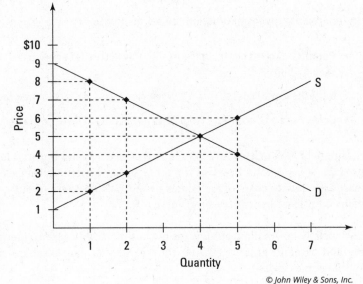

FIGURE 7-1:
Comparing costs and benefits using supply and demand curves.

© John Wiley & Sons, Inc.

Now look at the second unit of output. Going up to the demand curve tells you that people are willing to pay $7 for that unit, while going up to the supply curve tells you that the second unit costs $3 to produce. Again, benefits exceed costs. Again, this unit of output *should be* produced.

By contrast, look at the fifth unit of output. You can see that the costs as given by the supply curve for producing the fifth unit are $6, while the benefits as given by the demand curve are only $4. Because the costs of producing this unit exceed what anyone is willing to pay for it, this is a unit of output that *shouldn't be* produced.

In other words, producing the fifth unit of output would destroy value. Why? Because making it involves converting $6 worth of resources into something that's worth only $4 to consumers. Producing it would make the world worse off. Better to redirect the resources that would be necessary to make a fifth unit of this product toward the production of something that will generate net benefits to consumers.

Determining the socially optimal output level

A graph showing both the supply curve and the demand curve can tell you precisely what quantity (*q*) of output should be produced. That's because the supply and demand curves let you quickly compare costs and benefits for every possible output level.

There are only three cost–benefit relationships:

>> **Benefits exceed costs.** In Figure 7-1, this occurs for every bit of output such that $q < 4$.

>> **Benefits equal costs.** This occurs at exactly $q = 4$ units in the graph.

>> **Costs exceed benefits.** This occurs for all output levels where $q > 4$.

Economists look at this and conclude that the socially optimal level of output to produce is $q = 4$ units because for these units, benefits either exceed costs or at least are equal to costs. By producing the first four units of output, society either gains or at least isn't made any worse off.

TIP

The socially optimal output level is always incredibly easy to identify on any supply and demand graph: It's just the quantity produced where the demand and supply curves cross.

REMEMBER

Economist Adam Smith's big insight was to realize that competitive free markets produce exactly the socially optimal output level on their own without anyone having to direct them to do the right thing. This insight was the basis of Smith's metaphor of an invisible hand that seems to guide markets toward the socially optimal output level, despite the fact that each individual in the market may well be looking out only for his or her own interests. This result greatly simplifies life because it eliminates the need to have a government official or any other sort of central planner constantly checking whether the right amount of output is being produced.

The proof of Smith's assertion is almost trivial. All you have to do is look at Figure 7-1 and realize that the *market equilibrium quantity* — which happens when the market price is free to adjust so that the quantity supplied by sellers equals the quantity demanded by buyers — is determined by where the supply and demand curves cross (to understand why, see Chapter 8). Thus, the market equilibrium quantity is exactly equal to the number of units you'd want to produce if you were using the demand and supply curves to compare benefits and costs.

Measuring everyone's gains with total surplus

Economists use a concept called *total surplus* to add up the gains that come from producing the socially optimal output level. The gain, or *surplus*, comes from the fact that benefits exceed costs for the units of output that are produced.

The total surplus turns out to be divided between consumers and producers. The part of the total surplus that goes to consumers is (naturally) called *consumer surplus*, and the part that goes to producers is called *producer surplus*.

In the subsections that follow, I tackle consumer surplus first and then move on to producer surplus. After I explain each separately, I add them together to explain total surplus. (And I hope that when you're done with this section, you feel like you've received at least a *little* consumer surplus.)

Measuring the consumer surplus of a discrete good

Consumer surplus is the gain people receive when they can buy things at a price that is lower than what they were willing to pay. The easiest way to understand consumer surplus is by first looking at a discrete good. A *discrete good* is a good that comes only in whole units. For instance, you can buy 1 car or 57 cars, but you can't buy 2.33 cars. You can purchase 1 horse or 13 cows but not fractional amounts of livestock (at least if you want them alive!).

Look at Figure 7-2, which shows the demand for cows. Because cows come in discrete units, you don't get a smooth, downward-sloping curve. Rather, you get what mathematicians call a *step function*. The way to understand it is that people are willing to pay $900 for the first cow, $800 for the second cow, $700 for the third cow, and so on.

Now imagine that the market price of cows is $500, which is why I've drawn a horizontal dotted line at that price. Compare that price with what people are willing to pay for each cow.

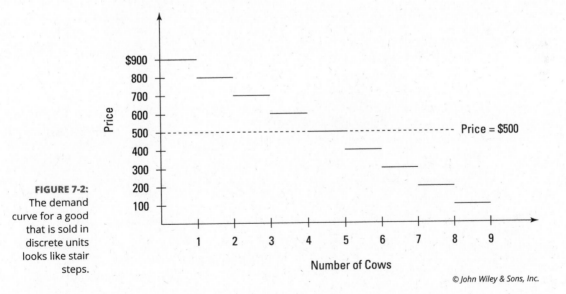

FIGURE 7-2: The demand curve for a good that is sold in discrete units looks like stair steps.

For the first cow, people are willing to pay $900. Because the market price of cows is only $500, these buyers come out ahead because they're able to purchase a cow for $400 less than they were willing to pay. Or, as economists like to say, the *consumer surplus* on the first cow is $400.

Next, look at the second cow. People are willing to pay $800 for it, but because the market price is only $500, they receive a consumer surplus for that cow of $300. Similarly, for the third cow, people get a consumer surplus of $200 because they are willing to pay $700 for it but have to pay only the market price of $500.

For the first four cows, there's a positive consumer surplus, but on the fifth cow, people just break even because they're willing to pay $500 and the cow costs $500. This means that people will want to buy only five cows. (Economists always assume that when the price equals your willingness to pay, you go ahead and buy.)

To calculate consumer surplus for a discrete good such as cows, you need to total the surpluses that people get on each unit that they choose to buy. In this case, the total is $1,000 ($400 for the first cow, plus $300 for the second cow, plus $200 for the third cow, plus $100 for the fourth cow, plus $0 for the fifth cow).

I show this $1,000 of consumer surplus in the graph in Figure 7-3 by shading in the area below each step and above the horizontal price line at $500. The staircase-shaped area equals $1,000.

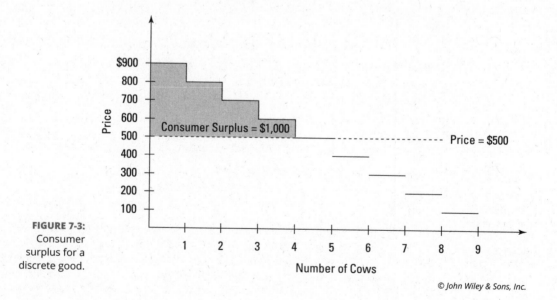

FIGURE 7-3: Consumer surplus for a discrete good.

© John Wiley & Sons, Inc.

Measuring the consumer surplus of a continuous good

Consumer surplus can be computed for continuously measured goods and services — things like land or cooking oil or hours of music lessons, which aren't necessarily sold in discrete units. In other words, you can buy fractional amounts of continuously measured goods, such as 78.5 acres of land, 6.33 gallons of cooking oil, or 2.5 hours of music lessons.

The demand curves for continuously measured goods are much nicer than the step functions that you get for discretely measured goods. In fact, the demand curves for continuously measured goods are smooth, downward-sloping lines (such as the ones in Chapter 4).

Because of the smoothness of such demand curves, when you graph consumer surplus for a continuously measured good, you get a triangular area that lies below the demand curve and above the market price. You can see this wedge illustrated in Figure 7-4, which depicts the cooking oil market.

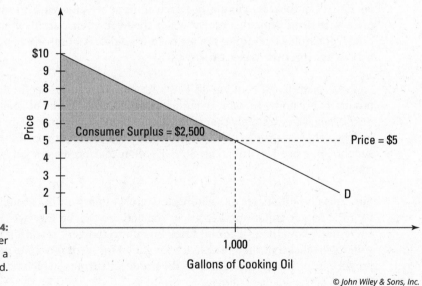

FIGURE 7-4: Consumer surplus for a continuous good.

© John Wiley & Sons, Inc.

In Figure 7-4, the price of cooking oil is $5 per gallon. At that price, people want to buy 1,000 gallons of cooking oil. For each of those 1,000 gallons, the demand curve lies above the horizontal, $5 price line. That implies that buyers are made better off by buying those 1,000 gallons because each of those 1,000 gallons is worth more to its buyer than the $5 per gallon that it costs to buy it.

TIP

To calculate consumer surplus for a continuous good, you total up all the gains that people receive when buying for less money than they are willing to pay — just as you would do for a discrete good. But because you're now dealing with a triangle, totaling up requires a bit of geometry. Simply use the formula for the area of a triangle ($1/2 \times$ base times height) to find the total surplus. In this case, you multiply $1/2 \times 1{,}000$ times $5 = \$2{,}500$.

Measuring producer surplus

Producer surplus measures the gain that firms receive when they can sell their output for more than the minimum price that they would've been willing to accept. You can calculate producer surplus for both discrete and continuous goods, just as you can calculate consumer surplus for each. In this section, I offer an example of calculating producer surplus for a continuous good.

You can get a good handle on producer surplus by looking at Figure 7-5, which shows the supply curve, S, for cooking oil. This supply curve is crucial for determining producer surplus because each point on the supply curve tells you the minimum that you would have to pay suppliers for them to give you the associated amount of output. By comparing each minimum value with the higher market price that firms actually receive when they sell their output, you can compute producer surplus by finding the area of a triangle. (For more on supply curves and how to interpret them, see Chapter 4.)

Suppose the price of cooking oil is \$5 per gallon. You can see in Figure 7-5 that producers are going to want to supply exactly 1,000 gallons of cooking oil at that price. They want to supply that much because for each drop of oil up to and including the very last drop of the 1,000th gallon, the production costs as given by the supply curve are less than the \$5 per gallon that producers get when they sell the oil.

But crucially, producers are willing to supply almost all that cooking oil for *less than* the \$5 per gallon market price. You can see this by the fact that the supply curve lies below the horizontal price line up to the very last drop of the 1,000th gallon. The fact that they receive \$5 per gallon for all of it despite being willing to produce it for less is the source of the producer surplus, which is represented by the area of the shaded triangle.

TIP

Using the formula for the area of a triangle ($1/2 \times$ base $\times$ height), you can compute that the producer surplus in this example is \$2,000. Producers are \$2,000 better off after selling the 1,000 gallons of oil because the total cash they get from selling the 1,000 gallons is \$2,000 greater than the minimum amount that they would have been willing to accept to produce those units.

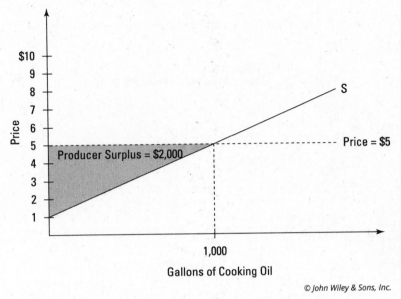

FIGURE 7-5:
Producer surplus for a continuous good.

Price

$10
9
8 — S
7
6
5 — — — — — Price = $5
Producer Surplus = $2,000
4
3
2
1

1,000

Gallons of Cooking Oil

© John Wiley & Sons, Inc.

Computing total surplus

REMEMBER

The *total surplus* that society receives from producing the socially optimal level of output of a certain good or service is simply the sum of the consumer surplus and producer surplus generated by that output level.

Figure 7-6 illustrates total surplus for a market in which the equilibrium price and quantity are, respectively, $p^* = \$5$ and $q^* = 4$. (If this graph looks familiar, that's because it's just like Figure 7-1.)

I've drawn the total surplus area so you can clearly see that it's made up of consumer surplus (the vertically striped area) plus producer surplus (the diagonally striped area). The two are separated by the horizontal line extending from the market equilibrium price ($5).

By again using the formula for the area of a triangle, you multiply $1/2 \times 4 \times 8$ to figure out that for this graph the total surplus is $16. The total gain to society of producing at this output level is $16.

Contemplating total surplus

Total surplus is important because it puts a number on the gains that come from production and trade. Firms make things to make a profit. People spend money on things because consuming those things makes them happy. And total surplus tells you just how much better off both consumers and producers are after interacting with each other.

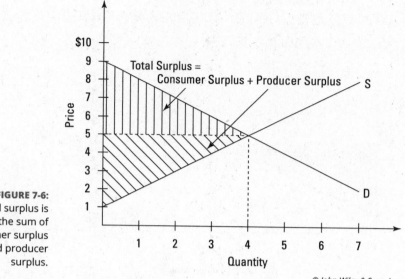

© John Wiley & Sons, Inc.

FIGURE 7-6:
Total surplus is
the sum of
consumer surplus
and producer
surplus.

REMEMBER

By putting a number on the gains made by their interaction, total surplus also provides a benchmark by which economists can measure the harm that comes from government policies that interfere with the market. It's one thing to say that, for instance, price subsidies hurt consumers. It's another thing to be able to say by exactly how many dollars consumers are harmed.

When Free Markets Lose Their Freedom: Dealing with Deadweight Losses

Anything that interferes with the market's ability to reach the market equilibrium and produce the market quantity reduces total surplus. Economists refer to the amount by which total surplus is reduced using the colorful term *deadweight loss*.

In this section, I give you detailed examples of deadweight losses caused by price ceilings and taxes. These types of market interference are both under the government's control, but you shouldn't think that deadweight losses are caused *only* by government policy. Anything that reduces output below the market quantity causes a deadweight loss. Monopolies and oligopolies can be to blame, as can asymmetric information and public goods problems — all things that I discuss in the next few chapters.

Coming up short: The deadweight loss from a price ceiling

Price ceilings are maximum prices at which sellers can legally sell their product (see Chapter 4 for details). Generally, price ceilings are intended to help buyers obtain a low price, but they cause a lot of harm. As an example of a deadweight loss, look at Figure 7-7 in which the government has imposed a price ceiling at P^C.

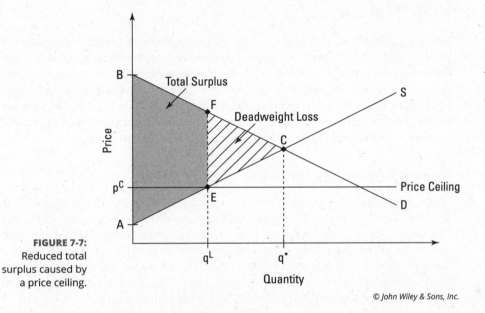

© John Wiley & Sons, Inc.

FIGURE 7-7: Reduced total surplus caused by a price ceiling.

To see the damage price ceilings inflict, first notice that at a maximum price of P^C, suppliers are going to want to sell only q^L units of output (the L stands for *low*). In other words, at that price, only the first q^L units of output are profitable to produce. By contrast, if no price ceiling existed and the market were left to its own devices, suppliers would choose to produce the market equilibrium quantity of output, q^*.

Consequently, if this were a free market, the total surplus would be represented graphically by the triangle defined by Points A, B, and C. But because only q^L units of output can be produced, the total surplus area is reduced down to the shaded area with corners at A, B, F, and E.

The difference between the total surplus generated by producing q^* versus q^L units of output is the diagonally striped triangle defined by Points E, F, and C. The area of this triangle illustrates the deadweight loss that comes from reducing output below the socially optimal level, q^*.

REMEMBER

The price ceiling is harmful because for all units between q^L and q^*, benefits exceed costs, meaning that such units should be produced. By tallying up the gains that should've come from producing and consuming these units, the deadweight loss triangle can precisely measure the harm that results from interfering with the market.

Death and taxes: Finding the deadweight loss of a tax

Taxes on goods and services can also cause deadweight losses. This happens because such taxes raise the costs of producing and consuming output. When these costs are artificially raised by the tax, people respond by producing and consuming fewer units of output than they did before the tax was imposed. Because each unit that had been consumed before the tax was imposed was a unit for which benefits had exceeded costs, the reduction in output that results from the tax necessarily reduces total surplus and causes a deadweight loss.

Seeing how taxes shift the supply curve

Taxes on production shift supply curves upward. Why? Because to the firms that are being taxed, taxes on production feel like increases in production costs. The firms know that the only way that they can at least break even is if they pass the cost of the tax on to buyers — just as they know that they must pass on to buyers the costs of any labor, capital, or other resources. So just as any increase in input costs shifts supply curves vertically, so does any production tax. Imposing a tax on sellers shifts the supply curve vertically by the amount of the tax.

Consider a concrete example — the supply of beef in a beef market in which the government is going to impose a tax of $1 per pound. Figure 7-8 shows two curves. (Well, actually they're straight lines, but humor me here.) The lower one, S, is the supply curve for beef. The higher one, labeled $S + tax$, is the supply curve after the tax is imposed. The important thing to realize is that the curve $S + tax$ is simply the original supply curve shifted up vertically by the amount of the tax, which in this case is $1.

The reason the supply curve shifts up vertically by the amount of the tax has to do with motivating suppliers. Each point on the supply curve tells you the minimum amount that suppliers must receive to get them to supply a particular quantity (see Chapter 4 for details). For instance, look at Point A. Because Point A is on the supply curve, you know that suppliers must receive $5 per pound if you want them to provide 10 million pounds of beef. Similarly, Point E tells you that suppliers must receive $4.50 per pound if you want them to supply 9 million pounds of beef.

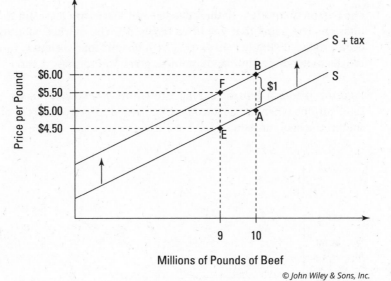

FIGURE 7-8:
Imposing a $1 tax on beef shifts the supply curve vertically by $1, from *S* to *S* + tax.

© John Wiley & Sons, Inc.

If the government comes in and imposes a tax of $1 per pound, it affects how much consumers must pay to get any given amount produced. In particular, there has to be enough money left over after paying the tax to motivate the suppliers. For instance, if consumers still want 10 million pounds of beef, they will have to pay the original amount required to motivate the suppliers to produce that much beef ($5 per pound), as well as enough money to pay the taxes on that much beef ($1 per pound).

Graphically, this means that Point *A* on supply curve *S* shifts up by the $1 amount of the tax to become Point *B* on the *S* + *tax* curve. For the same motivational reasons, Point *E* on the supply curve must shift up to Point *F* on the *S* + *tax* curve. That is, if you have to pay suppliers $4.50 per pound to motivate them to give you 9 million pounds of beef in a world in which $1 per pound must go to the government in taxes, you have to collect a total of $5.50 per pound. And that's exactly what happens at Point *F*.

Every point on the supply curve, *S*, must shift up vertically in the same way that Points *A* and *E* do, so the *S* + *tax* curve captures what the supply curve looks like after the tax is imposed. With this shift in mind, you're ready to discover how this sort of taxation causes deadweight losses.

Seeing how taxes cause deadweight losses

Deadweight losses are called *deadweight losses* because you can't say, "Your loss is my gain," in this situation. You aren't talking about something that passes from one person to another. Rather, deadweight losses are losses in the sense of anni-hilation. The gains that would've resulted if the market quantity of a good had been produced simply vanish; they're a weight that society is forced to bear as it strives to maximize human happiness given limited resources.

Figure 7-9 adds a demand curve, D, to Figure 7-8 so you can see what happens to total surplus when the government imposes a $1 per pound tax on the beef that's sold in the beef market.

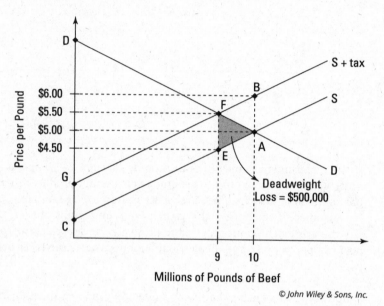

FIGURE 7-9: The deadweight loss caused by a $1 tax on beef.

Before the tax, the market equilibrium happens at Point A, where supply curve S crosses demand curve D. At that point, producers supply 10 million pounds of beef at a price of $5 per pound. The total surplus in this case is given by the triangle defined by Points C, D, and A.

After the tax is imposed, however, the equilibrium happens at Point F, where the S + tax curve crosses the demand curve. At that point, the price of beef is $5.50 per pound, and 9 million pounds are supplied. (Only 9 million pounds are supplied because after the government takes its $1 per pound in taxes, only $4.50 remains to motivate suppliers. You can see from the supply curve S that at that much money per pound, suppliers want to supply only 9 million pounds.)

Because of the tax, the amount of beef supplied falls from 10 million pounds to 9 million pounds. Furthermore, the total surplus is reduced to the triangle whose three corners are G, D, and F.

TIP

You can immediately see that this new total surplus is much smaller than the old total surplus. But before you start ranting about the evils of government, you need to take account of the fact that taxes are being collected. Taxes (theoretically, at least) benefit society, so you need to include this amount when calculating the total surplus of this good sold at this price. At the new equilibrium, $9 million in taxes will be collected because the 9 million pounds of beef sold will be taxed $1 each.

The $9 million in tax collections are represented graphically by the parallelogram whose corners are C, G, F, and E. This area was previously contained in the old total surplus triangle whose corners were C, D, and A. Consequently, this area that used to be part of the old total surplus hasn't been destroyed; it's merely been transferred to the government.

However, part of the old total surplus *has* been destroyed. This part is shown graphically by the shaded deadweight loss triangle (with corners at E, F, and A). This area captures the fact that society has been made worse off by the reduction in beef output from 10 million pounds to 9 million pounds. (Okay, *now* you can start ranting about the evils of government.)

Measuring the size of the deadweight loss using the formula for the area of a triangle ($1/2 \times \text{base} \times \text{height}$) tells you that the tax leads to a deadweight loss of $500,000. That's a big number representing a huge reduction in total surplus deriving from the fact that for each of the 1 million pounds of beef that are no longer being produced, benefits had exceeded costs. All those gains are lost when the tax is imposed.

Note: In certain special cases, a tax can reduce (rather than cause) a deadweight loss. The intuition is that if a product is being inefficiently overproduced, then imposing a tax can make things better: By shifting the supply curve upward, the tax causes production to decrease, thereby reducing the overproduction. I discuss these special cases in detail in Chapter 10.

Hallmarks of Perfect Competition: Zero Profits and Lowest Possible Costs

A wonderful thing about free markets and competition is that output is produced at the lowest possible cost. This fact is extremely important because it means that free markets are as efficient as possible at converting resources into the goods and services that people want to buy.

In addition, markets save society a lot of money because they produce efficiently without requiring human intervention. People don't have to pay big salaries to experts to make sure that markets run efficiently; markets do the job for free.

Understanding the causes and consequences of perfect competition

REMEMBER

To ensure that markets function efficiently, you need really strong competition among firms, a situation that economists refer to as *perfect competition*. Perfect competition exists when there are many firms within a given industry that are all producing identical (or nearly identical) products (see Chapter 6 for details). The following things are also true when perfect competition exists:

>> Every firm is a *price taker* (meaning that the firm must accept the market equilibrium price for what it produces) because its output is a very small fraction of the industry's total output (see Chapter 6).

>> Every firm has identical production technology.

>> Firms are free to enter or leave the industry as they please.

REMEMBER

When these requirements are met, perfect competition leads to two very excellent outcomes:

>> **Every firm in the industry makes zero economic profits.** This idea does not mean that businesses earn no money above the costs of doing business; if that were true, no one would go into business. Firms must earn enough money to keep entrepreneurs motivated to stay in business (and to attract other entrepreneurs to open new firms).

   So what does the first outcome mean? The *economic profits* earned by a firm are any monies collected above and beyond what is required to keep an entrepreneur interested in continuing in business. So the fact that perfect competition leads to zero economic profits means that managers just barely want to keep their current firms operating.

   It also means that nobody in the industry is getting filthy rich at anyone else's expense. Rather, they're doing just well enough to keep on supplying the output that society wants them to supply. This situation is great for society, because it'd be wasteful to pay entrepreneurs more than necessary to get them to do what society wants.

>> **Every firm produces output at the minimum possible cost**. This outcome is good for society because it means that the least possible amounts of resources are consumed while producing the output that society wants.

Peering into the process of perfect competition

REMEMBER

How does perfect competition actually work? The following four steps explain:

1. **The market price of the output sold by every firm in the industry is determined by the interaction of the industry's overall supply and demand curves.**

2. **Each firm takes the market price as given and produces whatever quantity of output will maximize its own profit (or minimize its own loss if the price is so low that it's not possible to make a profit).**

3. **Because each firm has an identical production technology, each will choose to produce the same quantity and will consequently make the same profit or loss as every other firm in the industry.**

4. **Depending on whether firms in the industry are making profits or losses, firms will either enter or leave the industry until the market price adjusts to the level where all remaining firms are making zero economic profit.**

The fourth point in this process — firm entry and exit — is very important. To understand it clearly, I break it into two cases: one where every firm in the industry is making a profit because the market price is high and another where every firm in the industry is making a loss because the market price is low:

>> **Attracting new firms by making profits:** If every firm in an industry is making a profit, new firms are attracted to enter the industry, too, in hopes of sharing the profits. But when they enter, total industry output increases so much that the market price begins to fall. As the price falls, profits fall, thereby lowering the incentive for further firms to enter the industry.

The process of new firms entering the industry continues until the market price falls so low that profits drop to zero. When that happens, the incentive to enter the industry disappears, and no more firms enter.

>> **Losing existing firms when making losses:** If every firm in an industry starts out making losses because the market price is low, some of the existing firms exit the industry because they can't stand losing money. When they do, total industry output falls. That reduction in total supply, in turn, causes the market price to rise. And as the market price rises, firms' losses decrease.

The process of firms leaving and prices rising continues until the remaining firms are no longer losing money.

REMEMBER

The fact that firms can freely enter or leave the industry means that after all adjustments are made, firms always make a zero economic profit. In other words, if there is perfect competition, you don't have to worry about firms exploiting anyone; they just barely make enough money to stay in business.

The other important result of perfect competition — that competitive firms produce at minimum cost — becomes apparent if you flesh out the four-stage process of perfect competition by using cost curves. I encourage you to take a look at Chapter 6 before moving on to the next section. If you haven't read that chapter, this section may cause your eyes to cross (and you know what your mother said about the dangers of crossing your eyes).

Graphing how profits guide firm entry and exit

In this section, I use firm cost curves to demonstrate how market forces automatically cause firms to produce output at the lowest possible cost. To make this process clear, I present two cases. In the first, firms begin by making profits. In the second, firms begin by making losses. Either way, adjustments happen so that they end up making zero economic profits and producing at minimum costs.

Visualizing firm entry when there are profits

To see how an industry adjusts when it starts off making profits, look at Figure 7-10, which consists of two graphs. The one on the left gives the market demand curve, D, and the initial market supply curve, S_0, for tennis balls. The one on the right gives the cost curves for one of the many identical firms that make tennis balls.

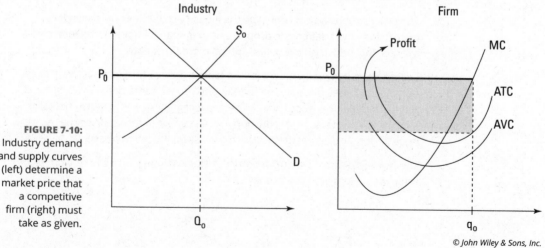

FIGURE 7-10:
Industry demand and supply curves (left) determine a market price that a competitive firm (right) must take as given.

© John Wiley & Sons, Inc.

Because the firms in this industry are identical, they all have the same cost structures. In particular, they all have the same marginal cost curve (MC). This point is important because a competitive firm's marginal cost curve is its supply curve, as I show in Chapter 6.

The example firm takes the market price, P_0, that's determined by supply and demand in the left graph and uses it to figure out its profit-maximizing output level in the right graph. (To emphasize that P_0 is the same in both graphs, I've drawn a solid horizontal line that goes all the way across both graphs.)

TIP

Each firm chooses to produce the output level at which the horizontal price line intersects the MC curve. In the right-hand graph, I label the output level q_0. In the left-hand graph, you can see that the industry's total supply is Q_0. The industry's total supply is simply each individual firm's output, q_0, times the total number of firms in the industry.

Next, focus on the fact that each firm runs a profit when the market price is P_0. The profit is shown by the shaded rectangle in the right graph.

REMEMBER

This profit is important because it attracts entrepreneurs to enter the industry. They realize that they can set up yet more identical firms and make some nice profits. As economists like to say, profits attract entrants.

SEEING HOW NEW ENTRY REDUCES PROFITS

Figure 7-11 shows what happens when the new entrants to the industry arrive. Their new production increases overall production so that the total supply curve shifts from S_0 to S_1 in the left-hand graph. That lowers the market equilibrium price from P_0 to P_1.

FIGURE 7-11:
New entrants increase industry supply, drive down price, and reduce profits.

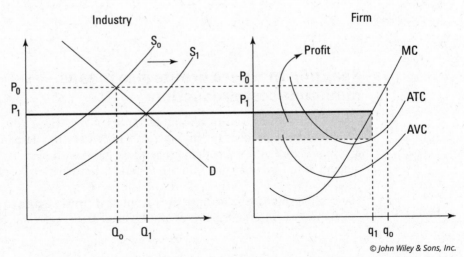

© John Wiley & Sons, Inc.

Each of the price-taking firms reacts to the lower price by producing a lower output level, q_i, which you can see illustrated in the right-hand graph. More importantly, the firms' profits decrease, which you can see by comparing the shaded profit rectangles in Figures 7-10 and 7-11.

The new entry results in smaller profits. The smaller profits are less attractive to entrepreneurs. So although the fact that some profits are still available will still cause new entry, there won't be as much new entry as when profits were larger.

SEEING HOW ENOUGH ENTRY DRIVES PROFITS TO ZERO

As more firms enter the market, entry continues until prices fall so far that all profits are driven away. This situation is illustrated in Figure 7-12, in which new entry has increased supply still more, to S_2. The result is that the market price falls to P_2, which results in zero profits. (Note that there's no shaded profit rectangle in the right-hand graph.) Because profits fall to zero, entry ceases.

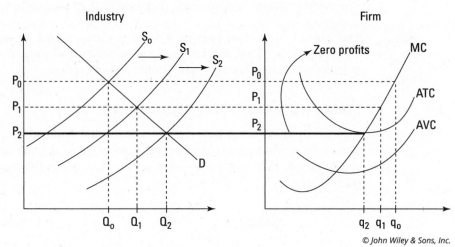

FIGURE 7-12: Eventually, new entry drives prices down so far that profits disappear.

© John Wiley & Sons, Inc.

Realizing that zero profits also means minimum-cost production

When profits are driven to zero by the entry of new firms, the cost per unit at which output is produced is minimized. You can see this fact in the right-hand graph of Figure 7-12 by noticing that when faced with price P_2, firms choose to produce at the quantity that minimizes per-unit production costs.

You can tell this is true because the output that firms choose to produce, q_2, lies exactly at the minimum point of the U-shaped average total cost (*ATC*) curve.

When output is produced at that level, the average cost per unit is lower than at any other output level. (In other words, any other output level results in a higher average total cost.)

This is a wonderful thing because it means that each firm is being as efficient as possible, producing output at the lowest possible cost per unit. Moreover, each firm is voluntarily choosing to produce at that level without any need for coercion.

REMEMBER

What's going on here is that profits serve as a self-correcting feedback mechanism. High profits automatically attract new entrants who automatically increase supply and drive prices down. That process continues until there are no more profits and no more new entrants. But more importantly, it continues until each and every firm is producing output at the most efficient, least-cost output level. This is truly Adam Smith's invisible hand at work.

Visualizing firm exit when there are losses

A competitive industry in which firms are losing money is an industry that should reduce its output level. Firms lose money only when the output that they produce is worth less than the cost of the inputs used to produce it. Reducing production solves this problem because a reduced quantity of output has a higher average value to consumers (as you can see by sliding down any demand curve and noting that successive units are worth successively less to consumers).

A fortunate thing about perfect competition is that it provides a feedback mechanism that leads to zero profits and efficient production whenever an industry starts out making losses. To see this, take a look at Figure 7-13, where the initial supply curve, S_3, interacts with the demand curve, D, to produce a very low market price of P_3.

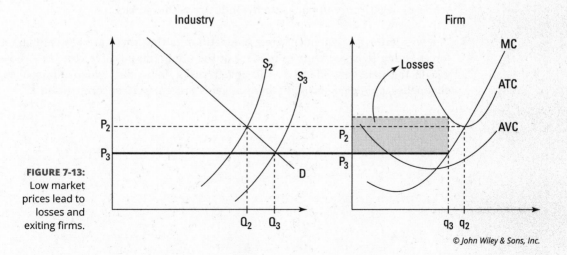

FIGURE 7-13: Low market prices lead to losses and exiting firms.

© John Wiley & Sons, Inc.

At this market price, you can see in the right-hand graph that each firm in the industry is making a loss, which is shown by the shaded rectangle.

REMEMBER

This loss discourages all the firms in the industry, and those in the weakest financial condition begin to exit. As that happens, the industry supply curve in the left-hand graph shifts left (because supply decreases). That shift raises the market price and reduces the losses made by firms remaining in the industry. But as long as there are losses, firms continue to exit until the supply curve moves all the way back to S_2, at which point the market price is P_2, and firms are making zero profits as in Figure 7-12.

When the market price reaches P_2 and firms are making zero profits, firm exits stop and, more importantly, each firm is producing at the least-cost output level, q_2.

Understanding that entry and exit don't happen instantly

Market pressures always push perfectly competitive firms to produce at the lowest possible per-unit cost (see the preceding sections). Keep in mind that this nice result doesn't happen overnight. When firms are making profits or sustaining losses, it takes time for new firms to enter (if there are profits) or for existing firms to leave (if there are losses).

Depending on the industry, these adjustment processes may take anywhere from a few weeks to a few years. For example, setting up new power plants takes a while because building a new power plant takes at least a year. Similarly, even if agricultural prices fall and farmers are making losses, those farmers who drop out of the industry won't do so until the next growing season. On the other hand, if producing U.S. flags suddenly becomes really profitable, you can be sure that scores of new firms will pour into the industry within weeks.

The wonderful thing about perfect competition is that there are always market forces acting to drive firms to produce at the minimum possible cost. As I show you in the next few chapters, this lovely result falls apart when monopolies, oligopolies, public goods, and other problems prevent perfect competition.

» **Maximizing profit**

» **Benefiting society (in certain situations)**

» **Abiding by regulations**

Chapter **8**

Monopolies: Bad Behavior without Competition

A firm that has no competitors in its industry is called a *monopoly*. Monopolies are much maligned because their profit incentive leads them to raise prices and lower output in order to squeeze more money out of consumers. As a result, governments typically go out of their way to break up monopolies and replace them with competitive industries that generate lower prices and higher output.

At the same time, however, governments also very intentionally create monopolies in other situations. For instance, governments issue patents, which give monopoly rights to inventors to sell and market their inventions. Similarly, in many places, local services such as natural gas delivery and trash collection are also monopolies created and enforced by local government.

In this chapter, I explain why society forbids monopolies in some situations and promotes them in others. First, I show you that profit-maximizing monopolies compare unfavorably with competitive firms because they set higher prices and produce less output than competitive firms. Then I explain how these problems may, in certain cases, be outweighed by other factors — the need to promote innovation, for example, and the odd fact that in some cases having a lot of competitors is just too annoying.

Examining Profit-Maximizing Monopolies

Essentially, this chapter is one big exercise in cost–benefit analysis. Monopolies aren't all evil. Neither are they utterly good. Whether you want to have one in any particular instance depends on whether, in that situation, the benefits outweigh the costs. This section goes into detail about the costs associated with monopolies.

Zeroing in on the problems monopolies cause

REMEMBER

In an industry that has only one monopoly firm rather than lots of small competitive firms, three socially harmful things occur:

>> The monopoly firm produces less output than a competitive industry would.

>> The monopoly firm sells its output at a higher price than the market price would be if the industry were competitive.

>> The monopoly's output is produced less efficiently and at a higher cost than the output produced by a competitive industry.

Although all these things are harmful to consumers, keep in mind that monopolies don't do these things to be jerks. Rather, these outcomes are simply the result of monopolies' acting to maximize their profits — which is, of course, the very same thing that competitive firms try to do.

REMEMBER

The difference in outcomes between a competitive industry and a monopoly industry doesn't have anything to do with bad intentions. Rather, it results from the fact that monopolies are free from the pressures that lead competitive industries to produce the socially optimal output level (see Chapter 7 for info on these pressures). Without these pressures, monopoly firms can increase prices and restrict output to increase their profits — things that competitive firms would also love to do but can't.

The lack of competitive pressure also means that monopoly firms can get away with costly, inefficient production. This is a real problem that you should take seriously when considering whether the benefits of a monopoly outweigh its costs. I talk more about this issue later in the chapter.

Identifying the source of the problem: Decreasing marginal revenues

REMEMBER

All the bad outcomes generated by a monopoly derive from the same source: The monopolist faces a downward-sloping marginal revenue curve. *Marginal revenue* is the increase in total revenue that comes from selling each successive unit of a product. This simple fact causes monopolies to charge more, produce less, and produce at higher costs than competitive firms.

How can one little curve cause such mayhem? A downward-sloping marginal revenue curve implies that each additional unit that the monopoly sells brings less revenue than the previous unit. For instance, although the 10th unit sold may bring in $8, the 11th brings in only $3. Obviously, such a situation reduces the incentive to produce a lot of output.

This situation stands in stark contrast to the marginal revenue situation facing competitive firms (see Chapter 6). Competitive firms face horizontal marginal revenue curves, meaning that whether they sell 11 units or 11,000, each unit brings in the same amount of money. Naturally, that's much more of an inducement to produce a lot of output.

Facing down demand

Why is there such a difference between the marginal revenue curves facing monopolists and competitive firms? A monopoly is free to choose the price it wants to charge along the demand curve it faces for its product. A competitive firm, on the other hand, has to take the market price as given.

A monopoly firm can choose its price because as the only firm in its industry, it controls all the output in that industry. As a result, it can create a relatively high price by producing only a few units, or it can induce a relatively low price by flooding the market. By contrast, each firm in a competitive industry is such a small part of its industry that its choice of output makes too small a difference in total output to cause price changes. (See Chapter 7 for more on why competitive firms can't affect prices.)

REMEMBER

The monopolist's ability to control the price by altering its output level means that the firm has to step back and consider what output level to produce. The firm's goal is profit maximization, so it has to figure out what level of output will maximize its profits. It turns out that a monopolist's profit-maximizing output level is defined by the same condition as that of a competitive firm: Produce at the output level where the marginal revenue curve crosses the marginal cost curve.

Deriving marginal revenue from the demand curve

REMEMBER

For a monopoly, the marginal revenue of each successive unit of output is less than the marginal revenue of the preceding unit because demand curves slope downward. The monopoly's marginal revenue curve has a precise relationship with the demand curve for the monopoly's output: If the demand curve is a straight line, the slope of the marginal revenue curve is twice as steep as the slope of the demand curve, meaning that marginal revenue falls quite quickly as output increases.

To see how this works, take a look at Figure 8-1, which draws out a demand curve and its associated marginal revenue curve.

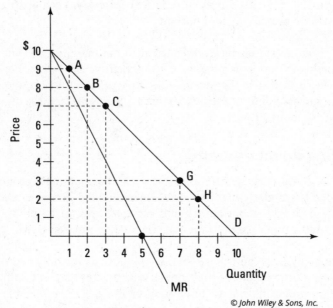

FIGURE 8-1:
The MR curve for a monopolist facing a straight-line demand curve has a slope twice as steep as that of the demand curve.

© *John Wiley & Sons, Inc.*

I provide the data needed to draw these two curves in Table 8-1. The first column contains output levels ranging from zero to ten units. The second column shows the price per unit that can be charged at each output level. The third column shows the total revenue that the monopoly would get for producing and selling each output level — the price per unit times the number of units. And the final column gives the marginal revenue — the change in total revenue — that happens as you increase output by one unit.

TABLE 8-1

Price and *MR* for Various Output Levels

Output	Selling Price	Total Revenue	Marginal Revenue
0	$10	$0	
			$9
1	$9	$9	
			$7
2	$8	$16	
			$5
3	$7	$21	
			$3
4	$6	$24	
			$1
5	$5	$25	
			−$1
6	$4	$24	
			−$3
7	$3	$21	
			−$5
8	$2	$16	
			−$7
9	$1	$9	
			−$9
10	$0	$0	

To clarify that marginal revenue represents the *change* in total revenue, the entries in the marginal revenue column are displayed between the two total revenue figures to which they correspond. For instance, total revenue increases from $0 to $9 as you move from producing no output to one unit of output. That's why I place the marginal revenue of $9 between the total revenue entries of $0 and $9.

As you see in Figure 8-1, the marginal revenue (MR) curve starts at the same point as the demand curve, but it falls with twice the slope. It hits the horizontal axis at an output level of $q = 5$ instead of the $q = 10$ output level at which demand hits the horizontal axis (where q stands for quantity produced).

Relating marginal revenue to total revenue

You can get a handle on why the monopolist's marginal revenue curve falls so quickly if you first examine total revenue, or *TR*. The total revenue that the monopolist can get is simply the output it produces times the price at which it can sell its output. That is, $TR = p \times q$. However, the price at which a monopolist can sell depends on how much the firm produces.

The relationship between output produced and the price at which the product can be sold depends on the demand curve. For instance, consider Point *A* on the demand curve in Figure 8-1. At that point, one unit is being produced, and it can be sold for $9. Consequently, the total revenue at that point is $9. Next, look at Point *B*, at which two units of output are being sold. At that output level, each unit can be sold for $8. Consequently, total revenue is $8 × 2 = $16. And at Point *C*, where three units can be sold for $7 each, total revenue is $21.

The important thing to notice is how total revenue changes as you move from *A* to *B* to *C* and output increases from one to two to three units. Total revenue goes from $9 to $16 to $21. Obviously, total revenue increases. But look more deeply. Moving from *A* to *B*, *TR* increases by $7 (from $9 to $16). But moving from *B* to *C*, it increases by only $5 (from $16 to $21). Each successive increase in total revenue is smaller than the preceding increase. In other words, marginal revenue declines as the monopoly increases production.

If you look at Table 8-1, you can see that marginal revenue continues to fall for each successive unit. In fact, it becomes negative for all units after the fifth. You can see why by looking at Points *G* and *H* in Figure 8-1 as examples. At Point *G*, the monopolist can sell seven units of output for $3 each. That makes for a total revenue of $21. But if he increases output to eight units at Point *H*, he can sell these units for only $2 each, implying a total revenue of $16.

Increasing output from seven units to eight units means decreasing total revenue from $21 to $16. That's the same thing as saying that marginal revenue is *negative* $5 as you move from seven to eight units of output.

Sliding down the demand curve: Higher output, lower prices

The reason marginal revenue keeps declining and even becomes negative is that the demand curve slopes downward, meaning that the only way to get people to buy more stuff is to offer them a lower price. You have to offer them a lower price not just on additional units but on all previous units as well. In other words, if the monopolist wants to sell only one unit (see Point A), he can get $9 for it. But if the monopolist wants to sell two units (see Point B), he has to lower the price down to $8 per unit for *both* the first unit *and* the second unit.

Because total revenue equals price times quantity *(TR = p × q)*, you can see that the monopolist faces a trade-off as he increases production and slides down the demand curve. As he produces more, the quantity *q* obviously goes up, but the price *p* must fall. What happens to *TR* depends on whether the increases in *q* (output effects) are bigger than the decreases in *p* (price effects).

You can see from Table 8-1 that as the monopoly increases production through the first four units, total revenue keeps increasing, meaning that the gains from selling more units more than offset the declines from getting less money per unit. At an output of five units, the two effects cancel each other out. And for higher outputs, total revenue falls because the negative effect of less money per unit overwhelms the positive effect of selling more units.

REMEMBER

Because marginal revenue *(MR)* tells you how total revenue *(TR)* changes as you increase output, the changes in *TR* caused by increasing output show up in *MR* as well. If you look at Figure 8-1, you can see that *MR* is always declining. That's because the negative price effect of getting less per unit keeps getting stronger and stronger relative to the positive quantity effect of selling more units.

TECHNICAL STUFF

For straight-line demand curves (like the one you see in Figure 8-1), the *MR* curve is a straight line that has twice as steep a slope as the demand curve. If you know calculus, you can prove that the *MR* curve falls twice as fast as the demand curve: First take the equation of the demand curve shown in Figure 8-1, $p = 10 - q$, and substitute it into the total revenue equation, $TR = p \times q$. That gives you $TR = (10 - q)q = 10q - q^2$. Then take the first derivative with respect to output, *q*. Because marginal revenue is *dTR/dq*, you find that $MR = 10 - 2q$, meaning that *MR* has the same *y*-intercept as the demand curve but twice as steep a slope.

When you understand the marginal revenue situation facing a monopolist, you can combine it with the firm's marginal cost curve to figure out its profit-maximizing output level. As I show you in the next section, this level is less than that chosen by a competitive firm — a behavior that leads to a social harm that can be quantified using the method of deadweight losses.

Choosing an output level to maximize profits

A monopoly is no different from a competitive firm when it comes to the costs of producing output. Just like a competitive firm, a monopoly has fixed costs, variable costs, and marginal costs (see Chapter 6). More importantly, these costs all behave in exactly the same way, whether a firm is competitive or a monopoly. This means you can use costs to help analyze the decision-making process of a monopoly in the same way that you use them to analyze the decision-making process of competitive firms.

The key difference, however, is that the monopoly faces a downward-sloping marginal revenue curve. In this section, you see how this factor causes a profit-maximizing monopoly to produce less output than would a profit-maximizing competitive firm.

Setting a monopoly's marginal revenue equal to marginal cost

The monopoly goes about maximizing profits in much the same way as a competitive firm. To see this, take a look at Figure 8-2, which draws a monopoly's average total cost (*ATC*) and marginal cost (*MC*) curves on the same graph as the monopoly's demand curve and marginal revenue (*MR*) curve.

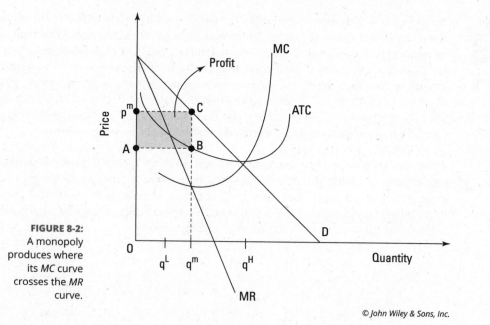

FIGURE 8-2:
A monopoly produces where its *MC* curve crosses the *MR* curve.

© John Wiley & Sons, Inc.

For every output level, q, the *ATC* curve gives the average total cost per unit of producing q units of output. This curve is U-shaped because average total costs first fall due to increasing returns and then increase due to diminishing returns. The *marginal cost curve* gives the cost of producing one more unit of output; that is, it tells you how much total costs rise if you increase output by one unit.

REMEMBER

The profit-maximizing monopolist's optimal output level, q^m, is determined by where the *MR* and *MC* curves cross. As with a competitive firm, choosing to produce where marginal revenues equal marginal costs $(MR = MC)$ either maximizes profits or minimizes losses, depending on whether demand is strong enough for the firm to be able to make a profit (see Chapter 6 for details).

You can see why q^m is optimal by looking at two different output levels, q^L and q^H, where L stands for low and H stands for high:

>> **Low output:** At output level q^L, you see that *MR* at that output exceeds *MC*, meaning that if you produce and sell that unit, it will bring in more in revenue than it costs to produce. Clearly, this is a good unit to produce. Because a similar relationship holds true for all output levels less than q^m, the monopolist should keep increasing output until it reaches q^m.

>> **High output:** On the other hand, the monopolist does not want to increase output beyond q^m. To see why, examine output level q^H. At that output level, marginal costs are much bigger than marginal revenues, meaning that if you produce that unit of output, the cost of producing it will exceed the money you could get selling it. In other words, if you produce that unit, you'll lose money.

If you're a monopolist, you want to produce exactly q^m units because for all units up to q^m, marginal revenues exceed marginal costs, meaning that you receive more money selling such units than you spend producing them.

TIP

To figure out what the price of each unit of output should be for a monopoly, use the demand curve. The monopolist's profit-maximizing output level is q^m, the value of q where the *MR* and *MC* curves cross. At q^m, go up to the demand curve. In Figure 8-2, you can see that at output level q^m, the monopolist can charge price p^m.

Eyeing the monopoly's profit

A monopoly's profit is the difference between total revenue and total costs. In Figure 8-2, the profit that the monopolist makes is shown by the shaded rectangle with corners at A, p^m, C, and B. As I discuss in Chapter 10, such profit rectangles are derived by comparing the two rectangles that give, respectively, total revenues and total costs.

TIP

The basic trick is to remember that the area of a rectangle is defined as a product — the product of its length times its width. Total revenue and total costs are also products — the price (or average cost) per unit multiplied by the number of units. Therefore, on a graph showing price along the y-axis and quantity along the x-axis, total revenue and total costs are represented as rectangles:

>> **Total revenue:** For the monopolist maximizing profits by producing q^m units and selling them for p^m dollars, total revenue is price times quantity: $TR = p^m \times q^m$. Consequently, total revenue is the area of the rectangle whose length is equal to the price and whose width is equal to the quantity. That is, TR is the area of the rectangle that has corners O, p^m, C, and q^m.

>> **Total costs:** Total costs are also a product — a product of the average cost per unit times the number of units. If you go up from Point q^m until you hit the ATC curve, you get to Point B. The vertical distance up to Point B gives the average cost per unit of producing output q^m. So if you multiply that amount by the output q^m, you get total costs. Geometrically, that means that total costs are given by the rectangle whose corners are O, A, B, and q^m.

In Figure 8-2, the total revenue rectangle (O, p^m, C, q^m) is bigger than the total cost rectangle (O, A, B, q^m), meaning that the monopoly is earning a profit. That profit is given by the shaded rectangle whose points are A, p^m, C, and B, which represents the difference in areas between the total revenue and total cost rectangles.

Understanding that monopoly doesn't guarantee profitability

Just because a firm has a monopoly doesn't mean that it's guaranteed a profit. If demand is weak relative to costs, then the monopoly price will be too low to generate a profit.

To see an example of this situation, look at Figure 8-3, where demand curve, D_1, leads to a marginal revenue curve, MR_1. The monopoly again sets marginal revenue equal to marginal cost to find the optimal output level, q^m_1. But because of demand being low relative to costs, the monopoly operates at a loss represented by the area of the shaded rectangle.

One way to see that the shaded rectangle gives a loss is to compare the total revenue rectangle with the total cost rectangle, as I did for Figure 8-2. Here in Figure 8-3, the total cost rectangle exceeds the total revenue rectangle by the amount of the shaded rectangle.

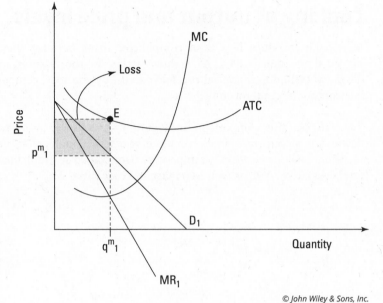

© John Wiley & Sons, Inc.

FIGURE 8-3: A monopoly facing weak demand can sustain a loss.

TIP

A different way to understand where the loss comes from is by comparing the monopoly's average total cost per unit with the price per unit it gets when producing and selling at output level q^m_1. At that output level, you find the price per unit, p^m_1, by starting on the horizontal axis at q^m_1 and then going up to the demand curve. As you can see, you have to go up even farther to get to the ATC curve, meaning that the average total cost per unit to make q^m_1 units exceeds the price per unit you get from selling these units. This fact implies that the firm will lose money producing at output level q^m_1.

As I show in Chapter 6, a firm in such a situation can't do any better. That is, any other output level besides q^m_1 would produce an even bigger loss. If the monopoly can't figure out a way to either reduce costs or increase demand, it will quickly go bankrupt.

Comparing Monopolies with Competitive Firms

In this section, I compare a profit-maximizing monopoly with a profit-maximizing competitive firm. This comparison comes off very badly for the monopoly because competitive firms deliver socially optimal output levels. Because monopolies always end up producing less than competitive firms, their output levels are always less than socially optimal.

Looking at output and price levels

Monopolies produce less than competitive firms because they have different marginal revenue curves. As I show earlier in the chapter, monopolies face downward-sloping marginal revenue curves. By contrast, competitive firms face horizontal marginal revenue curves.

You can see the comparison in Figure 8-4, where I've drawn in both the downward-sloping marginal revenue curve of a monopoly, MR^m, and the horizontal marginal revenue curve of a competitive firm, MR^c. The graph also has an average total cost curve, ATC, as well as a marginal cost curve, MC.

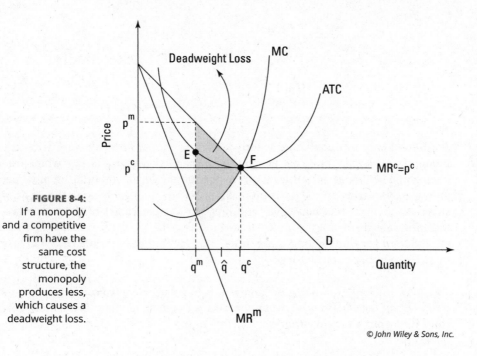

© John Wiley & Sons, Inc.

FIGURE 8-4:
If a monopoly and a competitive firm have the same cost structure, the monopoly produces less, which causes a deadweight loss.

Figure 8-4 assumes that the competitive firm and the monopoly have the same cost structure, which is why I show only one MC curve and one ATC curve. By assuming that both firms have the same cost structure, I can isolate the effect that the difference in marginal revenue curves has on each firm's output decisions.

Maximizing profits for each firm

The marginal revenue curve for a competitive firm, MR^c, is a horizontal line set at the market price, p^c. This is the case because a competitive firm is such a small part of its industry that the firm can't affect the market price. As a result, it can sell as many or as few units as it wants at p^c, meaning that the marginal revenue it gets for every unit it chooses to produce is p^c. As I show in Figure 8-4, $MR^c = p^c$ for a competitive firm.

Market forces adjust supply and demand until the market price is equal to the minimum average total cost at which a firm can produce. Geometrically, this means that the horizontal $MR^c = p^c$ line just touches the bottom of the U-shaped ATC curve. (Refer to Chapter 7 for more information.)

REMEMBER

Monopolies and competitive firms follow the same basic rule to maximize profits: They each produce where their marginal revenue curve intersects their marginal cost curve. But because they have different marginal revenue curves (as in Figure 8-4), they produce different outputs. The competitive firm produces q^c, and the monopoly produces q^m.

Understanding why the monopoly produces less

A competitive firm produces more than the monopolist because the competitive firm doesn't have to worry about reducing its revenue per unit if it increases output. No matter how much it produces, it always receives $MR^c = p^c$ on every unit sold because its output is too small relative to total output to affect the market price.

By contrast, the monopolist faces the market demand curve, meaning that every additional unit it sells lowers the price per unit that it receives on all units sold. Graphically, this appears as a downward-sloping MR^m curve that leads the monopoly to restrict output because it knows that the more it produces, the less money per unit it gets.

Because the monopoly restricts output compared to the competitive firm, the monopoly price, p^m, is also higher than the competitive price, p^c. This fact really irks consumers, but as I show you in the next section, the real harm comes from the reduction in output.

Deadweight losses: Quantifying the harm caused by monopolies

Monopolies cause harm because they reduce output below the socially optimal level produced by competitive firms. Take a look at Figure 8-4 and consider whether it would be good for society if all the units of output between the monopoly output level, q^m, and the competitive output level, q^c, were produced. For instance, look at unit $q^\wedge$. At that level of output, the demand curve is above the marginal cost curve. That implies that people are willing to pay more for that unit of output than it costs to make it. In other words, benefits exceed costs for that unit of output. Because this is true for all units between q^m and q^c, monopolies hurt society by failing to produce units of output for which benefits exceed costs.

The harm caused to society when the monopoly fails to produce output level q^
can be quantified as the vertical distance between the demand curve and the marginal cost curve at output level q^. That vertical distance is a dollar amount — the number of dollars by which benefits would exceed costs for that unit if it was produced and consumed. If you go through the same exercise for each and every unit between q^m and q^c, you can total up the harm caused by the failure of the monopoly to produce all of those units. Graphically, the total harm measured in dollars is equal to the area of the shaded deadweight loss region in Figure 8-4.

The deadweight loss region demonstrates that when monopolies restrict output in order to maximize their profits, they fail to produce units for which benefits exceed costs. That harms society.

Losing efficiency

Another problem with monopolies is that they are not efficient producers. You can see this in Figure 8-4. Competition leads competitive firms to produce at q^c, the output level that puts them at the bottom of the average total costs (ATC) curve. You can see this output level and cost as Point F.

TIP

That output level minimizes production costs per unit of output, which you can see by comparing q^c with any other output level. Whether you produce more or less than q^c, average costs per unit will be higher due to the U shape of the ATC curve.

In particular, look at the monopoly output level, q^m. At that output level, you get to Point E on the ATC curve. Because the vertical distance between the horizontal axis and E is greater than the vertical distance between the horizontal axis and Point F, you know for certain that total costs per unit when producing the monopoly output level, q^m, are higher than those when producing the competitive output level, q^c. Consequently, the monopoly is less efficient than the competitive firm — despite having identical costs.

REMEMBER

This bad result is yet another example of monopolists facing downward-sloping marginal revenue curves. The competitive firm's horizontal marginal revenue curve implies that it can sell as many units as it wants at the competitive price p^c. Consequently, the competitive firm has an incentive to increase output all the way to q^c because doing so lowers per-unit production costs without reducing per-unit revenue. The same cost-reducing incentive exists for a monopolist to increase its output; but the cost reduction is more than offset by declining marginal revenue as the monopoly moves down along its downward-sloping marginal revenue curve. As a result, the monopolist's profits are maximized at q^m, even though q^c is the lowest-cost output level.

Considering Good Monopolies

In some cases, the benefits of monopolies actually outweigh their costs. This section takes a closer look at these instances, where the goal is to encourage innovation, cut redundancy, and keep costs low.

Encouraging innovation and investment with patents

The most obvious place where monopolies do society a lot of good is patents. Patents give inventors the exclusive right to market their inventions for 20 years, after which time their inventions become public property. That is, patents give inventors the right to run a monopoly for 20 years.

REMEMBER

Without patents, an inventor is unlikely to ever see any financial reward for her hard work because copycats will steal her idea and flood the market with rip-offs, thereby collapsing the price. Consequently, in a world without patents, far fewer people would bother to put in the time, effort, and money required to come up with new inventions.

To remedy this situation, nations all over the world have established patent offices to issue patents to inventors. The result is faster innovation, much more rapid economic growth, and much faster increases in living standards. Indeed, it's hard to think of any more socially beneficial monopolies than those that arise from patents.

Reducing annoyingly redundant competitors

Societies have also stepped in to create monopolies in situations where competition means annoying redundancies. Consider the following examples:

>> **Trash hauling:** Garbage trucks are extremely loud and annoying. If one company has a monopoly on hauling trash, you have to endure a loud, annoying truck only once per week. But if, say, seven different trash-hauling companies compete, you may have to endure one each day if you and six of your neighbors each choose to use a different company that picks up on a different day of the week.

>> **Fiber-optic Internet access:** If ten different companies offering fiber-optic Internet access competed for your business, neighborhoods would have to have ten different sets of fiber-optic cables running through them — at much greater expense than running just one set of cables.

>> **Natural gas:** Laying the pipes that deliver natural gas is expensive, and laying down multiple grids of gas pipe in one area would be wasteful.

Consequently, most towns and cities have decided that there will be only one trash-hauling company, one company laying fiber-optic cables, and one natural gas company. Each company is given a monopoly and is then regulated to make sure that it doesn't exploit customers. (See the upcoming "Regulating Monopolies" section.)

Keeping costs low with natural monopolies

Another place where society may decide it's better to have a monopoly rather than competition is in the case of what economists refer to as *natural monopoly industries*, or *natural monopolies*. An industry is a natural monopoly if one large producer can produce output at a lower average cost per unit than many small producers. A good example is electric power generation. Due to engineering constraints, a 10-megawatt power plant can produce energy at a far lower per-unit cost than a 1-megawatt power plant can.

To see how this leads to a natural monopoly, imagine that a town needing 10 megawatts of power is initially served by ten of the small, 1-megawatt power plants. But then a big corporation comes along and builds a 10-megawatt power plant. Because the big plant can produce at a lower per-unit cost than the smaller, less efficient plants, the big plant offers lower prices and steals all the customers — meaning that the smaller plants quickly go bankrupt.

Such an industry is called a *natural monopoly* because it naturally becomes dominated by a single, low-cost producer. The perplexing problem here for policymakers is what to do with a natural monopoly. On one hand, everyone welcomes the fact that the big plant is much more efficient: It burns less fuel and causes less environmental damage. But because it has crushed all competition, people now have to worry that the new monopoly will charge high prices and produce less than the socially optimal output level.

These conflicting good and bad points typically mean that governments allow the natural monopoly to stay in business as the only firm in its industry, but at the same time, they regulate it so that people don't have to worry about high prices or low output levels. By doing so, society gets the benefits brought by the most efficient production method without having to worry about the problems that would otherwise result if the monopoly were left unregulated.

Regulating Monopolies

Governments have to decide when to support and when to suppress monopolies. For instance, patents support an inventor's monopoly right to produce and sell her invention for 20 years. After that, the production and sale of the invention is thrown open to competition.

In other situations, various regulatory institutions have been developed either to destroy a monopoly by breaking it apart or to regulate it after deciding to let it continue to be the only firm in its industry. In this section, I present several of these regulatory schemes and explore what they do to improve the behavior of monopolies.

Subsidizing a monopoly to increase output

A profit-maximizing monopoly produces less than the socially optimal level. In particular, a profit-maximizing monopoly produces where its downward-sloping marginal revenue curve, MR^m, intersects its upward-sloping marginal cost curve, MC (see Figure 8-4). This output level, q^m, is less than the socially optimal output level that would be produced by a competitive firm, q^c (for why, see "Comparing Monopolies with Competitive Firms," earlier).

REMEMBER

One way to get the monopoly to produce more is to subsidize its production costs so that the marginal cost curve in effect shifts down vertically. Doing so causes the marginal cost and marginal revenue curves to meet at a higher level of output. And if the subsidy is big enough, the monopoly can be induced to increase output all the way to q^c.

Some governments use this type of subsidy to get gas, electric, and phone companies to serve more people, especially poor people. If the monopoly firms' costs of hooking up customers are subsidized, the firms are willing to hook up more customers than they would without the subsidy. Some people object to subsidizing a monopolist, so this sort of solution isn't necessarily the most popular politically. But it is effective in increasing output.

Imposing minimum output requirements

Another way to get a monopoly to produce more is simply to order it to produce more. For instance, in many areas telephone companies are required to provide land-line telephone service to everyone — even to people who cannot pay for it themselves. (The idea is to make sure that everyone is able to call for help if they have an emergency.) The same is often true of companies that provide heating in the winter; in some jurisdictions, you can't turn off someone's heat for nonpayment of bills.

Minimum output requirements can force a monopoly to produce the socially optimal output level. They are often very politically popular because many people think of monopolists as evil and exploitative and don't mind seeing them ordered to produce more.

Any forced increase in output also means a reduction in the monopoly's profit. Therefore, such programs are also popular because many people consider a monopoly's profits to be ill-gotten given the fact that the firm doesn't have to compete to earn them.

Regulators have to be careful, though, not to bankrupt the monopolies they are regulating. Depending on a monopoly's cost curves, it's quite possible to force a monopoly to produce at an output level where it loses money. Because regulators don't want to bankrupt monopolies and deny consumers access to the products they produce, regulators are careful to take a monopoly's cost structure into account when considering minimum output requirements.

Regulating monopoly pricing

Perhaps the most common way to regulate a monopoly is to set the price at which it can sell each and every unit of output that it produces. This approach works because it changes the monopoly firm's marginal revenue curve from sloping downward to being horizontal. Therefore, it eliminates the monopoly's usual problem that the more it sells, the less it can charge per unit.

However, regulators have to pay close attention to a monopoly's cost structure when choosing the regulated price so they don't bankrupt the monopoly.

Marginal cost pricing: Benefit society but risk bankruptcy

REMEMBER

A monopoly doesn't produce as much of a product as it'd be socially beneficial to produce (see the earlier section "Comparing Monopolies with Competitive Firms" for details). Therefore, a well-intentioned regulator may want to get a monopoly to produce every single unit of output for which benefits exceed costs. *Marginal cost pricing* is a method of regulation in which the regulated price is set where the marginal cost curve crosses the demand curve.

Consider the monopoly whose cost curves are given in Figure 8-5. Left unregulated, the monopoly will choose to produce the profit-maximizing output level q^m, defined by where *MR* (marginal revenue) crosses *MC* (marginal cost). From the demand curve, you can see that the firm will be able to charge price p^m per unit for that amount of output.

A regulator may want to get the monopoly to produce output level q^{mc}, defined by where the downward-sloping demand curve intersects the *MC* curve. It's socially beneficial to produce each unit up to and including q^{mc} because for each of those units, benefits exceed costs. We know that because the amount that people are willing to pay to consume one of those units (given by the vertical distance from the horizontal axis up to the demand curve) exceeds the marginal cost of producing it (given by the vertical distance from the horizontal axis up to the *MC* curve).

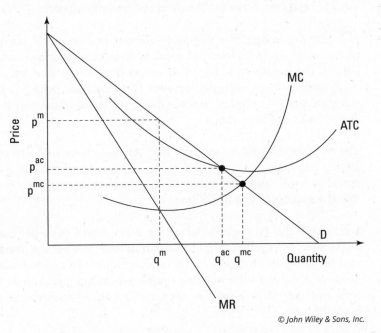

© John Wiley & Sons, Inc.

FIGURE 8-5:
Regulating a monopoly using average cost pricing and marginal cost pricing.

To motivate the monopoly to produce q^{mc} units of output, the regulator can set the price at p^{mc}. At that price, the demand curve tells you that consumers will want to purchase q^{mc} units of output. Better yet, the monopoly will want to supply that level of output because the marginal revenue from selling each unit exceeds the marginal cost of producing it.

There is, however, a big problem with this policy given this particular monopoly's cost structure: The monopoly will go bankrupt. That's because at output level q^{mc}, the firm's total costs will exceed its total revenues.

You can see this problem on a per-unit basis by noting that the average total cost per unit at output level q^{mc} (given by the vertical distance from the horizontal axis to the *ATC* curve) is more than the regulator-imposed revenue of p^{mc} per unit. Because average total costs per unit exceed revenues per unit, the monopoly will be operating at a loss. And unless the regulator relents and allows a higher price, the monopoly will eventually go bankrupt unless the government steps in to subsidize the firm by giving it a cash grant equal to the amount of its loss.

Average cost pricing

REMEMBER

Because marginal cost pricing can cause a monopoly to lose money, a more common alternative is *average cost pricing*, which sets the regulated price where the average total cost curve (*ATC*) intersects the demand curve.

In Figure 8-5, a regulator using average cost pricing would set the price at p^{ac}. At that price, you can see from the demand curve that consumers demand q^{ac} units of output. The monopoly is happy to supply that output level because for each and every unit up to q^{ac}, marginal revenue (the regulated price per unit, p^{ac}) exceeds marginal cost — meaning that the monopoly gains financially by producing each and every one of these units.

The main benefit of this system is that you don't have to worry about the monopoly's going bankrupt (or where to get the money to subsidize a monopoly that would go bankrupt under marginal cost pricing). Average cost pricing guarantees that the monopoly will break even.

You can see this fact by comparing the average total costs per unit at output level q^{ac} with the revenue per unit at that output level. You get the average total cost per unit by going up until you hit the average total cost curve. Because that vertical distance is equal to the regulated price per unit, p^{ac}, you know that the average total costs per unit are equal to the regulated price per unit — so the firm must be breaking even.

The downside to average cost pricing for this monopoly is that all the socially beneficial units between q^{ac} and q^{mc} don't get produced. On the other hand, the only way to keep this monopoly in business to produce those units if you imposed marginal cost pricing would be to subsidize it. Using average cost pricing eliminates any worries associated with providing subsidies. In particular, you don't have to worry about any potential harm that you may cause when raising the taxes that have to be imposed somewhere else in the economy in order to subsidize the monopoly.

Breaking up a monopoly into several competing firms

One solution to the problem of a monopoly is to destroy it by breaking it up into many competing firms. In the United States, the most famous case of this solution was the division of American Telephone and Telegraph Corporation (AT&T) into a bunch of smaller competitors in 1984.

Before 1984, AT&T was a nationwide monopoly. If you wanted to make a telephone call anywhere in the United States, you had to use AT&T because it was the only telephone company in the country. It was highly regulated, with both quantity requirements to provide everyone a phone and price requirements that encouraged it to provide a high quantity of telecommunication services. But it was still a monopoly, and a judge ruled in 1984 that it should be broken up into numerous local firms in order to foster competition.

The policy change worked extremely well. There was soon a very competitive market for telephone services between firms that had been part of AT&T. More recently, the telephone service industry has become even more competitive due to the arrival of cellphone companies, Internet telephony companies, and even cable TV companies offering phone services. This robust competition eliminates the problems associated with monopolies and ensures that telecommunication services are provided at low cost and in large quantity.

Creating competition is also a handy way to deal with a monopoly because it eliminates the costs associated with having to continually monitor a regulated monopoly. Competition gets you to the socially optimal output level without any sort of central control (for info on why, see Chapter 7). That stands in stark contrast to regulated monopolies, which typically require expensive bureaucracies to develop and enforce laws and regulations.

Chapter **9**

Oligopoly and Monopolistic Competition: Middle Grounds

The two most extreme forms that an industry can take are perfect competition (with many small competitive firms) and monopoly (where there's only one firm and hence no competition). I cover those cases in Chapters 6 and 8. This chapter concentrates on two interesting intermediate cases: oligopoly and monopolistic competition.

An *oligopoly* is an industry in which there are only a small number of firms — two, three, or a handful. The word itself is Greek for "few sellers." A diverse group of industries looks like this, including soft drinks and oil production. For instance, Coke and Pepsi dominate the soft drink market, vastly outselling other carbonated beverages. Similarly, just four or five countries produce the majority of the world's oil.

Oligopoly industries are interesting because depending on specific circumstances, the firms can either compete ruthlessly with each other or unite to behave almost exactly like a monopoly would. This means that in some cases, oligopolies can be left alone because competition ensures that they produce socially optimal output levels; in other cases, government regulation is needed to prevent them from acting like monopolies and behaving in socially undesirable ways.

The second type of intermediate industry is *monopolistic competition,* a sort of hybrid between perfect competition and monopoly. The key thing that sets firms in this type of industry apart from firms in a perfectly competitive industry is *product differentiation* — the fact that each firm produces a slightly different product than the others.

This chapter starts with a detailed look at oligopolies and the decisions that firms in this type of industry have to make. I then move on to monopolistic competition and show why product differentiation doesn't necessarily translate into tidy profits.

Oligopolies: Looking at the Allure of Joining Forces

In industries where only a few firms operate, firms have a choice about whether to compete or cooperate. This situation is very different from perfect competition (which I discuss in Chapter 7). In perfectly competitive markets, there are so many firms, and each firm is such a small part of the market, that their individual outputs don't have any effect on the market price. As a result, competitive firms just take the market price as given and adjust their output levels accordingly to make as large a profit as possible.

However, in a market in which there are only a few sellers, each one produces enough of the total output to be able to affect the market price. Each company can increase output and lower its own price in an attempt to gain more customers at the expense of its rivals, or the firms can work together to limit production and keep prices high to maximize their combined profits. This section explores the firms' incentives to work together and the possible benefits of acting like a monopoly. Later, in "Understanding Incentives to Cheat the Cartel," I explain why collusion usually doesn't go as planned.

Sharing power over prices

When only a few firms are in an industry, the decisions that any one firm makes about how much to produce or charge for its own output almost always affect the outputs and prices of the other firms in its industry.

As an example, consider that only two major producers of cola-flavored sodas operate in the United States: the Coca-Cola Company and PepsiCo. These two corporations produce such large fractions of the total output that if either one were to suddenly increase supply, the market price of cola-flavored soda would drop dramatically. One company's increase in output causes the price to decrease for other companies in the market as well.

In other words, if Pepsi produces twice as much of its product and floods the market, the price of Pepsi will drop dramatically. But most people aren't 100 percent loyal to one brand or the other, so if the price of Pepsi drops dramatically, a lot of regular Coke drinkers are going to switch brands and drink Pepsi. As a result of this decline in the demand for Coke, the price of Coke will drop, too.

Cartel behavior: Trying to imitate monopolists

REMEMBER

When firms are involved in a situation where each of their supply decisions affects not only their own sales but those of their competitors as well, economists say the firms are in a *strategic situation* because the firms involved have to decide which type of strategy to pursue. In particular, they have to decide whether to compete or collude:

>> **Compete:** If they compete, they'll both try to increase production to undercut each other on price and capture as many customers as possible.

>> **Collude:** If they collude, they'll jointly cut back on production to drive up prices and increase their profits. For producers, collusion is better than competition because it leads to profits that last as long as the firms keep colluding.

A group of firms that colludes and acts as a single coordinated whole is known as a *cartel.* Because a cartel acts essentially as one gigantic firm, it effectively turns a bunch of individual firms into a single big monopoly.

This fact makes understanding the profit-maximizing behavior of a cartel easy, because it's just like that of a monopoly. In fact, you can see what a cartel wants to do by looking at the figures in Chapter 8, which illustrate what a monopoly likes to do. In particular, a profit-maximizing cartel chooses to produce the monopoly's profit-maximizing output level of q^m units (where marginal cost equals marginal revenue), as in Figure 8-2. Producing that output level maximizes the cartel's collective profit. And better yet for the cartel, that monopoly profit will persist as long as the participating companies keep cooperating and producing a combined output of q^m.

What's really interesting, though, is that cartels often fail to maximize their collective profit because they can't sustain the cooperation needed to keep their collective output at the monopoly output level q^m.

Considering the criteria for coordinating a cartel

For consumers, collusion is worse than competition because it leads to higher prices and lower output. You may assume that government intervention is called for in order to protect consumers from collusion. But such intervention is needed only if firms actually collude.

A fascinating thing about the real world is that collusion doesn't happen in a lot of industries where you might expect it to. For instance, Coke and Pepsi are fierce competitors that spend billions of dollars a year on advertising to try to steal each other's customers. Similarly, most cities have only a handful of competing cellphone networks. But instead of colluding, they compete so ruthlessly that many of them are constantly flirting with bankruptcy. The same holds true for the airline industry, where bankruptcies are routine.

REMEMBER

The big question that economists have to answer is "Why do we see so little collusion in industries where you would expect more of it?" The answer is that it's often very difficult to get all the firms to coordinate so they're collectively producing the monopoly output level, q^m. To get the individual firms to cooperate and produce exactly q^m units of combined output, you have to get them to agree on two related things:

>> **How to share the profits:** Obviously, every firm wants as large a share as possible.

>> **Output quotas:** The firms must agree, and abide by, how much of the total output (q^m) each firm will produce. Each firm will constantly be tempted to produce more than its quota because doing so would bring higher revenues.

Understanding Incentives to Cheat the Cartel

To the extent that cartels work and create monopoly profits, they also create temptations for cartel members to cheat. You can best understand the behavior of cartels and their incentive to cheat using the insights of game theory.

Game theory is a branch of mathematics that studies how people behave in strategic situations — situations in which people take account of others' actions or anticipated actions and then modify their own actions accordingly. For instance, chess and checkers are strategic situations because what I do on my current move changes what my opponent does in subsequent moves. Even more importantly, what I think my opponent will do in response to each of the moves that I may make right now helps me to choose the best thing to do.

Cartels are strategic situations because each firm has to take into account what it thinks all the other firms are going to do before deciding what it should do. Consequently, game theory models are probably the best way to understand the motivations and temptations that guide the behavior of cartel members. This section introduces a game theory model called the Prisoner's Dilemma to explore decisions about whether to cheat. It then applies the model to the OPEC oil cartel.

Fleshing out the Prisoner's Dilemma

Understanding why cartels cheat is easy if you apply the Prisoner's Dilemma. The *Prisoner's Dilemma* is a game theory model in which two criminal partners have to individually decide whether to cheat on their previous agreement to not talk to the police.

It works in this way: Imagine Jesse and James have just robbed a bank. The police know this but don't have any hard evidence against them. Rather, the only way of getting a conviction is to get one or both of the bank robbers to confess to the crime and give evidence against the other. Fortunately for the police, they do have some leverage because they managed to catch Jesse and James committing other unrelated, minor crimes. These other crimes carry with them a one-year prison sentence. The police are hoping to use the threat of a year in prison to get one or both of the bank robbers to implicate his partner in exchange for immunity from prosecution.

Jesse and James both swore to each other several days before that they'd never rat on each other, but what happens when push comes to shove?

Comparing the payoffs of confessing or remaining silent

Following standard procedure, the police separate Jesse and James, questioning them in separate interrogation rooms. The police offer each of them the chance to give evidence against the other in exchange for immunity.

REMEMBER

The problem for each man is that what happens to him depends not only on what he does but on what his partner does as well. Each man can trade a confession for immunity, but he gets the deal only if his partner doesn't confess at the same time in the other interrogation room. Four outcomes are possible:

» **Both stay silent.** If the men both keep their pact not to talk and neither confesses to robbing banks, each man gets only a year in jail for the minor offense.

» **Only Jesse confesses and gives evidence.** If Jesse confesses and agrees to give evidence against James while James remains silent, Jesse goes free because he cooperated with police, but James gets ten years for bank robbery.

» **Only James confesses and gives evidence.** If James gives evidence while Jesse remains silent, James goes free while Jesse goes to prison for ten years.

» **Both confess and give evidence.** If both men admit to the crime, both get five years in prison. Why five years each? If both confess, the police don't need to make such a generous deal; they don't need to give either man immunity in order to get evidence against the other. On the other hand, the police want to give each criminal an incentive to confess, so they send each man to prison for only five years instead of the ten years he'd get if he remained silent while his partner gave evidence.

Figure 9-1 contains a payoff matrix. It illustrates the outcomes that each bank robber receives in terms of prison time, depending on the decision that each man makes about whether to remain silent or confess.

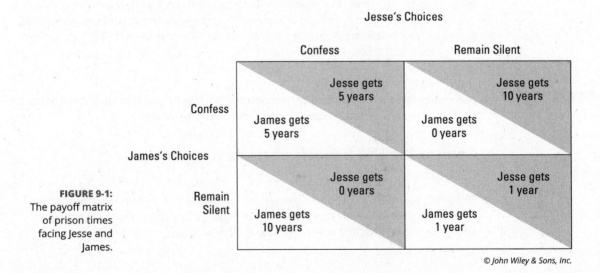

FIGURE 9-1:
The payoff matrix of prison times facing Jesse and James.

© John Wiley & Sons, Inc.

The columns give Jesse's options, the rows give James's options, and the four rectangles in the grid show the prison times that result from each of the four possible combinations of their individual decisions about whether to confess. For instance, the upper-left rectangle represents what happens if both confess. It's divided diagonally in half, with Jesse's payoff of five years in prison given in the upper shaded triangle and James's payoff of five years given in the lower unshaded triangle. Similarly, the upper-right rectangle gives each of their payoffs if Jesse remains silent while James confesses: Jesse gets ten years in prison while James gets zero years because he gave evidence against Jesse.

Determining the dominant strategy for each prisoner

The Prisoner's Dilemma is famous because it illustrates that with the way the police have set up the potential payoffs, each criminal has an incentive to confess — no matter what the other criminal does. For instance, concentrate on James. Should he confess or remain silent? Well, first examine which is the better option for him if his partner in the other interrogation room confesses. Looking at the left column of payoffs, you can see from the upper-left rectangle that if James confesses while Jesse confesses, James gets five years. On the other hand, the bottom-left rectangle tells you that if James remains silent while Jesse confesses, James gets ten years.

Clearly, the best thing for James to do if Jesse confesses is to also confess. But consider whether it's better for James to confess or remain silent when Jesse remains silent in the other interrogation room. Begin with the upper-right rectangle, which shows that if James confesses while Jesse remains silent, James gets zero years in jail. By contrast, the bottom-right rectangle tells you that if James remains silent while Jesse is also silent, James gets one year in jail. Clearly, if Jesse remains silent, the best thing for James to do is confess and get zero years in jail rather than one year.

In other words, it's *always* better for James to confess. If James confesses when Jesse confesses, James gets five years rather than ten. And if James confesses when Jesse remains silent, James gets zero years rather than one. So James should *always* confess no matter what Jesse is saying or not saying to the police in the other room. Because the payoff for confessing is always better for him than the payoff for not confessing, game theorists refer to confessing as James's *dominant strategy*, by which they mean superior strategy.

If you go through the payoffs from Jesse's perspective, you find that confessing is also Jesse's dominant strategy, because no matter what James is doing, the payoffs to Jesse if he confesses are always better than those from remaining silent.

Confessing is thus a dominant strategy for both players — you should expect both of them to separately confess. If they do so, they end up in the upper-left box of the payoff matrix, where they both get five years in prison.

Realizing that the dominant strategy leads to a lousy outcome for both players

Typically, both men go with their dominant strategy and confess. But because both separately decide to confess, they each end up getting five years in prison — a much worse outcome than if they had both kept their promise to each other to remain silent. If they had both kept their promise, they each would've gone to jail for only one year. The logic of the dominant strategy is so compelling, though, that they each break the agreement and end up going to prison for five years rather than one.

REMEMBER

Cartel members also face a Prisoner's Dilemma because they must decide whether to obey the cartel agreement (to reduce output to the monopoly level) or cheat and overproduce. The temptation for cartel members to overproduce and break their cartel output agreement is just as strong as the temptation for prisoners to confess and break their agreement not to talk to the police.

Enforcing the agreement: Resolving the dilemma with credible threats

REMEMBER

One way to get a pair of criminals to stay quiet — or to get a group of firms to stick to a cartel agreement — is to set up a strong threat against cheaters.

Mafia movies illustrate a bloodthirsty but effective system that mobsters developed to prevent people from confessing. The system is called *omerta*, which is Sicilian for "silence." Basically, what the mafia does is change the payoffs to the Prisoner's Dilemma so that the dominant strategy switches from confessing to remaining silent. The mob does this by explaining to their criminal members that if they talk to the police and confess to anything or implicate anyone else, they're going to die.

The mafia also makes sure that everyone knows that this threat is credible and not just talk. Otherwise, the mafia's members wouldn't alter their behavior.

The mafia's credible death threat totally rearranges the payoffs to the Prisoner's Dilemma. Instead of just comparing prison times, as in Figure 9-1, prisoners now have to factor in death, as in Figure 9-2. In Figure 9-2, you find that the dominant strategy for both players is now to remain silent because if either talks, the mafia will hunt him down and kill him no matter what the other guy does. The result is that both Jesse and James will go to prison for only one year each because they'll both keep their mouths shut.

Jesse's Choices

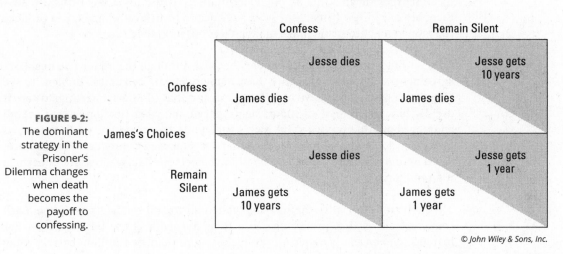

FIGURE 9-2:
The dominant strategy in the Prisoner's Dilemma changes when death becomes the payoff to confessing.

© John Wiley & Sons, Inc.

Paradoxically, the death threat benefits the two criminals. Even though the threat of death is scary, it actually serves their individual interests because it means that they'll go to jail for only one year instead of five. If you're going to be a criminal, you want to be part of a criminal organization that has enough power to bully you around and keep you from defecting on your agreements with your fellow criminals.

Seeing that OPEC is trapped in a Prisoner's Dilemma

The basic version of the Prisoner's Dilemma (discussed in the preceding section) is set up for just two people. But mathematicians have developed more advanced versions of the Prisoner's Dilemma that you can use to analyze the behavior of larger numbers of participants. These models are invaluable for understanding oligopoly industries with several firms and the incentives that firms in such industries face when they try to form cartels. The basic conclusion of these multi-firm models is that the dominant strategy is usually to cheat on cartel agreements.

This result goes a long way toward explaining why the OPEC oil cartel has a hard time when it tries to achieve its goal of raising oil prices by reducing oil production. Quite simply, cheating on OPEC cartel agreements is a dominant strategy for OPEC member countries.

OPEC stands for the Organization of Petroleum Exporting Countries. Although OPEC is a dull name, it represents a very lively group that includes Saudi Arabia, Iraq, Venezuela, Nigeria, Kuwait, Angola, and several other key oil-exporting nations. Together, these nations control the vast majority of the world's oil reserves, meaning that they occupy an oligopoly industry with only a few firms. Because there are only a few firms, they have a chance to form a cartel and try to produce the monopoly output and make monopoly profits. Do they succeed?

On the whole, no. I say "on the whole" because although the nations do negotiate agreements about oil production, these agreements are constantly broken. To see why that happens, you have to first understand that OPEC has meetings where it decides how much total oil should be produced and what fraction of that overall amount should be produced by each country. At the meetings, each country is given a *quota* — a maximum amount that it's supposed to produce. For instance, Saudi Arabia may have a quota of 10 million barrels per day, whereas for Venezuela it's 1 million barrels per day.

The problems start after the meetings when all the oil ministers go home. Each country realizes that producing more than its quota is the best strategy. For instance, Venezuela is better off producing more than its 1 million barrels a day quota no matter what the other countries do:

>> If the other countries obey their quotas, Venezuela is better off producing more than its quota because it can sell lots of oil at a high price. (The high price is caused by the fact that the other countries are obeying their quotas.)

>> If the other countries break their quotas and overproduce, the price of oil will be low, meaning that Venezuela should also overproduce its quota. There is no reason to obey the quota if prices are low due to everyone else's cheating.

Because each country faces the same temptation to overproduce its quota, the OPEC cartel doesn't typically work very well. Overproducing is a dominant strategy and is simply too tempting to resist given the payoffs.

Using an enforcer to help OPEC members stick to quotas

REMEMBER

OPEC could benefit if it had some way of threatening its members for violating their quotas. Because the member countries are sovereign nations, death threats aren't an option as they are in the mafia. Rather, Saudi Arabia has sometimes tried to provide an economic threat against quota violators.

The economic threat comes in the form of super low oil prices. Saudi Arabia is in the best position to make such a threat for two reasons:

>> **It's always been the world's first or second largest oil producer.** Saudi Arabia produces about 13 percent of the world's oil, just a bit behind the United States, which produces about 15 percent of the world's oil.

>> **It's the world's lowest-cost oil producer.** Saudi Arabia can produce profitably even if the price of oil falls down to $9 per barrel. (Oil is typically priced at between $40 and $100 per barrel, and most other countries, including the United States, need a price of at least $20 per barrel to break even.)

These two facts mean that if other countries cheat on their quotas, Saudi Arabia could potentially increase its production so much that the price of oil would fall very low. For instance, suppose the price fell to $9 per barrel. Saudi Arabia would be the only OPEC member making a profit at that price; everyone else would be losing money.

As a result, Saudi Arabia appears to be in a position to threaten other OPEC members with bankruptcy if they violate their quotas. Unfortunately, the threat doesn't work that well in the real world. The problem is that Saudi Arabia has limited pumping capacity. Although Saudi Arabia may be able to produce an extra 10 or 20 percent more oil per day than it normally does, that much of an increase wouldn't be enough to drive the price down to $9 per barrel and bankrupt the other OPEC nations. Therefore, the Saudi Arabian threat isn't nearly strong enough to switch the dominant strategy from cheating on the quota to obeying it. And because OPEC has never figured out a way to effectively threaten quota violators, the cartel doesn't work very well.

Regulating Oligopolies

In some industries, cartels *are* effective at reducing output and raising prices. Typically, these are industries where one firm is large enough and powerful enough to truly threaten other firms with bankruptcy.

In some cases, the industry will be broken up into even more firms to promote competition, but in others, regulations may be installed that regulate the prices firms can charge or the quantities they can produce. The specific policy often depends intimately on the circumstances of the firms in the industry and what policymakers think will best promote the general welfare.

Breaking up dominant firms

One important strategy for regulating an oligopoly is for the government to break it up into many smaller companies that will then compete with each other. In the 19th century, cartels were called *trusts* — for example, the Sugar Trust, the Steel Trust, the Railroad Trust, and so on. Therefore, laws that broke up monopolies and cartels were called *antitrust laws*. The most famous of these in the United States was the Sherman Anti-Trust Act. Most countries have now passed similar legislation to break up monopolies and cartels.

In U.S. history, the Standard Oil Company run by John D. Rockefeller during the 19th century dominated an oligopoly industry. It controlled something like 90 percent of the oil sold in the United States, and if a competitor didn't do what Rockefeller wanted, he would simply bankrupt the other firm by offering oil at a ridiculously low price that the competitor couldn't match.

Rockefeller would lose money temporarily while taking this action, but by bankrupting the competitors who disobeyed him, he was able to convince the remaining firms to help him restrain output and make huge profits. Indeed, because Standard Oil exerted so much control, its industry was much more like a monopoly than an oligopoly.

Rockefeller's effectiveness, however, soon brought a governmental response. Standard Oil was broken up into dozens of smaller, independent oil companies, none of which was large enough and powerful enough to dominate its industry and enforce collusion the way that Standard Oil had.

Attempting to apply antitrust laws

A big problem with antitrust laws is deciding when to regulate oligopolies or break them up to promote competition. The first sign that there may potentially be a cartel is, of course, when you see only a few firms in an industry. But because of the Prisoner's Dilemma, in some cases even a two-firm industry won't be able to form an effective cartel. Consequently, prosecutors typically have to do more than just show that there aren't many firms in an industry.

REMEMBER

Typically, there has to be concrete proof of collusion. In other words, if one day every firm in an oligopoly industry decides without coordination to cut its output in half and thereby raise prices, that may not be illegal. But if even a single text message from a manager of one firm to a manager of another firm is found saying that the firms should enter into a cartel, that is illegal and enough for a prosecutor to hang a case on.

Studying a Hybrid: Monopolistic Competition

An interesting form of competition that's found in some industries has the odd name of *monopolistic competition*. In such industries, you find characteristics of both monopolies (see Chapter 8) and competitive firms (see Chapter 7). This section provides an overview of monopolistic competition.

Benefiting from product differentiation

Like competitive firms operating in free markets, industries featuring monopolistic competition have lots of firms competing against each other. But unlike competitive free markets where all the firms sell an identical product, in monopolistic competition each firm's product is slightly different.

Think of the market for gasoline. Any large city has dozens, if not hundreds, of gas stations — all selling gasoline that is pretty much the same. But if you look at each gas station with a little wider scope, you notice that each one sells a product that's at least slightly different from the products sold by its competitors. For instance, some stations have mini-marts, and others have car washes or provide fuel with special additives designed to improve engine performance. And crucially, each gas station is clearly differentiated from all the others because it has a unique location — something that's very important to people who live nearby.

REMEMBER

Economists use the term *product differentiation* to describe the things that make each firm's product a little bit different from its competitors' products. The overall result of these differences is that they slightly decrease the intensity of competition. Your local gas station, for instance, may be able to get away with charging you one or two cents more per gallon than its competitors if it has nice facilities and the next-closest competitor is several miles away.

On the other hand, there's still a lot of competitive pressure in the industry. Although your local station may be able to use its unique characteristics to get away with charging you a little more, it couldn't charge you a lot more — if it tried to do that, you'd take your business to one of its competitors.

Similarly, all the restaurants in your neighborhood have to worry about what the other restaurants are charging, even if the others specialize in completely different cuisines. Although you may be willing to pay 20 percent more for something exotic, you wouldn't likely be willing to pay 90 percent more. Product differentiation lessens but does not eliminate price competition.

Facing profit limits

You may think that because monopolistically competitive firms can use their unique characteristics to raise prices, they're guaranteed nice profit margins. After all, in pure competition where firms all sell the same product and have no way of differentiating themselves from their competitors, prices fall so low that firms end up earning zero economic profits (see Chapter 7). If monopolistically competitive firms can raise prices above the competitive price, it seems like a no-brainer that they should be guaranteed to make profits. Unfortunately for them, this isn't the case.

REMEMBER

As pointed out by Cambridge economist Joan Robinson during the 1930s, monopolistically competitive firms still face competition. In particular, they face the prospect that if they're making tidy profits, those profits attract new entrants to their industry. When the new entrants begin producing, they take business away from the established firms and ruin their previously tidy profits. In fact, new entrants continue to arrive until profits have been driven all the way back to zero.

Dealing with downward sloping demand

Joan Robinson was able to show how this process works by slightly modifying the monopoly model that I introduce in Chapter 8. To see what she did, look at Figure 9-3, which shows a single monopolistically competitive firm initially making a profit. The figure shows the firm's marginal cost curve, MC, and average total cost curve, ATC, along with its demand curve, D_1, and the associated marginal revenue curve, MR_1.

Because of product differentiation, the firm in Figure 9-3 faces the downward sloping demand curve, D_1. Its demand curve is downward sloping because, like a monopoly, it has some control over its price. Product differentiation means that the firm can choose whether to set a higher or lower price. At a higher price, the quantity demanded of its product falls because some customers will not think that the unique characteristics of the firm's product are worth the extra money. At a lower price, the quantity demanded increases because the lower price steals customers away from the firm's competitors.

By contrast, competitive firms that sell identical products have no control over the prices they set. Because competitive firms sell identical products, the only thing that matters to consumers when choosing among them is who offers the lowest price. The result is that all firms have to sell at the same price, the *market price*, which is determined by where the overall industry supply curve crosses the industry demand curve. The demand curve for an individual competitive firm's product is a horizontal line at the market price (see Chapter 7). This line stands in sharp contrast to the downward sloping demand curve facing the monopolistically competitive firm in Figure 9-3.

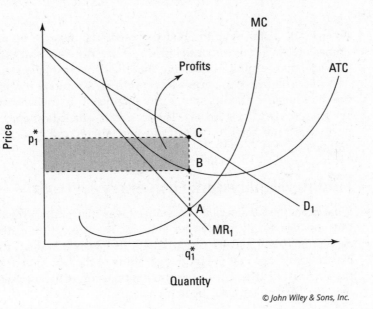

FIGURE 9-3:
A monopolistically competitive firm making a profit equal to the area of the shaded rectangle.

© John Wiley & Sons, Inc.

An important consequence of the downward sloping demand curve, D_1, is that the marginal revenue curve, MR_1, associated with demand curve D_1 is also downward sloping. Why is this so? The additional, or marginal, revenue that the firm can get from selling an additional unit of output is less than the marginal revenue it gets from selling the previous unit.

Declining marginal revenue is a natural consequence of a downward sloping demand curve. Because the only way to get consumers to buy more of your product is to entice them with a lower price, the marginal revenue you get has to fall with every additional unit you sell.

The monopolistically competitive firm optimizes profits by choosing to produce at Point A, where the downward sloping marginal revenue curve, MR_1, crosses the upward sloping marginal cost curve, MC. Producing the associated quantity, q^*_1, will either maximize the firm's profit (if it's possible to make a profit) or minimize its loss. Whether making a profit is possible depends on the position of the firm's demand curve — on how much demand there is for the firm's product.

In Figure 9-3, demand is strong enough that the firm makes a profit. You can see this by comparing the firm's average total cost per unit at output level q^*_1 with its selling price per unit at that output level. The average total cost per unit is found by going up vertically from the horizontal axis at output level q^*_1 until you hit the ATC curve at Point B. The price per unit that the firm can charge at output level q^*_1 is found by going up vertically until you hit the demand curve at Point C.

Because the distance up to Point C exceeds the distance up to Point B, you can immediately determine that the firm's selling price per unit exceeds the total cost of production per unit — meaning that the firm must be making a profit on each unit sold. The size of the firm's total profit on all units is the profit per unit times the total number of units sold, so its total profit is equivalent to the area of the shaded rectangle in Figure 9-3. The area of the shaded rectangle is the width of q^*_1 units times the height of the profit per unit — the vertical distance between Points B and C.

Finding equilibrium: Firm entry and exit

What economist Joan Robinson realized was that profit attracts new entrants to the monopolistically competitive industry. Each new entrant steals some business away from existing firms. Graphically, this means that the demand curve for any existing firm, like that of Figure 9-3, shifts to the left. At each possible price that the firm may charge, it sells fewer units than before because some of its old business has been stolen away by new entrants.

REMEMBER

Furthermore, new entrants continue to enter the industry and shift demand curves to the left until profits are driven all the way down to zero. Only then does the entry of new firms come to a halt.

You can see this sort of equilibrium in Figure 9-4. There, the demand curve has shifted left all the way to D_2, where it is just tangent to the ATC curve at Point B. As the demand curve moves left, so does the marginal revenue curve, which now lies at MR_2. Consequently, when the firm optimizes its production level by producing where the MC curve crosses MR_2, it will produce at output level q^*_2.

At this output level, profits are zero. You can see this by using the graph to show that the average total cost per unit of producing output level q^*_2 is equal to the price per unit that the firm can get selling those units. Go up vertically from the horizontal axis at Point q^*_2 to Point B. Because Point B lies both on the demand curve, D_2, and the average total cost curve, ATC, the vertical distance from the horizontal axis at Point q^*_2 to Point B represents both the average total cost per unit as well as the price per unit that the firm can charge. They are equal, so the firm is making zero profits.

If for some reason the firms in a monopolistically competitive industry are making losses, some firms will exit the industry. As each of them exits, the remaining firms gain more business, and the demand curves for firms still in the industry shift to the right. Exit continues until you reach an equilibrium like that of Figure 9-4, in which all firms are making zero profits.

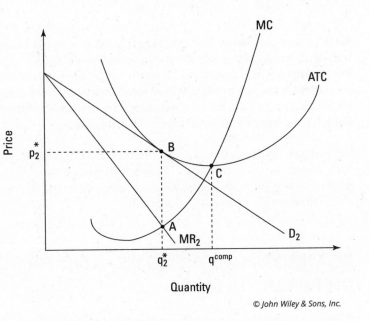

© John Wiley & Sons, Inc.

FIGURE 9-4:
A monopolistically competitive firm makes zero profits after entry (or exit) has shifted its demand curve until it's tangent with its *ATC* curve.

Producing inefficiently

A key thing to notice about the equilibrium in Figure 9-4 is that it implies that each firm produces less efficiently than would firms in a competitive industry. The best way to see this fact is to compare the monopolistically competitive firm's output level when the industry is in equilibrium, q^*_2, with the output level that would be produced by a firm with the same cost curves that was operating in a fully competitive industry in which all firms sold an identical product. I've labeled this output level as q^{comp} in Figure 9-4.

In Chapter 7, I explain how market forces push competitive firms to produce at q^{comp}, and why it ends up being exactly the level of output at which the *ATC* curve hits its minimum — that is, q^{comp} is the output level at the bottom of the U-shaped *ATC* curve. The socially significant implication of this fact is that competitive firms produce at the lowest possible average total cost per unit. That makes them as efficient as possible in terms of minimizing per-unit production costs.

By contrast, a monopolistically competitive firm operating in an industry where product differentiation allows it to have some control over the prices it charges will end up producing at a higher average total cost per unit. This is clearly the case in Figure 9-4 because the vertical distance from the horizontal axis up to Point B is longer than the vertical distance from the horizontal axis up to Point C. That fact implies that the firms in a monopolistically competitive industry are not as efficient as they would be if they were in a perfectly competitive industry.

Some look at this result and conclude that society would be better off if it could transform monopolistically competitive industries into competitive industries. But the cost savings might not be worth the loss of product differentiation. After all, variety is the spice of life. Would you really want every single restaurant to be identical in every way, to serve the same food in the same type of room, under the same lights, with identical furniture? Probably not.

But you have to decide for yourself whether you think the higher costs associated with variety are worthwhile — and in what situations. Although they may be worth it to you for restaurants, you may have a different feeling about the product differentiation found among gas stations.

COMMUNISM, WENDY'S, AND PRODUCT DIFFERENTIATION

One of the funniest TV commercials ever produced made its debut in 1987, at the height of Soviet communist power. It depicts a communist fashion show. A woman walks down the runway in a drab gray factory worker's uniform, and the announcer shouts, "Day wear!" Then she marches down the runway again in the same outfit but this time holding a flashlight. The announcer shouts out, "Evening wear!" Next, she marches down the runway again — still in the same uniform — holding an inflatable beach ball. "Swimwear!"

The commercial made fun of the fact that the central planners who ran communist countries didn't care much about product differentiation. They typically made only one design of any given product in order to be able to mass produce it at the lowest possible cost. The result was a society in which there was so much sameness that the Wendy's commercial was only a modest exaggeration.

The commercial helped to hammer home to U.S. consumers the idea that they should embrace the fact that the food produced by Wendy's was different from that produced by its main rivals, McDonald's and Burger King. Unlike the rigidly planned Soviet economy, free market U.S. capitalism allows for huge amounts of product differentiation.

3

Applying the Theories of Microeconomics

IN THIS PART . . .

Explore how externalities create socially inefficient outcomes and how societies reckon with the Tragedy of the Commons.

Find out why markets depend on full disclosure, how secrets can ruin a market, and why markets can't always provide public goods.

Understand why health insurance faces special challenges and how out-of-pocket costs encourage healthy self-rationing.

Probe the fascinating area of behavioral economics, including evolutionary irrationality, heuristics and cognitive biases, prospect theory, myopia, framing effects, and altruism.

Chapter **10**

Property Rights and Wrongs

conomist Adam Smith came up with the *invisible hand,* the idea that even though individuals pursue their own interests, the common good is achieved if you allow markets to allocate resources. Smith was quite aware, however, that you achieve this nice result only if society's property rights are set up correctly before people start to trade goods and services in markets. In fact, he spent a good deal of his famous book, *The Wealth of Nations,* talking about how governments must properly define property rights if they want markets to yield to socially beneficial outcomes. (Chapter 7 discusses this idea in more depth.)

The gist of the problem is that if property rights are not set up correctly, a person won't fully take into account how his or her actions affect other people. For instance, consider two pieces of land. One is privately owned, and the other is wilderness land that nobody owns and everyone is free to use as they please. If you want to dump your trash on the privately owned land, you have to pay the owner for the right to do so. (In other words, the owner is running a trash dump.) But like everyone else, you can dump trash for free on the wilderness land because nobody has the right to stop you.

Naturally, the difference in property rights with respect to the two pieces of land leads people to dump a lot more on the wilderness land because it's less costly personally to do so. But the problem is that although it's less costly personally, lots of costs are imposed on others. For example, what could've been a very nice park is now a heap of rotting garbage. Bad property rights lead to bad outcomes.

In this chapter, I talk about positive and negative *externalities* — situations where one person's behavior results in either benefits or costs to other people, but where the property rights are so badly defined that the costs and benefits aren't properly accounted for. I also show you how most cases of endangered or extinct species are the result of nonexistent property rights, and how redefining property rights can save species from oblivion.

Allowing Markets to Reach Socially Optimal Outcomes

For markets to achieve socially optimal outcomes, they must take into account all the costs and benefits involved in any activity, regardless of who feels the effects of those costs and benefits. If markets do this, the demand curve captures all benefits, the supply curve captures all costs, and the market equilibrium quantity ensures that only units of output for which benefits exceed costs are produced.

Look at Figure 10-1, which shows a demand curve and a supply curve. The market equilibrium quantity is q^*, and the market equilibrium price is P^*. The important thing to realize is that it's socially beneficial to produce every unit up to and including q^*. The reason for this can be seen by examining unit q_o. You can see from the demand curve that buyers are willing to pay price P_o for unit q_o, but it costs suppliers only C_o to produce unit q_o.

What does this mean? The overall happiness of society is improved by making unit q_o because it's clearly worth more to people to have it than the cost of the resources used in making it. Because the demand curve is above the supply curve for all units up to and including q^*, all those units are socially beneficial to produce.

REMEMBER

The wonderful thing about markets is that supply and demand just happen to cause the socially optimal level of output, q^*, to be produced. The fact that this happens entirely as the result of people pursuing their own selfish interests is, of course, why markets are so amazing. It's as though the invisible hand of some kindly deity magically turns the pursuit of individual goals into a socially optimal outcome.

What I show you next is that this nice result happens only if property rights are *full and complete,* meaning that the demand curve captures all the benefits that people are willing to pay for and the supply curve captures all the costs associated with production. As you'll see, if property rights aren't full and complete, markets won't generate socially optimal output levels like q^*. In such cases, the invisible hand turns out to be *really* invisible — it isn't there!

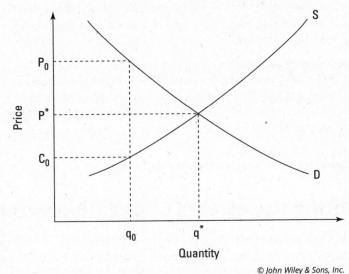

FIGURE 10-1:
With full and complete property rights, the market quantity produced, q^*, is socially optimal.

© *John Wiley & Sons, Inc.*

Examining Externalities: The Costs and Benefits Others Feel from Your Actions

Property rights give owners control over their property. For instance, I can paint my car any color I want. I can modify the engine or the tailpipe. I can even install big, shiny 19-inch wheels to try to disguise the fact that, like most economists, I'm not actually very hip.

On the other hand, property rights aren't unlimited. Society does restrict what I can do with my car. For instance, I can't be a source of noise pollution by removing the muffler. I can't drive it 90 miles per hour past an elementary school. And it's also illegal for me to play my 2,000-watt stereo at full volume late at night. I'm not legally allowed to do these things because I don't live on an island by myself. Rather, I live in a community with many other people, and making lots of noise or driving really fast affects their quality of life. The way economists describe this situation is by saying that my actions cause externalities.

REMEMBER

An *externality* is a cost or a benefit that falls not on the person(s) directly involved in an activity but on others. Externalities can be positive or negative:

>> **Positive externality:** A positive externality is a benefit that falls on a person not directly involved in an activity. Think of a beekeeper. She raises bees to sell the honey, but the bees also happen to fly around pollinating flowers for local farmers, thereby increasing their crop yields and providing them with a positive externality.

>> **Negative externality:** A negative externality is a cost that falls on a person not directly involved in an activity. Think of a steel mill that, as a byproduct of producing steel, puts out lots of soot and smoke. The pollution is a negative externality that causes smog and pollutes the air breathed by everyone living near the factory.

This section takes a closer look at externalities.

Noting the effects of negative externalities

Goods and services that impose negative externalities — that is, costs on third parties — end up being overproduced. This happens because negative externalities and the costs that they impose on others aren't taken into account when people make decisions about how much to produce.

For example, in the case of a polluting steel mill, the mill's managers take into account only their private costs of raw materials and running the plant.

If someone owned the atmosphere, the mill's managers would have to pay for the right to emit pollution. And if the atmosphere were owned by the people who would have to breathe in the mill's pollution, the firm would be forced to pay those people for the right to pollute and would be forced to take into account the harm that the pollution causes them. But because nobody owns the atmosphere, and firms don't have to pay to pollute into it, there's no mechanism for making the mill's managers take into account the costs of pollution that fall onto members of the broader community. The result is that the firm overproduces steel.

The following subsections explain how negative externalities such as pollution cause overproduction by shifting supply curves. When these shifted supply curves interact with demand curves, you can determine exactly how much overproduction will occur and how much harm results from each unit that is overproduced.

Looking at differences in private and social costs

In Chapter 6, I explain that a competitive firm's supply curve is equal to its marginal cost curve. If a steel mill doesn't take into account the marginal costs that its production of steel imposes on others, its marginal cost curve (its supply curve) is too low and leads to an overproduction of steel.

You can see this situation in Figure 10-2, where I've drawn in two supply curves. The lower one is labeled *Private MC* because the firm's supply curve is its private marginal cost curve, which takes into account only the firm's own costs of producing steel. The higher curve takes into account not only the firm's private costs but also the external pollution costs, which I've labeled *XC* (for external costs). This higher curve is called the *Social MC* curve and is useful because it captures all costs associated with producing steel — both the firm's costs of making it and the costs imposed on others as negative externalities.

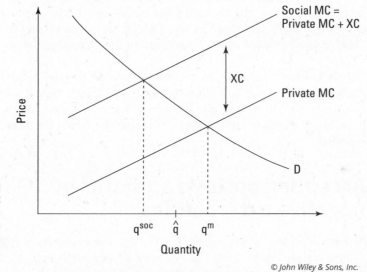

© John Wiley & Sons, Inc.

FIGURE 10-2: The market overproduces a good that has a negative externality.

Producing units for which costs exceed benefits

Overproduction is the result of the Private *MC's* curve failure to take account of external pollution costs. In particular, the market equilibrium features overproduction because it occurs where the demand curve intersects the Private *MC* curve rather than the Social *MC* curve.

To see why this leads to overproduction, first examine the market equilibrium in Figure 10-2, where the demand curve, *D*, crosses the Private *MC* curve. That equilibrium results in a quantity q^m of steel being produced, where *m* stands for market.

On the other hand, the socially optimal amount of steel to produce is q^{soc}, where *soc* stands for social. The socially optimal quantity is determined by where the Social *MC* curve crosses the demand curve. You can tell that q^{soc} is socially optimal because for every unit up to and including q^{soc}, the demand curve is above the Social *MC* curve, meaning that the benefits of producing these units exceed the costs of producing them. That's true when taking into account not only private costs but the external costs that fall on third parties as well.

REMEMBER

The problem with producing all the units from q^{soc} up to q^m is that although the benefits do exceed the firm's private production costs, they don't exceed the total costs when you take into account *XC*, the cost of the negative externality.

For instance, look at output level $q^\wedge$, which lies between q^{soc} and q^m. You can see by going up from $q^\wedge$ to the demand curve that the price that people are willing to pay for that level of output does exceed the private marginal cost of producing it. (That is, the demand curve is above the Private *MC* curve at output level $q^\wedge$.) But if you go up even farther, you see that what people are willing to pay for that level of output is actually less than the total, social cost of producing that much output. (That is, the Social MC curve is higher than the demand curve at output level $q^\wedge$.)

Output level $q^\wedge$ shouldn't be produced because the total cost of producing it exceeds what anyone is willing to pay for it. That's why it's unfortunate that output level q^m is, in fact, produced in a market economy. Every unit of output produced in excess of output level q^{soc} is a unit for which the total costs exceed the benefits.

Accepting positive amounts of negative externalities

REMEMBER

A very important thing to realize is that the common reaction to negative externalities — outlaw them! — is almost never socially optimal. The goal isn't to eliminate negative externalities. Rather, the goal is to ensure that when *all* costs and *all* benefits are weighed, the benefits from the units of output that are produced outweigh the costs of producing them — including the costs of the negative externalities.

In Figure 10-2, for all units of output up to and including q^{soc}, the total benefits are at least as great as the total costs, meaning that society as a whole benefits if these units are produced. Note in the figure that the socially optimal output level q^{soc} is a positive number. That is, it's socially optimal to produce steel even though some pollution will be produced along with it.

To understand the intuition behind this fact, think about automobiles. Cars pollute. And the only way to totally get rid of their pollution is for society to totally ban cars. But do you really want to do that? Although it's true that big, gas-guzzling cars produce prodigious amounts of pollution without justifiable benefits, do you really want to get rid of all cars, including ambulances and fire trucks? Not at all, because although these vehicles do emit pollution, the costs imposed on society by the pollution are more than compensated for by their social benefits — the life-saving activities in which the vehicles are engaged.

The same holds true for the pollution being produced by the steel factory at output level q^{soc}. The only way to totally eliminate the pollution from the steel factory is to shut it down. But that means removing from society all the benefits that steel can provide, such as earthquake-proof buildings and crash-resistant safety cages in automobiles.

The next thing to consider is how to make sure that only q^{soc} units are produced when the market wants to overproduce goods with negative externalities.

Dealing with negative externalities

There are basically three ways to deal with negative externalities:

>> **Pass laws banning or restricting activities that generate negative externalities.** For instance, most cities now forbid you to dispose of your trash by burning it.

>> **Pass laws that directly target the negative externality itself (rather than the underlying activity that leads to the externality).** For instance, steel mills are now required to install smokestack scrubbers that filter out most of the pollution before it goes into the atmosphere.

>> **Impose costs, such as taxes, on people or firms generating negative externalities.** For instance, governments can charge companies for each ton of pollution they emit. This solution is appealing to economists because it's the one that is most likely to lead to the production of the socially optimal output level.

You can see why economists like pollution taxes by looking back at Figure 10-2. Recall that *XC* is the external cost of the steel mill's pollution on others. If the government imposes a tax of *XC* dollars on every unit of steel produced by the firm, the tax raises the firm's cost curve up from Private MC to Social MC.

Setting the pollution tax at exactly *XC* dollars causes the firm's marginal cost curve to lie exactly where the Social MC curve lies. Because a firm's marginal cost curve is its supply curve, the result is that when demand and supply now interact, the socially optimal output level q^{soc} is produced. That is, by imposing exactly the right tax on steel, the government can sit back and let the market do the rest. That makes this sort of pollution-reducing policy attractive compared to other potential solutions.

Compare this solution with a system where firms are ordered to install smoke-stack scrubbers to reduce pollution. In such a system, you need to hire inspectors to constantly monitor factories to make sure they aren't cheating. This sort of system is much more costly to implement than simply imposing a tax on the mill's easily measured steel output and then letting supply and demand set the socially optimal output level. On the other hand, it may be difficult to figure out exactly how big the tax XC should be, so the pollution tax solution isn't without problems, either.

Calculating the consequences of positive externalities

REMEMBER

Externalities can be positive as well as negative. The key thing to understand about positive externalities is that goods and services that provide positive externalities to third parties end up being underproduced.

Underproduction is typical for goods that generate positive externalities. Because property rights are set up in such a way that the recipients of the positive externalities don't have to pay for them, the producers of goods that generate positive externalities have no incentive to provide extra units of output for the benefit of those receiving the positive externalities.

To see why goods that have positive externalities are underproduced, consider a beekeeper named Kate. Kate raises bees so she can sell the honey and make some money. The people who buy her honey do so because the honey brings them utility when they eat it. But because Kate's bees go around pollinating the flowers of local farmers, these farmers also benefit from her beekeeping activities.

But — and here's the crucial point — the farmers don't pay Kate for the benefits that her bees bring them; the bees just fly in and out of their fields, and there's no way to keep track of them. The result is that Kate is going to raise fewer hives of bees than she would if the farmers were paying her for the benefits that her bees bring them.

You can see how this situation works in Figure 10-3. Kate's supply curve is her marginal cost curve, and I've labeled it $S = MC$. I've labeled the demand for her honey by the customers who pay for it as *Private Demand*. Where the supply curve and the Private Demand curve intersect gives the market equilibrium quantity of honey, q^m.

But this output level doesn't take into account the benefits that bees bring to farmers. Suppose that these benefits have a dollar value of *XB*, which stands for external benefits. Then the total social demand for Kate's honey is given by the *Social Demand* curve, which is the Private Demand curve shifted up by *XB* dollars to take account of the fact that honey production benefits the farmers as well as Kate's honey-loving customers.

The socially optimal output level, q^{soc}, would be where the Social Demand curve crosses Kate's supply curve because for each unit of output up to and including q^{soc}, the total social benefit is at least as great as Kate's cost of production.

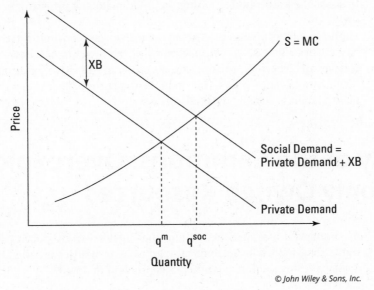

© John Wiley & Sons, Inc.

FIGURE 10-3:
The market underproduces a good that has a positive externality.

As you can see, the market equilibrium quantity produced, q^m, is less than the socially optimal output level, q^{soc}. In other words, because the market mechanism has no way of taking account of the positive externality, Kate produces less honey than is socially optimal.

Subsidizing things that provide positive externalities

Because markets tend to underproduce goods and services that have positive externalities, people have come up with ways to encourage higher levels of production.

The most common way to encourage higher production of goods that generate positive externalities is with a *subsidy*, a payment of money by a government to an individual or firm to encourage it to produce more of a given type of output. Crucially, the government does not receive anything back from the recipient of the subsidy in return for the payment; the beneficiaries are the consumers who receive the additional output.

In the case of Kate's beekeeping business, the government may pay her a honey subsidy of, say, 20 cents per pound to encourage her to keep more hives. The result is more bees pollinating more flowers leading to higher output levels for the farmers. In fact, the government may even tax the farmers to get the money to subsidize Kate's honey. Doing so would make the program pay for itself.

Similarly, governments also often subsidize the planting of trees in and around cities. They must do so because many of the benefits of trees — shade, cooling, cleaner air, less soil erosion, and so on — are positive externalities that aren't taken into account by the markets. Without the subsidy, fewer trees would be planted than is socially optimal.

Tragedy of the Commons: Overexploiting Commonly Owned Resources

An important economic problem that results from poorly defined property rights that don't take account of negative externalities is called the *Tragedy of the Commons.* This section examines this problem in detail.

Overgrazing on a commonly owned field

The *Tragedy of the Commons* refers to a resource being overexploited due to the perverse incentives created by common ownership. Under common ownership, the resource is open for all to use as they please. These circumstances make rapid use and overexploitation likely because each person has an incentive to use up as much of the resources as possible before others can.

To understand the Tragedy of the Commons, think of a farming town in which most of the land is privately owned. However, there's one large field of *common land* where anyone can graze their cattle. In a private field, the owner has an incentive to limit the number of cattle that he puts out to graze. That's because if he puts too many beasts in the field, they quickly eat up all the grass and ruin the field for later grazers. Consequently, the owner of a private field puts only a few cattle out to graze. Doing so reduces his short-run profits (because he restricts the current number of cows) but maximizes his long-run profits (because the field stays in good shape, and he can keep grazing cattle well into the future).

With the commonly held field, however, everyone is going to put some cattle out there because the personal cost of doing so is nothing. Nobody has a personal incentive to preserve the field's future usability. The incentives are actually horribly perverse because if the common field is currently lush with grass, your incentive is to put as many of your cattle out there as quickly as possible to eat all the grass before the field is ruined. Everyone else sees things the same way, so there is a mad rush to put as many cattle out to graze as quickly as possible. The result, of course, is that the field is rapidly ruined for everyone. So although there's no personal cost to putting a cow out to graze on a common field, there *is* a social cost. Each additional cow causes damage to the field that reduces the future productivity of the field.

REMEMBER

The difference between what happens to the private field versus the common field is totally the result of the different property rights governing the two types of land. In the case of privately owned fields, farmers have an incentive to weigh the costs as well as the benefits of putting more cattle out to graze. In particular, they take into account how much future profits will be reduced if current overgrazing ruins the future usability of the field.

Extinctions and poor property rights

Many environmental problems are caused by Tragedy of the Commons situations in which nobody owns the property rights to a given resource. Notably, most animal extinctions are the result of an absence of property rights.

For instance, think of tuna swimming in the open ocean. By international treaty, nobody owns the open ocean. Hence nobody owns the tuna swimming in the open ocean. On the other hand, if you catch a tuna and pull it up onto your boat, you then have a property right over it and can sell it for money. That is, the only way to economically benefit from a tuna is to kill it.

The result is that tuna and many other fish species are hugely overfished, with many near extinction. That's because each fisherman has the incentive to harvest as many fish as quickly as possible before anyone else. This quickly leads to an extinct species, and fishermen are very aware of the problem. But because of the way that property rights are set up in this case, no individual fisherman can do anything to prevent the calamity. If one guy decides to hold back and take fewer fish in the hope that by doing so the species will survive, someone else just comes in and catches the fish that he spared. The species will go extinct anyway. As a result, nobody has an incentive to hold back.

Avoiding the tragedy

REMEMBER

When an economist sees a Tragedy of the Commons situation, his first instinct is to change the property rights system governing the resource in question. Instead of commonly held property rights in which each person has an incentive to take as much of the resource as possible before anyone else does, economists suggest private ownership so there will be an incentive to preserve the resource. Here are a couple of solutions:

>> **Area-based property rights:** In the case of overfishing, one solution has been to give fishermen private property rights to an entire fishing ground — to all the fish in an area while they're still alive. That gives the new owners the proper incentive to manage the stock on a sustainable basis. Furthermore, because only one person has the right to fish in a given area, there's no longer a mad rush between competing fishermen to harvest as many fish as possible before anyone else can get to them.

>> **Permits:** For fish species that migrate freely between different areas, a different solution has been developed. In such cases, biologists first determine the maximum number of fish that can be sustainably harvested each year. The government then auctions off fishing permits for exactly that amount of fish. This method prevents the Tragedy of the Commons by creating a new sort of property right — the fishing permit. It also has the nice benefit of creating a self-sufficient government program. The money raised from auctioning off the fishing permits can be used to hire game wardens to prevent unlicensed fishing, as well as for conservation and wildlife management programs.

>> **Local collective management:** Nobel Prize–winner Elinor Ostrom studied instances in which the resource-users in particular areas were able to prevent the Tragedy of the Commons by developing local collective-management systems that restrained overuse.

Herders sharing pastures in Africa and farmers sharing irrigation water in Nepal have been able to avoid overexploitation by setting up systems in which outsiders can be excluded from exploiting the resource, insiders can be monitored against overuse, mechanisms exist for punishing those who take more than their allotted shares, and collective-choice arrangements allow most insiders to participate in the decision-making that regulates the system.

Chapter **11**

Asymmetric Information and Public Goods

Markets provide nearly everything that people consume. But markets sometimes fail to provide certain products that people want, or markets provide either too much or too little of a particular good or service. Economists refer to such situations as cases of *market failure*, and in this chapter, I discuss two of the most interesting and common causes of market failure:

» **Asymmetric information:** This situation occurs when either the buyer or the seller knows more about the thing he's bargaining over than the other party knows. The classic example is a high-quality used car: The owner who's trying to sell the vehicle knows all about the car's high quality and reliability, but the potential buyer can only take the owner's word for it. Because the potential buyer has no reason to trust the seller's assertions that the car is really good, he assumes the worst and offers a low price just in case the car turns out to be a low-quality "lemon." But because the owner knows that the car is of high quality, he rejects the low offer, and the car goes unsold — all because there's no cheap and easy way to prove the car's high quality to the potential buyer.

>> **Public goods:** These kill off markets in a different way. That's because the very nature of a public good makes it extremely difficult for private sellers to charge users. The classic example is a lighthouse. After it's up and running, it benefits all nearby ships, regardless of whether they pay for the service. That being the case, each and every ship owner tries to avoid paying for the service in the hope that somebody else will pay for it. But with no one paying, the lighthouse soon goes bankrupt, and society is denied a valuable service.

In this chapter, I discuss these two causes of market failure further, show you how pervasive they are, and describe some of the clever solutions that people have come up with to remedy them. So don't expect any asymmetric information here — I'll make sure that you end up knowing everything I do.

Please note that asymmetric information and public goods are not the only things that can cause markets to fail. Market failures also result from monopoly (Chapter 8), oligopoly (Chapter 9), and externalities (Chapter 10).

Facing Up to Asymmetric Information

In many real-life situations, buyers and sellers don't share the same information. Regardless of which party is better informed, economists refer to these situations as cases of *asymmetric information* because one side has more information than the other.

For instance, sellers of used cars are much more knowledgeable about the true quality of the vehicles than the buyers are. On the other hand, the buyers of auto insurance policies are much better informed than insurance companies about whether or not the buyers are bad drivers.

In this section, I provide more in-depth information about asymmetric information.

Realizing that asymmetric information limits trade

Asymmetric information is very important in the real world because it limits what goods and services can be successfully traded in markets. The fundamental reason is that if you know that the other guy is better informed, you're afraid that he'll use his information to take advantage of you.

In the case of used cars, buyers are afraid that sellers who know that their cars are bad will keep that fact to themselves and try to negotiate high prices, as if their cars were good. In the case of insurance, insurance companies are afraid that people who know they're high insurance risks will pretend to be low insurance risks so they can get lower rates.

Depending on how bad the asymmetric information gap is, markets may even collapse completely. That is, if you have huge worries that the seller of the used car is exaggerating the value of the vehicle he's trying to sell you, you probably won't buy. That sounds like a reasonable thing to do, but that fear prevents the sale of good cars because everybody's worried about bad cars. Similarly, if insurance companies can't figure out a way to tell the good insurance risks from the bad ones, they may charge high rates to everybody as though everyone were a high risk. And that, typically, causes the low-risk people not to buy insurance because they know they're being overcharged.

REMEMBER

In extreme cases, asymmetric information can lead to what economists call *missing markets* — situations in which there's no market for a good or service. In these situations, markets are absent because many potential participants have been scared off by the fact that better-informed market participants may use their informational advantage to exploit less-informed market participants.

In less extreme cases, asymmetric information only hobbles but does not completely eliminate a market. I explore how this happens in the next section.

Souring on the lemons problem: The used car market

Berkeley economist George Akerlof got the Nobel Prize in Economics in 2002 for a famous paper he wrote called "The Market for Lemons." The paper, first published in 1970, is all about asymmetric information and market failure, and it was especially memorable because Akerlof used the market for used cars as his primary example. What Akerlof correctly explained was that poor-quality vehicles, or lemons, dominate the market because asymmetric information drives away sellers who want to part with high-quality used cars.

To make the intuition behind the result clear, imagine that there are only three kinds of used cars for sale: good, okay, and bad. They all look the same on the outside and even test-drive pretty much the same, but they have major differences in terms of how much longer they're going to last before the engine gives out. Because of the difference in engine quality and how long the cars are likely to last, the good cars are worth $15,000, the okay cars are worth $10,000, and the bad ones are worth $5,000.

The problem that leads to market failure is the asymmetric information that exists between buyers and sellers. In particular, although each seller knows how good her own car's engine is, the buyers have no way of knowing.

Buyers could, of course, ask sellers to be truthful about the quality of their cars, and no doubt many sellers — probably most — would tell the truth. But there's no way to *know* whether they're telling the truth. Consequently, when a particular seller tells you that her car is good, you're still going to be nervous about being cheated.

As I show you in the following subsections, this very reasonable fear causes nearly all good and okay cars to be withdrawn from the market. The result is a used car market that's dominated by bad cars; as Akerlof put it, the used car market ends up becoming "a market for lemons."

Seeing how quality used cars are driven from the market

Imagine that you want to buy a used car, but you don't want to overpay for it. You know that there are only three types of cars: good, okay, and bad. In addition, you happen to know that one-third of all used cars on the road are good, one-third are okay, and one-third are bad. How much would you be willing to pay for a used car?

Well, given the fact that good cars are worth $15,000, okay cars are worth $10,000, and bad cars are worth $5,000, and also given the fact that you don't know which cars are which, imagine that you'd be willing to pay no more than $10,000. Why $10,000? Because that's what the okay used car — the car of average quality — is worth.

Because sellers have no way of proving to you how good their cars are, a sensible thing to do when presented with a used car is to assume that it's of average quality and, therefore, worth $10,000. So you offer $10,000. And so do all the other buyers presented with used cars because they, like you, can't tell the quality of used cars apart. Now look at how different sellers react to the $10,000 offer depending on the true quality of their vehicles:

» If a seller knows his car is bad and worth only $5,000, he happily accepts your offer.

» If a seller knows his car is okay, he also accepts because you're offering what the car's actually worth.

» If a seller has a good car, he won't accept unless he's in some sort of dire circumstance. He knows the car is worth $15,000, so he won't accept your $10,000 offer unless he's really desperate to raise cash in a hurry (perhaps to pay off some gambling debts).

The result is that nearly all the good cars on the market are withdrawn, leaving only bad and okay cars. Now consider how that situation changes what buyers are willing to offer. If all the good cars are withdrawn from the market, there's now a 50/50 chance that a car is okay or bad. In such a case, how much would you offer to pay if you were a buyer? Well, with a 50/50 chance of the car being worth either $10,000 or $5,000, you'll probably offer the average of these two values: $7,500. But when you do, the market becomes even more dysfunctional. After all, how are the sellers of okay cars going to react to being offered $7,500? They're going to reject the offer and withdraw their vehicles from the market, too.

The sad result is that with the good cars and then the okay cars withdrawn from the market, the only cars left are the bad ones, the lemons. Because of the asymmetric information problem, the used car market ends up being a market for lemons. Buyers know this, so they offer only $5,000 for any car on the market. And because only bad cars are offered, sellers accept the $5,000. So although it's true that bad cars end up being priced correctly in the used car market, no market exists for good or even okay used cars.

That's a problem because people — both buyers and sellers — want to trade good and okay cars, and they would be much happier if they could. But unless some solution can be found to the asymmetric information problem, they're all left out in the cold.

Making lemonade: Solutions to the lemons problem

The fundamental issue driving the lemons problem is that the sellers of good and okay cars have no way of convincing buyers that their cars are as good as the sellers know them to be. The whole problem could be resolved if sellers had some way to convince buyers that a good car is, in fact, a good car and an okay car is, in fact, an okay car.

In the next four subsections, I discuss ways to achieve this goal. These methods don't work perfectly, but because they offer some reassurance to buyers, buyers are willing to offer enough to get sellers to part with higher-quality automobiles.

BUYING INFORMATION FROM TRUSTED THIRD PARTIES

Several companies now specialize in selling vehicle history reports to people looking to purchase used cars. Potential buyers can enter the vehicle identification number (VIN) of the car they're interested in and obtain a report that notes mileage, reported accidents, service and repair visits, the number of owners the car has had, whether the car has ever been leased, and so on.

Although these vehicle history reports aren't guaranteed to be exhaustive or perfectly accurate, they're an inexpensive method by which potential buyers can help themselves identify problem vehicles. The reports reduce the likelihood of market failure by helping make information more symmetric between buyers and sellers.

OFFERING A WARRANTY

One way a seller can convince a buyer that she really has a good car is to offer the buyer a warranty. The seller knows that her good car won't break down after she sells it, meaning that she'll never have to pay for any repairs.

A warranty is convincing because only the seller of a good car would be willing to offer a warranty. By contrast, the seller of a bad car would never offer a warranty because he knows that his car will probably break down and that he'll have to pay for the repairs. Consequently, if someone is willing to offer you a warranty, she almost certainly has a good car. That's why you see so many used car dealers offering warranties on the vehicles they sell. If they didn't offer warranties, the lemons problem would quickly take over, and prices would fall so low that only bad cars would be bought and sold on the used car market.

BUILDING A REPUTATION

Another way to solve the lemons problem is to reassure buyers by setting up a market in such a way that sellers can build a reputation for honesty and fair dealing. This is why most good used cars are sold through used car dealers rather than directly between individuals.

Compare a used car dealership with an individual selling her used car online. Who has more of an incentive to tell the truth about car quality? The used car dealer makes his living selling used cars, so if he overcharges one customer by pretending a bad car is good, he gets in trouble. When that car starts to break down, the buyer becomes angry and uses social media to tell all his friends that the dealer cheated him. And that loss of reputation cuts into the dealer's future sales. In fact, he'll quickly go bankrupt if he develops a reputation for lying.

By contrast, an individual selling her used car doesn't have to worry about developing a reputation for lying. Her main source of income isn't selling cars. If she cheats you and you get mad and tell all your friends, it won't affect her much because she's not in the business of selling used cars. The result is that she has much more of an incentive to lie than does the used car dealer, who has to worry about his reputation. As a result, many good used cars are sold through used car dealers. (But even at used car dealers, people still need some reassurance, which is why most used car dealers also offer warranties.)

GETTING AN EXPERT OPINION

Because the heart of the lemons problem is asymmetric information, another method of resolving the problem is for skeptical buyers to hire an expert who can give them the information they need to distinguish good, okay, and bad cars. Many car buyers employ this strategy when they have doubts about a seller's honesty.

For a relatively small fee, a buyer can hire a disinterested third-party expert —for instance, a professional mechanic — to inspect the vehicle and make a list of repairs that will most likely be needed in the near future. In this way, the buyer can get a better picture of the car's quality and what a fair price would be.

This method doesn't fully resolve the asymmetric information problem because the expert probably can't discover *everything* that may be wrong with the car. To the extent that this is true, buyers may still be suspicious, and there may still be some potential for market failure. That's why you often see buyer-initiated inspections used in conjunction with other methods of resolving asymmetric information, such as warranties and sales by dealers who have a reputation to protect.

Issuing insurance when you can't tell individuals apart

An insurance company faces an asymmetric information problem of its own. Its problem is that the people buying insurance know more than the company does about the risks they face.

Consider automobile insurance. Who needs it more: good drivers who hardly ever get into accidents or bad drivers who get into lots of accidents? Now, clearly, even good drivers want insurance because they're sometimes involved in accidents for which they're not to blame. But bad drivers want insurance even more to help pay for all the accidents they know they're going to cause because of their poor driving.

REMEMBER

An asymmetric information problem faces the insurance companies because although individual drivers know whether they're good or bad, the insurance companies can't easily tell them apart. If they *could* tell them apart, insurance companies would simply charge the good drivers a low rate for insurance and the bad drivers a high rate.

But because they can't tell the good and bad drivers apart, the insurance companies run a serious risk of going bankrupt. To see why, imagine that insurance companies offered the same low rate to everyone, as though they were *all* good drivers. This would soon lead to bankruptcy because the insurance companies wouldn't be collecting enough in premiums to pay off all the damage caused by the bad drivers.

To avoid bankruptcy, the insurance companies could go to the other extreme, charging everyone as though they were bad drivers. But then the good drivers wouldn't bother buying insurance because for them it would be overpriced. The result would be that only bad drivers would sign up for insurance.

This is a very poor result socially because you want everyone to be able to buy insurance at a rate that fairly reflects their driving ability. Good drivers should be able to get insurance at a fair rate. And because good drivers make up most of the drivers in the real world, insurance companies lose out on lots of potential profits unless they can figure out a way to separate the good drivers from the bad drivers.

Grouping individuals to help tell them apart

Insurance companies have come up with a paradoxical way of dealing with the fact that they can't tell whether an individual is a good or bad driver. Instead of focusing on the individual, they look for clues about the individual based on the groups to which he or she belongs. Doing so often gives the insurance companies a pretty good idea about whether the individual is a good or bad driver.

For instance, government data indicates that males under 25 get into many more serious accidents than females under 25 do. So if two people walk into an insurance company and one of them is a 23-year-old male and the other is a 22-year-old female, chances are that the male is a worse driver than the female. Consequently, you charge the male a higher insurance rate.

This situation has the nice result of making sure that everybody can get insurance at what is *likely* to be a fair price given the fact that, on average, males under 25 get into many more accidents than females under 25.

TIP

In reality, this nice result isn't the compelling reason behind insurance companies' decisions to infer as much as possible about their customers by looking at which groups they belong to. These companies really have no choice; competition *forces* them to do so.

Why is this true? Consider two insurance companies, only one of which uses group membership information to help set rates. The company that doesn't use group information has to set very high rates because it's afraid that all its customers may be bad drivers. Doing so drives away the good drivers who don't want to pay bad-driver rates for their insurance.

But the company that uses group information can offer multiple rates, such as high ones to young men and lower ones to young women. Doing so allows it to capture the business of many good drivers who don't want to deal with the first insurance company that sets only one high rate for everyone. The result is that insurance companies are always looking for ways to estimate an individual's unknown risk profile based on the well-known risk profiles of the groups to which he or she belongs.

This process can lead to some rather unfair conclusions. The oddest is that good-driving young males end up paying higher rates than good-driving young females because the only thing insurance companies have to go on is gender. But such a system is still better than the even more unfair alternative in which *all* good drivers would have to pay bad-driver rates, which is what would happen if insurance companies were banned from using group membership information to try to distinguish their customers. The closer insurance companies can get to fully distinguishing good and bad drivers using group membership information, the fairer rates will be.

Keep in mind that the drivers for whom insurance companies have the greatest need to use group membership information are new drivers. Because insurance companies don't have any accident or violation records for new drivers, there's a pressing need to try to separate the good from the bad drivers using group membership information. As drivers get more experience, the insurance companies can get increasingly accurate accident and violation information that distinguishes the good from the bad.

Avoiding adverse selection

Using the groups to which a person belongs to estimate his or her individual insurance risk goes only part of the way to resolving the asymmetric information problem that exists between insurance companies and their customers. Obviously, there's still a lot of individual variation within any group. For instance, even if young women are, on average, better drivers than young men, some young women are bad drivers. This leads to a very difficult problem known as *adverse selection.*

If an insurance company sets a premium for young women on the basis of how often young women *on average* get into accidents, insurance will be more attractive to young women who are really bad drivers than to young women who are really good drivers.

REMEMBER

As a result, young female bad drivers will be more prone to sign up for insurance than young female good drivers. This tendency is known as *adverse selection* because it's as though the bad, or adverse, insurance risks self-select into buying insurance policies. The result is a customer pool that contains a disproportionately high number of bad drivers.

Adverse selection is a difficult problem because it feeds on itself. The insurance company has to raise rates to take account of the fact that bad drivers are more likely to sign up than good drivers. But when it raises rates, the problem just gets worse because the higher rates make insurance even less attractive to good drivers, meaning that the pool of applicants is going to be even more disproportionately dominated by bad drivers.

TIP

One solution to adverse selection is for an insurance company to offer a large group of people one rate — on the condition that nobody can opt out. For instance, at the school where I teach, our health insurance company offers the school one low rate for every employee on the condition that every employee must be enrolled. By enrolling everyone, there's no chance that the insurance pool is dominated by the sickly because all the healthy have declined to be enrolled.

Another solution is to force everyone to purchase insurance. For example, all 50 states now require drivers to buy auto insurance. By forcing all drivers to purchase insurance, governments can relieve insurance companies from having to worry about the adverse selection problem. On the other hand, many people consider these laws to be coercive because they force drivers to purchase insurance whether they want to or not. In addition, good drivers may be forced to subsidize bad drivers because both may now be grouped together by insurance companies.

Mitigating moral hazard

A big problem facing insurance companies is called *moral hazard.* Moral hazard arises because buying insurance tends to change people's behavior. For instance, if I didn't have car insurance, I would drive much more carefully, knowing that I would have to use my own money to pay for any damage I cause. But because I do have insurance, I drive faster and more recklessly knowing that if something goes wrong, the insurance company is going to be stuck with the bill. (Please know that when I say "I" in examples like this one, I don't actually mean me. You see, *I* am above moral hazard.)

The way car insurance companies deal with moral hazard is by offering discounts in exchange for high deductibles. For instance, if I get into an accident, the $1,000 deductible that I've chosen means that of any bills that ensue from the accident, I have to pay the first $1,000.

The deductible serves as a strong inducement for me not to give in to moral hazard and drive recklessly. And because the insurance company knows that my high deductible gets rid of most of my moral hazard problem, it's willing to offer me insurance at a lower rate than if I'd opted for only a $100 deductible. Deductibles are a clever way of reducing moral hazard problems and helping to make insurance more affordable for responsible drivers.

GROUP DISCRIMINATION, INDIVIDUAL IDENTIFICATION

The idea of grouping individuals to help sort them extends beyond insurance. For instance, companies want hard-working employees but can't tell when you walk in for an interview if you are, in fact, hard-working. So they try to estimate the chances that you are by seeing which groups you belong to.

For instance, nearly all straight-A students are hard-working. Therefore, if you're a straight-A student, a company is going to be much more likely to hire you. You may actually be lazy, but by seeing what group you belong to, the firm improves its odds that you're not.

The practice of using information about the groups to which an individual belongs to try to figure out personal characteristics is referred to as *statistical discrimination*. Although this practice typically improves economic outcomes, you have to decide for yourself whether — and in what cases — you think it's fair or unfair.

Providing Public Goods

Public goods are products that can't be profitably produced by private firms because there's no way to exclude nonpayers from using them. The inability of private firms to profitably produce public goods derives from the fact that they have two very special characteristics. Public goods are both nonrival and nonexcludable:

» **Nonrival:** Nonrival means that one person's using the good doesn't diminish another person's ability to enjoy the good. Think of an outdoor fireworks display, a statue in a park, or a television show broadcast over the airwaves. Your consumption doesn't in any way diminish that of others. This stands in stark contrast to most goods, where if you consume more, less remains for others. (Think of cookies.)

» **Nonexcludable:** Nonexcludable means that it's hard to prevent nonpayers from consuming a good or service. For instance, when you produce an outdoor fireworks display, everyone in the vicinity gets to see it for free no matter how much you'd like to charge them for it. A more serious example is an army: When it's in place to provide national defense, it provides national defense for everybody, including those who don't want to contribute to the cost of the army's maintenance.

REMEMBER

The nonrival and nonexcludable characteristics of public goods make it very hard for private firms to make any money producing them. Think about trying to get people to buy tickets to an outdoor fireworks display. Because people know that they're going to be able to see it for free, they won't buy tickets. Because they won't buy tickets, there's no way to raise the money needed to put on the display.

This sort of chicken-and-egg problem is frustrating, because although people don't want to pay for something they can get for free, they actually do like fireworks displays — meaning that they're fundamentally willing to pay something to see them. The problem is figuring out how to get them to pay.

Taxing to provide public goods

The most common solution to the problem of how to provide public goods has been for governments to step in and use tax money to pay for them. In the case of fireworks, because nearly everybody likes fireworks, there's no problem getting enough political support for spending tax money on displays. And after they've been funded by the taxpayer, everyone can enjoy them.

National defense has historically been provided for by the government because it, too, is very much a nonexcludable, nonrival public good. For instance, because protection from foreign invaders is nonexcludable, there's always a temptation to not help pay for it because you know that if someone else does pay, you get to enjoy safety from foreign invaders for free. And because national defense is nonrival, you know that the safety you enjoy is of just as high a quality as the safety everyone else enjoys. This fact, too, lessens your incentive to pay. As a result, governments force people to share the expense for national defense by levying taxes.

Taxes and a good portion of government spending are often derided as wasteful (and often are wasteful), but keep in mind that in many cases, taxes are the only way to fund the wide variety of public goods you enjoy. Although nobody likes taxes, you probably wouldn't want to trade a reduced tax burden for no public parks, no national army, no public roads, no public sewers, and so on. Without the government's ability to force people to pay for these things, you'd likely not have them — at least not in the quantity and variety that you currently enjoy.

Enlisting philanthropy to provide public goods

Although most public goods are paid for through taxation by the government, some are paid for privately. So don't think that governments are absolutely necessary to provide public goods. They aren't. However, governments are a much more reliable way to provide public goods because you don't have to rely upon the philanthropic largesse of the rich, who are under no obligation to spend their wealth on public rather than private goods.

WARNING

Don't make the common mistake of thinking that public goods are called *public* because they're typically provided by the government rather than the private sector. Economists call them public goods because private firms can't profitably produce them, not because they have to be produced by the government. Private philanthropy can produce public goods without any help at all from the government.

For example, in the middle of Los Angeles, where I grew up, there's a huge and beautiful mountain park called Griffith Park. The land for it was donated by a millionaire named Griffith J. Griffith. That is, he provided a public good at personal expense.

The desire for fame or recognition may help encourage the philanthropic provision of public goods. Rich people often trade million-dollar donations to hospitals, universities, and charities for having a building named after them. And corporations often sponsor cultural public goods such as fireworks displays, arts festivals, and parades in order to obtain name recognition and goodwill.

Providing a public good by selling a related private good

Broadcast radio is a public good. After a radio signal has been sent out over the airways, it's nonrival: My listening to a radio program doesn't reduce anyone else's ability to tune in. It's also nonexcludable: There's no way to stop anyone with a radio from tuning in. So given that radio programming is very much a public good, how is it that so much radio programming is produced and broadcast every day by privately owned and operated radio stations?

The answer is that the broadcast industry figured out that although radio itself is a public good, the commercials that they play on the radio are very much private goods for which radio stations can charge a lot of money. That is, if a car maker or beer maker or the publisher of a revolutionary new economics book with a yellow and black cover wants an ad to to be broadcast to the millions of listeners who tune in for free to the public good known as radio, the company has to pay for commercial air time.

SUPPORTING FREE INFORMATION WITH ADVERTISING

Google is currently the world's largest and most popular Internet search engine. But when it first started in business, it lost money hand over fist. Its problem was that it was providing Internet search results for free, as a public good. People went to google.com, typed in a search term, and got ranked results without having to pay anything. This service was very helpful to users, but Google would've soon gone bankrupt if it hadn't stumbled onto a way to generate income from its services.

The solution was the same one that broadcast TV stations and newspapers had long used. Google would charge advertisers for the right to have their ads appear next to Google's free search results. Thus, for instance, if a person were using Google to search for the word "dog," the free search results would be accompanied by ads paid for by companies selling products related to the word *dog* — for instance, hot dogs, dog food, and concert tickets for Snoop Dog.

Google's search ads had an unintended casualty: They began to kill off newspapers. This happened because Google's targeted search ads were much more cost-effective for advertisers than newspaper print ads. For example, if a company that wanted to sell dog collars took out a full-page ad in *The New York Times,* only a very small percentage of that paper's readers would've had any interest in that ad because the vast majority of them would've had no current need to buy a dog collar. But if that same company placed its ads only next to Google search results that were generated for people who had been searching for "dog collars," then nearly every person who saw the ad might be in the market for a dog collar.

In the decade after Google introduced search ads, newspaper advertising revenues fell by more than half, and hundreds of newspapers went bankrupt or were forced to merge with other newspapers to survive. Newspapers have attempted to adjust to the Internet Age by publishing online and attempting to capture online and mobile ad revenues. But because the news agencies' ads aren't as well targeted as those accompanying Google search results, they don't command very high rates.

The trick behind broadcast radio is that the privately sold good called advertising pays for the freely provided public good called radio. To a more limited extent, many newspapers and magazines work the same way. Although they raise some money from subscription fees or the newsstand price, a substantial chunk of their revenue comes from the advertising they sell.

Ranking new technology as a public good

You live in an age of rapidly rising living standards. Why is this the case? Because institutions are fostering the creation of new and better technologies that allow people to produce more goods and services from the same old resources, or to produce entirely new goods and services that were previously impossible to produce.

Technological progress is a public good. And because it is, society has had to come up with ways to make sure that technological progress happens given the fact that private individuals and firms have little incentive to invent new technology.

Patenting to turn public goods into private goods

To understand how new technologies are public goods, consider the invention of the movable-type printing press by Johannes Gutenberg in 1435. Before Gutenberg, books were copied by hand. But after he invented the printing press, it was much cheaper to make new copies by printing them. Furthermore, think about how simple the technology really is. The printing press is basically just a big version of the rubber stamps that little kids like to play with. The invention was immediately understandable to anyone and everyone who heard about it, which meant that they could make their own printing presses as soon as they heard about it.

So how does this invention satisfy the characteristics of a public good?

>> It's nonrival because my building and using a printing press doesn't in any way lessen your ability to build and use a printing press.

>> It's basically nonexcludable because the cost of communicating the new idea to another person is so low — just a short conversation does the trick.

The result is that unless society creates some sort of an institution to reward the creation of new ideas, there's not going to be much of a profit incentive to go into the invention business. In fact, what happened to Gutenberg was that everyone copied his idea and didn't pay him for it. So unless you can come up with a way to financially reward the creation of new inventions, you're not likely to get many of them.

REMEMBER

The solution has been the creation of *patents.* By giving inventors the exclusive right to market and sell their inventions for 20 years, patents provide a financial incentive to get people to invest the time and energy necessary to come up with new technologies that benefit everyone. It's no coincidence that economic growth took off after government-enforced patents became widely available in Western Europe in the 18th century.

Subsidizing research into technologies that can't be patented

Not every new innovation can be patented. That's because you can patent only something you invent, not something you discover. For instance, if you think up a chemical that's never existed before and then synthesize it, you can patent it. But if you merely discover an existing chemical that's been floating around the sea or lying in the soil, you can't patent it.

This is a big problem for things like cancer research because many potential cures are chemicals derived from plants and animals, chemicals that have existed in nature for eons. These chemicals have huge potential benefits, but because they can't be patented, nobody has a strong financial incentive to try to discover them.

As a result, the government and many private philanthropic groups fund research into areas of science where the public goods problem would otherwise limit research. This solution is very important to an economist because providing public goods is an economic problem that markets and the invisible hand can't fix. Other types of market failure, like asymmetric information, have pretty decent private sector solutions (as I discuss in the section "Making lemonade: Solutions to the lemons problem," earlier in the chapter).

conditions

» Comparing global healthcare expenditures

» Focusing on why out-of-pocket costs encourage good self-rationing

» Understanding how Singapore delivers world-class care at world-lowest cost

Chapter **12**

Health Economics and Healthcare Finance

O f all the goods and services that modern science and technology can provide, those that can extend someone's lifespan, guard against infirmity, and repair the injuries caused by diseases and accidents are among the most highly prized and intensely demanded. In addition, many people consider access to healthcare a basic human right. However, nothing is free. Any resources devoted to providing healthcare are resources that can't be devoted to producing other products — including public education and affordable housing, which many people also consider basic human rights. Thus, scarcity applies to healthcare as much as it does to any other good or service.

Because economics studies how people cope with scarcity, its insights are useful when considering the trade-offs that governments and individuals face. How can they best structure medical institutions to provide the highest-quality care to the greatest number of people at the lowest possible cost? As I explain in this chapter, incentives matter profoundly.

After defining health economics and health finance, this chapter introduces the mechanics and limitations of health insurance before examining which countries' healthcare systems provide the best results at the lowest costs. I then investigate the economic incentives that Singapore's healthcare system provides and how those incentives underpin its ability to provide top-quality care at extremely low costs. I conclude with a discussion of how effective those incentive systems have been when tried in other places.

Defining Health Economics and Healthcare Finance

Health economics is the study of how resources are allocated toward healthcare. Thus, health economics investigates wide-ranging topics, including the best methods for funding medical research, whether providing medical care through central hospitals or local clinics is more cost-effective, how advertising for prescription drugs affects consumer behavior, and how medical spending affects worker productivity.

A major focus of health economics is *health finance,* the study of how healthcare is paid for. One method is for people to simply pay for it themselves, directly with their own funds — as most people pay for food, clothing, shelter, entertainment, and so on. But many medical procedures are both hard to plan for and extremely expensive — for instance, life-saving emergency care after a serious car accident or coronary bypass surgery to save an ailing heart. Both the high costs and unexpected nature of these types of procedures make them very difficult for individuals to cope with individually.

One solution is health insurance, which helps people to pool resources to cope with these problems collectively. But health insurance is not without problems. In particular, both private health insurance and government-provided health insurance create incentives for inefficiency and artificially high demand that may be better handled by alternative methods of health finance. I explore these problems with health insurance in the next section.

Noting the Limits of Health Insurance

Health insurance can be great way of dealing with uncertain future healthcare costs — but only if you start off with a group of people who are all currently healthy. In this scenario, the insurance company collects money from a large number of healthy people who are exposed to a risk — for example, cancer —and stores that money away to compensate or reimburse the minority who will suffer that risk in the future. Because only a few will eventually suffer the risk, the monthly premiums paid by everyone purchasing insurance can be quite low. This is because the future costs of treating the few who will get cancer are spread across the entire group.

But people do get sick. As a result, you're not going to find many groups in which everybody is currently healthy. This is problematic because a high proportion of sick people can ruin the ability of health insurance to deal with future medical costs. The higher the proportion of unhealthy people, the less functional health insurance becomes. Healthy people drop out when premiums are too high, and at some point, not enough healthy people are left in the group for their contributions to pay for the high future costs of the sickly.

This section explores the limits of health insurance. Recognizing that insurance has its limits is important because it helps you understand the difficulties faced by both private companies and governments when they attempt to use insurance as the primary means of funding healthcare expenditures. In addition, you can immediately grasp that a big selling point for other methods of funding healthcare is that they typically sidestep the problems that beset health insurance. But don't think that avoiding insurance solves every problem related to funding healthcare; those other methods typically have some very serious problems of their own.

Adverse selection: Looking at who buys insurance

People who already have medical problems have *preexisting conditions.* Health insurance has difficulty coping with preexisting conditions due to *adverse selection,* which occurs when insurance is disproportionately purchased by those who are more likely to need costly reimbursements in the future. Adverse selection can drive up insurance rates and even kill off an insurance market. (For details on adverse selection in auto insurance, see Chapter 11.)

To see how adverse selection wreaks havoc on health insurance markets, suppose an insurance company offers health insurance to a large group of people — say, the population of Massachusetts. For those with preexisting conditions, purchasing insurance is a no-brainer, because they're certain that their future healthcare bills will be larger than their insurance premiums. But the money to pay for their future medical bills has to come from somewhere. With all the sick people purchasing insurance, the insurance company knows that future treatment costs will be high. The only way to cover those costs is to charge high premiums, getting enough money out of those *without* preexisting conditions to pay the expected costs.

Those without preexisting conditions will react the same way people react to higher prices when considering any good or service: Some will stop buying the product. Their dropping out of the insurance market makes things even worse for the insurance company, because it'll be forced to raise premiums even higher. But by raising insurance premiums, even more healthy people will choose not to purchase health insurance, and premiums will go up again.

If this process is intense enough, all the healthy people will drop out, and the insurance company will stop offering insurance — in which case *nobody* will have access to health insurance. It's hard to get more adverse than that!

Combating adverse selection

Both the private and public sectors have taken on adverse selection head-on. This section highlights a few examples.

Charging different rates

An important private-sector solution to the adverse-selection problem is for insurance companies to charge different rates to different customers based on their likely future health costs. Those without preexisting conditions get a lower rate, and those with preexisting conditions get a rate that reflects their higher future health expenses. Unfortunately, this solution can work only if insurance companies have the same information about health conditions as their customers and are legally allowed to set different rates based on preexisting conditions. Here are some challenges that arise:

>> **Asymmetric information:** Due to medical privacy laws, most patients have a better idea about their preexisting conditions than do their insurance companies (see Chapter 11, where I discuss asymmetric information). Because of this, the strategy of setting different insurance rates for the healthy and the sick can be difficult to implement, because those with preexisting conditions can simply pretend not to have them and apply for coverage at the lower rate.

>> **Fairness:** Governments sometimes forbid insurance companies from charging different rates on the basis of preexisting conditions. These prohibitions are imposed for fairness reasons and assume that those with preexisting conditions are afflicted through no fault of their own.

However, this assumption is dubious for many diseases. Take diabetes. In most cases, obesity is a major factor contributing to Type 2 diabetes, and obesity is in turn caused by overeating and not getting enough exercise. For such diseases, critics argue that it *would* be fair to allow insurance companies to charge higher premiums because people have these conditions as the result of lifestyle choices. Indeed, banning insurance companies from charging higher rates could make people less healthy — if people know that their insurance rates won't go up if they gain weight, they may be less likely to eat properly and exercise.

However, many governments *have* imposed bans on charging higher rates to individuals with preexisting conditions. These bans make the multiple-rates solution to the adverse selection problem illegal and force insurance companies to search for solutions, such as group insurance.

Offering group insurance

Group insurance is a private-sector solution to the adverse selection problem. It avoids the fairness issues that arise when charging higher prices to those with preexisting conditions. Under *group insurance,* an insurance company offers insurance to a group whose members are selected for reasons other than whether they have any particular interest in obtaining health insurance.

For example, consider the employees of a large construction company. They were drawn to that employer because it offered jobs they liked. Thus, they probably consist of a fairly random mixture of healthy people and a few people with preexisting conditions. The group as a whole probably looks like the mixture of healthy and sick people found in society at large.

The insurance company approaches the construction company and tells its owners that they can buy health insurance for their employees but only if they purchase policies for *all* their employees. Doing so solves the adverse selection problem because if policies are bought for all employees, then there will be plenty of healthy people to help pay for the high healthcare costs of those in the group who have costly preexisting conditions.

Insurance companies also offer group insurance deals to other groups, including trade unions, professional associations, and even large clubs. Any group will do just as long as its members contain plenty of healthy people and everyone in the group is covered (so that the healthy cannot drop out and thereby leave the insurance company with a smaller, sicker group).

By mitigating the adverse selection problem, group insurance helps provide healthcare to tens of millions of people in the United States. Indeed, the large majority of Americans with private health insurance receive it as part of plans paid for by their employers. Unfortunately, however, the availability of group insurance can make insurance harder to get for those who aren't members of groups that can be easily solicited by insurance companies.

Insurance companies may shy away from offering insurance to individuals who aren't already covered by a group insurance plan for two reasons:

>> Signing up individuals one at a time is substantially more expensive.

>> Insurance companies have to worry that people who apply for insurance as individuals may be especially likely to have preexisting conditions.

This worry is not unfounded. Many people with costly preexisting conditions are too ill to hold down full-time jobs, so the fact that a person is not already covered by an employer-based insurance plan raises the likelihood that he or she has a costly preexisting condition. Therefore, some insurance companies charge high premiums to those seeking individual health insurance policies, and other insurance companies are reluctant to issue individual policies at all. Thus, the availability of group insurance can make things worse rather than better for those who aren't already members of insured groups.

Considering the public-sector response

The public sector has also taken on adverse selection and sought to do so in ways that do not raise concerns about fairness. Canada and some other governments, for instance, have made the purchase of insurance mandatory. Because both the healthy and the sick must buy insurance, adverse selection can't lead to either extremely high insurance premiums or a total collapse of the health insurance market. And because every single person must buy insurance, there are no worries about fairness or unequal treatment.

Another government-imposed solution to the adverse selection problem is to eliminate health insurance altogether and have the government provide all healthcare. This is how healthcare is provided in many countries, including, most prominently, the United Kingdom. These healthcare systems are owned and run by the government, cover every resident, and are paid for out of general tax revenues. Because no insurance is involved, adverse selection isn't an issue. And because every resident is covered, no problems with fairness arise with respect to coving those with preexisting conditions.

Both mandatory health insurance requirements and government-run healthcare systems aren't, however, without their problems. As I discuss in the upcoming section "Inflated Demand: Suffering from 'Free' and Reduced-Cost Healthcare," both systems tend to lead to excessive and inefficient spending on healthcare that in turn necessitates cost-control policies that are considered by many to be arbitrary, severe, and ironically unfair.

Comparing Healthcare Internationally

Looking at how different countries address healthcare costs is important because it gives you a good sense of which combinations seem to work best — and more importantly, *why* they work best. For instance, in 2014 the United States healthcare system was such that 79 percent of all healthcare spending was paid for by either private insurance (35 percent of the total) or government insurance (44 percent of the total, most of it via Medicare for the elderly and Medicaid for the poor). That same year, most other nations either had a national health insurance system that paid for virtually all healthcare spending (as in Canada) or a government-run national health service that provided healthcare for free to all residents (as in the United Kingdom).

Many other variations combine varying amounts of private and public health insurance with privately run hospitals and publicly owned-and-operated hospitals. Refer to Table 12-1 for a rundown on healthcare spending and the relationship to life expectancy and infant mortality.

TABLE 12-1   **Three Important Healthcare Statistics, 2014**

Country	Healthcare Spending as a Percent of GDP	Life Expectancy in Years	Infant Mortality per 1,000 Live Births
United States	17.1	80.0	5.8
France	11.5	81.9	3.2
Switzerland	11.7	82.6	3.6
Germany	11.3	80.8	3.4
Canada	10.4	81.9	4.5
Italy	9.2	82.3	3.3
Australia	9.4	82.3	4.3
United Kingdom	9.1	80.8	4.3
Japan	10.2	85.3	2.0
Singapore	4.9	85.2	2.4

Source: CIA World Factbook, United States Central Intelligence Agency

The first column of Table 12-1 lists healthcare spending as a percent of gross domestic product (GDP) for several developed countries in 2014. *GDP* is a measure of the total income earned within a country in a given year (see Chapter 13). Thus, the data in the first column tells how much of each country's total income was spent on healthcare. The numbers vary dramatically. The United States spent the most in 2014 at 17.1 percent of its GDP. Most countries spent between 9 and 12 percent of their respective GDPs, and Singapore spent just 4.9 percent of its GDP.

The second and third columns of Table 12-1 give each country's life expectancy at birth and infant mortality rate. Although the United States spends substantially more than others on healthcare, it doesn't achieve the best results on these two measures. In fact, it's in last place on both!

In contrast, Singapore does best on both measures despite spending far less. Even more remarkable: In almost every health-quality category monitored by the World Health Organization, Singapore is either number one in the world or near the top of the list. The natural conclusion is that it's possible to get very good healthcare without spending very much money.

Inflated Demand: Suffering from "Free" and Reduced-Cost Healthcare

The quantity demanded of any good or service — including healthcare — depends on the price faced by consumers. The lower the price, the more people want to buy. This relationship is called the *law of demand*, and it explains many of the cost and efficiency problems that result when healthcare is delivered with artificially low prices through either insurance systems or national health systems. This section explores the problems with an increased demand caused by artificially low prices.

Diverting funds to lower-value uses

REMEMBER

People stop self-rationing when prices are set at artificially low levels. When healthcare has an artificially low price, some of it will end up being devoted to lower-value uses, which reduces efficiency:

>> **Treating minor problems:** When visiting a doctor costs, say, $25, many people with minor problems will skip going to the doctor because they view their problems as not worth the cost of the office visit. But if visits are free, many people with minor problems such as colds and backaches will come in. This means that a large number of patients with very minor problems will be competing for the limited supply of medical services with people having more serious problems.

>> **Testing for uncommon diseases:** For many diseases, preventive care for a large number of people costs more than waiting for the relatively few people who will develop the disease to show symptoms. Doctors don't know who may be in danger, so they run the diagnostic tests on everyone — including those who wouldn't have ended up suffering from the disease anyway. Diagnostic tests are often quite expensive, so the costs of early detection often exceed the money saved by avoiding the treatment of the disease in its advanced stages.

>> **Performing elective surgery:** Artificially low pricing diverts resources to purely elective (rather than necessary) medical procedures. Consider knee surgery. At a price that reflects the full cost of performing surgery, only a relative few will opt to pay for elective knee surgery. But with surgery available at an artificially low price, many more will opt for the procedure. The resources required to perform those surgeries —operating room space, the time of doctors and nurses, anesthetics —could've been used to treat patients with more life-threatening problems.

>> **Choosing expensive new treatments:** Artificially low prices promote the use of costly new medical procedures that are only marginally better than older procedures. Consider radiation treatments for cancer. Old methods bombard tumors with X-rays; new methods bombard tumors with protons. Do protons work better? Nobody is sure. But artificially low prices make the two treatments appear to be about equally costly, so many patients and doctors opt for the costly new method.

The inefficiencies caused by artificially low healthcare prices are system-wide and lead to such massive increases in demand that severe rationing systems have to be imposed to prevent spending from spiraling out of control.

Rationing healthcare

Some government healthcare systems provide care free of charge to residents, so the price of healthcare as seen from the viewpoint of consumers is zero. Applying the law of demand, you can immediately understand that people demand a lot more healthcare at the zero price than they would if they had to pay even a moderate price.

The government must cope with the high demand induced by "free" healthcare. The problem, of course, is that healthcare is not actually free. Hospitals must be built and maintained, doctors and nurses must be paid, and medicines must be purchased. Thus, the government develops methods to limit the amount of healthcare supplied to a level that the government can actually afford. Each method is a different form of rationing. Here's how these methods work for the United Kingdom's National Health Service:

>> **Increased wait times:** The simplest rationing method is waiting. In 2017, patients in the United States waited an average of 3.5 weeks to see a specialist. By comparison, the United Kingdom's National Health Service that year abandoned its previous goal of getting patients to specialists within 18 weeks. The NHS was forced to abandon that target because so many patients had been waiting even longer and because the NHS was struggling to even get patients to general practitioners quickly enough. The long waiting times for both specialists and general practitioners imposed a nonmonetary cost that helped equalize the limited resources that the National Health Service could afford with the high quantity of services demanded by patients who thought of healthcare as being "free."

>> **Denial of service:** Another tactic is denial of service based on cost considerations. To that end, the National Health Service has established the National Institute for Health and Clinical Excellence — or the NICE committee, as it's better known. Just how nice is the NICE committee? Well that depends on your medical condition. The NICE committee has decided on a general limit of £30,000 (approximately $44,000) on the cost of extending a life for a year. Applying that rule to a specific situation, if an anti-cancer treatment would cost more than £30,000 to extend a cancer patient's life for a year, the National Health Service won't pay for it. This cost rule keeps a lid on expenditures, but it forces those with costly treatments to fund their own medical care.

Facing shortages and higher prices

Health insurance isn't free, because premiums must be paid by individuals, firms, or government. But at the moment of use, the effect of health insurance is to vastly increase the demand for healthcare by making healthcare look artificially inexpensive. This happens because most health insurance policies require only modest cost-sharing on the part of consumers. For instance, a patient who's prescribed a $1,000 treatment of medication may only have to pay 10 percent of the cost, or $100, out of her own pocket because the insurance company pays for the other 90 percent. The result is a stressed healthcare system that's overwhelmed by the levels of demand.

Note that this is the case whether the insurance system is completely government-run, as in Canada, or is largely in private hands, as in the United States. Increasing demand has two predictable effects:

>> **Shortages:** In government-run systems, where the government can fix prices, increases in demand cause shortages unless the government chooses to spend the money necessary to increase supply. The Canadian government has been unwilling to do that and has instead relied on rationing. It employs both long waiting times for various services as well as other regulations that deny care (see the preceding section). That said, Canada's strategy of delaying or denying care does limit spending. That's why Table 12-1 shows that Canada spent only 10.4 percent of its GDP on healthcare in 2014.

>> **Higher prices:** In systems where healthcare prices are free to rise in response to increases in demand, prices rise. For instance, the United States spent 17.1 percent of its GDP on healthcare in 2014 because its prices could respond to the increases in demand caused by low out-of-pocket costs. This dynamic has only gotten worse over time because the percentage of total healthcare spending that comes directly out of consumers' pockets fell from almost 50 percent in 1960 to only 11 percent in 2016. The lower the percentage falls, the more healthcare looks "free" at purchase. And the more it looks "free," the more of it people demand (including expensive new technologies), driving up prices further.

Combatting inefficiency with bureaucracy

With artificially low prices, people do not engage in enough self-rationing (as they would if prices were higher). But rationing must still happen in some form or another because quantities demanded exceed quantities supplied. As a result, insurance companies and national health systems have attempted to develop bureaucratic systems that should, ideally, address those inefficiencies. Specifically, they allocate the limited supply of care as efficiently as possible — that is, to the sickest and most deserving patients.

For example, one system forces patients to visit "gateway doctors" before getting access to expensive specialists. The gateway doctors are tasked with saying *no* to most requests on the basis of preapproved regulations. Unfortunately, these bureaucratic systems are often perceived as heartless, inflexible, and rule-bound by consumers who would prefer that their doctors be free of preapproved regulations when suggesting treatment options.

Even worse, the attempt to use a bureaucracy to allocate scarce resources efficiently appears to fail in most cases. (Check out the nearby sidebar on Gammon's law, which explains that many medical bureaucracies are so inefficient that allocating them more resources leads to *reductions* in measurable outputs of medical services!)

INPUT UP, OUTPUT DOWN

In the mid 1970s, an English medical doctor named Max Gammon noticed that, between 1965 and 1973, the number of hospital personnel within the United Kingdom's National Health Service (NHS) had increased by 28 percent while the average number of beds occupied each day had decreased by 11 percent, despite an ongoing shortage of beds. Thus, over an eight-year period, the NHS saw a substantial increase in staff numbers accompanied by a substantial decrease in the number of patients served. Nobel Laureate Milton Friedman would later summarize this finding in just four words: "Input up, output down."

Gammon argued that it was nearly impossible for the NHS's senior managers to get enough information about how the entire system operated to make effective rules for the system as a whole. Regulations designed at the center ended up contradicting each other or incentivizing undesirable and inefficient changes, such as doctors and nurses abandoning patient care because higher salaries and greater prestige were only available if they transitioned into administrative positions. Larger budgets only made this problem of "bureaucratic displacement" worse because larger budgets increased the size and complexity of the system — thereby necessitating additional rules and additional bureaucrats to administer those rules.

Bureaucratic displacement has continued to plague the NHS. When Tony Blair took over as the United Kingdom's Prime Minister in 1997, he promised both a massive increase in healthcare funding as well as 2 percent per year productivity growth at the NHS. He only delivered on the massive increase in funding. Between 1997 and 2008 the United Kingdom's real (inflation-adjusted) healthcare expenditures more than doubled, but hospital productivity declined by 1.7 percent per year. Even worse, the number of hospital beds fell nearly 18 percent, continuing the trend Gammon had identified back in the 1970s. They would fall by another 18 percent between 2008 and 2016, even as the inflation-adjusted NHS budget increased by an additional 30 percent, to more than £133.3 billion per year. This is especially perplexing because bed shortages are an ongoing problem.

How does one avoid bureaucratic displacement? Singapore offers some hints. As pointed out in Table 12-1, Singapore runs the world's lowest-cost healthcare system. Max Gammon would not be surprised to learn that it's also highly decentralized, with an unusually high fraction of decision-making undertaken by doctors and patients (rather than by central planners). The results in terms of efficiency are startling. Singapore uses fewer doctors, nurses, and dentists per capita relative to any other developed nation while generating what are arguably the world's best overall healthcare outcomes. Relative to other healthcare systems, it achieves "Input down, output up."

Investigating Singapore's Secrets

Offering "free" healthcare, reduced-cost care, and health insurance all have drawbacks (see the earlier sections in this chapter). However, Singapore has managed to create a set of medical institutions that delivers world-class healthcare while somehow spending 50 percent less than Canada and 70 percent less than the United States. This section explains how.

Exploring cost-saving features

The secret to Singapore's success has been a unique blend of private and public medical funding that keeps costs down by paradoxically making people pay a lot of money out-of-pocket for their care. It also ensures that the poor will be cared for.

REMEMBER

Singapore's healthcare system has three main cost-saving features:

>> **Government mandates to encourage competition:** Singapore encourages competition by requiring hospitals to post prices for each of their services on the Internet. Armed with this information, patients can shop around for the best deal. The government also publishes the track record of each hospital on each service so that patients can make informed decisions about quality as well as price.

>> **High out-of-pocket costs for consumers:** Singapore insists upon high out-of-pocket costs to avoid the overconsumption and high prices that result when insurance policies pick up most of the price for medical procedures. Indeed, out-of-pocket spending represents about 92 percent of all private healthcare spending in Singapore, compared to just 11 percent in the United States.

>> **Laws requiring people to save for future health expenditures:** Having to pay for most medical spending out of pocket means that Singapore's citizens are faced with having to pay for most of their healthcare themselves. How can this be done without bankrupting the average citizen? The answer is mandatory health savings accounts.

Singapore's citizens are required to save about 6 percent of their incomes into MediSave accounts. MediSave deposits are private property, so people have an incentive to spend the money in their accounts wisely. But the citizens of Singapore also know that they won't be left helpless if the money in their MediSave accounts runs out. The government subsidizes the healthcare of those who have exhausted their MediSave accounts as well as the healthcare of the poor and others who have not been able to accumulate much money in their MediSave accounts.

Singapore's health ministry is still very much involved in policing doctors and hospitals for safety and in providing healthcare to the poor. In fact, about one-third of all healthcare spending in Singapore is paid for by the government on behalf of the poor. But Singapore restricts its direct management of the healthcare system by allowing high-out-of-pocket costs to ration care and direct the entrepreneurial efforts of medical researchers.

Weighing costs and benefits of medical procedures

Crucially, the prices patients pay in Singapore are not artificially low. Unlike in the United Kingdom, where healthcare looks free, or the United States, where it looks artificially inexpensive due to insurance's picking up most of the bill, the residents of Singapore are faced with the full prices of medical procedures. This causes them to self-ration, voluntarily choosing not to go to the hospital for minor problems. That frees up resources for doctors and nurses to concentrate on treating serious cases.

Singapore's residents typically make very sensible decisions when weighing the costs and benefits of various medical procedures. In fact, having to pay high out-of-pocket costs *encourages* good-decision making because people who have to pay their own money for healthcare generally spend a lot more time educating themselves about their options.

Supporting cost-cutting innovations

Singapore's system of individual self-rationing has meant that Singapore has not had to set up a bureaucracy to ration care. The absence of such a bureaucracy promotes innovation because instead of red tape, there are profit incentives. These incentives are especially helpful in motivating medical entrepreneurs to figure out innovative methods for reducing costs.

To see the power of profits, consider the fact that a medical doctor in the United Kingdom who comes up with an innovation will get no reward from that country's National Health Service. Indeed, her innovation will probably never be implemented, because dozens of committees would have to give their approval before her idea could be carried out. By contrast, a doctor with such an idea in Singapore could put it into practice quickly.

REMEMBER

Self-rationing affects the types of medical research in Singapore versus in other countries. With individual self-rationing, more research is devoted to reducing costs so that consumers can pay less. Typically, that has nothing to do with inventing a new way of treating a disease but rather with figuring out how to make an effective older treatment less expensive. Thus, some hospitals in Singapore can do an open-heart surgery for only $20,000, versus about $100,000 in the United States.

By contrast, the incentives facing medical researchers in the United States are very different. In the United States, most research is funded by the government and directed toward developing new treatments. Success is measured by whether the new method works in the sense of curing the disease or healing the wound; whether it does so substantially better than currently available methods when costs are taken into account is not a high priority.

The incentives facing the United States' medical research system lead to a paradox: On one hand, they result in the United States having the world's most cutting-edge medical technologies. On the other hand, many are hideously expensive and only marginally better than what was available before. From a cost-benefit perspective, the development of such technologies is wasteful.

Trying to copy Singapore's success

No other country has copied all three of Singapore's cost-reducing policies. But recent experiments suggest that huge savings can result from implementing just one: high out-of-pocket costs. A couple of examples, one a state government and one a private company, show some promise.

In 2007, Indiana introduced a new healthcare option for state employees. Any employee choosing this option received $2,750 in a health savings account plus an insurance policy that covers 80 percent of any medical expenses between $2,750 and $8,000 and 100 percent of any expenses above $8,000. Thus, any employee volunteering for the plan had to pay 100 percent of all spending up to $2,750 from his or her health savings accounts.

These high-out-of-pocket expenses encourage prudence. Indeed, those who opted for the plan visited doctors and emergency rooms two-thirds less often than they did before, were half as likely to be admitted to a hospital, and spent $18 less per prescription than state employees who opted to stick with the state's traditional health insurance option.

These changes in behavior led to a 35 percent decline in total healthcare spending for those who volunteered for the new plan versus those who stuck with the traditional option. An independent audit showed that participants in the new plan weren't cutting corners by skimping on cost-effective preventive care like annual physicals and annual mammogram screenings. Thus, the savings appear to be permanent and sustainable. The program is also popular, with positive personal recommendations causing voluntary participation to rise from 2 percent of state employees in the program's first year to 70 percent of state employees in the program's second year.

Similar programs implemented by private companies like Whole Foods Market also show 30 to 40 percent cost reductions. Thus, it's clear that substantial costs savings can be achieved by simply confronting consumers with nonsubsidized prices that must be paid for with out-of-pocket spending.

Even greater savings can presumably be achieved by implementing Singapore's two other cost-saving policies: encouraging competition and mandatory savings. Encouraging competition would likely lead to improved services at lower costs, and mandatory health savings would presumably make people even more cautious with out-of-pocket spending because they would be aware that they were very much spending their own money.

Widely implementing Singapore's innovations may be difficult, however. Many individuals and firms do very well financially under the healthcare systems currently in place. They may be reluctant to support innovations, as may the politicians who helped build the current systems.

» Explaining how evolution delivered a brain prone to systematic error

» Understanding heuristics and cognitive biases

» Probing prospect theory

» Focusing in on myopia and time inconsistency

» Assessing the evidence for fairness and non-self-interested behavior

Chapter **13**

Behavioral Economics: Investigating Irrationality

R emember that Victorian-era historian, Thomas Carlyle? He was the one who skewered economics as "the dismal science" in the late 19th century. Fortunately for everyone, behavioral economics popped onto the scene in the late 20th century. Within a few short years, a lot of the dismal became dazzling.

Explaining the Need for Behavioral Economics

Conventional 20th-century neoclassical economics makes many accurate predictions about human choice behavior and how it responds to financial incentives and incrementally changing prices. But when the decisions involve uncertainty and require the chooser to risk or commit or trust, neoclassical predictions often fail.

The key underlying problem is that real people are often irrational. That's problematic for neoclassical economics because neoclassical economics *assumes* that people are rational. Because rationality is at the heart of why neoclassical economics sometimes fails, let's begin our review of behavioral economics by precisely defining rationality.

REMEMBER

Rationality is defined by economists as decision-making that avoids systematic errors.

A *systematic error* is an error that you do over and over, as if you can never learn from your mistakes. A rational decision maker would not be subject to systematic errors. She would learn from her mistakes and figure out how to get what she wants for the least cost and effort. Outside factors might still derail things, but anything that the rational decision maker could have done to maximize her chances of success would have been learned and applied.

If people were always rational, then standard, mid-20th century neoclassical economics would have always generated reliable predictions about human decision-making. But people regularly and repeatedly engage in behaviors that reduce their likelihood of achieving what they want. They engage in systematic errors. Behavioral economics attempts to explain these systematic errors by combining insights from economics, psychology, and biology. The goal is to develop theories that can deliver more accurate predictions about human choice behavior, including all the irrational stuff.

Decades of research have allowed behavioral economists to develop theories that can explain why our brains employ error-prone mental shortcuts, why we don't save enough for retirement, why we fall for marketing gimmicks, and why higher incomes rarely lead to permanent happiness. Armed with those insights, behavioral economists have in some cases been able to develop beneficial correctives. And, least dismally of all, behavioral economists have found extensive evidence that people are not purely self-interested.

Complementing Neo-Classical Economics with Behavioral Economics

People aren't always irrational. They are sometimes very rational, and as a result, neoclassical economic models often make very good predictions about decision-making. That's why you should think of behavioral economics and neoclassical economics as *complementary* methods for trying to explain why people make the choices that we observe.

At the same time, it's important to realize that the two sets of theories are often radically different both in content and in what they imply about how we should approach the world. In particular, they end up having very different approaches to how we can help people to improve their situations.

In cases where people are being rational, a very simple way to help them is to offer them more options. After all, if they always act rationally and select the best option from whatever is available, they can only be made better off by offering them more options. Thus, neoclassical economists often try to solve consumers' problems by presenting them with additional options.

But in situations where people are making systematic errors, adding more options is unlikely to make things better. It may even worsen the situation because a systematic error would now have more options to play with. As just one example, if you have an impulse-eating problem, your life is not improved if your mom sends you a package of cookies in addition to a package of brownies. That's why behavioral economists focus on helping people make better choices from already available options.

Behavioral economists also tend to assume that complex decision-making situations will tend to be best explained by a combination of neoclassical economics and behavioral economics.

Let's analyze how people shop at a supermarket:

>> Neoclassical economics tells us that *incentives matter*. Customers care about prices. When prices go up, they buy less. When prices go down, they buy more.

>> Behavioral economics gives us the additional understanding that people tend to buy what they happen to see. This behavior is called *impulse buying*, and it falls outside of the neoclassicists' notion that the consumer calculates marginal utilities and compares prices. It also explains why grocery stores put the milk cooler at the back of the store — to force you to walk past lots of

other items and thus be more likely to see something tempting and make an impulse buy. And it's why they stock candy bars by the checkout lines — to tempt you with an impulse buy just as you are probably quite hungry from looking at everything else in the store.

But how did we end up with brains that need both rational, neoclassical models as well as irrational, behavioral models to explain? The answer is: four billion years of evolution.

Examining our Amazing, Efficient, and Error-Prone Brains

The most complex object in the known universe is the human brain, which has 100,000,0000,000 neurons sharing 10,000 times as many connections. This incredibly dense web of computing power allows us to observe our environments, think creatively, and interact with people and objects.

But despite all that processing power, the brain is quite prone to glitches. This is the result of four billion years of evolution having to deal with the fact that the world was a very tough place for our ancestors. Evolving bigger, smarter brains helped our ancestors survive, but bigger brains were costly in terms of calories. The modern brain, for instance, represents just 5 percent of your body weight but consumes about 20 percent of all your calories. So although there was evolutionary pressure to develop bigger brains, there was also a strong limiting factor in that finding enough calories to feed a bigger brain was very difficult before agriculture, fire, and modern hunting tools.

In response to the caloric constraint, evolution did two things: To the extent possible, it evolved a bigger (and hungrier!) brain. But it also generated many low-energy mental shortcuts, or *heuristics*, to help get the most decision-making power out of each ounce of brain tissue.

Deciphering heuristics

REMEMBER

Because they're shortcuts, heuristics aren't the most accurate mental processing options. But in a world where calories were hard to come by, a low-energy "good enough" heuristic was better than a "perfect but costly" alternative. In economic terms, there were diminishing returns to deploying additional units of brain power. Heuristics developed because the opportunity cost of perfection was too high.

The brain employs heuristics for nearly every type of action and decision that we make. Three examples will give you the general idea about how these mental shortcuts help to economize on calories and calculations:

>> **The gaze heuristic:** You're a centerfielder, and a baseball is hit in your general direction. If you lock your eyes on the ball and run so that the ball remains at the same angle above the horizon that it was at when you first locked your eyes on the ball, then provided you're fast enough, you will end up running wherever you need to be to catch the ball. This is the method actually used by people when catching fly balls. They don't use physics equations or an app to predict where to run to. They simply lock their gaze and run so as to keep the angle constant. It's a simple solution to a difficult problem.

>> **The steering heuristic:** You're riding a bicycle and moving forward. If you start to fall and you reflexively steer in the direction you're falling, you'll generate enough centrifugal force to stay upright long enough to steady the bike. This is what novice bike riders subconsciously learn to do: If falling to the right, steer right; if falling to the left, steer left. Will this basic rule always work? Not on ice, it won't. And not if you're standing still. But if you're moving forward, it gets the job done very nicely indeed.

>> **The recognition heuristic:** You're asked to guesstimate whether Munich or Stuttgart has the larger population. Most people don't know enough about Germany to give an informed answer to this question. But they'll often give the correct answer by choosing the city with the more recognizable name. The recognition heuristic often works because there's a positive relationship between population size and how often cities are mentioned in books, conversation, and social media.

Heuristics help us make decisions rapidly and at low cost. But the fact that they're hardwired means that expecting to avoid or unlearn them isn't practical. For the most part, we're stuck with them and prone to do whatever they suggest.

WARNING

This hardwiring can leave us vulnerable to being played by those who understand heuristics and are willing to use them against us. On the other hand, we can be helped by those who would like to place us in situations in which heuristics tend toward desirable outcomes. But if we cynically consider which of those two alternatives is more likely, we can see the wisdom of shoring up our defenses with more information about how our brains are structured and how their decision-making systems work.

Deconstructing brain modularity

The modern human brain has evolved with a modular structure, so that specific areas deal with specific sensations, activities, and emotions such as vision, breathing, and anger.

Located in the back of the head, adjacent to the entry of the spinal cord into the skull, the older parts of the brain control subconscious activities like breathing and sweating as well as automatic emotional reactions such as fear and joy.

Located up front, near the forehead, are the newer parts of the brain that allow creative thought, imagination about the future, and keeping track of your social network (Mark Zucker*who*?). These newer areas are largely under conscious control.

The differences between the older and newer brain modules allow us to think about decision-making as being controlled by two interrelated systems that were given really creative names: System 1 and System 2.

>> **System 1** is controlled by the older brain modules at the back of the head. System 1 produces quick, unconscious reactions and "gut instincts."

>> **System 2** is controlled by the newer brain modules up front. System 2 works more slowly, "thinks things over" deliberately, and delivers conscious calculations about how to handle various situations.

Some decisions are the result of your brain combining suggestions from System 1 and System 2. But you need to keep in mind that a large body of evidence suggests that the vast majority of decisions are probably either fully or mostly the result of System 1. That's very important because System 1 decision-making is prone to a wide variety of systematic errors.

Cogitating on cognitive biases

REMEMBER

Cognitive biases are the misperceptions or misunderstandings that produce systematic errors. Cognitive biases fall into two categories:

>> Those resulting from faulty heuristics.

>> Mental-processing errors that are the result of attempting to use brains that evolved in much simpler times to solve modern problems. Our brains evolved before modern complexities such as calculus, computer science, and trying to figure out how to more "likes" on social media. So our brains simply haven't developed the tools necessary to solve these problems very well.

Imagine a vicious underworld populated by thinking mistakes, and you're looking at a line-up of "the usual suspects." Do you see some familiar bad guys here (and can you give personal examples of each of these biases)?

>> **Confirmation bias** is the common human tendency to pay attention only to information that agrees with, or confirms, one's preconceptions. This causes information that contradicts one's preconceptions to be ignored completely or rationalized away, and the incorrect opinion persists.

>> **Self-serving bias** refers to people's tendency to attribute their successes to personal effort or personal character traits but their failures to factors outside of their control. This bias makes it difficult for people to learn from their mistakes.

>> **The overconfidence effect** refers to people's tendency to be overly confident about the correctness of their opinions and judgments and to act without taking time to verify their initial hunches.

>> **Hindsight bias** occurs when people retroactively believe that they were able to predict past events. A faulty "I-knew-it-all-along" perspective causes many people to overestimate their predictive abilities.

>> **The availability heuristic** causes people to base their estimates about the likelihood of an event not on objective facts but on whether mental images of similar events are quickly and readily brought to mind. Events that carry vivid and emotionally charged mental images are presumed to be much more common than events that bring to mind dull or boring mental images. Shark attacks are in fact very rare, but the mental image of being attacked by a shark is extremely vivid for most people.

>> **The planning fallacy** refers to the tendency people have to substantially underestimate the time needed to complete a task. When a student waits until 2 a.m. to start cramming for an 8 a.m. exam and when Congress waits until right before its August recess before trying to pass a long-awaited reform, both are up against the planning fallacy.

>> **Framing effects** have to do with providing context, or framing, for a decision. Framing effects are in play when a change in context (frame) causes people to change their decision-making, and changes in context can cause extraordinary changes in behavior. When experimenters tagged an area with graffiti and scattered trash around, ordinary people were twice as likely to litter, steal, and trespass. Upscale retail marketers play the opposite game, spending on expensive packaging, displays, and even architecture to increase the perceived value of their merchandise — and, you guessed it, how much customers are willing to pay.

Surveying Prospect Theory

Neoclassical economics focuses much of its attention on consumer-choice situations in which people have to choose between different "goods," as when selecting items at a supermarket. But in the real world, people have to make choices that involve the possibility of "bads" as well — they have to deal with uncertainty and the possibility of bad outcomes as well as good ones.

REMEMBER

Prospect theory makes predictions about how people will make decisions when presented with both potential gains and potential losses. It's based on three key factors that influence how people choose in these situations:

» People judge good things and bad things in relative terms, as gains or losses relative to their current situation, or *status quo*.

» People experience both diminishing marginal utility for gains (each successive unit of gain feels good, but not as good as the previous unit) as well as diminishing marginal disutility for losses (each successive unit of loss hurts, but less painfully than the previous unit).

» People experience *loss aversion,* meaning that for losses and gains near the status quo, losses are felt much more intensely than gains — in fact, about 2.5 times more intensely.

In addition to shedding important light on how consumers weigh their prospects, prospect theory also provides insights into how advertisers select their tactics, how manufacturers decide on pricing, why people tend to save too little for retirement, and why people often can't stick to weight-loss programs.

To better see why psychologist Daniel Kahneman was awarded the Nobel Prize in Economics for developing prospect theory, this section reviews instances of consumer behavior that would be hard to explain without it.

RUNNING ON THE HEDONIC TREADMILL

Just as a person running on a treadmill gets nowhere, people trying to make themselves permanently happier by consuming more also get nowhere because they end up getting used to any higher level of consumption. Economist Richard Easterlin coined the term *hedonic treadmill* (pleasure treadmill) to describe this phenomenon. And in fact, surveys indicate that except for the extremely poor, people across the income spectrum report similar levels of happiness and satisfaction with their lives. This has led several economists, including Robert Frank, to argue that we all should stop trying to consume more because doing so doesn't make us any happier.

Shrinking packages and loss aversion

Because people see the world in terms of gains and losses relative to the status quo situations they're used to, businesses have to be careful about increasing the prices they charge for their products since consumers will tend to treat any price increase as a painful loss. This has led firms to develop a "workaround" that can help them raise prices without angering consumers.

About 100 years ago, when the Hershey's chocolate brand was closely identified with its 5-cent candy bar, the company would decrease the size of the nickel bar when the cost of raw materials rose and increase the size when the cost of raw materials fell. You might think of this as a way to shield customers from changes in raw materials prices. But if you think a little harder, you will realize that the input prices were still passed along as changes in how much (or little!) chocolate customers got for a nickel. The price *per ounce* still went up and down.

But Mr. Hershey understood that customers don't pay much attention to the price per ounce. They're fixated on the price per unit. He understood that any increase in the price per unit would be categorized mentally as a loss (higher prices!) relative to the 5-cent per unit status quo. Thus, he kept the price fixed at a nickel to avoid triggering people's sense of loss aversion.

This trick is now very well known, and many other brands including Haagen-Dazs, Kraft, Tropicana, and Bounty have reacted to rising input prices in recent years by reducing product sizes.

Framing effects and advertising

Because people evaluate situations in terms of gains and losses, their decision-making can be very sensitive to the mental *frame*, or context, that they use to evaluate whether a possible outcome should be viewed as a gain or a loss. In terms of prospect theory, the framing information defines the status quo and thus our sense of whether any possible outcome will be perceived as a gain or as a loss.

Here are two examples of *framing effects* and how changing the frame can flip your perception of whether a possible outcome is to be viewed as a gain or as a loss:

>> You're offered a salary of $100,000 per year. Nice! But what if you're used to earning $140,000 per year? Not nice.

>> You have a part-time job. Your boss walks in and says he's going to give you a 10 percent raise. Sweet! But then he says all the other part-timers will be getting a 15 percent raise. Sour!

WANNAMAKER'S WARNING

In the late 19th century, American entrepreneur John Wannamaker invented the department store, the price tag, and the money-back guarantee. But he was famously frustrated by marketing and advertising. "Half the money I spend on advertising is wasted — the trouble is, I don't know which half."

His frustration echoes today. Most advertising campaigns fail. Most movies flop. And 80 percent of new product launches are abandoned within three months. So while advertisers and marketers are constantly doing their best to get consumers to buy this or that — including trying to utilize behavioral economics to get people to do their bidding — we can go about our lives with a little smirk because most of their efforts seem to be pretty ineffective in altering our behavior.

Advertisers know how important context is and go out of their way to frame their offers as gains rather than losses. Think about ads for hamburger meat. If they say "80 percent lean," we think of the meat as offering gains to health; but if they say "20 percent fat," the same meat feels like a potential coronary.

REMEMBER

Any frame that alters gain-or-loss perceptions will affect purchasing decisions. So sellers go out of their way to frame potential purchases as gains rather than losses.

Anchoring and credit card bills

Before people can calculate their gains and losses, they must first define the status quo from which to measure those changes. Unfortunately, people's sense of the status quo can be distracted by irrelevant information, including irrelevant numbers.

Credit card companies know this trick, known as *anchoring*, because the irrelevant number can be used to anchor, or set, people's sense of what the status quo should be. Credit card companies do this by printing very small minimum payment amounts on monthly credit card bills.

The small minimum payment amounts can unconsciously set people's status quo in terms of how much they should pay each month. If that happens, then any higher amount would feel like a loss relative to the minimum monthly payment amount suggested by the credit card company. And that would make it harder to select a higher amount.

Getting you to select the very small minimum payment amount is in the better interest of the credit card company because they want you paying off your bill as slowly as possible so that they can charge you as much interest as possible. They try to anchor you at the very small amount they print as the minimum payment.

TIP

Here's a pro tip: Decide how much you want to pay before you see the bill. That way you can't be influenced by any information that might anchor you into paying too little.

Examining the endowment effect

If you show a person a new mug and ask him to put a price on it, he might say $10. But if you gift that guy the mug and then ask him how much you would have to pay him to buy it back, he will typically quote you a substantially higher price, like $15.

What's interesting is that the higher buy–back price isn't the result of his bluffing or attempting to drive a hard bargain. The way human brains are wired, people tend to put a higher valuation on anything that they currently possess, or are endowed with, than on identical items that they don't own but might purchase. This phenomenon is called the *endowment effect*. It shows up all over the place, including with home purchases.

It appears that loss aversion is the likely culprit behind the endowment effect. Once you possess something, having it becomes your new status quo. And that means the prospect of parting with it would be perceived as a potential loss relative to the status quo of retaining possession. Consequently, people demand more money to part with something they currently possess than they would to purchase the same item if they didn't own it yet.

That difference in perceived value can be a problem for negotiations between buyers and sellers. The sellers will on average be demanding more than the buyers are going to be willing to pay.

Stipulating status quo bias

Prospect theory also explains *status quo bias*, which is the tendency people have to favor any option that's presented to them as being the default, or status quo, option.

The effect of status quo bias can be massive. Consider organ-donation programs tied to driver's license applications and renewals. In countries where the default option is donating your organs if you die in a car accident, nearly 100 percent of people are registered as donors. By contrast, in countries where the default option is *not* donating if you die in a car accident, only about 10 percent of people are registered as donors.

Both cases would require finding and filling out a form to switch the applicant away from the default option. And in both cases, hardly anyone bothers to find and fill out the form. They just go with whatever option was presented as the default, or status quo.

Prospect theory explains such examples of status quo bias as a combination of the endowment effect and loss aversion. Put into a novel situation, people will treat the default option as an endowment and will regard any other option as a prospect with the potential for loss. Loss aversion then kicks in and reinforces the appeal of the default option. The result is a bias toward the status quo and sticking with whatever the default option is.

Status quo bias was put to good use by researchers who wanted a simple method for increasing retirement savings. They made automatic enrollment into a savings program the default situation for thousands of workers. Those workers ended up saving far more than workers whose default option was to not be enrolled.

TIP

Such research leads to a more general point: Because people for the most part tend to stick with whatever the status quo is, why not make the status quo helpful or useful?

Countering Myopia and Time Inconsistency

Our distant forbears had to be almost entirely focused on the present moment — on how to avoid diseases and predatory animals and starvation, for example, and on how to get through the next few weeks or months.

That's why part of our genetic inheritance is our difficulty with long-run planning and decisions that involve trade-offs between the present and the future. Two of our major stumbling blocks are myopia and time inconsistency.

Focusing on myopia

In medicine, *myopia* means nearsightedness. People with myopia can see nearby objects clearly, but everything farther away looks blurry. By analogy, economists use *myopia* to refer to the fact that our brains have a hard time conceptualizing the future: It seems fuzzy, out of focus, and hard to see. That's why we have great difficulty imagining, for example, the additional spending power that will be ours in 30 years if we begin saving money now.

A primary consequence of decision-making myopia is that when a consumer is forced to choose between one thing that will generate benefits quickly and another thing that won't yield benefits for a long time, he will have a strong tendency to favor the more immediate option even if the long-run option would be well worth waiting for.

Consider having donuts today versus having an athletic figure down the line. Those donuts are close and warm and very tempting. You can smell and see them now. But the benefits of being in great shape in three or four years (washboard abs!) will seem relatively vague and far less pressing. Your brain will tell you to eat the donut — or two donuts — and thus lower the likelihood of your having a great physique in three years, even if that's something you genuinely want.

Tattling on time inconsistency

We view the future myopically from the here and now. This leads to a tendency to make bad predictions about what we'll want to do at particular points in the future.

Consider your 10 p.m. self setting an alarm for 6 a.m. the next morning, to get up and go to the gym. Your 10 p.m. self assumes that your 6 a.m. self will be on board with going to the gym once the alarm goes off. After all, it's the same you. But when the alarm goes off at 6 a.m., your 6 a.m. self doesn't want to go — and even turns the alarm off, goes back to sleep, and never gets to the gym.

The underlying problem is that your 10 p.m. self myopically fails to see how painful getting up and going to the gym is going to be. But when that moment arrives, your 6 a.m. self can see the pain very clearly. Thus, your 6 a.m. self makes a decision in the moment that your 10 p.m. self did not correctly anticipate the night before.

Economists refer to situations like this as being examples of *time inconsistency*. It happens whenever our current selves don't understand what our future selves will want once the future becomes the present.

GETTING GREEN THE MYOPIC WAY

Myopia causes consumers to focus too strongly on the up-front costs of installing solar panels. They can't see far enough into the future to appreciate the massive long-run savings they could achieve if they paid for solar panels now in exchange for cheap electricity in the future.

A company called Solar City has figured out a way to work with, rather than against, people's myopia. It does so by offering leasing and financing options that eliminate the need for consumers to pay for the up-front costs of installing a solar system. Instead, Solar City pays for the upfront costs and then makes its money by splitting the resulting cost savings with consumers.

This arrangement actually benefits from myopia because consumers get to focus on their share of the savings, which is immediately available. It's a great example of working with, rather than against, a behavioral bias.

Beating self-control problems with precommitments

Time inconsistency is a major cause of self-control problems. The misperceptions and misjudgments entailed by time inconsistency will subtly encourage people to put themselves in temptation's way. You can say today that you're going to spend three hours tomorrow working on your tax return. But when tomorrow comes around, you binge watch your favorite show instead.

Fortunately, behavioral economists have developed some techniques to help us take actions today that can help control our rascally future selves.

TIP

One of the leading strategies for dealing with time inconsistency is to make *precommitments* that aren't easily reversed by your future self. This strategy may include tactics such as setting multiple alarm clocks so that you can't easily get back to sleep when you're supposed to go to the gym; signing up for automatic payroll deductions so you don't have to decide every two weeks whether to save for retirement or blow all the money on Pokémon cards; and joining a weight-loss competition so that there will be ongoing social pressure to help keep you committed to reaching your weight-loss goals.

Gauging Fairness and Self-Interest

Neoclassical economics assumes that people are purely self-interested. Adam Smith, the founder of modern economics, put this idea into words in *The Wealth of Nations* in 1776: "It's not from the benevolence of the butcher, the brewer, or the baker that we expect our dinner, but from their regard to their own interest. We address ourselves not to their humanity but to their self-love, and never talk to them of our own necessities but of their advantage."

Whoa, lighten up, Mr. Smith! That sounds like it could have been written by Ebenezer Scrooge or the Grinch.

Yet don't judge Smith too quickly. He was a philosopher before he was an economist, and in his other famous book, *The Theory of Moral Sentiments*, Smith wrote, "How selfish soever man may be supposed, there are evidently some principles in his nature which interest him in the fortune of others and render their happiness necessary to him though he derives nothing from it except the pleasure of seeing it."

REMEMBER

Was Adam Smith an old softie from the get-go, despite his more famously quoted statement on self-interest? It appears so. And it appears that he was right to feel that way. Behavioral economists have amassed a pile of evidence that indicates that there is an ever-present human tendency toward altruism and caring about one's fellow man. Although self-interest is also always present, most people do care deeply about others and about the fairness of their own behavior in interactions with other people. For that reason, economic transactions are heavily influenced by moral and ethical factors.

Defining fairness

REMEMBER

In economics, *fairness* is a person's sense of whether a price, wage, or allocation is considered morally or ethically acceptable. Any tendency toward pure self-interest is modified by people's sense of fairness. In some cases, people go so far as to act precisely the opposite of how you would expect a purely self-interested person to behave. Examples include giving anonymously to charity, obeying the law even when there is zero chance of getting caught, and being willing to pay a premium price to purchase a "fair-trade" product.

Examining the experimental evidence for fairness

In recent decades, experimental games have been created to test people's feelings about fairness. One key feature is that the games are played for real money, so that participants have a strong incentive to act in a self-interested manner so as to win as much money as possible.

Another key feature is that players interact anonymously via computer screens. Economists provide that anonymity to give each player the chance to be a jerk without having to fear retaliation either during the game or afterward. That freedom from retaliation liberates players to use whatever strategies are most likely to maximize their own winnings during the game. The question is whether players will use that freedom to act in a purely self-interested manner — or behave more nicely.

The dictator game and the ultimatum game are two of the most famous. Each game involves two players.

Dishing on the dictator game

The experimental researcher who runs this game puts up a fixed amount of money, say $10, and designates one of the two players as the "dictator." The dictator's job is to determine the split — be it $10/$0 or $8.67/$1.33 or another division — between the dictator and the other player. The dictator chooses the division. The researcher executes it, paying each player his or her share. And the game ends.

The dictator game has been played hundreds of thousands of times all over the world. A review of the outcomes shows that roughly one-third of dictators keep all of the money for themselves. The other two-thirds of dictators show generosity by allowing the other player some money — on average, $4.20. Seventeen percent of all dictators split the money evenly, and 5 percent of all dictators give the entire amount to the other player.

REMEMBER

From such experimental results, behavioral economists have come to believe that some people are incredibly selfish, others are incredibly generous, and most of us are somewhere in between. But the most important thing to remember is that the most common behavior is to give a perfectly anonymous stranger a substantial share of the money even though there are zero consequences for being entirely selfish.

Unraveling the ultimatum game

This game is a bit more complex, represents a more realistic money-splitting situation, and is often played for higher stakes than $10. In this real-money, two-person game, there is no dictator who can unilaterally decide what the split will be. Instead, both players must jointly agree on any proposed division of the money in order for the split to take place.

In real-world markets where buyers and sellers interact voluntarily, a transaction takes place only when a proposal made by one party is accepted by the other. In the ultimatum game, one player is randomly assigned to function as *proposer* and the other as *responder* — and both face the possibility that if they can't agree, both will forgo all possible benefits.

The proposer issues an offer (the ultimatum) in which she suggests a split — perhaps 70 percent for herself and 30 percent for the other player — and the responder gets to either accept it or reject it. If the responder accepts the proposed split, the split is made, the game ends, and both players go anonymously on their way. But if the responder rejects the proposer's suggested split, neither player gets anything, and the game ends without anybody getting any money at all.

Here's what typically happens: Almost no proposers suggest allocating the money perfectly unfairly, 100/0 percent in their own favor. The large majority of proposers suggest either a perfectly equal 50/50 split or something close to it, like 55/45 percent.

REMEMBER

The key thing to notice is that proposers in this ultimatum game are even more considerate in their proposed splits than are dictators in the dictator game. That happens because the responders in the ultimatum game can be active and reject, whereas the second players in the dictator game must be passive and just take whatever the dictator proposes. The ability of responders in the ultimatum game to reject offers means proposers must be careful not to offend responders, especially responders' sense of fair treatment. That leads proposers toward suggesting very equal splits.

Digesting the experimental evidence on fairness

A good way to interpret the behavior we observe in the dictator and ultimatum games is to notice that the two games support both the gentler instincts discussed in *The Theory of Moral Sentiments* and the power of self-interest that features so prominently in *The Wealth of Nations*:

REMEMBER

>> The fact that dictators who face no possibility of retaliation on average give quite a bit of the money to the other player in the dictator game is consistent with human beings having an intrinsic sense of fairness that causes them to help others even when there's nothing in it for themselves.

>> The fact that splits become more equal when there's a threat of rejection in the ultimatum game shows that incentives for good behavior can make people behave even more fairly than they do when left completely to their own devices without any threat of punishment or retaliation.

The increased equality of splits that we see when both parties must consent to them gives us another way to understand Adam Smith's metaphor of the *invisible hand*. When people are constrained by having to consider the needs and interests of others, they tend to behave in more mutually beneficial, socially optimal ways — as if guided to do the right thing by an invisible hand.

That's a powerful result from two simple games. And it's yet another illustration of the dazzling insights that behavioral economics has delivered since it burst onto the scene back in the 1980s.

WARNING

NUDGING PEOPLE TOWARD BETTER OUTCOMES

Behavioral economists have begun "nudging" people toward better decisions by using gentle reminders or mild peer pressure. Many nudges can be implemented at extremely low cost. Here are some examples:

- Weekly text-message reminders increased attendance at adult literacy classes in England by 33 percent.

- Letters that told taxpayers in Guatemala that most of their neighbors had already paid their taxes tripled collections.

- Personal savings was increased by a factor of seven in the Philippines by offering people commitment savings accounts which restricted people from withdrawing money either until a specific date or until the account reached a specific dollar amount.

- Households slashed their electricity consumption substantially after an electric company started printing sad-face icons like ☹ on the bills of high-consumption households.

But before applauding these efforts too loudly, consider for yourself whether nudges are ethical. Would you be okay with being subconsciously manipulated if the manipulation helped you get something you desired?

4

Macroeconomics: The Science of Economic Growth and Stability

IN THIS PART . . .

Discover gross domestic product — the total value of goods and services produced in a country.

Probe inflation, price indexes, and interest rates to see how inflation is caused by printing too much money.

Explore the business cycle and why recessions happen.

Find out what government should or shouldn't do to fight recessions using tools like stimulus spending and fiscal and monetary policy.

Understand that borrowing and debt drive price bubbles and financial crises and why fiscal and monetary policy don't work very well after a financial crisis.

Chapter **14**

How Economists Measure the Macroeconomy

Macroeconomics studies the economy as a whole. Seen from on high, either businesses or the government produces goods and services. Businesses produce the bulk of what people consume, but the government provides many goods and services, including public safety, national defense, and public goods such as roads and bridges. In addition, the government provides the legal structure in which businesses operate and also intervenes in the economy to regulate pollution, mandate safety equipment, and redistribute income from the rich to the poor. (For more on the division of tasks between private businesses and the government, see Chapter 3.)

To study production, distribution, and consumption with any real understanding, economists must keep track of exactly how much is produced and where it all ends up. Consequently, economists have developed a huge accounting apparatus, called *National Income and Product Accounts* (NIPA), to measure economic activity. This system produces many useful statistics, including the famous *gross domestic product* (GDP), which measures the total quantity of goods and services produced in a country in a given period of time.

The system can seem arcane, but knowing the accounting is indispensable — it's the basis for all the mathematical models that economists use to understand and predict the business cycle, inflation, economic growth, and monetary and fiscal policy. (I present some of these models in Chapters 16 and 17.) So make sure to take, uh, proper account of what I'm about to show you.

Getting a Grip on the GDP (and Its Parts)

REMEMBER

Gross domestic product, or GDP, is a statistic that calculates the value of all goods and services produced in a given country in a given period of time. In the United States, the Bureau of Economic Analysis at the Department of Commerce computes this statistic every three months, giving an idea of how much economic activity took place in the previous quarter. Add up the numbers for four consecutive quarters and you get GDP for a year.

GDP is very important because higher levels of output afford greater access not only to essentials like good food and quality healthcare, but to a wide variety of goods and services that bring people pleasure and enjoyment. I'm not saying that money is the only thing that matters, but economists evaluate economies by how successfully they maximize happiness — and although money can't buy you love, it can sure as heck buy you a lot of other things that make you happy, such as food, education, and vacations. So, a high and quickly growing GDP is preferable because it reflects lots of economic transactions that provide people with the goods and services they desire. (To examine some reasons GDP may *not* always reflect increased happiness, see the later section "Watching GDP rise with the good, the bad, and the ugly.")

Chapters 2 and 3 discuss how people's fundamental economic goal is to maximize happiness given limited resources. Because people like to consume goods and services, measuring GDP allows economists to quantify, in some sense, how well a country is doing at maximizing its citizens' happiness given the country's limited resources. Rising GDP indicates that a country is figuring out ways to provide more goods and services that make people happy.

In this section, I show how and why the economists who tabulate the National Income and Product Accounts (NIPA) divide GDP into its constituent parts. Breaking up GDP lets you analyze each part separately and get a good handle on the major factors that influence the production of goods and services. But first, I give you a short explanation of what GDP *doesn't* take account of.

Leaving some things out of GDP

REMEMBER

The GDP statistic counts only transactions that involve money, so if you do volunteer work for your parents or if a mother stays home to take care of an infant, that economic activity — though very productive and socially beneficial — doesn't get counted in GDP.

In economies like the United States', GDP is very good at capturing nearly all output that's produced because almost everything that's produced within the U.S. is subsequently sold. But in a largely rural and agrarian society of small farmers, most production is for consumption within the household. Consequently, most of their output never makes it to the official GDP statistics.

WARNING

As countries transition from rural agrarian economies with lots of household production to market economies where nearly everything produced is sold for money, GDP appears to rise because a lot of output is being counted for the first time. But this apparent change may not be an increase in output. These limitations can make comparing the GDPs of various countries misleading.

Tallying up what counts in GDP

Counting sales where money trades hands can get a little tricky because both a buyer and a seller are involved in every such transaction. The money that the buyer spends has to equal the money that the seller receives. Translated into economist lingo, income has to equal expenditure. Consequently, you can measure GDP by totaling all the expenditures in the economy or by counting up all the incomes in the economy. If your calculations are correct, both methods give you the same value for GDP.

REMEMBER

When thinking about GDP, you also have to consider the goods and services that are being traded for money. Economists simplify life by saying that households directly or indirectly own all the resources or factors of production of a society — land, labor, and capital (see Chapter 3). *Households* can be made up of one person or several — individuals or families. *Firms* buy or rent the factors of production from the households and use them to produce goods and services, which are then sold back to the households. This process sets up a *circular flow* for resources moving from households to firms and goods and services moving back the other way, as Figure 14-1 shows.

Moving opposite to the flow of resources and goods are payments in dollars. When firms buy factors of production from households, they have to pay money to the households. That money is *income* to the households. And when households buy goods and services from the firms, they pay for those goods and services with money, which in Figure 14-1 are *expenditures*.

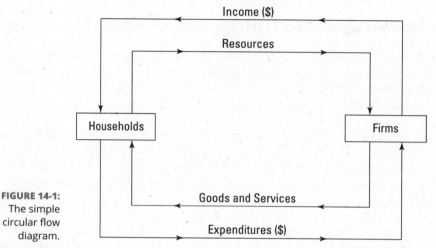

© John Wiley & Sons, Inc.

FIGURE 14-1:
The simple
circular flow
diagram.

REMEMBER

Households own firms; firms don't exist on their own. As a result, any money that a firm receives when it sells a good or a service flows on as income to some individual or group of individuals. Because of this, incomes in Figure 14-1 have to equal expenditures. Also, any resources that firms own — land, factories, mines, and so on — households also own because households own all the firms in the economy. Thus, all income generated by selling resources to produce goods and services flows directly or indirectly to households.

Accounting for streams of incomes, and assets

REMEMBER

Although you can use either incomes or expenditures to measure GDP, economists prefer to use incomes because governments make individuals and businesses keep track of every penny of income they receive so that it can be taxed. This requirement provides extensive, accurate data about incomes.

Tracing the flow of income

All the income in the economy flows into one of four categories:

>> Labor receives wages.

>> Land receives rent.

>> Capital receives interest.

>> Entrepreneurial ability receives profits.

Because you need land, labor, and capital to make things, you have to pay for them. That's why some of the income in the economy flows their way. But in a dynamic, competitive economy, you also need individuals who are willing to bear business risks like going bankrupt and who are willing to invest money in risky new technologies that may never catch on. To get them to do so, you have to pay them, so some income must also flow as profits to risk-taking entrepreneurs to compensate them for providing entrepreneurial ability.

Each of the four payments is a flow of money that compensates for a flow of services needed in production:

>> **Wages:** Workers charge wages for the labor services that they provide.

>> **Rent:** Owners of buildings and land charge rents to tenants for the services that real estate and physical structures provide.

>> **Interest:** Firms wanting to obtain the services of capital, such as machines and computers, must pay for them. This payment is considered interest because, for example, the cost of obtaining the services of a $1,000 piece of capital equipment is the interest payments that a firm must make on a $1,000 loan to buy that piece of equipment.

>> **Profits:** The firm's profits must flow to the entrepreneurs and owners of the firm, who risk that the firm may do badly or even go bankrupt.

Taking assets into consideration

What happens to the flow of income if a firm buys land and office space rather than rents it? Or if a firm owns its capital outright instead of borrowing money to buy it? If a firm owns these things, it no longer has to pay a flow of money to obtain a flow of services. Do expenditures still equal incomes? Yes: Incomes still equal expenditures. But you have to do some fancy accounting to see why. The key to this balancing act is understanding what an asset is.

REMEMBER

An *asset* is something durable that isn't directly consumed but that gives off a flow of services that you do consume. A house is an asset because it provides shelter services. You don't consume the house (just think of all the fiber!); you consume the services it provides. Similarly, a car is an asset because although you don't consume the car itself, it provides transportation services.

You often have a choice between buying an asset outright and thereby owning all the future services that the asset provides or letting someone else own the asset and sell you the services as they're produced. For example, you can buy a house and thereby get all future shelter services that the house provides, or you can rent the house and get those same services by paying for them each month. For this reason, an asset is considered to be a *stock*, and the services it provides are referred to as a *flow*.

REMEMBER

For all assets that a firm owns, accountants put a dollar value on the services that the assets provide based on what those same services would've cost if the firm had rented them. Accountants can then divvy up the firm's total income, calling some of it rent, some of it interest, and some of it profits, as though the owners of the firm were getting three streams of income.

Because the firm's owners provided the money to buy the firm's assets, part of their income is compensation for providing these goods and services, and the rest of their income is counted as compensation for providing entrepreneurship and taking on risk. Consequently, all the money expended on goods and services flows as income to somebody for providing land, labor, capital, or entrepreneurship (the four friendly factors of production). Under this methodology, incomes equal expenditures even if firms own their own assets.

Following the funds, around and around

The simple circular flow diagram of Figure 14-1 captures the fact that an income exists for every expenditure. However, because the diagram divides the economy only into firms and households, it misses a lot of the action that goes on in the real world. In Figure 14-2, you can see a much more realistic and detailed circular flow diagram that divides the economy into firms, households, and the government, with these entities making transactions in the following three markets:

» **Markets for factors of production:** Money is exchanged to purchase or rent the land, labor, capital, and entrepreneurship used in production.

» **Financial markets:** People who want to lend money (savers) interact with those who want to borrow money (borrowers). In these markets, the supply and demand for loans determine the *interest rate,* which is the price you have to pay to get someone to lend you his money for a while. Because most governments run deficits (in other words, they're always in the hole) and have to borrow a lot of money, they're major players in the financial markets.

» **Markets for goods and services:** People and the government buy the stuff that firms make.

In Figure 14-2, arrows show the flows of dollars throughout the economy. Firms make factor payments — rent, wages, interest, and profits — to households to obtain the factors of production — land, labor, capital, and entrepreneurial ability. (See the previous section "Accounting for the streams of incomes and assets" for details.) Households take the income they get from selling these factors and use it to pay for goods and services, to pay taxes, or to save. The government buys goods and services using either the tax revenues it takes in or the money it borrows in the financial markets. The financial markets also provide dollars for corporations to make investments. These dollars add to those that firms get from selling goods and services to households and the government.

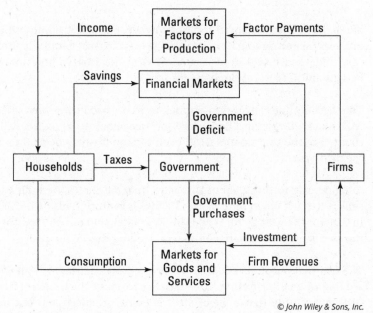

FIGURE 14-2
The detailed circular flow diagram.

© John Wiley & Sons, Inc.

REMEMBER

Not all transactions in the financial markets are relevant to the calculation of GDP. GDP measures currently produced output, and most transactions in the financial markets are trading property rights for stuff produced long ago. For example, a house that was built 30 years ago has nothing to do with current production, so the sale of the house doesn't factor into this year's GDP. Only the sales of newly constructed houses figure into this year's GDP.

Counting stuff when it's made, not when it's sold

Newly produced output is counted as part of GDP as soon as it's produced, even before it gets sold. That makes keeping track of the money associated with new production a little tricky.

For example, as soon as construction on a new house is completed, its market value of $300,000 is estimated and counted as part of GDP right then, even though the house may not be sold for months. Suppose construction is completed on December 29, 2020, adding $300,000 to the year 2020's GDP. If the house is sold on February 21, 2021, it doesn't count in the year 2021's GDP because double counting isn't allowed.

When the house is sold, it's considered old property and not new production. Economists just say that the property right to this now-old house has changed hands from the builder to the new owner. Because trading old assets obviously involves no new production, it doesn't count in GDP. Similarly, items such as used cars and used books don't count in GDP, no matter how many times they're bought and sold in resale markets.

This accounting convention applies to firms producing any sort of output good whatsoever. If Sony produces a TV on December 31, 2020, the value of that TV is counted in the year 2020's GDP, even though it won't be sold to a customer until the next year.

TIP

A handy way to think about this is to imagine that Sony builds the TV and then sells it to itself when putting the TV into inventory. This "sale" is what's counted in GDP for the year 2020. When the TV is later sold out of inventory to a customer, the sale is just an exchange of assets (trading the TV for cash).

WARNING

The fact that output is counted when it's produced rather than when it's sold is a red flag when interpreting GDP statistics to gauge the health of the economy. High GDP means only that a lot of stuff is being produced and put into inventory. It doesn't necessarily mean that firms are selling lots of stuff.

Economists who try to forecast where the economy is heading pay much more attention to inventory levels than they do to last quarter's GDP. Why? Because it's quite possible that although GDP is high, the economy is about to go into a recession because inventories are piling up and managers will soon cut back on production in order to get inventories back down to target levels.

Watching GDP rise with the good, the bad, and the ugly

Generally speaking, higher GDP is better than lower GDP because more output produced means higher potential living standards, including better healthcare for the sick and more money to aid the needy. But higher GDP doesn't guarantee that happiness is increasing, because GDP often goes up when bad things happen. For instance, if a hurricane destroys a big section of a city, GDP goes up as reconstruction kicks into gear and lots of new output is produced to replace what was destroyed. But wouldn't it have been better not to have had the hurricane in the first place?

Similarly, higher GDP may be possible in certain situations only if you're willing to tolerate more pollution or greater income inequality. Countries experiencing the early stages of industrialization and quickly rising living standards often also get dirtier environments and more social unrest because some people are getting richer much faster than others. The GDP number doesn't reflect these negative outcomes.

GDP also doesn't count the value of leisure. Many of my favorite times have been when I was neither producing nor consuming anything that would count in GDP — sitting on the beach, climbing a mountain, taking a walk, working out with friends. Moreover, an increase in GDP often comes at the price of sacrificing these leisure activities — meaning that when you see an increase in GDP, overall well-being or happiness hasn't necessarily improved. So although policies that raise GDP are generally beneficial for society, you must always examine the costs involved in creating the rising output.

Diving In to the GDP Equation

Now's the time for you and GDP to make friends so you can understand all of GDP's little secrets — in particular, its constituent parts and how they behave. The discussion in this section is interesting by itself, but it's doubly useful because it makes the standard Keynesian macroeconomic model (which I introduce in Chapter 16) much easier to understand and manipulate.

In the section "Tallying up what counts in GDP," earlier in this chapter, I explain that you can measure GDP either by adding up all the expenditures made on purchasing goods and services or by adding up all the incomes that are derived from producing goods and services. The two numbers have to be equal, so this switch to the expenditure method of counting up GDP is totally kosher. (It's also the perfect opportunity for you to understand the economy from the point of view of where money is spent, as opposed to who gets to keep what's earned.)

REMEMBER

The expenditure equation for totaling up GDP adds together the four traditional expenditure categories — consumption (C), investment (I), government spending (G), and net exports (NX). Their sum is abbreviated with the symbol Y and is equal to the value in dollars (or whatever currency a given country is using) of all goods and services produced domestically in that country during a given period of time (typically a quarter or a year). In terms of algebra, the GDP equation looks like this:

$$Y = C + I + G + NX$$

Here's a quick look at the four expenditure variables that total up to GDP:

>> **Consumption:** C stands for consumption expenditures made by households on goods and services, whether produced domestically or abroad.

>> **Investment:** I stands for investment expenditures that firms make on new capital goods, including buildings, factories, and equipment. I also contains changes in inventories, because any goods produced but not sold during a

period have to go into firms' inventories and are counted as inventory investments.

» **Government expenditures:** *G* stands for government expenditures on goods and services (they've got to buy paperclips for all those government documents).

» **Net exports:** *NX* stands for net exports, which are all a country's exports *(EX)* minus all its imports *(IM),* or $NX = EX - IM$. *EX* is the number of dollars of your nation's output that foreigners are buying. *IM* is the number of dollars of their output that your country is buying.

These four expenditures make up the GDP because, as a group, they buy every last bit of output produced in your country in a given period. The following subsections give more detail about each one.

"C" is for consumption (that's good enough for me!)

Household consumption spending accounts for about 70 percent of GDP — far more than the other three GDP components combined. Many factors affect how much income households decide to spend on consumption and how much of it they decide to save for the future.

Microeconomists spend a lot of time studying the various factors that affect such decisions, including expectations about whether the future looks bright or dark and how high or low the rates of return are on savings. (See Part III of this book for info on microeconomics.) Macroeconomists, on the other hand, step back from these factors because, when studying the economy as a whole, what matters is the amount of total consumption across the entire economy rather than the consumption decisions of particular households or individuals.

TIP

Macroeconomists model consumption very simply, as a function of people's after-tax, or *disposable*, incomes. You can derive disposable income algebraically using this handy three-step process:

1. **Start with *Y*, the total income in the economy.**

In Keynes's equation, *Y* equals total expenditures, but because income equals expenditures, you can use it for income as well. Remember that any money you spend is income to someone else.

2. **Figure out how much taxes people have to pay.**

   For simplicity's sake, assume that the only tax is an income tax and that the income tax rate is given by t. For instance, $t = 0.25$ would mean a tax rate of 25 percent of people's incomes. Consequently, the total taxes people pay, T, will be given by $T = tY$ — the tax rate times the total income in the economy.

3. **Subtract people's taxes, T, from their incomes, Y, to figure out their after-tax incomes.**

   Economists refer to this value as *disposable income* and write it algebraically as YD. Subtracting taxes from income looks like this:

   $$Y_D = Y - T = Y - tY = Y(1-t)$$

After you derive disposable income, you use a very simple model of the consumption expenditures households make. The model says that consumption, C, is a function of disposable income and a couple other variables, C_o and c.

$$C = C_o + cY_D$$

Lowercase c is called the *marginal propensity to consume*, or MPC. It's always a number between 0 and 1 that indicates the rate at which people choose to consume income rather than save it. For instance, if $c = 0.9$, then you consume 90 cents of every dollar of disposable income that you have after paying taxes. (You save the other ten cents.) The value of the marginal propensity to consume, c, is determined by the individual and varies from person to person, depending on how much of their disposable incomes they like to save.

You can think of C_o as how much people consume even if they have zero disposable income this year. (If you assume that $Y_D = 0$ in the equation $C = C_o + cY_D$, then that equation reduces to $C = C_o$.) But where does the money come from to pay for C_o if you have zero disposable income? It comes from your personal savings, which you've piled up over the years, or from borrowing from other people who've saved over the years.

TIP

What the overall equation $C = C_o + cY_D$ says is that the total consumption expenditure in an economy is the amount people consume even if they have no income (C_o), plus a part of their disposable income (cY_D).

For the rest of this book, I assume that the equation $C = C_o + cY_D$ is a good-enough model of how consumption expenditures are determined in the economy. It's not perfectly realistic, but it does show that higher tax rates reduce consumption and that people make decisions about how much of their disposable incomes to save or consume. The equation allows you to analyze the effects of policies that change tax rates and the effects of other policies that encourage people to spend higher or lower fractions of their incomes.

"I" is for investment in capital stock

REMEMBER

Investment is vital because the economy's capacity to produce depends on how much capital is available to make output. The capital stock increases when firms purchase new tools, buildings, machines, computers, and so on to help produce consumption goods. Investment is a flow that increases the capital stock of the economy.

Of course, capital wears out as it's used. Some of it rusts. Some of it breaks down. Some of it's thrown away when it becomes obsolete. Economists call all these flows that decrease the capital stock *depreciation.*

Naturally, firms must make some investments just to replace the capital that has depreciated. But any investment in excess of depreciation causes the overall size of the capital stock to increase, creating more potential output for people to consume.

REMEMBER

The flow of investment spending over any period of time depends on the comparisons that firms make between the potential benefits and the costs of buying pieces of capital. The potential benefits are measured in terms of potential profits, and the costs of buying are measured by the interest rate, regardless of whether a firm takes out a loan to buy a given piece of capital.

Why does the interest rate matter so much? Naturally, if a firm needs to take out a loan to buy capital, higher interest rates make the firm less likely to borrow money because the loan repayment costs will be high. However, even if a firm has enough cash on hand to buy a given piece of equipment, higher interest rates force the firm to decide between using the cash to buy the equipment and lending it to someone else. The higher the interest rates, the more attractive loaning it out becomes. Consequently, higher interest rates discourage investment regardless of whether firms have to borrow to fund investment. (See Chapter 2 for why higher interest rates increase the opportunity cost of investing.)

Economists model the amount of investment expenditure that firms desire to make, I, as a function of the interest rate, r, which is given as a percentage. The equation that I use here is standard in introductory books on macroeconomics (although notation does vary from book to book):

$$I_r = I_o - I_r r$$

This equation is similar in spirit to the consumption equation in the preceding section except for the minus sign, which indicates that when the interest rate rises, I falls.

The parameter I_r tells you how much I falls in an entire economy for any given increase in interest rates. For instance, suppose that r rises by 1 percentage point. If I_r is, say, 10 billion, you know that each percentage point increase in interest rates will decrease investment by \$10 billion.

The parameter I_0 tells you how much investment would occur if interest rates were zero. In truth, interest rates almost never fall all the way to zero, but suppose that they did. Then the second term in the equation would be equal to zero, leaving you with $I = I_0$.

TIP

The equation as a whole says that if interest rates were zero, investment expenditures would max out at I_0. But as interest rates rise above zero and keep on rising, investment falls more and more. In fact, rates could potentially rise so high that investment spending would fall to zero.

REMEMBER

The relationship between interest rates and investment is one reason the government's ability to set interest rates has great bearing on the economy. By setting interest rates, the government can determine how much businesses want to spend buying investment goods. In particular, if the economy is in a recession, the government can lower interest rates in order to raise firms' expenditures on investment and (hopefully) help improve the economy.

The big "G" (government, that is)

In most countries, the government consumes a huge portion of GDP. In the United States, government at the local, state, and federal levels consumes about 35 to 40 percent of the GDP. In many other countries, the proportion is even higher. In most of Europe, for instance, it's closer to 50 percent.

REMEMBER

The government gets the money to buy all that output from taxation and borrowing. If a government's tax revenues are exactly equal to its expenditures, it has a *balanced budget.* If tax revenues are greater than expenditures, it's running a *budget surplus.* But if the government's expenditures exceed its tax revenues (which the government can arrange for by borrowing the difference on the financial markets), the government will be running a *budget deficit.*

Governments borrow by selling bonds. A typical bond says that in exchange for \$10,000 right now, the government will give you back \$10,000 in ten years and, in the meantime, pay you \$1,000 per year for each of the intervening years. If you accept the deal and buy the bond, you're in effect lending the government \$10,000 right now and getting a 10 percent per-year return until the government gives you back your \$10,000 in ten years.

A huge amount of political maneuvering goes into determining how much a government is going to spend in a given year. Many groups lobby for special programs to benefit their hometown or their industry, and no matter what, governments have to provide for essential governmental functions such as national defense and law enforcement.

However, economists largely ignore the political machinations that go into determining government expenditures because the economic effects of government expenditure, G, depend on how big the expenditure turns out to be — not on how it got to be that size. So, for the rest of this book, I make the simplifying assumption that government expenditures can be denoted as

$$G = G_o$$

G is equal to some number, G_o, that the political process determines. G_o may be high or low depending on politics, but in the end, you care only about how big or small it turns out to be and can ignore where it came from.

TIP

G includes only government expenditures on newly produced goods and services. It doesn't include government expenditures that merely transfer money from one person to another. For instance, when the government taxes me and gives the money to a poor person, that transaction has nothing to do with currently produced goods and services and consequently doesn't count as part of G. So remember that when I talk about G, I'm talking about only the government's purchases of currently produced goods and services.

Measuring foreign trade with "NX"

When your country sells domestically made goods and services to someone or some firm in another country, such sales are called *exports*, or *EX*. When someone in your country buys something produced abroad, such purchases are called *imports*, or *IM*. Net exports, or *NX*, is simply the total value of all exports minus the total value of all imports during a given period of time (mathematically, $NX = EX - IM$). When using the expenditure method for totaling up GDP, you add in net exports, *NX*. But why add in only *net* exports?

The whole point of totaling up expenditures to get GDP is to figure out how many total dollars were spent on products made in your own country. Most of that expenditure is made by locals, but foreigners can also buy your products. That's exactly what happens when they pay you for the goods that you export to them. Consequently, you have to add in *EX* if you want to get a correct measure of expenditures made on stuff you produce domestically.

You have to subtract imports of foreign goods to differentiate the total expenditures that domestic residents make on *all* goods and services from their expenditures on *domestically made* goods and services. Total expenditures on all goods and services, both domestic and foreign, are C (as covered earlier). To get just the part that's spent on domestically made stuff, you subtract the value of imports, *IM*, because all money spent on imports is money that's *not* spent on domestically made goods and services. So C – IM gives the amount of money that domestic residents spend on domestically produced output.

The result is that you can write your GDP expenditures equation that totals up all expenditures made on domestically produced output as follows:

$$Y = C - IM + I + G + EX$$

But the equation normally puts the exports and imports next to each other:

$$Y = C + I + G + EX - IM$$

TIP

Rearranging the GDP expenditures equation to include *EX – IM* quickly reveals your country's *trade balance*. When *EX – IM* is positive, you're exporting more than you're importing; when it's negative, you're importing more than you're exporting. Economists like to present the math in a way that tells a little story. International trade is hugely important, and you should understand not only why trade balances can be positive or negative but also why you shouldn't necessarily worry if it's negative (covered next).

Making Sense of International Trade and Its Effect on the Economy

Modern countries do a huge amount of trading with other countries — so huge, in fact, that for many countries, imports and exports equal more than 50 percent of their GDPs. So now's as good a time as any to focus a little more deeply on the *NX* part of the GDP expenditure equation, $Y = C + I + G + NX$.

TIP

Understanding how international trade affects the economy is essential if you hope to have a complete understanding of macroeconomics. This understanding is also important because politicians are constantly suggesting policies, such as tariffs and exchange rate controls, that are aimed squarely at international trade but whose effects reverberate throughout the domestic economy.

This section explains why trade deficits (negative values of *NX*) aren't necessarily bad and why engaging in international trade — even when it means sustaining trade deficits — is typically hugely beneficial.

"Trade deficit" ain't fightin' words

If your exports exceed your imports, you have a *trade surplus,* and if your imports exceed your exports, you have a *trade deficit.* Unfortunately, the words *surplus* and *deficit* carry strong connotations that make surpluses sound like they're necessarily better than deficits. That's just not true, but you wouldn't know it from the rhetoric that politicians throw around. They make trade deficits sound as though they only lead to calamity.

WARNING

To focus on whether a trade deficit or surplus exists is to miss the point that international trade is a rearrangement of assets that makes everyone happier — even the country running the trade deficit. As long as international trade is voluntary, all trades enhance happiness, even if politicians say otherwise.

Consider two individuals who want to trade. Each person starts with $100 cash, and each produces a product for sale. The first guy grows and sells apples for $1 each. The second guy grows and sells oranges, also for $1 each. Each of them produces 50 pieces of fruit.

Next, suppose that the guy who grows apples really likes oranges and wants to buy 30 of them for $30, and suppose that the guy who grows oranges wants to buy 20 apples for $20. Each guy is happy to satisfy the other guy's desires, so the apple grower spends $30 buying oranges from the orange grower, and the orange grower spends $20 buying apples from the apple grower.

Their trades shouldn't cause any alarm bells to ring, but when people start looking at their trades using the terms *trade surplus* and *trade deficit,* they often come to the false conclusion that only one of the guys benefits from the trades that, in reality, they both were quite eager to make. To see where the confusion arises, notice that in the vocabulary of international trade, the apple guy exports only $20 worth of apples but imports $30 worth of oranges. The orange guy exports $30 worth of oranges but imports only $20 worth of apples. So, you have a situation in which the apple guy is running a $10 trade deficit and the orange guy is running a $10 trade surplus.

Does this mean that the apple guy is worse off than the orange guy? No. Each person started with $150 worth of stuff: their respective $100 cash piles plus $50 each worth of fruit. When they finish trading, they each still have $150 worth of stuff. The apple guy has $90 of cash plus $30 worth of apples and $30 worth of oranges. The orange guy has $110 of cash plus $20 worth of oranges and $20 worth of apples.

Saying that their trading has made either one poorer is way off the mark. In fact, both are happier with their arrangements of wealth after trading than they were before because their trades were voluntary. If the apple guy would've been happier keeping his initial $100 cash and 50 apples, he wouldn't have traded for oranges — and the same goes for the orange guy.

Considering assets — not just cash

To people who hate trade deficits, changes in cash holdings seem alarming. But when gauging whether trade is beneficial, you need to consider the value of the traded assets, not just how much cash each party ends up with. For instance, the fact that the apple guy's cash pile (see the preceding section) falls from $100 before the trade to only $90 after the trade looks spooky to deficit-haters because they're focused on the fact that the apple guy is $10 poorer in terms of cash after trading with the orange guy. And they're even more peeved because that $10 ends up with the orange guy, giving him a commanding $110-to-$90 advantage in terms of cash piles.

This perspective misses the fact that the apple guy's overall wealth is still $150 and he now has a distribution of assets that's more pleasing to him than what he had before. Deficit-haters respond to this by asking you what happens after the apple guy eats his 30 apples and 30 oranges and after the orange guy eats his 20 apples and 20 oranges. In the end, all that the two guys have left are their cash piles. Because the apple guy has $20 less cash than the orange guy, he must be worse off by running a trade deficit.

Again, this reasoning misses the point that the apple guy was happier trading and ending up with $90 of cash than he would've been not trading and having $100 in cash. If not for trade, he would've had a boring diet of only apples.

Opponents of trade deficits really make things seem scary when they start talking about land trading hands due to international trade. ("Oh no!" they say. "The foreigners are taking over our country!") To see their point, imagine that instead of starting with $100 each of cash, the fruit farmers each start with 100 acres of land worth $1 per acre. The only way for the apple guy to come up with $10 of cash to pay for his trade deficit is by selling 10 acres of land to the orange guy. That is, the overall exchange that they engage in is 20 apples plus 10 acres of land worth a combined $30 in exchange for 30 oranges worth $30. Because 10 of the apple guy's acres of land now belong to the orange guy, deficit haters think the apple guy sold out his country — literally.

Such transfers of property do happen in real life. During the 1980s, the United States ran huge trade deficits with Japan. The result was that Japanese corporations and individuals ended up owning many famous U.S. buildings and companies. This really spooked many jingoistic U.S. politicians, but they missed the point that all trading in life — be it with foreigners or fellow citizens — is designed to make both parties happy. After all, what good is keeping all your 100 acres of land if you're happier trading 10 of them for foreign-made goods? Or in the case of the United States during the 1980s, what good is continuing to own Times Square or Columbia Pictures if you'd rather trade them for Honda Accords and Sony VCRs? (The anti-Japanese hysteria at the time was even sillier given that the largest group of foreign owners of U.S. property was, and still is, the British!)

Much to the chagrin of economists, the argument that the point of trade is to make you *happier* doesn't always fly well. Many people view trade as an antagonistic contest to dominate other countries by running trade surpluses so that you eventually own all the other guy's assets. They argue for restrictions on trade designed to rig trade relations so that their own countries always run surpluses. But such policies inevitably fail because anytime you put up a tariff barrier or an import tax to discourage imports and improve your trade balance, other countries can do the same. The result of such trade wars is that all the barriers, restrictions, and taxes imposed by both sides reduce international trade to a trickle. No one comes out ahead, and no one's happy.

Consequently, for the last 70 years, national governments have increasingly pushed for fewer and fewer restrictions on international trade. This *free trade* movement has resulted in hundreds of millions of new jobs and a vast improvement in living standards and happiness because people all over the world are free to trade and buy whatever it is that makes them happiest — even if that means buying from a foreigner.

Wielding a comparative advantage

The argument that even countries running trade deficits are better off because they get to consume a mix of goods and services they couldn't get otherwise rests solely on the benefits of trading things that have already been produced. But an even better argument for international trade is that the trade actually increases the total amount of output produced in the world — meaning that there's more output per person, so overall living standards rise.

English economist David Ricardo developed this argument, known as *comparative advantage,* in 1817 as a forceful rebuttal against the import tariffs known as the *Corn Laws,* which heavily taxed imports of foreign-grown grain. These laws kept the price of grain high, so the nobility that owned the vast majority of farmland favored keeping them. Naturally, the poor were opposed because the laws drove up the price of their basic food supply: bread.

Ricardo pointed out that abolishing restrictions on international trade would, in addition to helping England's poor, actually make England and all the countries it traded with richer by encouraging them to specialize in the production of goods and services that each of them could produce at the lowest possible opportunity cost (in terms of other goods and services forgone). He demonstrated that this process of specialization would increase total worldwide output and thereby raise living standards.

You can most easily understand the logic behind the comparative advantage argument by thinking in terms of people rather than countries. Consider a patent lawyer named Heather and her brother Adam, a bike mechanic. Heather is very good at filing patents for new discoveries and is also very good at repairing bicycles — in fact, she's faster at that than her brother. Adam is a smart guy and can file patents, too, although not as quickly as Heather can. Table 14-1 lists how many bike repairs and patent filings each of them could do in one day if they put all their efforts into only one of the activities.

TABLE 14-1   ## Productivity for Heather and Adam per Day

Person	Patent Productivity	Bike Repair Productivity
Heather	6	12
Adam	2	10

In one day's work, Heather can produce 6 patents or repair 12 bikes; Adam can file 2 patents or repair 10 bikes. She is more efficient at producing both patents and bike repairs because she can convert one day's labor into more of either good than Adam can. Heather has an *absolute advantage* over Adam at producing both goods. She's the more efficient producer of both; with the same amount of labor input (one workday), she can produce more than her brother. Before David Ricardo came up with the idea of comparative advantage, the only thing anyone knew to look at was absolute advantage. And when they saw situations like that of Heather and Adam, they concluded (incorrectly) that because Heather is more efficient at both tasks, she has no need to trade with him.

In other words, people used to believe that because Heather is better than Adam at repairing bikes, not only should she work hard as a patent attorney filing lots of patents, but she should also fix her own bike whenever it breaks down. Ricardo pointed out that this argument based on absolute advantage is bogus and that Heather should, in fact, *never* fix bikes, despite the fact that she's the most efficient bike repairperson around. The nifty thing Ricardo realized is that the world is better off if each person (and country) specializes.

WARNING

Comparative advantage's insight is that the measure of cost when considering whether you should produce one good or another isn't how many hours of labor input it takes you to produce each one (which is the logic behind absolute advantage). The true cost is the opportunity cost of how much of the production of one good you have to give up to produce a unit of the other good.

To produce one patent, Heather must give up the chance to repair two bikes. To make one patent, Adam would have to give up the chance to repair five bikes. Heather is the lower-cost producer of patents and therefore should specialize in filing patents. And Adam should specialize in bike repairs because he's the lower-cost producer of bike repairs. In economic terminology, we say that Heather has a *comparative advantage* in the production of patents, whereas Adam has a *comparative advantage* in the production of bike repairs.

On a larger scale, countries should specialize in the production of goods and services that they can deliver at lower opportunity costs than other countries. If countries are free to do this, everything that's produced comes from the lowest-cost producer. Because this arrangement leads to the most efficient possible production, total output increases, thereby raising living standards.

Politicians often argue that countries shouldn't be "dependent" on other countries for various goods and services. Any policy that takes this warning seriously by impeding trade and specialization increases costs and makes total output fall. Rather, by letting comparative advantage guide who makes what, free trade increases total world output and thereby raises living standards. In free trade, each country specializes in its area(s) of comparative advantage and trades with other countries for goods and services it desires to consume.

REMEMBER

Don't be tricked by absolute advantage. Having an absolute advantage means you can make something at a lower cost as measured in inputs (Heather requires fewer hours of labor input to file a patent than Adam does). But what matters in life are outputs — the things people actually want to consume. By focusing on costs as measured in terms of alternative types of output that must be given up to produce a certain product, comparative advantage assures that you're focusing on being efficient in terms of what really matters: output.

Chapter **15**

Inflation Frustration: Why More Money Isn't Always Good

I nflation is the word economists use to describe a situation in which the general level of prices in the economy is rising. Although some prices may stay the same and a few may fall, the large majority of prices rise.

Inflation is typically mild, with the overall level of prices rising only a small percentage each year. But people dislike even mild inflation because — face it — who likes paying higher prices? Mild inflation also causes problems such as making retirement planning difficult. After all, if you don't know how expensive things will be when you retire, calculating how much money you need to be saving right now is hard.

Things can go from bad to worse if inflation really gets out of control and prices begin rising 20 or 30 percent per month — something that has happened in more than a few countries in the past century. Such situations of *hyperinflation* usually accompany a major economic collapse featuring high unemployment and a major decrease in the production of goods and services. (For more on prices and how they affect the economy, see Chapter 16.)

The good news is that economists know exactly what causes inflation and how to stop it. The culprit is a money supply that grows too quickly, and the solution is to slow or halt the growth of the money supply. Unfortunately, some political pressure is always exerted in favor of inflation so that simply knowing how to prevent inflation doesn't necessarily mean it won't develop.

In this chapter, I tell you about money and inflation, including why governments are often tempted to print a lot of money to pay for budget deficits, why doing so is actually a form of taxation, and why some constituency is always encouraging the government to go ahead and print a ton of money. I also show you why printing lots of money causes inflation, how to measure inflation, and how to measure the effect that inflation has on interest rates. One thing I don't tell you is how to print your own money — this ain't *Counterfeiting For Dummies*.

BEATING BARTER: SHOW ME THE MONEY!

Historically, people have used a wide variety of things as money:

- Seashells were used as money in ancient China, throughout the Pacific, and also by Native Americans.

- Boxes of cigarettes were used as money in prisoner-of-war camps during World War II.

- Various agricultural products, such as barley or cattle, were used as money by many cultures.

- Huge, doughnut-shaped stones were used as money on the island of Yap in the Pacific.

Eventually, most of the ancient world realized that metal made the best money. Metal doesn't wear out or shatter like seashells; it doesn't get moldy like barley; and it can easily be carried around in your pocket, unlike giant doughnut-shaped stones.

Shaping metal money into coins was a later innovation. The first metal monies had other shapes. Early Celts preferred ring money; ancient Mesopotamians liked long, helical ribbons of metal; and the ancient Chinese used metal monies cast in the shapes of knives and spades. Regardless of the shape or substance, nearly every society designated some good or other to serve as money. If they hadn't, they would've been stuck with barter — a fate everyone wanted to avoid.

Buying an Inflation: When Too Much Money Is a Bad Thing

I don't think I can overstate how important money is to the proper functioning of the economy. Without it, you'd waste most of your time *bartering*, or arranging trades of one good for another — kind of like in kindergarten ("I'll trade you my sandwich for your brownie"). Bartering works well only in the rare circumstance that you run into somebody who has what you want and who wants what you have.

In contrast, money provides a medium of exchange that allows you to trade for the brownie from the kid next to you, even if you don't have a sandwich. *Money* can be any good, object, or thing, but its defining characteristic is that it's accepted as payment for all other goods and services. In today's economy, people pay for things using a wide variety of monies, including government-issued coins and cash, checks drawn on private bank deposits, and electronic payments facilitated by debit cards and so-called crypto currencies. Because money affects nearly every economic transaction that takes place, money is at the heart of *macroeconomics*, the study of the economy as a whole.

As with everything in life, balance is essential. If a government prints too much money, prices go up, and you get inflation. If a government prints too little, prices go down, and you get deflation. But how much money is the right amount? And why does printing too much or too little cause inflation or deflation? In this section, I go into more detail about these money matters.

Balancing money supply and demand

Basically, money's value is determined by supply and demand (which I discuss in detail in Chapter 4):

>> The *supply* of money is under government control, and the government can very easily print more money anytime it wants to.

>> The *demand* for money derives from its usefulness as a means of paying for things and from the fact that having money means not having to engage in barter.

For any given supply of money, supply and demand interact to set a value for each unit of money. If money is in short supply, each piece of money is very valuable; fewer pieces of money translate into fewer chances to avoid having to engage in barter. But if the government greatly increases the supply of money, then each individual unit of money loses value because getting enough money together to avoid barter is easy.

CROESUS AND KUBLAI: THE KINGS OF MONEY

King Croesus of Lydia is usually given credit for solving the problem of bogus metal money. In the sixth century BC, Croesus issued the first government-certified coins that guaranteed purity and weight.

Lydia was located in what is now western Turkey, and soon all the major trading nations of the Mediterranean were using the new Lydian coins because they were by far the most trustworthy medium of exchange available. The new coinage gave Lydian traders a major advantage, and the kingdom soon became very wealthy, so much so that Croesus was considered the richest man in the world — even richer than King Midas (of *Midas touch* fame), whose gold Croesus minted into coins.

But coins are hard to carry around in large amounts, and it was up to the Chinese emperor Kublai Khan to create the first paper money in the 13th century. This paper money was actually a kind of precious metal certificate; people holding one of these certificates could go to a government vault and redeem it for gold. Consequently, the pieces of paper were as good as gold, but a stack of paper was a whole lot easier to carry than a heavy bag of coins.

Paper money was such a radical innovation that when Marco Polo came back from China and told Europeans about it, they laughed, unable to conceive of anything other than gold or silver coins serving as money. Their incredulity was hard to overcome, and after paper money fell out of favor in China, it would be centuries before another government issued any again.

TIP

Prices and the value of money are *inversely related*, meaning that when the value of money goes up, prices go down (and vice versa). To see how this relationship works, suppose that money is in short supply and is consequently very valuable. Because it's very valuable, it buys a lot of stuff. For instance, 1 dollar may buy 10 pounds of coffee (that's 10 cents per pound). But if money's very common, then each unit isn't very valuable. In this case, 1 dollar may buy only 1 pound of coffee (that's 1 dollar per pound). So the greater the supply of money, the higher the prices.

The demand for money tends to grow slowly over time. Growing economies produce more stuff, and consumers demand more money with which to buy the available stuff. Depending on how a government reacts to consumer demand for more money, three scenarios are possible:

>> **The government increases the supply of money at the same rate as the growing demand for money.** In this case, prices don't change. In other

words, if supply and demand for money grow at equal rates, the relative value of money doesn't change.

>> **The government increases the supply of money faster than the demand for money grows.** Here, inflation results as money becomes relatively more plentiful and each piece of money becomes relatively less valuable. With each piece of money possessing less value, you need more pieces of money to buy any particular item — which is the same as saying that the item's price will rise.

>> **The government increases the supply of money slower than the demand for money grows.** In this case, deflation results because each piece of money grows relatively more valuable. Buying any given good or service requires less money.

REMEMBER

You may be wondering whether there's any way to know exactly how much inflation you can expect from printing any given amount of extra money. You're in luck! The *quantity theory of money* states that the overall level of prices in the economy is proportional to the quantity of money circulating in the economy. *Proportional* just means that things go up by equal ratios or proportions, so the quantity theory can also be stated this way: If you double the money supply, you double prices.

PREVENTING INFLATION WITH A GOLD STANDARD

Until the early 1970s, printing new bills was difficult because most of the world's paper currencies were backed by a valuable metal, such as gold. Under this system, every piece of paper money circulating in the economy was convertible into a specific quantity of gold so that anyone holding cash could redeem their cash for gold anytime they wanted. For instance, in the United States, you could bring $35 cash to the U.S. Treasury and get exactly 1 ounce of gold.

This *gold standard* made it difficult for the government to devalue the currency by printing too much money because it first had to get more gold with which to back the new money. Because purchasing gold is expensive, governments were effectively restrained from increasing their money supplies.

But in 1971, President Nixon took the United States off the gold standard and on to the *fiat system,* in which paper currency isn't backed by anything. People just have to accept the currency as though it has value. In fact, *fiat* is Latin for "Let it be!" So when you say *fiat money,* you're basically referring to how a government creates money simply by ordering it into existence. The problem with a fiat money system is that nothing limits the number of little pieces of paper that the government can print to pay its debts.

But *why* would any government want to cause inflation or deflation of any size whatsoever? For the answer to that question, read on!

Giving in to the inflation temptation

Inflation is caused primarily by governments' printing more paper money or producing a large amount of cheap-metal coins, which vastly increases the supply of money and makes each piece of money less precious. As sellers demand higher prices to make up for the fact that each piece of money is worth less, you get inflation.

REMEMBER

So why in the world would governments ever opt to increases in the money supply so fast that inflation will result? Good question. Historically, governments circulate more money in three circumstances:

>> When governments can't raise enough tax revenue to pay their obligations

>> When governments feel pressure from debtors who want inflation so they can repay their debts using less valuable money

>> When governments want to try to stimulate the economy during a recession or depression

As you find out more about these three reasons for increasing the money supply, keep the following in mind: If the supply of money increases faster than the demand for money, inflation results. (For more on this, see the earlier section "Balancing money supply and demand.") Consequently, no matter what reason a government has for increasing the supply of money, it runs the risk of inflation. And that's true both for good reasons, such as wanting to help the economy out of a recession, and for bad reasons, such as helping debtors repay their loans using less valuable money.

Paying bills by printing bills: Hyperinflation

Governments almost always have debts, and printing extra money can be a tempting way to pay them. Quite often, a government may want to spend more money than it's collecting in tax revenue. One solution is to borrow the shortfall, but another is to simply print new bills to cover the difference.

The trouble with allowing a government to pay its debts and obligations by printing money is that as soon as the newly printed money begins to circulate, people spend it, drive up prices, and cause inflation. And if the government prints successively more money, you end up with people offering shopkeepers and producers successively more cash for the same amount of goods and services. It's like a giant auction where everybody bidding on items keeps getting more and more money to bid with.

REMEMBER

If a government gets into the habit of rapidly printing new money to pay its bills, inflation can soon reach or even surpass 20 or 30 percent per month, a situation referred to as a *hyperinflation*. Economists (and everyone else) hate hyperinflation because it greatly disrupts daily life and ruins the investment climate. Hyperinflation does the following:

>> **Causes people to waste huge amounts of time trying to avoid the effects of rising prices:** During the Weimar hyperinflation in Germany (which I discuss in the sidebar "Hyperinflation and Hitler"), men working at factories were paid two or even three times a day because money lost its value so quickly. Their wives waited at the factories to immediately take the money to the nearest shops, trying to spend the pay before it lost most of its value. Shopping may be fun, but not when you're desperately racing against outrageously rising prices!

>> **Destroys the incentive to save:** The only sensible thing to do with money during a hyperinflation is to spend it as quickly as you can before it loses even more of its value. People whose life savings were in German marks during the Weimar hyperinflation soon found that what they had worked so hard to amass had become worthless. And people thinking about saving for the future were greatly discouraged because they knew that any money they saved would soon lose all value.

>> **Harms businesses:** The discouragement of saving causes major business problems because if people aren't saving, then no money is available for businesses to borrow for new investments. And without new investments, the economy can't grow.

Feeling printing press pressures: Inflation politics

Even if the government isn't trying to use inflation to increase tax revenues (see the preceding section), a certain political constituency will always pressure it to circulate more money. You may even be a member of this group — they're called *borrowers*. To understand the politics of inflation, understand that one of the functions of money is to act as a *standard of deferred payment*. What does that mean?

Imagine that you borrow $1,000 to invest on your farm, promising to pay the bank back $1,200 next year. For the past several years, prices in the economy have been stable, and, in particular, the pigs that you raise have sold for $100 each. Essentially, your loan lets you borrow the equivalent of 10 pigs with the promise to pay back 12 pigs next year.

HYPERINFLATION AND HITLER

History's most infamous hyperinflation hit Germany in the 1920s, during the economically incompetent Weimar Republic. It so badly ruined the German economy that Germans would later vote Adolph Hitler into power because he promised to fix things.

At the end of World War I, Germany faced the prospect of paying off massive debts taken on during the conflict in addition to all the ongoing costs of running a government. Most of its debts were in its own currency, the German mark.

Because the German government had the exclusive right to produce German marks, the debt proved an irresistible temptation to begin printing money to pay its bills. If the government owed a billion marks to a certain firm, it simply printed up a billion crisp, new mark bills and handed them over. If a bunch of schoolteachers hadn't been paid the previous month, the Weimar government simply printed up enough new cash to pay them.

Soon, all the new money caused a wild hyperinflation. In fact, the rate of inflation in Weimar Germany in 1922 was well over 100 percent per month — it reached nearly 6,000 percent by the end of year!

Then things *really* got out of control. Prices went up 1,300,000,000,000 times (this is not a misprint!) in 1923. That year, Germans paid 200,000 marks for a loaf of bread and 2 million marks for a pound of meat. Prices rose so rapidly that waiters at restaurants had to pencil in new prices on menus several times a day. And if you ate slowly, you were sometimes charged twice what was printed on the menu because prices had gone up so much while you were eating! In some places in Germany, people stopped bothering to take the time to count out money. Instead, they tied paper bills into huge bricks and weighed the bricks of cash. For instance, it may have cost 2 pounds of cash to buy a chicken.

But you've got an idea. You lobby your congressman to lobby the government to print more money. All that new money causes inflation, after which the price of pigs rises to $200 each. Now you have to sell only six pigs to pay back the $1,200 loan, leaving you with more pigs, you pig!

Lenders, of course, oppose the inflationary desires of borrowers. If you were the bank, you would do everything in your power to stop the inflation. If it goes through, not only are your profits ruined, but you're an outright loser. In the first year, your loan of $1,000 is the equivalent of ten pigs. But after the inflation, you get paid back the equivalent of only six pigs. You take a 40 percent loss on the value of your loan. Too much inflation, and a lender ends up being a pig in a poke.

As long as economies use money, lenders and borrowers will always be lined up against each other, both trying to sway the government.

Stimulating the economy with inflation: Monetary policy

A legitimate reason for governments to print more money has the very respectable name of monetary policy. *Monetary policy* refers to the decisions a government makes about increasing or decreasing the money supply in order to stimulate or slow down the economy.

I go into monetary policy in detail in Chapter 17, but the basic idea is that if the economy is in a recession, the government may print up some new money and spend it. All the goods and services it buys with the new money stimulate the economy immediately. All those businesses that received money from the government can now also go out and spend that new money themselves. And whoever receives the money from them will also go out and spend it to buy things. In fact, this can theoretically go on forever and stimulate a lot of economic activity — enough to lift an economy out of a recession.

REMEMBER

If this sounds too good to be true, it is. Why? Inflation. When people start spending all that new money, it drives up prices. Eventually, the only effect of the government's good intentions is that prices rise and no additional goods are sold. For example, if the government doubles the money supply, businesses will double the prices they charge because each piece of money is worth half as much as before. Consequently, the total amount of goods and services sold will be the same as before because although twice as much money is being spent, prices are also twice as high.

The sad upshot is that an increase in the money supply stimulates the economy only when it's a surprise. If the government can print the money and start spending it before people can raise prices, you get an increase in the amount of goods and services sold. Eventually, of course, people figure it out and raise prices, but until they do, the monetary stimulus works.

Unfortunately, fooling people over and over is tough. You can surprise people once, but it's much harder the second time and even harder the third time. In fact, if the government keeps trying to surprise people, people begin to anticipate the government's actions, and they raise prices even before the government prints more money. Consequently, most modern governments have decided against using this sort of monetary stimulus and now strive for zero inflation or very low inflation.

Tallying up the effects of inflation

In the United States, prices rise only a small amount each year. However, even moderate inflation causes problems by cutting into the practical benefits of using money instead of barter. You can get a better sense of this fact by looking at the four functions that economists generally ascribe to money and the ways in which inflation screws up each of them:

» **Money is a store of value.** If I sell a cow today for one gold coin, I should be able to turn around and trade that gold coin back for a cow tomorrow or next week or next month. When money retains its value, you can hold it instead of holding cows, or real estate, or any other asset.

Inflations weaken the use of money as a store of value because each unit of currency is worth less and less as time passes.

» **Money is a unit of account.** When money is widely accepted in an economy, it often becomes the unit of account in which people write contracts. People start using phrases like "$50 worth of lumber" rather than "50 square feet of lumber," or "$1 million worth of shirts in inventory" instead of "20,000 shirts in inventory."

This practice makes sense if money holds its value over time, but in the presence of inflation, using money as a unit of account creates problems because the value of money declines. For instance, if the value of money is falling fast, how much lumber, exactly, is "$50 worth of lumber"?

» **Money is a standard of deferred payment.** If you want a cow, you probably wouldn't borrow a cow with the promise to repay two cows next year. Instead, you'd be much more likely to borrow and repay in terms of money. That is, you'd borrow one gold coin and use it to buy a cow, after promising to pay back two gold coins next year.

The progressive devaluing of money during a period of inflation makes lenders reluctant to use money as a standard of deferred payment. Suppose a friend asks to borrow $100, promising to pay you $120 in a year. That seems like a good deal — after all, it's a 20 percent interest rate. But if prices are rapidly rising and the value of money is falling, how much will you be able to buy with that $120 next year?

Inflations make people reluctant to lend money. Potential lenders fear that when the loans are repaid, the repayment cash won't have the same purchasing power as the cash that was lent. This uncertainty can have a devastating effect on the development of new businesses, which rely heavily on loans to fund their operations.

» **Money is a medium of exchange.** Money is a *medium* (literally meaning "something in the middle") of trade between buyers and sellers because it can be directly exchanged for anything else, making buying and selling much easier. In a barter economy, an orange farmer who wants to buy beer may have to first trade oranges for apples and then apples for beer because the guy selling the beer wants only apples. Money can eliminate this kind of hassle.

But if inflation is bad enough, money is no longer an effective medium of exchange. During hyperinflations, economies often revert to barter so buyers and sellers don't have to worry about the falling value of money. For example, in a healthy economy, the orange seller can first sell oranges for cash and then trade the cash for beer. But during a hyperinflation, between the time he sells the oranges for cash and buys the beer, the price of beer may have skyrocketed so high that he can't buy very much beer with the cash. During a hyperinflation, economies have to resort to cumbersome bartering.

REMEMBER

Another effect of inflation is that it functions as a giant tax increase. This seems strange because you normally think of governments taxing by taking away chunks of people's money, not by printing more money. But a tax is basically anything that transfers private property to the government. Debasing the currency or printing more money can have this effect.

Suppose that the government wants to buy a $20,000 van for the post office. The honest way to go about this is to use $20,000 of tax revenues to buy a van. But a sneakier way is to print $20,000 in new cash to buy the van. By printing and spending the new cash, the government has converted $20,000 of private property — the van — into public property. So printing new cash works just like a tax. Because printing new money ends up causing inflation, this type of taxation is often referred to as an *inflation tax.*

Not only is the inflation tax sneaky, it unfairly targets the poor because they spend nearly all their incomes on goods and services, the prices of which go up greatly during an inflation. By contrast, because the rich have the opportunity to save a lot of their incomes, proportionately they're less affected by an inflation tax. By investing their savings in assets whose prices go up during an inflation (such as real estate), the rich can insulate themselves from a great deal of the harm caused by inflation.

Measuring Inflation

Inflation can cause lots of problems, so for the government to keep inflation under control, it needs a way to measure inflation accurately.

The value of money is determined by the interaction of the *supply* of money with the *demand* for money (as I explain in the earlier section "Buying an Inflation: When Too Much Money Is a Bad Thing"). The supply of money is under the government's control, but the government can't directly ascertain the demand for money; it has to look at how supply and demand interact in order to determine how much to increase or decrease the money supply:

>> If inflation is in effect, the government knows that the supply of money is increasing faster than the demand for money. If it wants to tame the inflation, it should reduce the supply of money.

>> If deflation is in effect, the government knows that the demand for money is increasing faster than the supply of money. If it wants to end the deflation, it should increase the supply of money.

TIP

Because inflation is a *general* increase in the overall level of prices, the best way to look for it is by seeing whether the cost of buying a large collection of many different goods and services rises over time. If, instead, you look at only one or two prices, you may end up confusing a *relative* price increase for an increase in the overall, general level of prices. (A *relative price increase* is when a single price increases when compared to other prices, which remain unchanged or even fall.)

REMEMBER

Economists arbitrarily define some large collection of goods and services and refer to it as a *market basket.* They then measure inflation by finding out how much money it takes to buy this basket at various times. The best-known market basket is monitored by the Bureau of Labor Statistics. This basket is called the *Consumer Price Index,* or CPI. It consists of what the Bureau thinks a typical family of four buys in the United States each month.

In this section, I show you how this process works by creating a market basket, noting how it can be used to measure inflation, and normalizing it to a given base year so that calculating inflation rates between any two years is a breeze. (If I've piqued your interest with this talk of market baskets and the CPI, feel free to check out the Bureau of Labor Statistics' CPI Web site at www.bls.gov/cpi.)

Creating your very own market basket

The Consumer Price Index involves a large number of products and services — it's a big market basket. Understanding price indexes is easier if you create a simplified index with a small market basket. In this section, I look at a *very* small market basket containing pizza, beer, and textbooks — typical purchases of college students. I call it the Collegiate Price Index.

For each of the three items in the Collegiate Price Index, I've created prices for 2021, 2022, and 2023 and listed them in Table 15-1.

TABLE 15-1

The Collegiate Price Index

Item	Number Bought	2021	2022	2023
Pizza	5	$20	$18	$18
Beer	30	$4	$4	$4.50
Textbooks	1	$120	$160	$170

In 2021, one medium cheese pizza costs $20, a cold bottle of beer costs $4, and an overly long, incomprehensible introductory economics textbook costs $120. The next year, the price of a medium cheese pizza actually falls to $18 because a new pizza parlor opens up next to the old one, causing a price war. Beer still costs $4, but the college bookstore decides that it can really stick it to students, raising the price of the textbook to $160. (Don't worry about the 2023 column yet. I give you a chance to dig in and calculate inflation using the 2023 numbers later in the chapter.)

So far, so good. But in evaluating the index, you also have to keep track of how many of each item is bought by the typical student each year. For the sake of simplicity, assume that a typical student buys 5 cheese pizzas, 30 beers, and 1 economics textbook each year.

Calculating the inflation rate

To calculate how much inflation your college economy has (or deflation, if the price of this basket happens to go down), first total up how much the market basket costs each year using Table 15-1. In 2021, it costs $340: $100 on pizza (5 pizzas at $20 each), $120 on beer (30 beers at $4 each), and $120 on economics textbooks (1 textbook at $120). The cost of buying the same market basket in 2022 is $370, so the cost of buying the same market basket has gone up by $30.

Now that you've done the addition, you need some simple algebra. Economists use the capital letter P to denote how many dollars the defined market basket costs. So in this case, P_{2021} means the cost of buying the market basket in 2021 and P_{2022} is the cost of buying the market basket in 2022. Economics has a standard practice of denoting the rate of inflation with the Greek letter π (pronounced "pie").

To calculate the rate of inflation, you use a very simple formula:

(1) $\pi = (P_{Second\ Year} - P_{First\ Year}) / P_{First\ Year}$

In the case of the Collegiate Price Index, the formula becomes:

(2) $\pi = (P_{2022} - P_{2021}) / P_{2021}$

Substituting in $P_{2021} = \$340$ and $P_{2022} = \$370$, you find that $\pi = 0.088$. Convert this number into a percentage by multiplying by 100, and inflation in the Collegiate Price Index is 8.8 percent between 2021 and 2022. So on the basis of this number, a student needs 8.8 percent more money in 2022 to buy the simple market basket.

Setting up a price index

The collegiate market basket (see Table 15-1) is a simple example. When government statisticians compute the Consumer Price Index, they basically do the same thing, just using a lot more goods. They also introduce the concept of a *price index* (or *price level index*) to make calculating and interpreting inflation rates over several years much easier. To set up a price index, statisticians first establish a base year, or index year. Continuing the example from Table 15-1, suppose that 2021 is the base year for the Collegiate Price Index. You can then make a handy mathematical transformation so that the price level in 2021 is fixed at the number 100 and the price levels of every other year are set up so that they're relative to the 100 of the base year.

TIP

To make $P_{2021} = \$340$ your base year, divide it by itself. That, of course, gives you 1, which you then multiply by 100 to get 100 ($100 \times 1 = 100$). This may seem like an idiotic thing to do until you realize that if you do the same thing to the other years, you end up with something very useful. Divide P_{2022} by P_{2021} and then multiply that quotient by 100 to get 108.8. This number is easy to interpret: It's 8.8 percent larger than 100. Or put differently, the price level in 2022 is 8.8 percent larger than the price level in 2021.

You can keep going, using the numbers for 2023 that appear in Table 15-1. For instance, $P_{2023} = \$395$. If you divide P_{2023} by P_{2021} and multiply by 100, you get 116.2; the price level in 2023 is 16.2 percent bigger than the price level in 2021.

Figuring the rate of inflation between 2022 and 2023 using these index numbers is also easy. Because the price index level for 2022 is 108.8 and the price index level for 2023 is 116.2, inflation is simply $(116.2 - 108.8) / 108.8 = 0.068$, or 6.8 percent. (You're using equation [1] here, but you're inputting index numbers instead of the actual costs of market baskets.)

Figure 15-1 charts the actual values of the Consumer Price Index from 1983 to 2016. The index was set to a level of 100 using prices that consumers paid on average over the two-year period from 1982 to 1984.

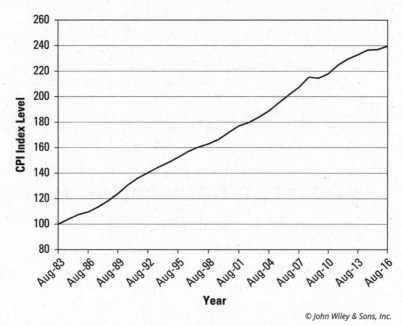

© John Wiley & Sons, Inc.

FIGURE 15-1:
Consumer Price
Index, 1983–2016.

You can see that the Consumer Price Index grew from its initial level of 100 in 1983 to a level of 240 in 2016. That is, to buy what a typical family of four consumes, you would have needed an additional 140 percent more money in 2016 than you did in 1983. Increases in the money supply caused the price level in the United States to more than double over those 33 years.

Determining the real standard of living with the price index

REMEMBER

Beyond making inflation easy to measure and interpret, price indexes also make it simple to measure the very important difference between real prices and nominal prices. *Nominal prices* are simply money prices, which can change over time due to inflation. Because nominal prices can change, economists like to focus on *real prices,* which keep track of how much of one kind of stuff you have to give up to get another kind of stuff, no matter what happens to nominal prices.

For example, suppose that in 2021 you make $10 an hour working at a youth camp and that the cost of a museum ticket is $20. The *real cost* of a museum ticket to you is two hours of work. Suppose that the next year, the prices of all goods double. But your wages also double, so you're earning $20 an hour, and a museum ticket costs $40. The result is that you still have to work two hours to buy a museum ticket. So although the *nominal* price of a museum ticket has doubled, its *real* price in terms of labor — how much labor you have to give up to get a museum ticket — hasn't changed.

By constructing price indexes like the CPI, economists can tell how the *real standard of living* changes for people from year to year. In the Collegiate Price Index example from preceding sections (using data from Table 15-1), inflation is 8.8 percent between 2021 and 2022, meaning that the cost of living of a typical college student went up 8.8 percent. So if at the same time student incomes go up only 5 percent, students are actually worse off because costs have gone up faster than incomes. Real living standards — measured in terms of how much stuff you can buy with your income — have fallen.

Identifying price index problems

Using price indexes to track the cost of living isn't a flawless system. Here are three big issues:

>> **The market basket can never perfectly reflect family spending.** The Bureau of Labor Statistics tries to keep track of what a typical family of four purchases when calculating the Consumer Price Index (CPI). But families differ greatly, not only in terms of *what* they buy but also in terms of *how many* of each thing they buy.

>> **The market basket becomes outdated.** The Bureau of Labor Statistics often waits way too long before including new types of goods in the market basket. For instance, the Bureau took years to include paid movie downloads from the Internet even while paid downloads and streaming services were quickly replacing DVD movie rentals. If the CPI fails to include popular new products, it's not fully capturing the price changes that matter to consumers.

>> **The market basket can't account for quality.** Price isn't the only thing that matters to consumers. For example, what if a beer stays the same price but improves in quality from one year to the next? You're getting better beer for the same price, but this isn't reflected in the data. This problem is especially severe for things like computers, cellphones, and video games. For these products, quality improves dramatically year after year while prices either stay the same or go down.

Each of these problems troubles government statisticians, who are constantly coming up with better price indexes and statistical methods to try to overcome them. In the meantime, the Federal Reserve (the government agency charged with regulating the money supply in the United States) has estimated that the CPI overstates inflation by 1 to 2 percentage points per year. Most of the overstatement comes from the failure of the CPI to account for new goods and quality improvements.

The main consequence of this overstatement is that the government is overly generous with the cost-of-living increases it grants workers and retirees. Each year, government workers and retirees receive pay increases based upon increases in the CPI. These pay increases are designed to ensure that people's real incomes aren't eroded by inflation, but because the CPI is most likely overstating the rate of inflation each year, the cost-of-living increases are overly generous.

On the other hand, the rise of popular free Internet services has caused an opposite problem. Millions of people derive great enjoyment from the services provided by Facebook, Google, and other Internet companies. But those services are provided free of charge. So it's not at all clear how one would be able to incorporate them into a price basket or keep track of how inflation in the overall economy affects the demand or supply for these services — or how to account for quality improvements to free online services.

Pricing the Future: Nominal and Real Interest Rates

Because inflation erodes the value of a loan repayment (see the earlier section "Tallying up the effects of inflation"), economists have to distinguish between nominal interest rates and real interest rates. *Nominal interest rates* are simply the normal, money interest rates that you're used to dealing with; they measure the returns to a loan in terms of money borrowed and money returned. *Real interest rates*, however, compensate for inflation by measuring the returns to a loan in terms of units of stuff lent and units of stuff returned. This distinction is important because the *real* interest rate is what makes people want to save and invest. After all, what lenders really care about isn't how much money they get back but how much stuff they can buy with it.

Suppose that you borrow $1,000 with the promise to pay $1,100 to the lender in a year. Your nominal interest rate is 10 percent because you're paying back an additional $100, or 10 percent more dollars than you borrowed. But if inflation occurs, the amount of stuff that $100 can buy will decrease over time.

Say a nice meal for two with a bottle of wine costs $100 right now but will cost $105 next year. The lender is giving up 10 of these very good meals ($1,000 divided by $100 per meal) in order to give you the loan. Next year, when he gets repaid $1,100, he can buy 10.47 meals at the price of $105. He is giving up 10 meals now in exchange for 10.47 meals next year, meaning that the real rate of interest on the loan is 4.7 percent. Because of inflation, the real interest rate on the loan is substantially less than the nominal rate.

REMEMBER

When lenders and borrowers negotiate a nominal interest rate on a loan, they both try to estimate what the inflation rate will be over the period of the loan. This *expected rate of inflation* is denoted algebraically as π^e. (Don't confuse expected inflation, π^e, with actual inflation, π. Expected inflation is what people expect to happen ahead of time, while actual inflation is what actually ends up happening.)

In this section, I show how to estimate and use the expected rate of inflation.

Using the Fisher equation

Economist Irving Fisher came up with a simple formula that links nominal and real interest rates. Here's the *Fisher equation,* using *i* to denote the nominal interest rate and *r* to denote the real interest rate:

$$(3) \quad i = r + \pi^e$$

This equation simply says that the nominal interest rate is the real interest rate plus the expected rate of inflation. This relationship is very important to borrowers and lenders because although all loan contracts specify a nominal rate of interest, their goal is to achieve a specific real rate of interest, even after any subsequent inflation reduces the value of money. By using the Fisher equation, the borrowers and lenders can determine what nominal interest to charge now to achieve a given real rate of return, taking into account the expected rate of inflation.

Suppose that a borrower and lender agree that 6 percent is a fair real rate of interest, and they also agree that inflation is likely to be 3.3 percent over the course of one year. Using the Fisher equation, they write the loan contract with a 9.3 percent nominal interest rate. A year later, when the borrower repays the lender 9.3 percent more money than was borrowed, that money is expected to have only 6 percent more purchasing power than the borrowed money, given the expected increase in prices.

Realizing that predictions aren't perfect

Negotiations like the one described in the preceding section depend crucially on estimating the expected inflation rate, π^e, and lots of economists have job descriptions consisting primarily of trying to predict future inflation rates. Their predictions are widely reported in the business media, but every person comes up with inflation forecasts in his or her own way. Some listen to the experts, and others make estimates based on their own daily experiences.

During the period of low inflation starting in the early 1980s and extending through the many years of recovery after the Great Recession of 2007–2009, people's inflation expectations were remarkably accurate. For example, consumers polled by researchers at the University of Michigan each January were on average no more than a couple of percentage points off the actual rate of inflation over the next 12 months. In addition, the vast majority of those polled had very similar predictions about inflation. In that sort of an environment, people trusted their own inflation expectations and also tended to agree with other people's inflation expectations. Agreeing on the nominal interest rates to be charged on particular loans was consequently relatively easy for borrowers and lenders.

But during periods of high inflation, actual rates of inflation tend to be quite unpredictable and volatile — with, say, a 35 percent rate one year, followed by a 15 percent rate the next year, and then a 45 percent rate the year after. Thus, in periods of high inflation, individuals tend not to trust their own inflation forecasts or to agree with the inflation forecasts of others. In that sort of an environment, borrowers and lenders find it difficult to agree on the nominal interest rates to be charged on particular loans. The resulting declines in lending and borrowing can reduce investment, and consequently, the economy's ability to produce goods and services.

» **The ideal: Letting price adjustments eliminate recessions**

» **Reality: Coping with sticky prices and lingering recessions**

» **Linking slow price adjustments to slow wage adjustments**

» **Introducing the Keynesian model**

Chapter **16**

Understanding Why Recessions Happen

Macroeconomists' biggest task is to try to prevent — or at least shorten — *recessions,* those periods of time during which the economy's output of goods and services declines. Economists, politicians, and most other people who work for a living despise recessions because of the toll they exact in human suffering. That's because when output falls, firms need fewer workers. The typical result is massive layoffs, which cause significant increases in unemployment. In large countries such as the United States, millions of workers lose their jobs and their ability to support themselves and their families.

In this chapter, I use the *aggregate supply/aggregate demand* model to show you how economists analyze recessions. Typically, recessions begin with what economists like to call *shocks* — unexpected bad events such as terrorist attacks, natural disasters, the introduction of bad government policies, or sudden spikes in the cost of important natural resources such as oil.

The first big lesson of this chapter is that if the prices of goods and services in the economy were free to adjust to the changes in demand and supply that shocks cause, the economy would typically be able to recover quite swiftly. Unfortunately, the second big lesson is that not all real-world prices are free to adjust. Rather, some very important prices are quite slow to adjust — they are, as economists like to say, *sticky*. As a result, recessions can linger and cause a lot of harm unless the government intervenes to help the economy recover more quickly. (In Chapter 17, I discuss the best ways for governments to intervene.)

Introducing the Business Cycle

REMEMBER

Economies go through alternating periods during which the total output of goods and services expands and then contracts. The alternating pattern of economic expansion and contraction, illustrated in Figure 16-1, is often called the *business cycle* because businesses are so greatly affected by the changes in output.

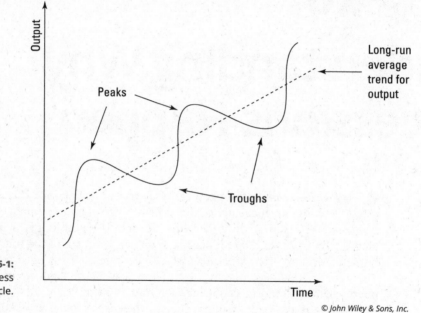

FIGURE 16-1:
The business cycle.

© John Wiley & Sons, Inc.

REMEMBER

The solid line in Figure 16-1 represents how the economy's total output of goods and services varies over time. It alternates between troughs and peaks, which helps you identify periods of recession and recovery. Here's how you can distinguish between the two:

>> **Recessions:** Recessions, or contractions, are the periods of time during which output falls — that is, after a peak and before the next trough.

>> **Recoveries:** Recoveries, or expansions, are the periods of time during which output increases — that is, after a trough and before the next peak.

The dotted line in Figure 16-1 represents the long-run, average growth trend for an economy's total output of goods and services. I've drawn Figure 16-1 so that it has an upward-sloping average growth trend, capturing the fact that the economies of most countries now have sustained economic growth. In other words, on average, total output tends to rise year after year. Because recessions still happen, however, the actual path given by the solid line fluctuates around the long-run growth path given by the dotted line.

In Figure 16-1, you can see that macroeconomic policy has two natural goals:

>> **Make the long-run average growth line as steep as possible.** The steeper it is, the faster (on average) total output and living standards rise.

>> **Reduce the size of business cycle fluctuations around the long-run average growth line.** Smaller distances between peaks and troughs translate into fewer people suffering through bouts of unemployment when output falls.

In Chapter 17, I explain the policies that economists think are best for achieving these two goals. But for Chapter 17 to make sense, I must first explain what causes the business cycle — especially recessions and the high rates of unemployment that accompany them. After all, if you don't understand what's wrong, you can't sensibly fix it.

Striving for Full-Employment Output

Before you can say whether an economy is doing well or doing poorly, you need some objective standard of what "doing well" is. Economists use the concept of *full-employment output* (which is represented by the symbol Y^*) as their measure of how well an economy should be doing.

REMEMBER

The idea of full-employment output revolves around the concept of *full employment*, by which economists mean a situation in which everyone who wants a full-time job can get one. Full-employment output is the total amount of goods and services produced in the economy when there's full employment in the labor market.

WARNING

Please don't confuse full-employment output with the economy's *maximum output*, which is the larger amount of goods and services that would be produced if everyone were forced to work as much as humanly possible. Also, don't assume that full employment is the same thing as having a zero unemployment rate. Even when everyone who wants a job can get one, some unemployment will always exist as people voluntarily quit one job to search for a better one. For the duration of their job search, these people are counted as unemployed. Economists call this situation *frictional unemployment,* as though the delay in finding a better job is due to some sort of friction slowing the process down.

TIP

As technology improves, full-employment output (Y^*) grows because better technology means that a fully employed labor force can produce more output. But to simplify their analyses, economists usually ignore the long-term growth trend and look only at whether actual output, Y, is currently above or below their best estimates of Y^* at that particular moment. (I follow this convention, too, for the rest of the chapter. You will find out how the economy adjusts to situations in which output is either above or below potential output at a given point in time.)

As I show you in this chapter, the economy naturally wants to adjust back to Y^* anytime it deviates from Y^*. If that adjustment process were rapid enough, you wouldn't have to worry about business cycles, recessions, and unemployment. If the economy reverted back to Y^* fast enough, recessions would be too brief to cause any serious negative consequences. Unfortunately, the natural adjustment process can be very slow, and as a result, recessions can be quite lengthy and awful.

Returning to Y*: The Natural Result of Price Adjustments

After an economic shock, such as a natural disaster or a spike in the cost of natural resources, price adjustments tend to return an economy to producing at full-employment output (Y^*) (see "Striving for Full-Employment Output" earlier in this chapter for details on full employment). That's right, I said *price adjustments* — not the president, and not the chairman of the Federal Reserve Board. Don't believe me? Read on.

Consider a situation in which the overall demand for goods and services in the economy falls off: Individuals, firms, and the government demand and buy less than the economy is currently producing. The result is an excess supply of output which, in turn, leads to lower prices. After all, what does any business do when it can't sell off everything it's producing at the prices it's currently charging? It has a sale. It lowers prices. The lower prices attract more buyers, and soon the business is able to sell off the rest of its output.

REMEMBER

This process repeats itself all over the economy during an economic downturn. When aggregate demand falls off due to an economic shock, firms lower prices to make sure they sell off their outputs. This process eventually leads to two outcomes:

>> Prices all over the economy fall.

>> The economy again produces at full-employment output, *Y**.

For this process to work well, prices must be able to change quickly; if they can, the economy very quickly returns to Y^*. If, however, price adjustments are slow, the economy may produce less output than Y^* for a significant amount of time. In other words, if prices don't adjust quickly, you can get a recession. And until prices do adjust, the recession lingers.

Responding to Economic Shocks: Short-Run and Long-Run Effects

Economists like to break the time period after an economic shock into two parts, which they call the *short run* and the *long run*:

>> **The short run:** The period of time in which firms haven't yet made price changes in response to an economic shock

>> **The long run:** The period of time after which firms have made all necessary price changes in response to an economic shock

These definitions are intentionally vague because the speed at which firms adjust prices varies from shock to shock. In this section, I show you the major differences between what happens in the short run and the long run.

Defining some critical terms

To see the difference between an economy responding to a shock in the short run versus the long run, begin by looking at Figure 16-2, which is a model of the macroeconomy. The horizontal axis measures the dollar value of the output of goods and services sold in the economy (Y). This number is the same as a country's gross domestic product (GDP), which I discuss in Chapter 14. The vertical axis measures the overall price level in the economy, P.

To understand the meaning of P, consider this: Although each individual good and service has its own price, and some of those prices may be going up while others are going down, an overall trend in prices exists for the economy as a whole. P is simply a measure of how the prices of goods and services as a whole behave. If P goes up, then on average prices are rising; if P goes down, then on average prices are falling. And if prices stay the same, then P (of course) stays the same. (See Chapter 15 for details about how economists measure P.)

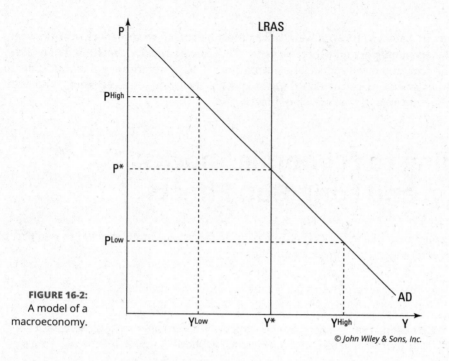

FIGURE 16-2:
A model of a
macroeconomy.

© John Wiley & Sons, Inc.

Now that you understand the meaning of P, you're ready to tackle the two curves that appear in Figure 16-2:

>> **Aggregate demand curve:** This curve represents the total amount of goods and services (Y) that people want to buy at any particular price level P, holding all other factors constant.

Notice that in Figure 16-2, the AD curve slopes downward. That's because there's an inverse relationship between the price level (P) and the amount of stuff that people want to buy (Y). *Inverse relationship* simply means that at the higher price level (P^{High}), people want to buy a low level of output (Y^{Low}). But if prices fall to P^{Low}, people demand a much greater amount of output (Y^{High}). The downward slope of the AD curve captures the fact that at lower price levels, people want to buy more.

>> **Long-run aggregate supply curve:** This curve represents the amount of goods and services that an economy will produce when prices have adjusted after an economic shock.

In Figure 16-2, you can see that the LRAS is a vertical line — it isn't a curve at all! (Do you feel cheated?) The LRAS is drawn above the point on the horizontal axis that represents the full-employment output level, Y^*. Why? Because in the long run, changes in prices *always* return the economy to producing at the full-employment output level.

The tao of P: Looking at price adjustments in the long run

In Figure 16-2, P^* represents the *equilibrium* level of prices in the economy. P^* is determined by the intersection of the *long-run aggregate supply curve* (LRAS) with the *aggregate demand curve* (AD). P^* is both the price level at which consumers demand exactly the amount of full-employment output (Y^*) as well as the price level to which the economy will naturally return if the price level ever deviates from P^*.

To see why the price level will always move back to P^*, look at price level P^{High} and its corresponding aggregate demand level, Y^{Low}. Obviously, Y^{Low} is less than the economy's full-employment level of output (Y^*). That's important because firms would rather produce at output level Y^*. In fact, they've invested in factories and equipment that'll be wasted if they produce at lower levels of output. Consequently, their response is to cut prices in order to increase sales. And they continue to cut prices until the overall price level in the economy falls down to P^*, because that's the price level at which consumers want to buy exactly Y^* worth of output.

Are you worried that all these price cuts will cause firms to lose money? Take heart: Firms don't necessarily lose profits in this situation because their costs are falling at the same time. That's because when the economy is producing at less than Y^*, there are a lot of unemployed workers and a lot of unused productive inputs, such as iron and oil. Unemployment puts downward pressure on wages; in other words, having lots of unemployed labor readily available means you can hire people at lower wages. And the larger the piles of unused productive inputs, the more their prices will fall, too.

Okay, so the lower prices attract more customers, increase sales, and cause firms to hire back unemployed workers. This process continues until prices fall all the way to P^*, at which point the economy is operating at full employment again, meaning all workers who want full-time jobs can get them.

In a similar fashion, prices can't remain below P^* for long. At price level P^{Low}, people want to buy Y^{High} worth of output. But that's more than firms can produce at full employment. The only way to produce that much output is if employees work more than the standard 40-hour work week. The only way to get them to do so is to pay them more, and the only way to give them higher wages is for firms to raise prices. So with demand exceeding supply, prices are raised until they reach P^*, at which price level the quantity demanded by consumers is exactly equal to the full-employment output level, Y^*.

As you can see, if prices have enough time to adjust, the economy always returns to producing at output level Y^*. Because I'm calling the time required for prices to adjust the *long run*, it makes sense to call the vertical line above Y^* the *long-run* *aggregate supply curve* because it shows how much output the economy will supply after prices have had enough time to adjust to equalize the supply and demand for goods and services. (For much more on supply and demand, see Chapter 4.)

A shock to the system: Adjusting to a shift in aggregate demand

What causes prices to be too high or too low in the first place? A shock to *aggregate demand* — the total amount of goods and services that people are willing to buy.

First, visualize what a shock to aggregate demand looks like: Figure 16-3 shows the aggregate demand curve shifting to the left from AD_0 to AD_1. A leftward shift of aggregate demand is called a *negative demand shock*, and it could be caused, for instance, by a decline in confidence in the economy that makes people want to save more and consume less. (A rightward shift of *AD* would be called a *positive demand shock.*)

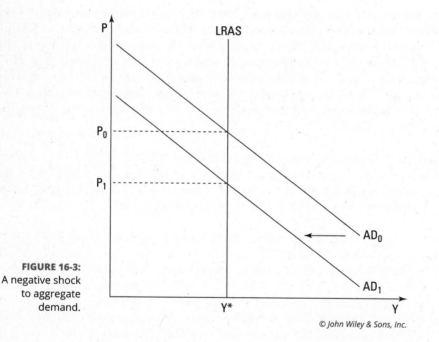

FIGURE 16-3:
A negative shock to aggregate demand.

© John Wiley & Sons, Inc.

The original price level, P_0, is determined by where the original AD_0 curve intersects the vertical *LRAS* curve. In the long run, after firms adjust to the demand shock, the new price level, P_1, will be where the new AD_1 curve intersects the vertical *LRAS* curve.

REMEMBER

The new price level (P_1) is less than the original price level (P_0). Why? Because the demand for goods and services decreases after the negative demand shock. The only way to entice consumers to again purchase full-employment levels of output (Y^*) is to lower the cost of buying that much output, so the price level has to fall. Firms may take a while to make the necessary price reductions, but when they do, the economy will again produce at Y^* in the long run.

Dealing with fixed prices in the short run

After an economic shock happens, prices eventually adjust to return the economy to full-employment output, Y^* (see the preceding sections). However, this process may take a while because in the short run, prices are essentially fixed. Even the managers of the most nimble firms need some time to decide how much to cut prices. And some firms aren't quite as nimble.

Suppose that a firm has printed up catalogs listing the prices of the things it sells. This firm distributes catalogs only once a year, which means it's committed to selling to customers at these prices until the next catalog is sent out. In such a situation, a firm adjusts its production to meet whatever amount of demand happens to come along at these fixed prices. If a lot of people show up to buy at these prices, the firm increases production, typically by hiring more employees. If very few people show up to buy, it reduces production, typically by hiring fewer employees.

Figure 16-4 depicts a situation in which firms have committed to a fixed set of prices and can respond to changes in demand only by adjusting their production levels. The figure shows the horizontal *short-run aggregate supply curve* (SRAS), which is actually a straight line. This "curve" corresponds to price level P_0 because the firms, in the short run, can't adjust their prices. Movements right and left along the *SRAS* curve capture the increases and decreases in output that firms have to make as demand for their products varies at the fixed price level.

TECHNICAL STUFF

Economists have various complicated ways of explaining how an economy adjusts to a demand shock. I'm cutting the discussion down to the bare bones, which means thinking of the *SRAS* curve as a horizontal line. In more elaborate explanations, the *SRAS* curve is an upward-sloping line. But don't be confused: The basic idea in either case is that the economy moves from having a perfectly horizontal aggregate supply curve right after a shock, to an upward sloping one a little later, to a perfectly vertical one — the *LRAS* — in the long run. I'm skipping the middle part in order to make the discussion as direct as possible. I use only the initial, horizontal curve and the final, vertical curve, calling the former the *SRAS* and the latter the *LRAS*.

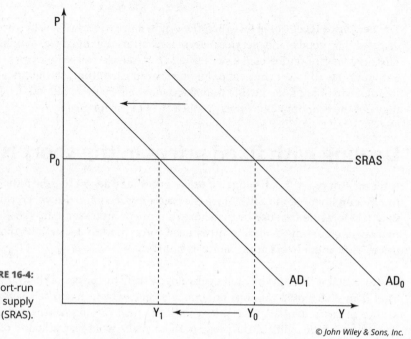

FIGURE 16-4:
The short-run
aggregate supply
curve (SRAS).

© John Wiley & Sons, Inc.

Figure 16-4 also has two aggregate demand curves, AD_o and AD_1, that again show what happens when aggregate demand is reduced as the result of a negative demand shock. The initial level of output that firms produce, Y_o, is determined by the intersection of the original aggregate demand curve, AD_o, with the SRAS curve. In other words, at price level P_o, people demand output level Y_o, and firms respond by supplying it.

When the negative demand shock strikes, it shifts aggregate demand leftward to AD_1. Reduced demand means that at the fixed price level, customers are willing to buy less output. Because firms can't change prices, their only recourse is to reduce production down to match the decrease in demand; this reduced level of output (Y_1) appears on the graph where the SRAS curve intersects AD_1. Because lower output means that firms need fewer workers, you end up with a recession: Output falls, and unemployment rises.

If you compare Figures 16-3 and 16-4, you can see that the leftward shift in aggregate demand has very different effects in the short run and the long run:

>> **In the short run, when prices are fixed:** Output falls and unemployment rises.

>> **In the long run, when prices can fall:** Output returns to the full-employment level.

ADJUSTING PRICES QUICKLY: WALMART AND Y*

The recessions of 1991 and 2001 were very mild — much milder, in fact, than most previous recessions in the United States. The exact reason for this isn't clear, but many economists believe that one factor was that starting in the 1980s, retailers got much better at quickly adjusting prices when supply didn't equal demand.

The leader in this regard was Walmart, which developed the most sophisticated inventory-management systems in the world. With these computerized systems, Walmart's managers could tell minute-by-minute what was selling and what was not. As a result, the prices of slow-moving items could be cut very quickly so that products didn't go unsold for weeks or months, as was the case in decades past when inventory was taken by hand once a month.

As a result of such innovations, prices could quickly adjust to equate supply and demand. In fact, individual prices could fall much more rapidly, thereby helping to get the economy back to producing at full-employment output ($Y*$) more quickly. Other things held equal, that means shorter, milder recessions.

This effect helped to moderate the severe recession of 2007–2009. That recession occurred when aggregate demand declined substantially after a collapse in real estate prices. Thanks to sophisticated inventory-management systems, retailers like Walmart and Amazon were able to quickly identify and respond to the decline in demand. They could ascertain which products were no longer popular and thereby reduce orders for those products immediately.

Its inventory-management system prevented huge accumulations of unsold products from building up in Walmart's inventories. Thus, when the economy began to finally grow again in 2009, Walmart and other retailers had to immediately increase their factory orders to keep up with the increase in demand — something that they wouldn't have chosen to do if large amounts of unsold inventories had built up during the recession.

Why the huge difference between the short run and the long run? Firms aren't forever stuck with their original catalog prices. Eventually, they print new catalogs with lower prices. The lower prices entice customers to purchase more, and soon the economy can return to producing at the full-employment output level, $Y*$.

Putting together the long and short of it

If you have both long-run and short-run responses to an economic shock tucked under your belt, you're ready to put the two very different responses together into one big picture. Figure 16-5 lets you see how an economy adapts to a negative demand shock both in the short run and in the long run. The economy begins at point A, where the original aggregate demand curve, AD_0, intersects both the *LRAS* and the *SRAS* curves. At Point A, the economy is in equilibrium because at price level P_0, the aggregate demand for output equals the full-employment level of output, Y^*. There is neither a surplus nor a shortage that could cause prices to change.

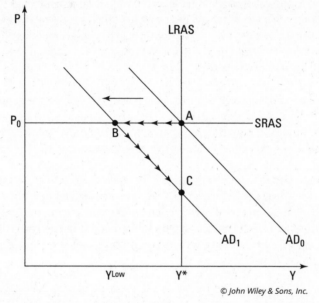

© John Wiley & Sons, Inc.

FIGURE 16-5:
Short-run and long-run responses to a negative demand shock.

REMEMBER

The *SRAS* curve is horizontal at price P_0 to reflect the fact that after the economy reaches its equilibrium (where AD_0 intersects the *LRAS* at output level Y^*), the prices that are determined at that level are fixed in the short run; they can't change immediately, even if a demand shock happens to come along.

For instance, suppose that the aggregate demand curve shifts left from AD_0 to AD_1 because of a negative demand shock of some sort. Because prices are fixed in the short run at P_0, the economy's first response is to move from Point A to Point B. In other words, because prices are fixed, production falls from Y^* down to Y^{Low} as firms respond to decreased demand by cutting production. (Small arrows indicate the movement of the economy from Point A to Point B.)

At Point *B*, the economy is operating below full employment, implying that a lot of workers are unemployed. This high level of unemployment causes wages to fall. As wages fall, firms' costs also fall, allowing them to cut prices in order to attract more customers.

Falling prices cause increased aggregate demand for goods and services, which eventually moves the economy all the way from Point *B* to Point *C* (arrows on the graph indicate this movement). When the economy reaches point *C*, it's once again producing at full employment, *Y**.

REMEMBER

The short-run and long-run effects of a negative demand shock are basically total opposites of each other:

>> **Short run:** In the short run, prices are fixed while output decreases.

>> **Long run:** In the long run, prices decrease while output returns to *Y*.

If prices don't stay fixed for very long, the economy can quickly move from *A* to *B* to *C*. But if prices are slow to adjust to the negative aggregate demand shock, the economy can take a very long time to get from *A* to *B* to *C*. In such cases, there's a long-lasting recession during which output remains below *Y** and many people are unemployed.

Heading toward Recession: Getting Stuck with Sticky Prices

When the economy encounters a negative demand shock like the one depicted in Figure 16-5, price flexibility (or lack of flexibility) determines both the severity and length of any recession that may result. If prices were infinitely flexible — if they could change within seconds or minutes after a shock — the economy would immediately move from Point *A* to Point *C*, and all would be right with the world. But if prices are fixed for any period of time, the economy goes into a recession as it moves from Point *A* to Point *B* before prices eventually fall and bring it back to full-employment output at Point *C*.

In the real world, prices are indeed somewhat slow to change, or as economists like to say, prices are *sticky*. Interestingly, prices tend to be stickier when going downward than upward, meaning that prices appear to have a harder time falling than rising.

The major culprit seems to be one particular price: wages. *Wages* are the price employers must pay workers for their labor. Unlike other prices in the economy, people are particularly emotionally attached to wages and how they change over time.

REMEMBER

Employees don't like to see their wages cut. They have a strong sense of fairness concerning their wages and usually retaliate against any wage cut by working less hard. As a result, managers typically find lowering wages to be counterproductive, even if a firm is losing money and needs to cut costs.

This section explains how firms' worries about worker motivation lead to the sticky output prices that prevent the economy from rapidly recovering from recessions. When sales fall as a result of the recession, output prices can't fall very much because firms choose to lay off workers rather than cut wages.

Cutting wages or cutting workers

During a recession, you see a large increase in unemployment but little decrease in wage rates. The fact that managers are unwilling to cut wages, however, has a nasty side effect: Not cutting wages makes it very hard for firms to cut the prices of the goods and services they sell (for more on this topic, see the next section).

Suppose that a negative demand shock hits an economy and greatly reduces sales at a particular company. The firm is losing money, so managers need to figure out a way to cut costs. About 70 percent of this company's total costs are labor costs (wages and salaries). Naturally, labor costs are an obvious target for cuts.

But the managers of the firm realize that if they cut wages, employees will get angry and work less hard. In fact, their productivity may fall off so much that cutting wages may make the firm's profit situation worse: Output may fall so much that sales revenues will decrease by more than the reduction in labor costs. Therefore, cutting wages isn't really a good option.

So instead, the managers lay off a large chunk of their workforce in order to reduce labor costs. For instance, if sales are down 40 percent, the firm may lay off 40 percent of the workforce. However, any workers who remain employed get to keep their old wages so that they aren't angry and their productivity doesn't fall.

Adding up the costs of wages and profits

Obviously, firms need to turn a profit in order to stay in business. And that means making sure that the price per unit that they charge for their products exceeds the cost per unit of making them.

During a recession, lower aggregate demand means that firms reduce production and sell fewer units. Wages are the largest component of most firms' costs — in fact, they're a full 70 percent of the average firm's costs. If a firm can't cut wages for fear of causing worker productivity to drop, it can't reduce its per-unit production costs very much, either. In turn, the firm can't cut its prices very much because prices have to stay above production costs if firms are to break even and stay in business. What does all this mean?

REMEMBER

When demand drops off, prices are typically sticky. They stay high even though there's less demand for output in the economy. That's the reason behind the economy's moving horizontally from Point A to Point B in Figure 16-5 after the negative demand shock. With prices sticky because firms can't quickly or easily cut wages, the negative demand shock results in a recession, with output falling and unemployment rising because so many workers get fired.

Worse yet, unless prices can somehow begin to fall, the economy won't be able to move from B to C to get back to producing at the full-employment output level (Y^*). Prices do *eventually* fall, but this process can take a long time, meaning that the negative demand shock can cause a long-lasting recession.

One way around this slow adjustment process is for the government to try to offset the negative demand shock. The next section covers how such attempts may be able to speed recovery by avoiding the need for prices to adjust to bring the economy back to producing at the full-employment output level.

Returning to Y* with and without government intervention

In Chapter 17, I explain in great detail how the government can use monetary and fiscal stimuli to get around the sticky prices problem by boosting aggregate demand. Here, I want to give you a preview of how that process works.

Imagine that after the negative demand shock depicted in Figure 16-5 moves aggregate demand leftward from AD_0 to AD_1, the government doesn't hang around waiting for prices to fall. Instead, it stimulates aggregate demand so that the aggregate demand curve shifts right and returns to where it started, at AD_0. Taking this action returns the economy to producing at full employment without having to wait for prices to fall.

What if the government doesn't act to stimulate aggregate demand in that fashion? What if the economy is at Point B and the government doesn't intervene? In such cases, prices do eventually fall because firms' production costs eventually fall.

Labor costs are very slow to fall because managers don't want to risk alienating workers by cutting their wages (see the earlier section "Cutting wages or cutting workers" for details). But because so many workers are unemployed when the economy is at Point B, wages eventually decline. Some firms hire unemployed people at lower wages, which reduces the firms' costs, meaning that they can undersell firms that keep wages high. Eventually, such competitive pressures mean that all firms end up cutting wages.

Other costs also decline because during a recession, with output so diminished, a significant portion of the economy's productive capacity is unused. There are unused factories, unused trucks, unused train cars, and unused ships. There are also large amounts of unused lumber, iron, oil, and other productive inputs.

The owners of these unused inputs lower their prices to try to sell them. As their prices fall, production costs also fall, thereby allowing firms to reduce the selling prices of their output. And as these selling prices fall, the economy moves from Point B to Point C in Figure 16-5, restoring the economy to producing at the full-employment output level (Y^*). See how nicely it all (eventually) works out?

Achieving Equilibrium with Sticky Prices: The Keynesian Model

John Maynard Keynes was the most influential economist of the 20th century. Why? He was the first economist to realize that sticky prices (caused by sticky wages) are the culprit behind recessions, an insight that changed the way people studied economies.

What inspired Keynes to have this insight? He was led to the idea by the horrible state that the economy reached during the Great Depression of the 1930s. Just the name itself — *Great Depression* — gives you some idea how bad things got. Normal economic downturns are called *recessions*. Really bad recessions are called *depressions*. What happened in the 1930s was so bad, people started calling it the *Great Depression* to indicate how severe it was.

The Great Depression started with a lingering recession from 1929 to 1933. The United States did not see its output return to its 1929 level until after entering World War II in 1941. To put the Great Depression in perspective, Table 16-1 gives data for the eight recessions the United States has experienced since 1960, plus (on the first line) the same data for the Great Depression.

As you can see, the Great Depression was far, far worse than any normal recession. Nearly 25 percent of the labor force was unemployed, and the initial downturn lasted about four times longer than the 11.6-month average duration of post-1960 recessions.

Total economic output as measured by real GDP (which I discuss in Chapter 15) also fell much more than in a normal recession. Because real GDP adjusts for inflation, it captures changes in the physical quantity of output produced. In recent recessions, real output has fallen at most 4.1 percentage points, with 0.5 to 2 percentage points being typical. During the Great Depression, real GDP fell 28.8 percent!

TABLE 16-1   **The Great Depression and U.S. Recessions since 1960**

Start (Month/Year)	End (Month/Year)	Duration (Months)	Highest Unemployment Rate	Change in Real GDP (%)
8/1929	3/1933	43	24.9	−28.8
4/1960	2/1961	10	6.7	2.3
12/1969	11/1970	11	5.9	0.1
11/1973	3/1975	16	8.5	1.1
1/1980	7/1980	6	7.6	−0.3
6/1981	11/1982	16	9.7	−2.1
6/1990	3/1991	8	7.5	−0.9
3/2001	11/2001	8	6.0	0.5
12/2007	6/2009	18	9.9	−4.1

Source: NBER, Economic Report of the President, Bureau of Labor Statistics

As a witness to the Great Depression, Keynes obviously wanted to figure out what could cause such a drastic economic downturn — and what could prevent such devastation from happening again. Keep reading for more on the Keynesian model.

WHAT MAKES A RECESSION A RECESSION?

I define a *recession* as a period of time during which output falls and unemployment rises. But this isn't the only definition. For example, you may read in a textbook or a newspaper article that an economy is in a recession if real GDP falls for two consecutive quarters. But if you look at Table 16-1, you notice that during certain recessions (such as the one that began in April 1960), real output actually went up rather than down. So why was that time period labeled a recession?

A lot of factors go into determining what gets labeled a recession. A group of economists at the National Bureau of Economic Research (NBER) in Cambridge, Massachusetts, gets to "officially" declare when recessions begin and end in the United States. This group has a long set of criteria that begins with falling output and rising unemployment and includes lots of other things, such as how fast factories receive new orders. Sometimes these other factors cause the NBER to feel that the economy has passed a peak and has entered a recession, even if output isn't falling.

Check out the NBER's website at www.nber.org for more information about business cycles and how the NBER goes about declaring recessions.

Adjusting inventories instead of prices

Not only did Keynes figure out that sticky prices cause recessions, but he also developed a hugely influential model that's still presented in many macroeconomics textbooks. This model is a small part of a larger approach to managing the macroeconomy that came to be called *Keynesianism* — an approach that favored large government interventions into the economy rather than the sort of *laissez-faire* policies of nonintervention preferred by other people. (For a discussion of the costs and benefits of having the government intervene in the economy, see Chapter 3.)

To be fair, I have to point out that Keynesianism has attracted a lot of critics and is not the be-all-end-all of macroeconomics. But the part of it I present here is not controversial. It explains how an economy adjusts to *equilibrium* — a place where aggregate supply matches aggregate demand — in the extreme short run after an economic shock, when prices can't change at all.

Look back at Figure 16-4 for a moment. The Keynesian model elaborates on exactly how an economy moves from producing at output level Y_o to producing at output level Y_1 when a shock to aggregate demand happens and prices are fixed at level P_o.

REMEMBER

Keynes's model focuses your attention on firms' inventories of goods that have been made but not yet sold. According to Keynes, changes in inventories guide firms to increase or decrease output during situations in which prices are sticky and can't serve as signals of what to do.

To see the novelty of Keynes's inventory idea, understand that if prices could change, then prices (not inventories) would guide firm decisions about how much to produce:

>> If prices were rising, a firm would know that its product was popular and that it should increase output.

>> If prices were falling, the firm would know that the product was not doing well and that it should probably cut output (and maybe get into another line of business!).

In an economy with fixed prices, however, firms need some other way of deciding whether to increase or decrease production. Keynes realized that the guiding force would be changes in inventories, as you can see in the following subsections.

Keeping an eye on target inventory levels

Inventories are constantly turning over, with goods flowing both in and out. New production increases inventories, while new sales decrease inventories. The two factors interact to determine if inventories are rising, falling, or staying the same.

For instance, if new production equals new sales, inventory levels stay constant. If new production exceeds new sales, inventories rise.

REMEMBER

The interaction of new production and new sales is important because each firm has a *target level* of inventories that it likes to keep on hand to meet situations in which sales temporarily run faster than the firm can produce output. The costs and benefits of having a bigger or smaller inventory on hand determine the target level.

Having less inventory than the target level is dangerous because the firm may not be able to keep up with sales spikes. Having more inventory than the target level is wasteful because there's no point in having stuff sitting around unsold, year after year. Each firm weighs these costs and benefits to come up with its own target inventory level.

Target inventory levels may vary from year to year, depending on whether firms are expecting strong or weak sales. If managers are expecting strong sales, they may plan on increasing inventories, whereas if they're expecting weak sales, they may plan on decreasing inventories.

REMEMBER

Keynes realized that aggregate demand shocks (which are, by definition, unexpected) would show up as unexpected changes in firm inventories:

>> Unexpectedly low aggregate demand means that sales slow so much, inventories increase to levels higher than firms had planned on.

>> Unexpectedly high aggregate demand means that sales increase so much, inventories decrease and reach levels lower than firms had planned on.

Increasing or decreasing output as inventories fluctuate

Unexpectedly large changes in inventories cause firms to change their output levels as follows:

>> If inventories rise above target levels, firms respond by cutting production. By reducing production rates to less than sales rates, inventories begin to fall down toward target levels.

>> If inventories fall below target levels, firms respond by raising production. By increasing production rates to more than sales rates, inventories begin to rise toward target levels.

The changes in output levels caused by changes in inventories are hugely important because they determine not only whether output *(Y)* is increasing or decreasing but also whether unemployment is rising or falling. For instance, if firms increase production because inventories have fallen below target levels, they need to hire more workers, so unemployment falls. If, on the other hand, firms decrease production because inventories rise above target levels, they need to lay off workers, so unemployment rises.

Adjusting inventories based on planned and actual expenditures

The Keynesian model differentiates between planned expenditures and actual expenditures as follows:

>> **Planned expenditures:** The amount of money that households, businesses, the government, and foreigners would like to spend on domestically produced goods and services.

>> **Actual expenditures:** What households, businesses, the government, and foreigners end up spending on domestically produced goods and services. The sum total of all these actual expenditures is equal to GDP.

REMEMBER

What happens when actual expenditures are different from planned expenditures? Inventories automatically change. For instance, if more money is spent on goods and services than planned, people are buying more output than is currently being produced. This situation is possible because firms sell (from their inventories) goods that were produced in previous periods. On the flip side, if people spend less money on goods and services than planned, firms' inventories rise because firms have to store all the output that they can't sell.

Keynes represented planned expenditures, *PE*, algebraically with the following equation:

(1) $PE = C + I^P + G + NX$

What do all these letters mean? Here's the short version (I discuss them in detail in Chapter 14):

>> *C* stands for the amount of output that consumers want to consume.

>> *I*^{P} stands for the amount of output that firms plan to buy as investment goods, such as new factories and equipment, as well as any inventory changes that firms plan to make.

If, later on, firms have to increase or decrease inventories more than they planned, then actual investment, *I,* will not equal planned investment, *I^P*.

» *G* stands for how much output the government wants to spend on things like building schools, paving roads, and ensuring an adequate supply of paper for paperwork.

» *NX* stands for *net exports* — the value of a nation's exports minus the value of its imports. *NX* tells you the net demand that the foreign sector of the economy has for stuff that your country makes domestically.

For actual expenditures, *Y,* Keynes used the same equation that you use to calculate gross domestic product (which I discuss in Chapter 14):

(2) $Y = C + I + G + NX$

TIP

Why can you use the GDP equation to calculate actual expenditures? Actual expenditures are equal to national income because every cent of expenditure made in the economy is income to somebody. Furthermore, actual expenditure is also equal to the dollar value of all goods and services produced in the economy because every bit of output that's produced is sold to someone. (Any output that a firm makes but can't sell to customers is counted as being "sold" by the firm to itself as it's placed into inventory. These inventory changes are known as *inventory investment* and are totaled up in GDP as part of the total investment, *I.*)

Having three ways of looking at *Y* is very handy as you become familiar with the Keynesian model. Sometimes understanding the model is easier if you think of *Y* as being actual expenditures; at other times, understanding is easier if you think of *Y* as being national income or output. I switch among these three definitions when doing so helps make understanding the model easier.

REMEMBER

The only difference between the right sides of Equations (1) and (2) is the investment variable, which is *planned investment (I^P)* in the first equation and *actual investment (I)* in the second. In other words, *Y* and *PE* differ only because of differences in investments caused by inventories' increasing or decreasing unexpectedly when sales are more or less than planned.

Bringing some algebra into the mix

You knew it was coming: It's time to get algebraic so you can identify the Keynesian model's economic equilibrium, using mathematical superpowers. (Now, where did I put those?)

First, you need to define a *consumption function* — a way to calculate total consumption — that you can substitute into Equation (1). In Chapter 14, I present the following formula for calculating consumption:

(3) $C = C_o + c(1-t)Y$

For now, what you really need to know about this formula is that higher income (Y) leads to higher consumption (C). If you substitute Equation (3) into Equation (1), you get the following:

(4) $PE = C_o + c(1-t)Y + I^P + G + NX$

If you look carefully, you can see that this equation shows that the total planned expenditures on goods and services in the economy *(PE)* depends on the total income in the economy (Y). The higher the total income, the more money people are going to plan to spend.

TIP

A good way to simplify the planned-expenditures equation is to create a variable called A and to define it as follows:

$A = C_o + I^P + G + NX$

If you do that, Equation (4) looks a little more palatable:

(5) $PE = A + c(1-t)Y$

The variable A stands for *autonomous expenditures,* by which economists mean the part of planned expenditures that doesn't depend on income (Y). The part of planned expenditures that does depend on income, $c(1-t)Y$, is known as *induced expenditures.*

To understand induced expenditures, realize that because t stands for the income tax rate, $(1-t)Y$ is what people have left over to spend after the government taxes them. And of that amount, the fraction c gets spent on consumption, so $c(1-t)Y$ tells you how much expenditure is "induced" by an income of size Y.

Figure 16-6 graphs Equation (5) and labels it the *planned expenditures line.*

To find the specific equilibrium of the Keynesian model, realize that the following equation captures all possible equilibriums:

(6) $PE = Y$

You can read this equation as "planned expenditures equal actual expenditures." (Remember that Y equals both total income and total expenditure in the economy because all expenditures are income to somebody.)

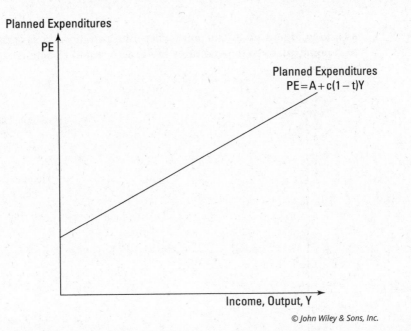

Planned Expenditures

PE

Planned Expenditures
PE = A + c(1 − t)Y

Income, Output, Y

© John Wiley & Sons, Inc.

FIGURE 16-6:
The planned
expenditures line.

REMEMBER

Any situation where $PE = Y$ is an equilibrium. Why? Because if the economy could get to the point where $PE = Y$, then nobody would have any reason to change their behavior. Consumers would be consuming as much as they planned to consume (*C*). The government would be buying up as much output as it wanted to buy (*G*). Foreigners would be buying as much stuff from your nation as they intended (*NX*). And most importantly, firms would be spending exactly as much on investment as they planned — implying that inventories aren't changing unexpectedly.

If planned expenditures equal actual expenditures, you truly have an equilibrium because everybody is getting what they want, and nobody has any incentive to change his or her behavior.

**TECHNICAL
STUFF**

You can solve for the equilibrium value of output, which I call $\tilde{Y}$, by substituting Equation (5) into Equation (6). If you do so, you get the following:

$$(7) \quad \tilde{Y} = \frac{1}{1 - c(1-t)} A$$

Showing equilibrium graphically

If Equation (7) from the preceding section is just too frightening, stick with me. Finding the Keynesian model's equilibrium graphically is much easier. To do so, you plot the $PE = Y$ equation on the same graph as the $PE = A + c(1-t)Y$ equation, as I do in Figure 16-7. The point where the two lines cross is the equilibrium. At that point, planned expenditures are exactly equal to actual expenditures in the economy.

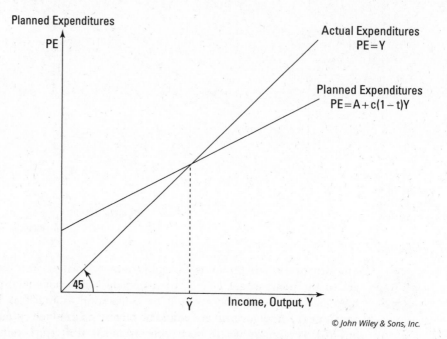

© John Wiley & Sons, Inc.

FIGURE 16-7:
The Keynesian model's equilibrium, $\tilde{Y}$.

This equilibrium is *stable,* by which I mean that if the economy starts out at any income level other than $\tilde{Y}$, it soon moves back to $\tilde{Y}$. The element that returns the output to $\tilde{Y}$ is inventory changes.

To see why this is true, look at Figure 16-8, which exploits a nifty geometric trick about the $PE = Y$ line to show how the economy behaves when it's not producing at the equilibrium output level, $\tilde{Y}$.

TIP

The trick is that the $PE = Y$ line shows up on the graph at a 45° angle, meaning that you can use it to draw squares — boxes whose sides all have the same length. That means you can transpose any value of Y onto the vertical axis. To do so, take any value of Y, go straight up until you hit the 45° line, and then go straight sideways until you hit the vertical axis. The point you hit represents as many dollars vertically as Y represents horizontally.

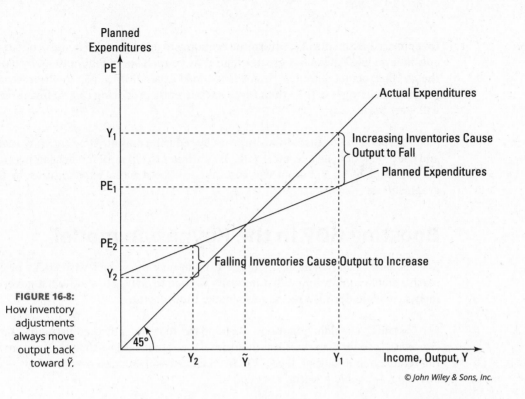

FIGURE 16-8:
How inventory adjustments always move output back toward Ỹ.

© John Wiley & Sons, Inc.

For instance, in Figure 16-8, start on the horizontal axis at output level Y_2, which is less than the equilibrium output level $Ỹ$. If you go up vertically to the 45° line and then to the left, you can plot output level Y_2 onto the vertical axis. Why is this useful? Because you can then compare Y_2 directly to the level of planned expenditures, PE_2, that you get by starting at output level Y_2 on the horizontal axis.

As you can see, $PE_2 > Y_2$, meaning that planned expenditures exceed output in the economy. This means that inventories will unexpectedly drop as firms sell part of their stockpiles of inventory to make up for the fact that people are buying up more stuff than firms are currently producing. This drop in inventories will return the economy to equilibrium.

As inventories fall unexpectedly, firms increase production. As a result, Y increases. Furthermore, actual expenditures continue to increase until Y reaches $Ỹ$, because for any value of $Y < Ỹ$, planned expenditures will continue to exceed output, as you can see from the graph.

Inventory adjustments also return the economy to equilibrium if it starts out at an output level like Y_1, which is greater than $\tilde{Y}$. As you can see in Figure 16-8, by using the 45° line, actual output, Y_1, exceeds planned expenditures, PE_1. In other words, people are buying less (PE_1) than firms are currently producing (Y_1), so inventories will start to rise.

Firms respond to increases in inventories by reducing output. They lay off workers and cut production. As a result, Y falls. It continues to fall until it reaches $\tilde{Y}$ because for any value of $Y > \tilde{Y}$, output will continue to exceed actual expenditures, as the graph shows.

Boosting GDP in the Keynesian model

Keynes didn't just invent his model to explain how economies with sticky prices reach a stable equilibrium. What he really wanted to do was to show what governments could do during a recession to make things better.

For instance, consider Figure 16-8. Suppose that inventory adjustments have carried the economy to equilibrium income, $\tilde{Y}$, but that $\tilde{Y}$ is less than the economy's full-employment output level, Y^*. In such a case, Keynes asked, what — if anything — should governments do?

REMEMBER

Governments could choose to do nothing. Eventually, because $\tilde{Y} < Y^*$, prices will fall and the economy will return to full employment (as it does moving from Point B to Point C in Figure 16-5). But Keynes argued that governments could speed up the recovery by boosting planned expenditures.

For instance, suppose that the government decides to increase G, government spending on goods and services. If it does so, then PE in Equation (4) clearly gets bigger. Because G is a part of autonomous expenditures (A), the increase in G means an increase in A in Equation (5). Graphically, a larger A means that the planned expenditure line shifts vertically from PE_1 to PE_2, as in Figure 16-9. Given that the actual expenditure line $(PE = Y)$ doesn't change, the vertical shift in the planned expenditure line causes equilibrium output to increase from $\tilde{Y}_1$ to $\tilde{Y}_2$.

What Keynes suggested doing was using government policy to increase planned expenditures by whatever amount was necessary to increase the economy's short-run, sticky-price equilibrium, $\tilde{Y}$, all the way to the full-employment output level, Y^*. In Chapter 17, I discuss such policies in greater detail, including why they don't always work so well in practice.

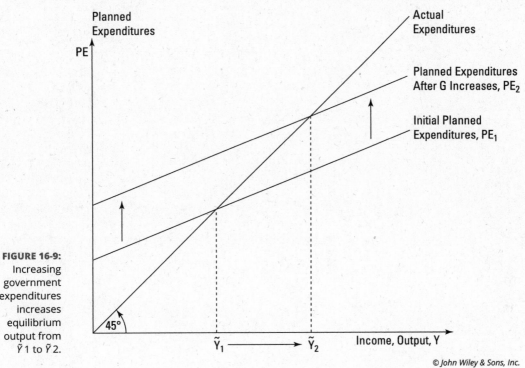

FIGURE 16-9: Increasing government expenditures increases equilibrium output from $\tilde{Y}1$ to $\tilde{Y}2$.

Planned Expenditures

PE

Actual Expenditures

Planned Expenditures After G Increases, PE$_2$

Initial Planned Expenditures, PE$_1$

45°

$\tilde{Y}_1$ ⟶ $\tilde{Y}_2$

Income, Output, Y

© John Wiley & Sons, Inc.

Chapter **17**

Fighting Recessions with Monetary and Fiscal Policy

Monetary and fiscal policy are two of the most important functions of modern governments. *Monetary policy* focuses on increasing or decreasing the money supply to influence the economy, and *fiscal policy* uses government spending and the tax code to influence the economy.

Thanks to the development of good economic theory, governments can use monetary and fiscal policy to mitigate the duration and severity of recessions. This theory is hugely important because it gives governments the chance to make a positive difference in the lives of billions of people. Good economic policy can make a nation prosperous, but bad economic policy can ruin it.

But monetary and fiscal policy are not without problems. In this chapter, I show you how well they can work in the best-case scenario and their limits and problems in the real world. By seeing the whole picture, you can decide when and how governments should use monetary and fiscal policy.

The information in this chapter can put you two steps ahead of many politicians and help you judge when politically biased economists are trying to pull a fast one. As Joan Robinson, one of the great economists of the 20th century, said, "The purpose of studying economics is not to acquire a set of ready-made answers to economic questions but to learn how to avoid being deceived by an economist." I totally agree. But don't worry, you can trust *me*.

If you haven't read Chapter 16, I encourage you to do so before tackling this chapter. Although my goal with this book is to make each chapter its own entity so that you can jump in and jump out wherever you need, I introduce and explain much of the terminology you encounter in this chapter in Chapter 16. You may find tackling monetary and fiscal policy easier if you have a basic understanding of how recessions work, which is the focus of that chapter.

Stimulating Demand to End Recessions

Before looking at monetary and fiscal policy in detail, realize that the purpose of both is to alter the aggregate demand for goods and services. (The *aggregate demand* is the total demand for goods and services in an economy.) In particular, both monetary and fiscal policy can increase aggregate demand during a recession. This section explains this concept more in depth.

Aiming for full-employment output

The ability to use monetary and fiscal policy to stimulate the economy is important because you always want to end a recession and return the economy to producing at the full-employment output level as quickly as possible.

The full-employment output level, Y^*, is the amount of output the economy produces at full employment, which occurs when every person who wants a full-time job can get one. If the economy goes into recession and produces less than Y^* worth of output, millions of people lose their jobs because firms need fewer workers to produce the smaller amount of output.

Worse yet, the unemployment rate remains high until output returns to the full-employment level. Monetary policy and fiscal policy are useful precisely because they can help return the economy to producing at Y^* as soon as possible and shorten the frustration and misery the unemployed have to endure.

Look at Figure 17-1, which shows how monetary and fiscal policy can stimulate aggregate demand and return an economy to producing at Y^* as quickly as possible after the economy is hit with a negative demand shock. (*Negative demand shocks* [see Chapter 16] are events that unexpectedly decrease aggregate demand, such as a drop in consumer confidence.)

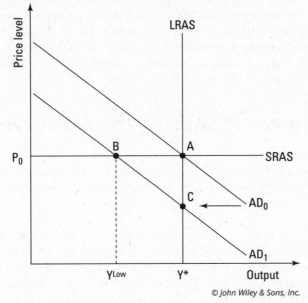

© John Wiley & Sons, Inc.

FIGURE 17-1:
How a negative demand shock affects the economy.

In Figure 17-1, the economy begins in equilibrium at Point A, where the downward-sloping aggregate demand curve AD_o intersects the vertical long-run aggregate supply curve, *LRAS*. Prices in the economy are fixed in the short run, so the short-run aggregate supply curve, *SRAS*, is horizontal at the initial price level (P_o), which is determined by the intersection of AD_o and *LRAS*. (As in Chapter 16, for simplicity's sake I'm using horizontal *SRAS* curves rather than the upward-sloping curves many other books use. If you're used to seeing upward-sloping *SRAS* curves, take a peek at that chapter.)

When the negative demand shock comes along, here's what happens:

» The aggregate demand curve shifts left to AD_1, reflecting the reduction in spending on goods and services.

» With prices fixed at P_0 in the short run, the economy's equilibrium shifts leftward from Point A to Point B, and output in the economy falls from Y^* down to Y^{Low}.

» As output falls, unemployment rises because firms don't need as many workers.

As you can see, the overall result of the demand shock is a recession: a period of declining output and increasing unemployment. Unfortunately, a recession can take a long time to resolve. If the government takes no action to end a recession, the only way for the economy to return to producing at the full-employment output level is for prices to drop so that the economy's equilibrium can slide down the AD_1 curve from Point B to Point C. That process is typically very slow because of sticky (slow-to-change) prices, especially sticky wages. As a result, the economy has high unemployment and takes a long time to get back to producing at Y^* unless the government becomes involved. Refer to Chapter 16 for more in-depth information.

Back to work: Shifting the AD curve right

REMEMBER

The trick that both monetary and fiscal policy accomplish is to increase aggregate demand, which eliminates the need to endure the slow adjustment process that takes the economy from Point B to Point C (see Figure 17-1). They do this by shifting the aggregate demand curve to the right.

For instance, if the government were able to shift the aggregate demand curve from AD_1 back to AD_0, the economy would jump back to equilibrium Point A. That's very nice because it gets the economy back to producing at Y^* without having to go through the slow adjustment process needed to get an economy to move from B to C. In human terms, this means that unemployment ends much sooner for millions of workers, who can once again find jobs and provide for themselves and their families. Unfortunately, implementing aggregate demand shifts to fight recessions isn't easy. Several problems can creep up involving inflation and people's expectations about how increases in aggregate demand affect prices.

Generating Inflation: The Risk of Too Much Stimulation

The best way to begin to understand the limitations of economic policies that stimulate aggregate demand is to note that in the long run, such policies can change only the price level, not the level of output. Why? No matter where the aggregate demand curve happens to be — no matter how much stuff consumers are willing (or unwilling) to buy — prices eventually adjust until the economy is once again producing at full-employment output (Y^*). The economy simply doesn't want to stray from Y^* indefinitely.

I explain the economy's affection for Y^* in Chapter 16, and you can see it in Figure 17-1 as well. The negative demand shock shifts the aggregate demand curve from AD_o to AD_1. If the government doesn't use some sort of stimulus, the economy slowly adjusts on its own from Point A to Point B to Point C. At Point C, the price level has fallen, and output has returned to Y^*.

But even if the government applies some sort of stimulus to move the aggregate demand curve to the right of AD_1, the long-run result is always that the economy comes to equilibrium at the point where the aggregate demand curve intersects the long-run aggregate supply (LRAS) curve. And as I show in Chapter 16, the *LRAS* is a vertical line that corresponds to the full-employment output level, Y^*.

In this section, I explain why changes in wages and prices prevent government stimulus from permanently pushing output above Y*. In particular, I show that an economy that has been temporarily stimulated into producing more than Y* is an economy in which workers are overworked and demanding wage increases — wages increases that will eventually drive up firm production costs, lower firm profits, and cause firms to reduce production. That feedback process continues until output falls back to Y*.

Trying to increase output beyond Y*

Because the economy always returns to producing at full-employment output (Y^*), the government can't for any significant period of time keep the economy producing more output than Y^*. To see why this is true, suppose that the government uses monetary and/or fiscal policy to shift the aggregate demand curve from AD_o to AD_1, as Figure 17-2 shows.

Before the shift, the economy is in equilibrium at Point A, where the original aggregate demand curve, AD_o, intersects the long-run aggregate supply curve (LRAS), which is a vertical line above Y^*. At that initial equilibrium, the price level is P_o, and because prices are sticky in the short run (see Chapter 16), the short-run aggregate supply curve, $SRAS_o$, is a horizontal line at P_o.

When the government stimulates the economy and shifts the aggregate demand curve to the right from AD_o to AD_1, the economy initially shifts from Point A to Point B. That is, because prices are fixed in the short run, the economy adjusts to a temporary equilibrium at B (where AD_1 intersects $SRAS_o$).

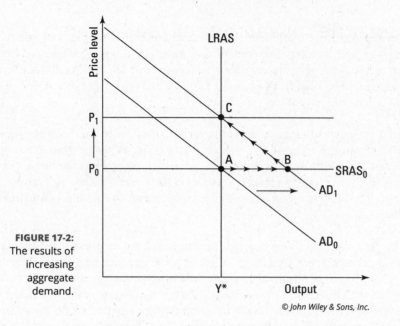

FIGURE 17-2:
The results of
increasing
aggregate
demand.

© *John Wiley & Sons, Inc.*

The economy's output level at Point *B* is greater than the full–employment output level, Y^*. Point *B* is only a temporary equilibrium because the only way the economy can produce more than Y^* is by using more labor than is used at Y^*. This can happen in only two ways, both of which increase wages:

» **Firms convince workers to work overtime.** To get existing workers to consistently work overtime, firms must pay them high overtime wages.

» **Firms increase the total number of workers by tempting people like retirees, not normally in the labor force, to take jobs.** To tempt people like retirees to join the workforce, firms must increase wages (because, obviously, these people weren't tempted to work at the old wages).

Either way, production costs rise. And as they do, firms pass them on to consumers by raising the prices they charge for goods and services. That's why the economy moves from Point *B* to Point *C* in Figure 17-2. As prices rise because wages are increasing, the economy moves up the *AD₁* curve (as the arrows indicate). Wages, and hence prices, continue to rise until the economy is once again producing Y^* worth of output at Point *C*. At that point, there's no need for further wage increases; the economy is once again producing at Y^*, and firms don't have to increase wages to try to produce more than that level.

Tracing the movement of real wages

In the movement from A to B to C in Figure 17-2 caused by the government's stimulus, you can see that the only long-run consequence is an increase in the price level from P_0 to P_1. After a period of increased production, the economy is back to producing at the full-employment output level, Y^*.

You can take two critical lessons away from this example:

» The government can't permanently keep output above Y^*.

» The government can't permanently keep more people employed than the number employed at Y^*.

These two lessons are true because of *real wages* — measured not in terms of money but by how much stuff workers can buy with the money they're paid.

REMEMBER

Real wages are crucial to understanding how government stimulus affects the economy because people don't work hard for money in and of itself — they work hard for the things money can buy. This distinction is important because as the economy reacts to the government's shifting of the aggregate demand curve from AD_0 to AD_1, real wages increase only temporarily. While they're higher, workers supply more labor. But when wages fall back down to their original levels, workers go back to supplying their original amount of labor.

Raising nominal wages while prices are stuck

To see the importance of real wages, consider the situation of a banana-loving worker named Ralph. When the economy is at Point A in Figure 17-2, Ralph is paid $10 per hour, and his favorite food, bananas, costs $1 per pound. This implies that his *real wages* — his wages measured in terms of what they can buy — are 10 pounds of bananas per hour. At that real wage, Ralph is willing to work full-time.

When the government stimulates the economy and shifts the aggregate demand curve from AD_0 to AD_1, workers like Ralph initially benefit because real wages initially rise. That's because to produce more output than Y^*, firms have to raise *nominal wages* (wages measured in money) in order to get workers to produce more. Because prices are initially sticky at price level P_0, the increase in nominal wages means an increase in real wages.

In Ralph's case, suppose that the price of bananas remains at $1 per pound because of sticky prices, but Ralph's nominal wage rises to $12 per hour because the company he works for needs more labor. Ralph's real wage increases from 10 pounds of bananas per hour to 12 pounds of bananas per hour.

This increase in real wages motivates workers to supply all the extra labor that's required to produce higher levels of output. (In Figure 17-2, this is what's going on at Point B.) Because nominal wages have gone up but prices haven't, the resulting increase in real wages causes workers to supply more labor, which in turn allows firms to produce an output level greater than Y^*.

Moving back to Y^* and to original real wages

Unfortunately, as firms begin to pass on the costs of increased nominal wages as higher prices, real wages begin to fall. Suppose that because of higher labor costs, the price of bananas rises to $1.10 per pound. At that price, Ralph's real wage falls from 12 pounds of bananas per hour down to 10.91 pounds of bananas per hour. (To get 10.91, divide Ralph's $12-per-hour money wage by the $1.10-per-pound price of bananas.)

REMEMBER

In Figure 17-2, the decrease in real wages happens as the economy moves along the aggregate demand curve from Point B to Point C. As prices rise, real wages fall. Prices continue to rise until real wages return to where they were at Point A before the government stimulated aggregate demand.

In Ralph's case, the price of bananas continues to rise until they cost $1.20 per pound. Now his higher nominal wage of $12 per hour once again buys him 10 pounds of bananas per hour; his real wage is back where it started.

This boomerang effect in the real wage makes sense. Because the economy returns to producing at Y^*, you only need to motivate workers to supply enough labor to produce Y^*, not anything extra. Workers like Ralph were willing to supply that much labor at Point A for a real wage of 10 pounds of bananas per hour. After the economy has moved to Point C, these workers will once again be willing to supply that amount of labor for the same real wage.

Not every worker is fixated on bananas like Ralph, but you get the idea: If both wages and prices rise by 20 percent, real wages remain unchanged, and consequently, the amount of labor that workers supply ends up unchanged.

REMEMBER

Because the amount of labor reflects real wages, government stimulus policies that shift aggregate demand from AD_o to AD_1 (as in Figure 17-2) can't permanently increase the amount of labor firms employ. Nor can these policies permanently increase workers' real wages. These effects are at best temporary; they last only as long as the economy takes to adjust from A to B to C.

Failing to stimulate: What happens when a stimulus is expected

Unfortunately, if people know about a stimulus ahead of time, the economy may adjust directly from A to C and eliminate the ability of the aggregate demand shift to stimulate the economy even temporarily. In this section, I show you that prices may adjust so quickly that the stimulus may fail to increase output at all, even temporarily.

Respecting the importance of price stickiness

As Figure 17-2 shows, any increase in output after aggregate demand shifts rightward from AD_0 to AD_1 depends on prices being sticky in the short run. In other words, the economy moves from Point A to Point B along the horizontal short-run aggregate supply curve, $SRAS_0$, only if the price level is fixed at P_0 in the short run.

A lot of evidence shows that prices have a hard time falling during a recession (see Chapter 16 for details). In particular, firms don't like to cut wages and insult their workers. The firms' managers know that if they cut wages, workers will become angry and refuse to work hard, and the resulting decline in productivity will make the firm's profit situation even worse.

As a result, the economy has a lot of *downward wage stickiness*, which means that nominal wages rarely decline. Downward wage stickiness leads to *downward price stickiness*, because firms can't cut their prices below production costs if they want to break even and stay in business. (Keep in mind that labor costs are, for most businesses, the largest part of production costs. If firms can't cut wages, they can't cut the price of their output.)

Realizing that prices aren't very sticky upward

In the preceding section, I talk only about *downward* stickiness; I don't say anything about prices or wages having trouble rising. In fact, there seems to be very little in the economy that can cause *upward* wage stickiness or *upward* price stickiness.

Wages and prices seem quite free to rise if demand increases relative to supply. Business and labor contracts may limit price and wage increases for a while, but as soon as these contracts expire, prices and wages are free to rise.

Anticipating (and undermining) a stimulus

REMEMBER

The lack of upward price stickiness implies two very important ideas for any government attempting to stimulate the economy into producing more than the full-employment output level (Y^*):

HELPING EMPLOYMENT WITH A LITTLE INFLATION

Economists have thought a lot about the best way to use monetary policy. Many have concluded that it should always be just a little bit overstimulating so that there's always a modest 1 or 2 percent inflation rate. The idea is that modest inflation helps smooth out the labor market by giving firms a sneaky way to increase profits if they run into a temporary slowdown in sales.

Wages are typically sticky downward because if you cut workers' wages, they get mad and give less effort. The result is that when the demand for a firm's output slows and labor costs need to be cut to restore profitability, managers usually fire a portion of the workforce and keep the remaining workers at their old wages instead of keeping all the workers on the job at lower wages.

The pressure to make such layoffs is lower in the presence of inflation, because inflation drives up the selling price of the firm's output. If managers keep nominal wages fixed while that's happening, profits improve and lessen the need to fire anyone.

But workers' real wages will fall, because while nominal (money) wages are fixed, the cost of living keeps rising due to the inflation. And because inflation helps firm profits along, firms see less of a need to lay off workers. So although the workers lose in some sense by their real wages falling, many still have jobs, whereas otherwise they would've been laid off.

» **If prices and wages can rise quickly, the economy will produce more than Y* only very briefly.** That is, the economy will move from A to B to C in Figure 17-2 very quickly — so quickly that the stimulus will cause output and employment to rise above Y* only briefly.

» **If people see a stimulus coming, that stimulus (which attempts to increase output beyond Y*) is likely to generate only inflation and no increase in output whatsoever.** If people anticipate an increase in aggregate demand, the economy may jump directly from Point A to Point C so that the price level rises without even a temporary increase in output.

This phenomenon is an example of *rational expectations*, a term that economists use to describe how people rationally change their current behavior in anticipation of future events. In this case, firms rationally decide to raise prices immediately when they find out that the government will be increasing aggregate demand from AD_0 to AD_1 in the future.

Indeed, firms' only rational course of action is to raise prices immediately because if firms were to leave prices alone at P_o, they'd be volunteering for the decrease in profits that results when the economy moves from Point A to Point B (when nominal wages rise while prices stay constant). By immediately raising prices and shifting the economy directly from A to C, firms can avoid that situation altogether.

REMEMBER

Rational expectations is one of the most important ideas in macroeconomics because it tells you that there are strong limits on the government's ability to control the economy. People don't just sit around like potted plants when the government announces a policy change; they change their behavior. And sometimes their behavioral changes completely ruin the government's ability to stimulate the economy — as is the case with firms' immediately raising prices when the firms' managers find out that the government is about to attempt a stimulus.

To see why this is true, suppose that the government preannounces a big stimulus package that will shift aggregate demand from AD_o to AD_1 in a few months' time (see Figure 17-2). Because workers and businesses can learn macroeconomics just as well as the politicians running the government, workers and businesses realize that the only long-run effect of the upcoming stimulus will be for prices to rise from P_o to P_1.

In addition, workers understand that real wages will remain unchanged in the long run because both their nominal wages and their cost of living (given by the price level) will increase by equal amounts. As a result, workers know that in the long run, the stimulus won't help them at all. Indeed, their only hope for gains is based entirely upon the short run, when nominal wages should go up and the price level should stay the same. In other words, they hope to benefit from the movement from A to B in Figure 17-2.

But firms aren't stupid. They don't want to have their profits reduced because wages are rising while prices are fixed, so firms simply anticipate everything. Because prices eventually have to rise from P_o to P_1 and wages eventually have to rise by an equal amount, firms get ahead of the wage increases by raising prices as soon as they can.

Nothing prevents firms from raising prices because nothing in the economy causes upward price stickiness. So if firms can see the stimulus coming ahead of time, they simply raise prices as soon as they can in order to make sure that prices and wages are going up at the same pace. As a result, the price level jumps from P_o to P_1.

Of course, at the same time, firms raise wages by an equal percentage in order to keep real wages the same. They want to keep workers motivated to supply the labor necessary to produce Y^* worth of output.

As you can see, if a government tries to stimulate the economy past producing at Y^*, and if everyone in the economy understands and anticipates the stimulus, it may not work at all. Prices and wages may simply jump from Point *A* to Point *C*, meaning that the stimulus fails to stimulate because output stays constant at Y^* while prices and wages go up simultaneously.

I explain monetary and fiscal policy in more detail in the rest of the chapter, where you can see other examples of rational expectations limiting the effectiveness of government policy. Be sure to notice how, in every case, changes in people's behavior reduce the impact of government policy initiatives.

Figuring Out Fiscal Policy

Fiscal policy concerns itself with how governments tax and spend. It overlaps macroeconomics because modern governments have many opportunities to increase aggregate demand by making changes in fiscal policy. These changes fall into two main categories:

>> **Indirect:** Increasing aggregate demand indirectly by lowering taxes so that consumers have larger after-tax incomes to spend on buying more goods and services

>> **Direct:** Increasing aggregate demand directly by buying more goods and services

The first category involves decreasing government revenues, and the second involves increasing government spending. Because the government's budget deficit is defined as tax revenues minus spending, both types of fiscal policy are likely to increase government budget deficits. This idea is important because large and ongoing budget deficits may lead to many economic problems, including inflation. As a result, the fear of large budget deficits constrains the magnitude of fiscal policy initiatives.

TIP

As you read about fiscal policy, keep the fear of large budget deficits in mind, because it limits the size of the aggregate demand shifts that a government can undertake. For instance, if you look back at Figure 17-1, the government may want to use fiscal policy to shift aggregate demand rightward from AD_o to AD_1, but if doing so would involve an overly large budget deficit, the government may have to settle for a smaller shift that moves the economy only part of the way back to producing again at full-employment output (Y^*).

Increasing government spending to help end recessions

If an economy gets into trouble, one of the first things that politicians call for is increased government spending. The idea is that if people are unemployed and unsold goods are sitting around gathering dust, the government can come in with a lot of money and buy up a lot of unsold products. The result is that the government generates so much demand that businesses start hiring the unemployed in order to increase output to meet all the new demand.

The hope is that this stimulus jump-starts further demand. When people who were unemployed start getting paychecks again, they start spending more money, which means demand rises. When this happens, the economic recovery should be self-sustaining so the government doesn't need to continue to spend so much money.

Paying for increased government spending

Politicians like suggesting increases in government spending because such increases make politicians look good, especially if they can get some of the new spending earmarked for their constituents. However, nothing in life is free.

The government can pay for increased spending in only three ways:

>> **The government can print more money.** Printing lots of new money to pay for increased government spending leads to large bouts of inflation, which bring with them economic chaos and recession (see Chapter 15). Consequently, governments nowadays rarely resort to printing money to pay for increased government purchases of goods and services.

>> **The government can raise taxes.** Raising taxes is problematic because if you're trying to get out of a recession, you want consumers to spend as much as possible on goods and services. If you raise taxes, consumers reduce their spending. You may offset some of the decreased private spending by immediately turning around and spending all the tax revenue, but clearly this isn't the way to stimulate aggregate demand in the long run. The government may as well just let its citizens spend their money in the first place.

>> **The government can borrow more money.** To combat recessions, governments have to figure out a way to increase their spending without decreasing private spending. The solution is borrowing.

Borrowing and spending: The most common solution

By borrowing and spending money during a recession, the government can increase its purchases of goods and services without decreasing the private sector's purchases. Who does it borrow from? You and other people like you.

At any given moment, people want to save a certain part of their incomes. These people can use these savings to buy many different kinds of assets, including stocks and bonds issued by corporations, real estate, mutual funds, and annuities. But people can also use their savings to buy government bonds, which are, in essence, loans to the government.

REMEMBER

By offering more bonds for sale, the government can redirect some of the savings that people are making away from purchases of other assets and into purchases of government-issued bonds. By selling bonds, the government can get hold of lots of money that it can spend on goods and services, thereby turning what otherwise would've been private spending on assets into public spending on goods and services.

Dealing with deficits

Increasing government spending and financing it through borrowing is clearly a good way to increase the overall demand for goods and services. But it has the potentially nasty side effect of creating a *budget deficit,* which is the dollar amount by which government spending exceeds tax revenues during the current year. Any current budget deficit adds to the *national debt,* the cumulative total of all the money that the government owes lenders.

The problem with budget deficits and the national debt is that they have to be paid back someday. Consider a ten-year bond that pays a 6 percent rate of return. When you buy the bond from the government, you give it $1,000. In return, the government promises to do two things:

>> Give you back your $1,000 in ten years

>> Give you $60 a year (a 6 percent return) until you get your $1,000 back

So the government gets $1,000 now to spend on goods and services to boost the economy, but it has to figure out where to get $60 per year for your interest payments and where to get $1,000 in ten years when the bond matures.

In this section, I explain how tax revenues and the government's ability to print money ensure that it should always be able to pay back its bonds.

Relying on the security of future tax revenues

Obviously, the only reason people are willing to lend the government any money by buying bonds is that the buyers believe that the government will eventually pay them back. They have confidence in repayment because governments have the exclusive right to tax things. Essentially, all government borrowing is secured by future tax revenues.

But the link between taxes and bond repayments is not direct. Just because a government has a lot of bonds coming due, it doesn't necessarily have to raise taxes suddenly to get the money to pay off the bonds. That's because governments often refinance the bonds that are coming due by issuing new bonds to get enough cash to pay off the old bonds. This process is referred to as *rolling over the debt* and is routinely practiced by governments everywhere.

But don't think that this is all just a huge scam to defer paying off the debt indefinitely. The only reason investors are willing to participate in a rollover is that they have confidence that the government can always use its future tax revenues to pay off its debts. Investor confidence allows governments to keep on borrowing, whether to fund new borrowing or to roll over old debt.

Paying the debt by printing money: A devastating choice

Sometimes, investor confidence in the government turns out to have been misplaced. Governments have another (rather diabolical) way to pay off their bonds besides using tax revenues: They can print lots of money.

A $1,000 bond obligates the government to pay you back $1,000 worth of money. The bond doesn't say where that $1,000 comes from. So the government is free to print $1,000 worth of new bills and hand them to you. This solution may seem okay at first, but when you and all the other bond holders with newly printed cash go out into the economy and start spending that new money, you drive up prices and cause an inflation.

Big inflations destroy economic activity, as Chapter 15 explains. Prices lose much of their meaning, and people are much more mistrustful and reluctant to engage in long-term contracts or make long-term investments because they don't know how much money will be worth in the future.

REMEMBER

Knowing the potential horrors of inflation, people tend to worry anytime they see a government running large budget deficits or piling up a very large debt. They worry that the government may find itself in a position in which it can't raise taxes high enough to pay off its obligations (or it isn't willing to anger voters by raising taxes that high). Investors worry that if this situation occurs, the government may resort to printing money to pay off its debts — and doing so would ruin the economy.

Printing money to pay government debts would also badly hurt most bondholders because most of them would get their cash after prices have gone up, meaning their cash won't buy much stuff. Consequently, when people really begin to worry that a government may start printing money to pay off its debts, finding anyone willing to buy government bonds gets harder. In such a situation, the only way for the government to get anyone to buy its bonds is to offer higher and higher interest rates as a compensation for people's worries that the money they'll eventually get back won't be worth much. These higher interest rates make the government's situation even more desperate because any debt rollovers have to be done at the higher interest rates.

Furthermore, because an inflation affects all bonds, not just the ones the government issues, interest rates all across the economy rise if people fear inflation is coming. This situation can have bad economic consequences immediately because higher interest rates dissuade consumers from borrowing money to buy things like cars and houses, and the interest rates also discourage firms from borrowing money to buy new factories and equipment. Consequently, just the expectation that a government may print money at some point in the future to pay off its bonds can cause immediate harm to the economy. (This is another example of rational expectations in action; see the section "Anticipating (and undermining) a stimulus," earlier in the chapter, for details.)

Most governments try to keep their debt level and their deficits under control so that no one seriously worries that the government will ever be tempted to print money to pay off its bonds.

Dissecting Monetary Policy

Monetary policy is the manipulation of the money supply and interest rates in order to stabilize or stimulate the economy. In modern economies, monetary policy is regarded as the most powerful mechanism that governments have at their disposal to fight recessions and reduce unemployment — even more powerful than fiscal policy.

Governments put monetary policy into practice by first changing the supply of money in order to manipulate interest rates. Because interest rates affect everything from consumers' demand for home mortgages to businesses' demand for investment goods, interest rates have a huge and pervasive effect on stimulating or depressing economic activity.

To give you a complete picture of how monetary policy functions, I first explain what money is. I then show you that having too much money is possible and how that idea is related to interest rates and inflation. That, in turn, gives you the insight necessary to understand how the government can affect interest rates by changing the amount of money floating around in the economy.

Identifying the benefits of fiat money over the gold standard

Money is an *asset,* meaning that it is a type of property that has value and which retains value over time. Other assets include real estate, precious metals such as gold, and financial assets such as stocks and bonds. But money is unique because it's the only asset that's universally acceptable as a means of payment for goods and services.

Money makes an economy much more efficient because it eliminates the need to engage in barter. But the need to verify the authenticity of money (so people are willing to accept it) means the responsibility for producing money and suppressing counterfeits falls to governments. That, in turn, brings up potential problems, because governments always face the temptation to print more money to pay off old debts or buy lots of newly produced goods and services.

Historically, one way to limit governments' ability to print more money to pay bills was to put money on a *metallic standard.* Under such a system, governments couldn't print more bills without backing them with a precious metal, such as gold. For instance, the United States used to have a gold standard under which people could redeem $35 for 1 ounce of gold. You could literally bring $35 of bills to the U.S. Treasury and exchange it for an ounce of gold.

What this meant for monetary policy was that the government couldn't arbitrarily increase the supply of paper money because for every $35 of new bills it wanted to print, it had to buy an ounce of gold with which to back them. The high cost of buying gold limited the money supply. Such a system is great for preventing big inflations because the only way you ever get a big inflation is if the government prints a huge amount of new money. (When that new money begins circulating, it drives up prices.)

WARNING

Preventing inflations is a good thing, but using a metallic standard turns out to have some big drawbacks. That's because using a metallic standard causes the supply of money to be pretty much fixed over time, meaning that even if the economy could use a little bit more or a little bit less money to make it work better, the government can't do anything because the supply of money is fixed by the amount of gold the government has in its vaults.

In particular, the metallic standard means that you can't use monetary policy to stimulate your economy if it gets into a recession. One of the reasons the Great Depression was so bad around the world was that nearly every country was on a gold standard when the calamity began. This meant that governments were unable to increase their money supplies to help their economies. It also explains why the countries that quit their gold standards earliest had the shortest and mildest recessions; after they quit, they were free to print new money to stimulate their economies. On the other hand, countries that stubbornly stuck to their gold standards, such as the United States and England, had the most prolonged and painful economic downturns.

Largely because of that experience and the desire to use monetary policy if needed, every country in the world has abandoned the gold standard in favor of *fiat money.* Under a fiat money system, the government simply prints up as many bills as it likes, declares them to be money, and puts them out in the economy. (*Fiat* means "let it be" in Latin.) The great benefit of this system is that the government can arbitrarily increase or decrease the money supply in whatever way will best help to regulate the economy.

REMEMBER

I use M to denote the total supply of money floating around the economy. For instance, "$M = \$1.3$ trillion" means that the sum of the face values of all the bills and coins in the economy is $1.3 trillion.

Realizing you can have too much money!

Monetary policy manipulates the supply of money in order to change the price of borrowing money, the interest rate. The key to making monetary policy work is that the demand for money depends on the interest rate.

You have $1 million and can do whatever you want with it. Suppose you're frugal and decide to save every penny, at least for a year, because you think that'll be enough time to figure out how to best blow the money. My question to you is: Should you keep it all in cash? The correct answer is "No!"

Holding wealth in cash is, to be blunt, not smart because it earns no interest. Even if you put the money into a checking account at a bank, you'd get at least a tiny bit of interest. Even 1 percent of interest on a million dollars is $10,000. Why would you give that up? Even better, if you use the cash to buy government bonds, you may get 5–6 percent in normal times. That's $50,000 or $60,000 more than you'd get if you kept your wealth in the form of cash.

Clearly, the higher the interest rate you can get on other assets, the more incentive you have to convert your cash into other assets. In fact, the only thing preventing people from converting all their wealth to other assets and never holding any cash is the fact that money lets them buy things. Beyond that function, money is not any better than any other asset; in fact, it's worse in terms of its rate of return because the rate of return on cash is always zero.

Figure 17-3's graph demonstrates how much money people demand to hold at any particular interest rate. I denote money demand as M^D. The nominal interest rate, i, is on the vertical axis. (For an explanation of nominal interest rates, see Chapter 15.) The horizontal axis is measured in dollars.

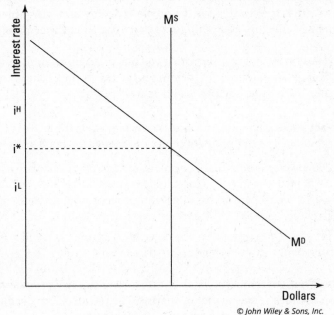

© John Wiley & Sons, Inc.

FIGURE 17-3:
The equilibrium interest rate is determined by the intersection of the money demand curve with the money supply curve.

REMEMBER

As you can see from the downward slope of the money demand curve, the higher the interest rate, the less money people want to hold. This graph simply represents the idea that cash, with its zero interest rate, is a worse and worse place to park your wealth if you can get higher and higher returns in alternative assets. In other words, the higher the interest rate on other assets, the more you're going to want to economize on your cash holdings.

Figure 17-3 also shows the vertical money supply curve, where M^S stands for money supply. This curve is vertical because the government can decide how much money it wants to print and circulate without regard to the interest rate.

The M^D and M^S curves cross at interest rate i^*. This interest rate is the *equilibrium* interest rate because it's the only one at which the total number of dollars of money that people want to hold is equal to the total number of dollars that the government has circulated. More importantly, i^* is a *stable equilibrium*, meaning that if interest rates ever deviate from it, they will be pushed back to i^* by market forces.

Getting the basics about bonds

The best way to see why the equilibrium interest rate constitutes a stable equilibrium (see the preceding section) is to understand how interest rates are determined in the bond market. Pay close attention because bond markets are *the* place where interest rates for the whole economy are determined. Bond markets have a huge effect on everything else that goes on in the economy.

A *bond* is a financial asset for which you pay a certain amount of money right now in exchange for a series of payments in the future. There are two kinds of payments, face value payments and coupon payments:

>> **Face value payment:** The face value is printed on the face of the bond certificate, and this payment comes on the date the bond expires.

>> **Coupon payments:** These payments are typically made twice per year until the bond expires. They're called *coupon payments* because before computerized recordkeeping, you'd literally clip a coupon off the bottom of the bond certificate and mail it in to receive your payment.

Typically, bonds expire after 1, 5, 10, or 20 years.

REMEMBER

Bonds do not guarantee any sort of rate of return. They promise only to make the coupon and face value payments on time. The rate of return depends on how much you pay for the right to receive those payments.

If you think I'm speaking in tongues right now, bear with me. Imagine a really simple kind of bond called a *zero-coupon bond* (so named because there are no coupon payments). The only payment this bond will ever make is the face value payment that comes when the bond expires. And to make things really simple, suppose that this bond will pay its owner exactly $100 exactly one year from now.

If you're the bond owner, the rate of return the bond will pay depends on how much you pay for it right now. Suppose that you were naive enough to pay $100 for the bond right now. Your rate of return would be zero percent because you paid $100 for something that will give you $100 in a year.

On the other hand, suppose you pay only $90 for the bond right now. Your rate of return will be about 11 percent because $(\$100 - \$90)/\$90 = 0.111$, or 11.1 percent. If you could buy the bond for only $50, your rate of return would be 100 percent because you'd double your money in a year's time.

TIP

The rate of return on a bond *varies inversely* with how much you pay for it. Because the amount of money you get in the future is always fixed, the more you pay for it right now, the less is your rate of return. Higher bond prices imply lower rates of return.

Seeing the link between bond prices and interest rates

The fact that bond prices vary inversely with interest rates is the key to understanding why i^* is a stable equilibrium in Figure 17-3. First, consider interest rates that are higher than i^*, such as i^H. When interest rates are higher than i^*, the amount of money supplied exceeds the amount of money demanded. What this means is that people have been given more of the asset called *money* than they want to hold. So what they do is try to reallocate their portfolio of assets by using the excess money to buy other assets.

Another asset is bonds. But with all this new money being thrown at the limited supply of bonds, the price of bonds rises. Now be careful. What happens to interest rates when bond prices rise? They *fall.* That's why if you start out at an interest rate that's higher than i^*, interest rates will fall back toward i^*. Excess money drives up the price of bonds, which lowers interest rates.

On the other hand, for interest rates like i^L that are lower than i^*, the amount of money demanded exceeds the amount supplied. Because people want more money than they have, they're going to try to get it by selling noncash assets such as bonds in order to convert those assets into the cash they want.

Imagine that everybody does this by trying to sell their bonds. With all the selling, bond prices fall, meaning interest rates will *rise.* In fact, bond prices will continue to fall and interest rates rise until they're back at i^*, because that's the only rate of interest at which people are satisfied holding the amount of money M^S that the government has decided to circulate.

REMEMBER

Movements back to the equilibrium interest rate, i^*, are quick. Any excess money demand or excess money supply never lasts very long because rapid adjustments in the price of bonds move the interest rate to its equilibrium.

An important consequence of the fact that interest rates adjust so quickly is that the government can print whatever amount of money it wants to, knowing that interest rates will adjust to get people to want to hold exactly that amount. This gives the government a very useful policy tool to manage the economy because it can think one step ahead and create whatever interest rate it wants by printing the appropriate amount of money.

Changing the money supply to change interest rates

Monetary policy works because governments know that interest rates adjust in order to get people to hold whatever amount of money the government decides to print. The interest rate is, in some sense, the price of money, and it reacts in a way similar to other prices. That is, if the money supply suddenly increases, the price of money falls, and vice versa.

You can see this in Figure 17-4, in which the government increases the money supply from M^S_0 to M^S_1. This action shifts the vertical money supply line to the right and lowers the equilibrium nominal interest rate from i^*_0 to i^*_1.

In the United States, changes in the money supply are controlled by the Federal Reserve Bank, which is often just referred to as *the Federal Reserve* or *the Fed.* The Fed has the exclusive right to print currency in the United States, which means that it could make M^S as big as it wanted to by printing more money and handing it out. However, the Fed actually relies on a more subtle method for changing the money supply, a method that economists call *open-market operations.*

REMEMBER

Open-market operations refers to the Fed's buying and selling of U.S. government bonds. That is, open-market operations are transactions that take place in the public, or open, bond market. Depending on whether the Fed buys or sells bonds, the money supply out in circulation in the economy either increases or decreases:

>> **If the Fed wants to increase the money supply, it buys bonds.** To buy bonds, the Fed must pay cash, which then circulates throughout the economy.

>> **If the Fed wants to decrease the money supply, it sells bonds.** The people to whom the Fed is selling the bonds have to give the Fed money, which the Fed then locks away in a vault so that it no longer circulates.

By buying or selling bonds in this way, the amount of money out in circulation (M^S) can be very precisely controlled, meaning that the Fed can, in turn, keep tight control over interest rates.

Lowering interest rates to stimulate the economy

The basic idea behind monetary policy is that lower interest rates cause both more consumption and more investment, thereby shifting the aggregate demand curve to the right. Here's how:

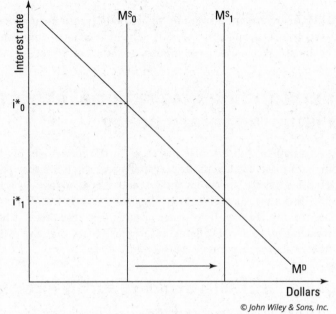

FIGURE 17-4:
Increasing the
money supply
lowers the
equilibrium
nominal
interest rate.

© John Wiley & Sons, Inc.

>> **Consumption spending:** Lower interest rates stimulate consumption spending by increasing the attractiveness of taking out loans for buying things such as automobiles and houses.

>> **Investment spending:** Lower interest rates stimulate businesses' investment spending because at lower interest rates, a larger number of potential investment projects become profitable. That is, if interest rates are 10 percent, businesses are only willing to borrow money to invest in projects with rates of return of more than 10 percent. But if interest rates fall to 5 percent, all projects with rates of return higher than 5 percent become viable, so firms take out more loans and start more projects. (For more on how interest rates affect investment, see Chapter 14.)

REMEMBER

When trying to remember how monetary policy works, keep in mind that it's actually a very simple three-step process. When the Fed wants to help increase output, it initiates the following chain of events:

1. **It buys U.S. government bonds to increase the money supply.**

2. **The increased money supply causes interest rates to fall because the prices of bonds get bid up.**

3. **Consumers and businesses respond to the lower interest rates by taking out more loans and using the money to buy more goods.**

The hard part is remembering that higher bond prices mean lower interest rates, which seems counterintuitive. But if you have a hard time remembering that, don't be embarrassed. Many economists get stuck on it, too.

Understanding how rational expectations can limit monetary policy

The government's ability to use increases in the money supply to stimulate the economy is limited by rational expectations and the fears that people have about inflation. Specifically, investors understand that increases in the money supply can cause inflation (as I discuss in Chapter 15). Whenever the Federal Reserve increases the money supply to lower nominal interest rates, it has to do so with some moderation to avoid causing inflationary fears that can offset the stimulatory effect of increasing the money supply.

Graphing the results of money supply increases

Look at Figure 17-5, which shows an economy in recession at Point A where aggregate demand curve AD_0 intersects short-run aggregate supply curve $SRAS_0$, which is fixed at price level P_0. The Federal Reserve then increases the money supply to lower interest rates and stimulate the economy, which causes the aggregate demand curve to shift rightward to AD_1.

At this point, two things can happen, depending on inflationary expectations:

» If people believe that the price level will remain fixed at P_0, the rightward shift in aggregate demand will move the economy's equilibrium rightward along the $SRAS_0$ curve from Point A to Point B.

» If people believe the price level will jump in response to the increase in the money supply, the short-run aggregate supply curve will shift up vertically by the amount that the price level is expected to increase. That means that the economy's equilibrium will move from A to C, where AD_1 intersects the new short-run aggregate supply curve, $SRAS_1$.

Because output increases less if the economy moves from A to C than if it moves from A to B, the Fed obviously has to be careful about inflationary expectations when trying to stimulate the economy by increasing the money supply. If people expect inflation to occur, their actions can offset some of the stimulus that an increased money supply is expected to bring with it.

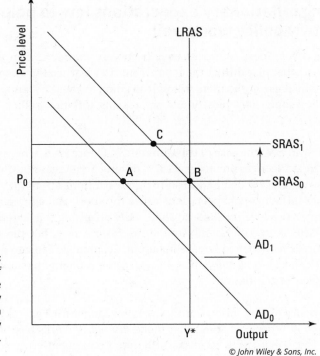

© John Wiley & Sons, Inc.

FIGURE 17-5:
The result of increasing the money supply depends on inflationary expectations.

Realizing how inflationary expectations affect interest rates

REMEMBER

The underlying problem with monetary policy is that the Fed has only partial control over interest rates. In particular, it controls money supply but not money demand. This is a problem because if people think that an increase in the money supply will cause inflation, they increase their money demand because they're expecting to need more cash to buy things at higher prices.

So while the increase in the money supply tends to lower interest rates, as in Figure 17-4, the increase in money demand caused by inflationary fears tends to increase interest rates. Because higher interest rates tend to decrease investment, any increase in interest rates caused by inflationary fears works against the stimulus that the Fed is attempting to apply to the economy by increasing the money supply.

This decrease in the effectiveness of monetary stimulus is why the big shift in aggregate demand in Figure 17-5 doesn't shift the economy back to producing at Y^*. With people expecting inflation, part of the stimulus ends up causing inflation rather than stimulating the economy to produce more output.

Keeping inflationary expectations low to help monetary policy work well

Since the 1970s, most countries have been very cautious when using monetary policy. That's because during the 1970s, countries learned the lesson that if people believe an increase in the money supply is going to cause inflation, an increase in the money supply may mostly end up causing inflation rather than providing stimulus.

You can see an extreme case of this situation in Figure 17-6, where output remains unchanged at the recessionary level Y^{Low} despite an increase in the money supply that causes aggregate demand to shift rightward from AD_0 to AD_1. The problem is that higher inflationary expectations cause the short-run aggregate supply curve to shift up vertically from $SRAS_0$ to $SRAS_1$, fully offsetting the increase in aggregate demand. The short-run equilibrium shifts from A to B, but the only effect is a higher price level with no increase in output. Economists came to refer to the situation in Figure 17-6 as *stagflation*, in which the economy has a stagnant output level coupled with inflation.

REMEMBER

The experience of stagflation during the 1970s taught the Federal Reserve (and its equivalents in other countries) that monetary policy works best if people believe that the Fed is *not* going to cause inflation. Consequently, these days, the Fed makes only moderate increases in the money supply when it wants to stimulate the economy. These increases end up being more effective than larger increases because they don't trigger inflationary fears.

Examining quantitative easing and the Great Recession

The worldwide Great Recession of 2007–2009 began when a housing bubble in the United States popped in 2006. Trillions of dollars had been invested in the financial markets on the premise that residential housing prices would never decline significantly. As the bubble burst and home prices began to plummet, dozens of large banks as well as many hundreds of financial firms were threatened with bankruptcy.

Lending ceased not only for home mortgages but for business loans, and if it hadn't been for aggressive interventions by governments and central banks, the entire worldwide financial system might have collapsed, such that nobody would have been able to obtain a loan for any purpose. Because the world economy is highly dependent on borrowed money to finance everything from credit card purchases to factory construction, another Great Depression loomed just over the horizon.

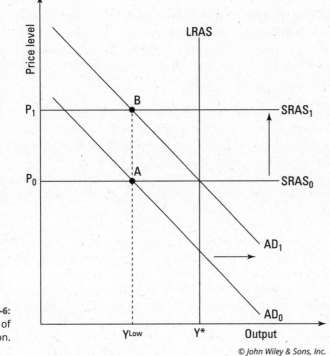

FIGURE 17-6:
An example of
stagflation.

© John Wiley & Sons, Inc.

To calm the immediate crisis, the Fed and other central banks became lenders of last resort, ensuring that businesses could still obtain financing directly from the Fed even if banks were reluctant to loan. The Fed also protected banks from banking panics by increasing the insurance limits offered to checking account depositors. These and other steps limited the recession to only being moderately severe.

That being said, the Great Recession was still much more severe than your typical recession. So it wasn't surprising that the Fed and other central banks undertook innovative new monetary policy measures to stimulate the economy. These came to be known as *unconventional monetary policy.*

Under conventional monetary policy, central banks like the Fed use open-market operations to purchase short-term (less than 1-year maturity) government bonds to increase the money supply and drive short-term interest rates toward zero in order to stimulate the economy. (For more, see the earlier section "Lowering interest rates to stimulate the economy.")

But given the severity of the Great Recession, the Fed and other central banks found that conventional monetary policy wasn't going to be enough to drive short-term interest rates to zero. Additional stimulus was needed. So the Fed and other central banks began to purchase trillions of dollars worth of longer-term government bonds (with 5-year, 10-year, and 20-year maturities), private-sector bonds (including mortgage-backed securities), and even stocks. The goal in all cases was to increase the quantity of money available to be loaned out. It was hoped that more borrowing and lending would take place, thereby stimulating both consumption and investment.

These policies became known as *quantitative easing* (or QE), since their goal was to ease the constraints on lending and borrowing by increasing the quantity of money in circulation. By contrast, conventional monetary policy targets not the quantity of money in circulation but rather the *price* of money — the interest rate. Conventional monetary policy attempts to simulate the economy by lowering the price of loans. Unconventional monetary policy (quantitative easing) attempts to increase the sheer volume of loans.

Another unconventional monetary policy was setting an explicit target for inflation, so that people would know how aggressive central banks were going to be with changes in the money supply. The inflation target was set at 2 percent in the United States, which could only be met if the Fed were increasing the money supply faster than any increase in money demand. By setting a 2 percent target, the Fed was committing itself to continually pushing the AD curve to the right and thus always attempting to stimulate the economy. This commitment was intended to give consumers and businesses confidence that the Fed would stimulate as long as necessary until the Great Recession was over and the economy had fully recovered.

IN THIS CHAPTER

» **Understanding that borrowing and debt drive price bubbles and financial crises**

» **Seeing how rising asset prices feed bubbles by increasing the value of loan collateral**

» **Examining how popping bubbles can take down the banking system**

» **Realizing that the post-bubble economy is hamstrung by high debt levels**

» **Identifying why fiscal and monetary policy don't work very well after a financial crisis**

Chapter **18**

Grasping Origins and Effects of Financial Crises

A *financial crisis* is a period of economic instability triggered by the failure of one or more major financial institutions to fulfill their promises. For instance, banking crises are triggered when banks fail to honor their legal obligation to redeem deposits on demand. And currency crises are triggered when national central banks break promises to maintain fixed exchange rates.

Financial crises can cause *recessions*, periods of decline in the total output of goods and services produced by the economy. Please understand, though, that not every bank failure or broken promise about an exchange rate triggers a recession. A recession follows a financial crisis only if previous events have led the economy into such a precarious situation that bank failures or exchange-rate collapses make a recession almost inevitable. That happened in the United States and

Europe in 2007, when the failure of many banks and investment companies to repay money that they'd borrowed to invest in real estate led to the most severe recession in over 70 years.

REMEMBER

So what sets the stage for a crisis? Massive amounts of debt. Financial crises are always preceded by economy-wide borrowing binges that fuel unsustainable asset-price bubbles, typically in stocks or real estate. These borrowing binges also fuel economic booms because a great deal of the borrowed money is used to purchase not only stocks or real estate but also goods and services.

As a boom continues, people start thinking it's permanent and that their incomes will keep rising rapidly. This encourages them to take on even more debt, so when the bubble eventually bursts, they find themselves with huge amounts of debt but much-lower-than-expected incomes. The economy then goes into a recession as people retrench, directing more of their reduced incomes to paying down debt and less to buying goods and services.

This chapter tells you how debt-driven bubbles develop, how they can cause misallocation of resources in the economy, and why recessions that occur after debt bubbles burst are so severe and hard for governments to deal with.

Understanding How Debt-Driven Bubbles Develop

Debt contracts, such as bonds and mortgages, are promises to repay particular amounts of money. When negotiating such contracts, lenders normally believe that those to whom they're lending will be able to repay — or else lenders wouldn't extend the loans. On the flip side, borrowers typically believe that they'll be able to repay — or else they wouldn't take out those loans.

However, a circular, self-reinforcing process can develop between the total amount of borrowing and the anticipated ability of borrowers to repay their loans. These situations drive *asset-price bubbles,* in which speculative purchases financed with borrowed money drive the price of an asset (such as real estate) upward.

As long as the bubble continues to expand and prices continue to rise, nearly every loan gets paid off — leading both borrowers and lenders to erroneously conclude that lending and borrowing are very safe. That drives the demand for even more borrowing and lending, further inflating the bubble. This continues until the bubble finally pops and prices collapse. In this section, I give more detail on how bubbles get started and expand, and I discuss price collapses later in "Seeing the Bubble Burst."

Embracing borrowing in a booming economy

REMEMBER

During the periods preceding financial crises, the expectations of both lenders and borrowers tend to be overly optimistic, usually because the economy has enjoyed a period of sustained growth in output and living standards. With the demand for goods and services high, jobs are plentiful and wages tend to grow strongly. Thus, both borrowers and lenders come to believe that the financial prospects of borrowers are very strong — and therefore that to borrow or lend successively larger amounts of money at successively lower interest rates wouldn't be overly risky.

The problem is that the lending and borrowing facilitated by the initial optimism can quickly become self-justifying, because when people spend borrowed money, that money stimulates the economy even more and causes an even higher level of optimism that justifies making even more loans.

Firms use the loans to expand factories, and individuals use borrowed money to purchase houses, cars, and durable goods. All this economic activity makes it easy for both borrowers and lenders to conclude that the boom will go on indefinitely and that paying back loans will always be easy for borrowers.

Offering larger loans as collateral values rise

The sharp increase in lending and borrowing that precedes a financial crisis is exacerbated by the fact that lending can drive up the value of the assets (such as real estate) that are used as collateral for loans. *Collateral* is property that a borrower pledges to a lender as security for a loan. People refer to the collateral as *security* because if the borrower fails to repay the loan, the lender receives the collateral. Thus, the collateral provides some financial security (safety) for the lender.

For instance, when a home buyer takes out a mortgage, the contract with the bank from which she's borrowing specifies that the house itself serves as collateral for the mortgage loan. Thus, if the borrower defaults on the loan, the home will become the property of the bank, which can then sell the home at auction to raise money to pay off the defaulted loan.

REMEMBER

Having houses serve as their own collateral helps fuel housing bubbles. Because rising home prices imply rising collateral values, banks feel comfortable lending successively larger amounts of money for home mortgage loans. But as loans become easier to obtain, more buyers take out loans, increase the demand for houses, and drive up home prices.

People then get into a self-reinforcing process as increased lending leads to higher demand, which leads to higher prices, which leads to increased lending because higher prices imply higher collateral values. This sort of process drove the real estate bubble in Japan during the late 1980s as well as the real estate bubbles in the United States, Ireland, and Spain from 2000 to 2006.

Relaxing lending standards

Beyond increasing collateral values, rising prices also cause lenders to become lax about their lending standards in an additional way. During normal times, lenders verify that borrowers can pay off their loans with their labor income. If you have a low labor income, then you normally aren't allowed to borrow very much money because you won't be able to afford large monthly loan payments.

This logic gets shunted aside during periods of rapidly rising real-estate prices. In fact, banks become increasingly willing to lend large amounts to anybody, including people with very low incomes, because rising real estate prices imply that borrowers should always be able to sell their houses for more than they paid for them.

For example, consider how willing a bank will be to give even a poor person a loan of $200,000 to purchase a house if the price of the house is expected to rise to $225,000 over the course of the next year. With the market price of the house expected to rise by $25,000, the bank will assume that the chance that the borrower will default on the loan is virtually zero because he'll always be able to sell the house for more money than he borrowed. Thus, in situations where home prices are expected to keep on rising, banks become willing to lend even to those with low incomes.

Borrowing more in hopes of profit

The willingness of banks to lend when home prices are expected to rise is matched by borrowers' desire to take out loans in attempts to profit from the rising real estate prices. For instance, if home prices are expected to rise from $200,000 to $225,000 over the next year, potential borrowers will assume that they can easily repay a $200,000 mortgage loan by selling the house the next year for $225,000. In fact, they'll expect to come out almost $25,000 ahead on the deal, even after accounting for accumulated interest on the loan.

The risk is that the house prices won't rise by as much as expected and may even fall, but during a housing-price bubble, many people become so convinced that home prices will rise that they feel that they're not really taking on any risk when they borrow money to purchase real estate.

Indeed, because the potential $25,000 gain looks like free money, many millions of people are tempted to take out loans to purchase houses that they'd otherwise have no reason to care about. Their goal isn't to live in those houses or to rent them out to tenants but rather to use borrowed money to "buy low and sell high," hoping to profit if home prices continue to rise.

Watching the process gain momentum

Both borrowers and lenders are willing to participate in a real estate bubble. The lenders think that rising real estate prices almost certainly guarantee that loans will be repaid, and borrowers think that rising real estate prices almost certainly guarantee that buyers can make money for nothing.

As soon as that process gains momentum, it can become temporarily self-sustaining. Lots of borrowed money drives up real estate prices, causing even more people to think that price increases will be sustained, which tempts both borrowers and lenders to increased borrowing and lending — thereby driving even further price increases. Sadly, though, there's no such thing as a party that never ends — or a party for which nobody has to pick up the tab.

Seeing the Bubble Burst

Debt-driven asset-price bubbles eventually pop because at some point, borrowing enough money to keep prices rising becomes impossible. Imagine that home prices start off at $100,000. At that price, potential buyers must be able to borrow $100,000 each if they're to purchase a home. But if home prices are driven up over time to $300,000, then any new potential buyers must get their hands on $300,000 of borrowed money to purchase a home. And if home prices rise to $500,000 per house, then potential buyers need loans of $500,000 each.

REMEMBER

Given the limited amounts of money available for borrowing, buyers will at some point face the reality that they simply can't find enough new money to borrow to drive prices up any higher. At that point, prices will peak.

In this section, I explain why asset-price bubbles pop quickly rather than deflate slowly. The end is rapid because the end of rising prices causes both a massive increase in supply as well as a massive decrease in demand. With supply rising and demand falling, prices fall rapidly.

Deleveraging: Trying to ditch debt as prices fall

People who've borrowed money to purchase assets are in a *leveraged position*, meaning that they've augmented (or in other words, *leveraged*) their own purchasing power with that of the money they've borrowed.

When a price bubble peaks, being in a leveraged position is extremely precarious. The problem is that if you're a borrower, you probably don't have enough labor income to pay off the loan. That's because you took out your loan in anticipation of future price increases. Your plan had been to sell your house for more than you paid for it, thereby getting enough money to pay off the mortgage loan while leaving any extra money as profit.

With prices unable to rise any further (due to new borrowers' being unable to borrow enough money to keep prices rising), you have no incentive to hold on to the property. You want to sell it, pay off your loan, and *deleverage* while the price of houses is still above your purchase price. Unfortunately, so does everyone else in your predicament.

The result is a massive increase in the supply of homes for sale. When prices start to fall due to the increase in supply, sellers begin to panic, undercutting each other on selling price because each one is desperate to sell before the price of houses falls below the price they paid (which is equal to the amount of money they borrowed).

Even worse, the demand for houses collapses at the same time. Why? Because during the bubble, the demand was mostly driven by the anticipation of future price increases. With prices now falling, speculators leave the market.

Taken together, the skyrocketing supply and collapsing demand cause prices to fall precipitously. The price bubble pops, and people who couldn't sell fast enough find themselves "underwater," owing more money on their mortgages than their properties are currently worth. Unless they have large enough labor incomes to make their monthly mortgage payments, they'll end up defaulting on their loans. At that point, the bubble can bring down the banking system and induce an economy-wide recession.

Comprehending bank collapses caused by bursting bubbles

Financial crises begin when bubbles burst. Because millions of borrowers owe more than their property is worth, thousands of banks and other lenders will be unlikely ever to collect on a large percentage of the mortgage loans they made during the bubble. Many of those lenders are likely to go bankrupt because their future income from loan repayments will be substantially less than what they need to meet their current and future financial obligations.

Consider commercial banks, which attempt to support themselves by borrowing money at a low interest rate and lending it out at a higher interest rate. In particular, the money that checking-account depositors place in their accounts at a particular commercial bank is in fact a loan to that bank. The bank pays these depositors a small amount of interest on their deposits and then lends their money out at a higher rate of interest to finance things such as home mortgages and small-business loans.

Normally, the vast majority of those loans for mortgages and small-business investments would be repaid on time. But many of the loans made during a bubble will never be repaid. And that means that the bank won't have enough money coming in from loan repayments to ensure that it can give back all the money that it owes to its checking-account depositors.

In legal terms, the bank is *insolvent*, owing more to the people from whom it has borrowed money than it can ever expect to get back from the people to whom it has lent money. Stated simply, an insolvent bank is a bank that can't honor its promises. The government typically takes over banks that have reached insolvency and uses taxpayer money to guarantee that all checking-account depositors will in fact get their money back. After the takeover, those banks cease to make new loans because they don't even have enough money to pay back their depositors.

Similarly, banks that aren't yet insolvent but feel threatened by that possibility also stop making new loans. They do this so that all the income that's flowing in from repayments on the loans that haven't gone bust can be saved up to guarantee the bank's ability to meet its obligations to its checking-account depositors.

The net result is that lending in the economy plummets as most banks stop making new loans either because they're already insolvent or because they may become insolvent.

Leading into a recession

After the asset-price bubble pops, the reduction in lending on the part of financially stressed banks reduces the aggregate demand for goods and services in two ways:

>> Entrepreneurs and businesses can't borrow nearly as much money as before to fund the purchase of investment goods such as machinery, computers, and so on.

>> Consumers aren't able to get nearly as many loans to finance the purchase of consumer goods.

Furthermore, many of the people who took on large amounts of debt during the bubble begin trying to pay off their loans. Repayment is possible only by devoting a larger chunk of their paychecks to paying off loans and a smaller fraction to purchasing goods and services. This reallocation of their incomes away from consumption and toward dept repayment reduces aggregate demand even more, thereby exacerbating the recession.

And that's how the collapse of an asset-price bubble can lead into a recession. After the bubble pops, credit dries up and reduces the total demand for goods and services. With less demand, firms sell fewer products. And then they start laying off employees who are made redundant by the low level of sales. Unemployment rises, spending slows, and GDP (gross domestic product; see Chapter 14) begins to decline.

After the Crisis: Looking at Recovery

An international historical examination of financial crises reveals that the recessionary periods that follow financial crises last several times longer than those following recessions that don't involve the building up of massive amounts of debt. This section examines why the recovery from post-bubble recessions tends to take so long and why government policies that can work well against normal recessions have trouble speeding up the recovery process after an asset-price bubble collapses. Here are the two main culprits:

>> A weak banking system that can't make many new loans

>> *Structural mismatches* between the goods and services that the economy's existing firms are capable of producing and the goods and services that consumers actually demand in the post-bubble period

Enduring a broken banking system

In the wake of a financial crisis, a nation's banking system tends to be weak and unable to extend many loans. Many banks become insolvent and are forced out of business as the borrowers default on their loans (see the earlier section "Comprehending bank collapses caused by bursting bubbles" for details). Other banks survive but are typically in weak financial condition because they made so many bad loans during the bubble.

As a result, the post-crisis banking system has very little capacity to make loans as the economy recovers from its post-bubble recession. The weak lending capacity prolongs the recession because even when consumers and firms regain confidence and want to borrow and spend again, they find very few banks willing to make loans.

By contrast, ordinary recessions tend to do very little damage to banks because ordinary recessions aren't preceded by asset-price bubbles. When the economy is recovering from a normal recession, loans are usually much more widely available. This speeds recovery by allowing firms and consumers to borrow and spend more freely.

Struggling with structural mismatches

Post-bubble recessions tend to be longer and more severe than ordinary recessions partly because of structural mismatches. An economy has a *structural mismatch* between its production capacity and the products consumers demand if the mix of goods and services that the economy's firms are capable of producing differs from what consumers want to purchase and consume.

Post-crisis economies often feature structural mismatches because of distortions to productive capacity that occur while bubbles are expanding. For example, consider the United States housing bubble of 2000–2006 and the subsequent recession of 2007–2009.

The U.S. housing bubble of 2000–2006 was the largest real estate bubble in world history. During the expansionary phase of that bubble, credit was easily available throughout the economy. This led to $2 trillion of excess housing being built and to many firms' borrowing trillions of dollars to fund new investment projects.

But even after the recession ended and the economy began to slowly grow again in the summer of 2009, unemployment remained very high and businesses were producing at levels far below their capacity. Some experts ascribed this to low aggregate demand caused by banks' reducing lending and consumers' reducing consumption in order to pay down debts.

Other experts, however, feared that the U.S. economy was suffering from a structural mismatch. Their reasoning was that during the bubble, firms had used their access to easy credit to build up lots of capacity to produce things that were popular during the boom — large new houses, fancy malls, and plenty of SUVs and large trucks. After the bubble popped, however, consumers didn't want lots of new houses or new SUVs or additional large trucks. Instead, they wanted products such as iPads, better touch-screen cell phones, and smaller cars, as well as the ability to do more of their shopping over the Internet instead of driving to shopping malls.

If that interpretation is correct, then recovering from the 2007–2009 recession entailed a much slower recovery process than recovering from a plain-vanilla cyclical recession. The added difficulty came from having to rejigger the economy's production capacity from making the products that were in demand while the bubble was expanding to producing the different goods and services in demand after the bubble burst.

Making that sort of a transition requires revamping old firms or starting new firms, moving workers away from dying industries into new industries, and undertaking the time and expense of retooling factories and restructuring supply chains. Making those adjustments all over the economy is not quick.

Noting the limits of government policy

Whether a recession is preceded by a bubble or not, governments almost always attempt to use both fiscal and monetary policy to increase aggregate demand (see Chapter 17). However, government stimulus policies often appear unable to significantly speed up the recovery process after a financial crisis. The policies are stymied by the debt that remains after the bubble pops.

REMEMBER

In particular, both fiscal and monetary policy are of limited effectiveness because post-bubble consumers want to deleverage, or get rid of their debt. Here's how the desire to deleverage hampers both fiscal and monetary policy:

>> **Fiscal policy:** Post-crisis fiscal policy comes in the form of massive increases in government spending that are intended to stimulate aggregate demand by having the government purchase lots of goods and services. The hope is that by increasing people's incomes, those initial purchases will spur further economic activity that will snowball into robust economic growth as consumers return to spending confidently.

But in the aftermath of a debt-driven bubble, fiscal policy's stimulatory effects may be limited because people often use increases in income to pay down debt (instead of using the money to purchase additional goods and services).

>> **Monetary policy:** The government attempts to use monetary policy to stimulate demand by lowering interest rates to encourage both consumers and firms to borrow and spend more.

However, monetary policy fails to work very well after a debt-driven bubble because highly leveraged consumers are in no mood to borrow more money. They're understandably more interested in paying down their current debts than in taking on additional debts.

If this situation sounds very dismal, it is. Until the debt level in the economy falls so that people do not need to devote so much of their incomes to paying off loans, economic growth is likely to remain stagnant, and government attempts at monetary and fiscal policy are likely to prove ineffective.

5

The Part of Tens

Discover ten common — but false — beliefs held about economics.

Get the scoop on ten valuable insights from economics.

Find out about some of the most famous economists who ever lived.

Chapter **19**

Ten Seductive Economic Fallacies

n this short chapter, I outline the most attractive and compelling incorrect ideas in economics. Some are logical fallacies. A few are myopic opinions that don't take into account the big picture. And others are poorly thought out examples of economic reasoning. All are to be avoided.

The Lump of Labor

The argument that there's a fixed amount of work that you can divide up among as many people as you want is often presented as a cure for unemployment. The idea goes that if you convert from a 40-hour work week to a 20-hour work week, firms will have to hire twice as many workers. In 2000, for instance, France reduced its work week to only 35 hours hoping that firms would hire more workers and cure the persistent unemployment problem.

It didn't work; such policies have never worked. One problem is that hiring workers involves many fixed costs, including training costs and health insurance. So two 20-hour-per-week workers cost more to employ than one 40-hour-per-week worker. What's more, two 20-hour-per-week workers don't produce any more output than one 40-hour-per-week worker.

So if laws were passed that forced firms to move from a 40-hour work week to a 20-hour work week, firms wouldn't double the size of their workforces. They'd hire fewer than twice as many workers because costs would go up.

In addition, even if cutting the work week in half actually did double the number of workers used, it would only hide the overall unemployment problem by spreading it around. If, for example, 100 percent of workers are working half-time, they are all 50 percent underemployed. In terms of the total amount of output that could be produced (and hence available for people to consume), that situation wouldn't be any better than having 50 percent of the population employed full-time and 50 percent totally unemployed.

REMEMBER

You really want a situation in which every worker who wants a full-time job is able to get one. Shortening the work week doesn't achieve this goal.

The World Is Facing Overpopulation

Various versions of this myth have been floating around since the late 18th century when Thomas Malthus first asserted it. He argued that living standards couldn't permanently rise because higher living standards would cause people to breed faster. He believed that population growth would outpace our ability to grow more food, so we would be doomed to return to subsistence levels of nutrition and living standards.

Even when Malthus first published this idea, lots of evidence indicated that it was bunk. For generations, living standards had been rising while birth rates had been falling. And because that trend has continued up to the present day, we're not going to breed our way to subsistence. Indeed, many nations now face an *under*population problem because birthrates have fallen below the replacement rate necessary to keep the population stable. The populations of Italy, Japan, and Russia, among others, have already begun to shrink.

A related problem is that rapidly falling birth rates are wreaking havoc on government-sponsored retirement systems because there aren't enough young workers to pay all the taxes needed to fund retirees' pensions.

Sequence Indicates Causation

Post hoc ergo propter hoc is a Latin phrase that translates roughly as, "Because you see one thing precede another, you think that it causes the other." That is, if A happens before B, you assume that A causes B. Such a deduction is false because

A and B often don't have any relationship. For instance, sometimes it rains in the morning, and I get a headache in the afternoon. That doesn't mean that the rain caused my headache.

Politicians try to pull this logical fallacy all the time when discussing the economy. For instance, suppose that politician A gets elected, and a recession begins a few months later. The two may have nothing to do with each other, but you can be sure that during the next election, politician B — an opponent of politician A — will claim that the recession was the result of politician A's policies. The only proof offered is that one event happened before the other.

Protectionism Is the Best Solution to Foreign Competition

Many trade unions and politicians argue in favor of trade barriers and taxes on imports on the grounds that these policies would benefit citizens and prevent jobs from being exported. The problem is that their arguments consider only the benefits of protectionism. Trade barriers and taxes on imports *do* protect the specific jobs that they're intended to protect. However, other jobs are often sacrificed in the process.

Another problem with protectionism is that citizens are consumers as well as producers. For instance, if the government prevents the importation of lower price, higher quality foreign automobiles, it preserves jobs in the domestic auto industry. But costs for domestic consumers rise as a result.

Protecting an unproductive industry that faces foreign competition only allows it to keep using resources that would otherwise be better used by more vibrant industries. Workers who would otherwise move to jobs in innovative, highly productive new industries instead get stuck in an industry so unproductive that it can survive only by having the government rig the economy in its favor.

Granted, the move from a dying industry to an innovative new industry can be rough for an individual worker. But rather than avoid the need for change by protecting unproductive industries, the government can help domestic workers more efficiently by providing retraining programs for employees. (In the case of older workers who have only a few years of employment left, early retirement programs may be more viable than retraining.)

The Fallacy of Composition

Assuming that what's good for one person to do is good for everyone to do all at once is another common fallacy. For instance, if you're at a sold-out sporting event and want to get a better view, standing is a good idea — but only if you're the only one who stands up. If everyone else also stands up, everyone's view is just as bad as when everyone was sitting down (but now everyone's legs are getting tired). Consequently, what was good for you to do alone is actually bad for everyone to do at the same time.

The fallacy of composition is false because some things in life have to do with relative position. For instance, if you start out as the lowest paid employee at your firm but then get a 50 percent raise while nobody else gets a raise, your relative position within the firm improves. However, if everyone gets a 50 percent raise at the same time, you're still the lowest paid person at the firm. If what matters to you is your relative standing within the firm, getting the same raise as everyone else doesn't make you any happier. (On the other hand, if you are more interested in where you stand relative to people who work at other firms, getting a 50 percent raise is good even if everyone else at your firm gets it, too!)

If It's Worth Doing, Do It 100 Percent

We all value safety. But was a famous U.S. politician really being sensible when he said that we should spend whatever money might be necessary to make flying on commercial airlines "as safe as possible"? Economists would say, "No!" The problem is that making commercial airline travel "as safe as possible" would mean making it prohibitively expensive.

The politician failed to apply *marginalism* — the idea that the best way to approach a problem is to compare marginal benefits with marginal costs. The first few airline safety innovations (such as seatbelts and radar) are sensible to undertake because the extra, or marginal, benefit that each brings is greater than the extra, or marginal, cost required to pay for it. But after the first few safety innovations are implemented, successive innovations become more costly and less effective. At some point, additional innovations bring only small marginal increases in safety while running up high marginal costs.

REMEMBER

When the costs for the extra safety innovations exceed their benefits, they *shouldn't* be implemented. You should add safety features only as long as the marginal benefits exceed the marginal costs — which means that you'll usually stop adding safety features long before you get anywhere near making things "as safe as possible."

Free Markets Are Dangerously Unstable

Free market prices and quantities often change extremely rapidly. They do so because supply and demand often change very quickly, causing rapid changes in equilibrium prices and quantities (which I discuss in Chapter 4). But rapidly changing prices and quantities should not be seen as a problem in and of themselves. The responsiveness of markets is actually one of their great benefits. Unlike a government bureaucracy that can never react quickly to anything, markets can adjust to huge changes in world events in only minutes.

The new equilibrium prices and quantities see to it that resources are allocated to their best uses and that society suffers from neither shortages nor gluts. So don't call markets unstable. Call them *responsive*.

Low Foreign Wages Mean That Rich Countries Can't Compete

Suppose that a U.S. factory pays its workers $20 per hour while a competing factory in a developing country pays its workers $4 per hour. People mistakenly jump to the conclusion that because the foreign factory's labor costs are so much lower, it can easily undersell the U.S. factory. But this argument fails to take into account two things:

>> What actually matters is labor costs per *unit,* not labor costs per *hour.*

>> Differences in productivity typically mean that labor costs per unit are often nearly identical despite huge differences in labor costs per hour.

To see what I mean, compare how productive the two factories are. Because the U.S. factory uses much more advanced technology, one worker in one hour can produce 20 units of output. The U.S. worker gets paid $20 per hour, so the labor cost *per unit of output* is $1. The factory in the developing country is much less productive; a worker there produces only 4 units in one hour. Given the foreign wage of $4 per hour, the labor cost per unit of output in the developing country is also $1.

Obviously, the developing country's lower hourly wage rate *per hour* does not translate into lower labor costs *per unit* — meaning that it won't be able to undersell its U.S. competitor.

People who focus exclusively on the difference in labor costs per hour never mention the productivity differences that typically equalize labor costs per unit.

And don't think that my example uses happy-happy numbers. Wage differences across countries really do tend to reflect productivity differences.

TIP

Keep in mind that governments can seriously screw up what would otherwise be a near equality of labor costs per unit by fixing artificially low exchange rates. For instance, if at an exchange rate of 8 Chinese yuan to 1 U.S. dollar labor costs per unit are equal, the Chinese government could make labor costs per unit look artificially low to U.S. consumers if it fixes its currency at, for instance, 16 yuan to 1 dollar. In such situations, the inability of U.S. workers to compete with Chinese workers is due to the currency manipulation, not to the lower wage rate per hour found in China.

Tax Rates Don't Affect Work Effort

Some politicians argue for raising income taxes as though the only effect of doing so will be to raise more money. But it's been demonstrated over and over again that beyond a certain point, people respond to higher taxes by working less. And that reduction in labor denies society all the benefits that would have come from the extra work. (Because people work less, the increased tax rate also doesn't bring in nearly as much revenue as expected.)

So if you see a politician arguing for an increase in income taxes, look into the details to make sure that the disincentive effects of the tax hike don't cause more mischief than the benefits that will be derived from spending the money raised by the tax increase.

Forgetting Unintended Consequences

When evaluating a policy, people tend to concentrate on how the policy will fix some particular problem while ignoring or downplaying other effects it may have. Economists often refer to this situation as *The Law of Unintended Consequences.* For instance, suppose that you impose a tariff on imported steel in order to protect the jobs of domestic steelworkers. If you impose a high enough tariff, their jobs will indeed be protected from competition by foreign steel companies. But an unintended consequence is that the jobs of some autoworkers will be lost to foreign competition. Why? The tariff that protects steelworkers raises the price of the steel that domestic automobile makers need to build their cars. As a result, domestic automobile manufacturers have to raise the prices of their cars, making them relatively less attractive than foreign cars. Raising prices tends to reduce domestic car sales, so some domestic autoworkers lose their jobs.

Chapter **20**

Ten Economic Ideas to Hold Dear

I n this chapter, I list ten economic ideas that all informed people should understand and be ready to use to evaluate the policy proposals made by politicians, pundits, and the media. Some of these ideas aren't true in all situations, but because they're usually correct, be wary if some guy wants you to believe that they don't apply to a particular situation. Chances are that he's wrong.

Self-Interest Can Improve Society

The idea that self-interest can improve society is basically Adam Smith's famous *invisible hand*. If all economic transactions in a society are voluntary on the parts of all parties involved, then the only transactions that will take place are those where all parties feel that they're being made better off. This concept doesn't mean that charitable acts are bad for society. Rather, it means that even philanthropy is generated by self-interest: People give because they enjoy helping others, so both givers and the people they help are better off. In addition, this concept motivates entrepreneurs to find ways to produce products you like at prices you like. Sellers must fear your power of choice — your right to walk away from any offer that you don't consider advantageous.

Free Markets Require Regulation

Economists firmly believe that voluntary transactions in free markets tend to work toward the common good. But they also believe that nearly every participant in the marketplace would love to rig the system in his or her own favor. Adam Smith was quick to argue that for markets to work and serve the common good, the government has to fight monopolies, collusion, and any other attempts to prevent a properly functioning market in which firms vigorously compete against each other to give consumers what they want at the lowest possible price. Government intervention may also be necessary to deal with asymmetric information, public goods, and externalities.

Economic Growth Relies on Innovation

The only way to have sustained economic growth and widespread increases in living standards is to invent more efficient technologies that allow people to produce more from the limited supply of labor and physical resources. To that end, societies should promote education and set up institutions such as patent rights, competitive markets, and copyright laws to promote innovation and increases in efficiency.

Freedom and Democracy Make Us Richer

Very good moral and ethical reasons exist for favoring freedom and democracy. But a more bottom-line reason is that because they promote the free development and exchange of ideas, free societies have more innovation and, consequently, faster economic growth. And they attract foreign investment.

Education Raises Living Standards

Not only do educated people produce more as workers — and get paid higher salaries — they produce innovative new technologies. Sustained economic growth and higher living standards are possible only if you educate your citizens well. You have, of course, other good reasons for getting an education, including the ability to appreciate high art and literature. But if all you care about is rising living standards, work hard to promote education in science and engineering, sectors where revolutionary technologies are created.

Intellectual Property Boosts Innovation

People need incentives to take risks. One of the biggest risks is leaving a secure job to start a new business or develop a great new idea. *Intellectual property rights,* such as patents and copyrights, guarantee that you'll be the only one making money off your hard, innovative work. Without this assurance, few would be willing to take the risks necessary to provide new technologies and products.

Weak Property Rights Cause All Environmental Problems

Environmental problems stem from poorly defined or nonexistent property rights that allow polluters to ignore the costs that they impose on others. Therefore, economists favor the creation and enforcement of property rights systems that force people to take all costs into account. People always need to do some polluting. After all, even if you don't want gas-guzzling SUVs causing lots of pollution, you probably still want ambulances and fire trucks to operate even though they, too, pollute the environment. The difference is that the benefits to society outweigh the costs of pollution in the case of the emergency vehicles. As I discuss in Chapter 10, strong property rights are the key to ensuring that people weigh the complete costs and benefits of causing pollution. Property rights force people to take into account not only personal costs but also the costs that their actions impose on others.

International Trade Is a Good Thing

Opening your country to international trade means opening your country to new ideas and innovations. Competition causes local businesses to innovate to match the best offerings of companies from around the world. Throughout history, the richest and most dynamic societies have been the ones open to international trade. Of course, what economists have in mind when they think of the benefits of international trade is *free trade,* where companies compete across borders to provide people with the best goods and services at the lowest prices. Economists strongly condemn the government subsidies and trade restrictions that impede free trade and that try to rig the game in one country's favor.

Government Can Provide Public Goods

Economists view the existence of public goods as one of the most important justifications for government intervention in the economy. Although private philanthropy can provide some public goods, many are so expensive that they can be provided only if the government uses taxes to fund them. Consequently, public goods are typically government-provided.

Private firms can provide goods and services only if they can at least break even doing so. To break even (or make a profit), whatever a firm is selling has to be *excludable*, which means that only those paying for the good or service receive it. As I explain in Chapter 11, some goods and services are not excludable. For instance, a lighthouse provides warning services to all ships in the vicinity regardless of whether the ships' captains pay the lighthouse keeper. The private lighthouse quickly goes bankrupt because only a few captains are fair-minded enough to pay for the service. Goods and services that are not excludable are *called public goods* because they're essentially open to the public and can't be kept private.

Because private firms can't make a profit producing public goods, you typically need governments to provide them. Governments can *force* people to pay for public goods. They do this by levying taxes and using the tax revenues to pay for public goods, such as national defense, police departments, lighthouses, public fireworks displays, basic scientific research, and so on.

Preventing Inflation Is Easy

High rates of inflation are caused by the government's increasing the money supply too rapidly. A growing economy always has a growing demand for money because with more stuff to buy, you need more money with which to buy it. To keep the overall level of prices constant, increase the money supply at the same rate that demand is increasing. If the supply of money increases faster than the demand, the value of money falls, creating an inflation. In other words, you need more money to buy the same amount of stuff as before, so prices go up. The way to prevent an inflation is to make sure that the government increases the money supply at the same rate that the demand for money increases. Modern central banks such as the Federal Reserve Bank in the United States can do this quite easily, so there's no excuse for high rates of inflation.

Chapter **21**

Ten (Or So) Famous Economists

This short chapter describes the ideas put forth by 12 of the best and most influential economists. (Ten wasn't enough.) Each either radically changed the way that economics conceptualizes the world or radically changed the way that politicians and government officials formulate public policy.

But don't think these guys did it all on their own. As with any science, a single person's breakthrough is built on the hundreds of contributions made by scores of researchers. In other words, there are a whole lot more than 10 — or even 12 — great economists. With any luck, this book has sparked your interest to learn more about economics, so you can come to know the stellar ideas of the many great economists who didn't happen to make this list.

Adam Smith

Adam Smith (1723–1790) developed the intuition that as long as firms are constrained by robust competition, their self-interested profit seeking inadvertently causes them to act in ways that are socially optimal — as though they are guided by an *invisible hand* to do the right thing.

But Smith was not naive. He believed that businessmen prefer to collude rather than compete whenever possible, and that governments have a very important economic role to play in fostering the robust competition needed for the invisible hand to work its magic. He also believed that governments must provide many essential public goods, like national defense, that aren't readily produced by the private sector.

David Ricardo

David Ricardo (1772–1823) discovered comparative advantage and argued correctly that international trade is a win-win situation for the countries involved. Comparative advantage destroyed the intellectual respectability of *mercantilism*, the mistaken theory behind colonialism that viewed trade as being one-sided and consequently argued that trade should be set up to benefit the mother country at the expense of its colony.

Ricardo correctly analyzed the economic phenomenon of diminishing returns, which explains why costs tend to increase as you increase production levels. He was also a strong early proponent of the quantity theory of money, the idea that increasing the money supply will increase prices.

Karl Marx

Karl Marx (1818–1883) was the foremost economist among 19th-century socialists. None of his major economic theories is now believed to be true, but because proponents of his Marxist ideas came to power in dozens of countries during the 20th century, he is surely one of the most influential economists who ever lived. (Marx gets the most space here not because he's the most important economist on this list, but because I have to take the time to explain his ideas before discrediting them. The ideas of the other economists on this list are already explained in detail in other places in this book.)

Marx's most important intellectual contribution is his idea that capitalism is a historically unique form of social and productive organization. In his book *Capital*, he analyzed capitalism as a brand-new form of social and economic organization based on capital accumulation and factory production. He called the owners of the factories "capitalists" and argued that they would be forced to exploit the workers who labored in their factories.

In particular, he believed that the only capitalists who would survive and whose businesses would grow were those who paid workers the minimum salaries necessary for the workers to survive. Thus, even as productivity and output rose rapidly, workers would endure permanent, grinding poverty out of which they could never rise except by means of a violent overthrow of the capitalists in which the workers would gain control over the factories.

Marx argued that this violent overthrow would be facilitated by what he saw as an inevitable tendency toward concentration and monopoly. When there was only one monopoly firm in each industry, it would be much easier for the workers to revolt and take over the system.

With more than a century of hindsight, we know that Marx was wrong in his economic thinking. In particular, workers' wages *do* rise over time — in fact, they rise on average as fast as technological innovation increases productivity levels. That's because capitalists compete over the limited supply of workers, and wages get bid up as quickly as productivity improvements allow one capitalist to bid higher wages to steal workers away from other capitalists. In addition, competition does *not* lead to each industry being dominated by a single monopoly firm. Rather, competition remains robust in most industries and consequently delivers all the benefits of Adam Smith's invisible hand.

Alfred Marshall

Alfred Marshall (1842–1924) invented the supply-and-demand method for analyzing markets. Applying mathematics to economic theory, he clearly differentiated between *shifts* of demand and supply curves and movements *along* demand and supply curves. In doing so, he cleared up 2,000 years of faulty reasoning. He also made the revolutionary prediction that the market price would be where the demand and supply curves cross.

Marshall went one more step and realized that by comparing points along demand and supply curves with the market price, you could quantify the benefits consumers and producers derive from market transactions: The sum of consumer surplus and producer surplus is the total economic surplus.

This method of quantifying the benefits of production and consumption is still used today and forms the basis of *welfare economics,* which studies the costs and benefits of economic activities. This method also happens to illustrate the intuition behind Adam Smith's invisible hand. The free market equilibrium, where demand and supply cross, is exactly the same as what a benevolent social planner would choose to do to try to maximize social welfare by maximizing total economic surplus. In other words, a free market does indeed act "as if moved by an invisible hand" to promote the common good.

John Maynard Keynes

John Maynard Keynes (1883–1946) invented modern macroeconomics and the idea of government-provided economic stimuli overcoming recessions. Much of the rest of 20th-century macroeconomics was a response to his ideas.

His most famous ideas were developed in response to the long agony of the Great Depression of the 1930s. He first asserted that the Great Depression was the result of a collapse in the expenditures being made on goods and services. He then asserted that monetary policy had been ineffective in combating the decline in expenditures. And he finally concluded, given his dismay about monetary policy, that fiscal policy was the only remaining source of salvation. In particular, Keynes believed that the best way to increase expenditures in such dire circumstances was for the government to spend heavily to pay for programs that would buy up lots of goods and services in order to get the economy moving again.

Keynes's policy prescriptions were adopted during the Great Depression in many countries, including the United States. And although many of his ideas about the cause of the Great Depression and the best policies for dealing with recessions are no longer embraced, his underlying idea that governments are responsible for taming the business cycle remains very much with us today.

Kenneth Arrow and Gerard Debreu

Kenneth Arrow (1921–2017) and Gerard Debreu (1921–2004) mathematically proved that Adam Smith's intuition about the invisible hand was, in fact, correct. Not only do competitive firms provide society with the utility-maximizing combination of goods and services, they do so efficiently, at minimum cost. Since this proof came in the 1950s, it served to disprove the assertions of totalitarians and communists that centrally planned economies were more productive or more efficient than market economies.

Milton Friedman

Milton Friedman (1912–2006) convinced economists that the quantity theory of money is, in fact, true: Sustained inflations are the result of sustained increases in the money supply (printing too much money). This insight put limits on using monetary policy to stimulate the economy.

Friedman also argued that the Great Depression was chiefly a monetary disaster and that its severity was the result of a gruesomely tight money supply that kept real interest rates much too high. This diagnosis of the cause of the Great Depression is now the standard explanation, meaning that the intellectual ammunition for Keynes's solution to recessions — large increases in government spending — has lost much of the sway that it once had. It has also led economists to conclude that monetary policy is more important than fiscal policy for regulating the economy and preventing recessions.

Paul Samuelson

Paul Samuelson (1915–2009) has made many contributions. Perhaps the most important was crystallizing the idea that all economic behavior can be thought of as consumers and firms maximizing either utility or profits subject to a set of constraints. *Constrained maximization* has become the dominant paradigm that governs how economists conceive of economic behavior.

Samuelson also developed a judicious blending of Keynesian and classical ideas about the proper use of government intervention in the economy. Keynes argued for large government interventions to mitigate recessions. Smith and Ricardo argued for minimal government interventions, fearing that government interventions tend to make things worse. Samuelson's *neoclassical synthesis* states that during recessions the government should be willing to make large interventions in the economy to get it moving, but when it's operating at full potential, the role of government is to provide public goods and take care of externalities. Many economists embrace this view.

Robert Solow

Robert Solow (b. 1924) has made huge contributions to the understanding of economic growth and rising living standards. In addition to developing innovative models of how economies grow, he showed that the dominant long-run force propelling economic growth is technological innovation.

Before Solow, the economic profession believed that increases in output were the result of increases in inputs. In particular, increases in output were solely the result of either using more workers or more capital (such as bigger factories). What Solow demonstrated was that *at most* 50 percent of the long-run growth of living standards can be explained by increases in labor and capital. The rest has to be the result of technological innovation.

This created a huge paradigm shift among economists that has resulted in the study of technological innovation and how it can be improved by government policies like patents and copyrights. It also opens up the refreshing possibility that technological innovation will allow us to enjoy higher living standards without having to constantly increase use of the earth's resources.

Gary Becker

Gary Becker (1930–2014) has been hugely influential because he has pushed economics into areas that were previously immune to economic thinking. His first major contribution was to argue that free markets would tend to work *for* equality and *against* racial and gender discrimination. The intuition is that firms that refuse to hire the best qualified workers because of their race or gender put themselves at a competitive disadvantage relative to nonbiased firms. Becker backed up this intuition by showing that industries that are more competitive do, in fact, employ more minorities and women.

Another significant contribution Becker made was to model families as economic units in which family members tend to act on the basis of cost–benefit analyses. As societies became richer and paid employment became more plentiful (and better paying), Becker predicted that more women would choose to work rather than stay home. He provided an economic explanation for a huge change in the labor force that otherwise would have been explained only in terms of sociological considerations (such as changing gender roles).

Similarly, he was the first to model criminal behavior in terms of how criminals view the potential costs and benefits of committing a given crime. If the expected benefits exceed the expected costs, the criminal will most likely attempt the crime. This theory of criminal behavior is radically different from previous explanations, and it led Becker to propose the very influential idea that the best way to deter crime is to raise the costs relative to the benefits.

Robert Lucas

Robert Lucas (b. 1937) showed that people are sophisticated planners who constantly modify their optimal strategies in response to government policy. If you assume that people only very slowly change their behavior in response to policy changes, you'll overestimate the results of those changes.

Monetary policy loses most of its effectiveness if people rationally plan for it. Suppose the government announces that in three months it's going to double the money supply in an attempt to stimulate increased purchases of goods and services. If store owners keep prices the same even though more money is on the way, the economy will be stimulated because people will buy more stuff with that new money. But if shop owners double their prices in anticipation of the doubling of the money supply, the policy change won't result in any increase in the amount of goods and services sold. With prices twice as high, twice as much money will only allow customers to buy as much as before.

Lucas's idea came be known as *rational expectations,* and it brought with it a new humility about the extent to which government policy — monetary policy in particular — can influence the world.

Appendix

Glossary

This glossary contains common economics terms. Words set in *italic* type are terms that are defined separately in this glossary.

absolute advantage: When a person or nation can produce more output from a given amount of resource inputs than can another person or nation.

aggregate demand: Total demand for goods and services in an economy.

aggregate supply: The total supply of goods and services in an economy.

allocatively efficient: When an economy's limited supply of resources is allocated to the production of the goods and services that consumers most greatly desire to consume.

anchoring: The tendency people have to anchor (base) the value that they assign an item on recently viewed, but logically irrelevant, information.

antitrust laws: Laws that regulate *monopolies* and *cartels*.

asset-price bubble: A situation in which the price of an asset rises above its true value; usually driven by speculative purchases financed with borrowed money.

asymmetric information: A situation in which either the buyer or the seller knows more about the quality of the good that he or she is negotiating over than does the other party.

behavioral economics: The branch of economic theory that deals with irrational decision making and *systematic errors*.

capital: Machines, factories, and infrastructure used to produce output.

cartel: A group of firms that colludes and acts as a single coordinated whole to restrict output and drive up prices; formerly called trusts.

collateral: An asset pledged to guarantee the repayment of a loan in the event that the borrower fails to make his or her contractually obligated loan payments on schedule.

command economy: An economy in which all economic activity is directed by the government.

comparative advantage: Occurs when a person or nation can produce a good or service at a lower opportunity cost (in terms of other goods and services that must be forgone) than another person or nation.

Consumer Price Index (CPI): The Bureau of Labor Statistics' *market basket* (bundle of goods and services) used to measure changes in the prices of goods and services bought by a typical family of four.

consumer surplus: The benefit consumers get when they can buy something for less than the maximum amount that they're willing to pay for it.

deadweight loss: The amount by which *total surplus* (the sum of *consumer surplus* and *producer surplus*) is reduced whenever output is less than the *socially optimal output level*.

deflation: When the overall level of prices in the economy is falling.

demand: The whole range of quantities that a person with a given income and preferences will demand at various possible prices.

demand curve: A line on a graph that represents how much of a good or service buyers will consume at various prices.

depreciation: A decrease in the economy's stock of *capital* caused by wear and tear or obsolescence (when an older machine or tool, despite being in good working order, is no longer wanted because it's been made outdated by new technologies).

dictator game: A *behavioral economics* game in which one person (the dictator) gets to anonymously split a sum of money with a second player. Provides evidence of a human tendency for fairness because most dictators share at least some of the money with the other player.

diminishing marginal utility: A situation in which each additional, or *marginal*, unit of a good or service that you consume brings less *utility* (happiness) than the previous unit.

diminishing returns: A situation in which each additional unit of a resource used in a production process brings forth successively smaller amounts of output.

economic costs: Total costs, including money spent on production and *opportunity cost* (the value of the best alternative forgone).

economic profits: Any monies collected by a firm above and beyond what is required to keep an entrepreneur owner interested in continuing in business.

economics: The study of how people allocate scarce resources among alternative uses.

endowment effect: The tendency people have to put a higher dollar value on items they possess as compared with identical items that they do not possess. Explained by *prospect theory* and *loss aversion*.

entrepreneur: Individuals who supply *entrepreneurial ability* to firms.

entrepreneurial ability: The human resource, distinct from *labor*, that combines the other three *factors of production (land, labor,* and *capital)* to produce new products or make innovations in the production of existing products. Without entrepreneurial ability, we'd be stuck making the same things the same way, forever.

equilibrium: A situation where every party involved in an economic interaction has no reason to change his or her current behavior.

externality: A cost or benefit that falls not on the person(s) directly involved in an activity but on others; externalities can be positive (benefits) or negative (costs).

factors of production: Inputs (resources) used to create goods and services, including land, labor, capital, and entrepreneurship.

financial markets: Markets in which either people trade the property rights to assets (such as real estate or stocks) or savers lend money to borrowers.

fiscal policy: A government's policy on taxes and spending; increased government spending and/or lower tax rates help to fight recessions.

fixed costs: Costs that have to be paid even if a firm isn't producing anything.

framing effects: Changes in decisions that are caused by making potential options that were once viewed as losses look like gains, and vice versa. Explained by *prospect theory.*

full employment: When every worker who wants a full-time job can obtain one.

full-employment output (Y^*): The quantity of output produced in the economy when there's *full employment* in the labor market.

gross domestic product (GDP): The value of all goods and services produced in the economy in a given period of time, usually a quarter or a year; the sum (denoted by the variable Y) of expenditures on consumption, investment, government purchases, and exports less expenditures on imports, or $Y = C + I + G + EX - IM$.

human capital: The knowledge and skills that people use to help them produce output.

hyperinflation: A very high rate of *inflation;* defined by some authors to be a rate of inflation in excess of 20 or 30 percent per month.

increasing returns: A situation in which each additional unit of a resource used in a production process brings forth successively larger amounts of output.

inflation: When the overall level of prices in the economy is rising.

inflation rate: A measure of how the overall level of prices in the economy changes over time; if the inflation rate is positive, prices are rising; if the inflation rate is negative, prices are falling.

insolvent: Being unable to honor one's financial obligations because one's financial obligations exceed the combined value of current assets and future income.

interest rate: The price someone has to pay to borrow money.

investment: Spending to increase the economy's stock of *capital* as well as the value of any increases in inventories.

invisible hand: Adam Smith's famous idea that when firms are constrained by competition, each firm's greed causes it to act in a socially optimal way, as if guided to do the right thing by an invisible hand.

laissez faire: See *market economy.*

law of demand: The fact that for most goods and services, price and quantity demanded have an inverse relationship (as one goes up, the other goes down).

long-run shutdown condition: A situation in which a firm's total revenues exceed its *variable costs* but are less than its total costs; the firm will operate until its *fixed cost* contracts expire (in the long run).

loss aversion: The tendency people have to avoid potential losses relative to their current *status quo* situation. Explained by *prospect theory.*

macroeconomics: The study of the economy as whole, concentrating on economy-wide factors such as interest rates, inflation, and unemployment; macroeconomics also encompasses the study of economic growth and how governments use monetary and fiscal policy to try to moderate the harm caused by recessions.

marginal cost: How much total costs increase when you produce one more unit of output.

marginal utility: The change in total *utility* (happiness) that results from consuming the next unit of a good or service; marginal utility can be positive or negative.

market basket: A bundle of goods and services selected to measure inflation; economists define a market basket, such as the *Consumer Price Index,* and then track how much money it takes to buy this basket from one period to the next.

market economy: An economy in which the private decisions of consumers, resource suppliers, and firms determine how resources are allocated, with only limited interventions from the government; often referred to as a *laissez-faire* ("to leave alone") economic system.

market failures: Situations in which markets deliver nonoptimal social outcomes; common causes of market failure are *asymmetric information, monopoly, externalities,* and *public goods.*

microeconomics: The part of economics that studies individual people and individual businesses; for people, microeconomics studies how they behave when faced with decisions about where to spend their limited budgets; for businesses, it studies how profit-maximizing firms behave individually and how they behave when competing against each other in markets.

monetary policy: Using changes in the money supply to change interest rates in order to stimulate or slow down economic activity.

monopolistic competition: A situation in which many firms with slightly different products compete; production costs are above what could be achieved by perfectly competitive firms, but society benefits from the product differentiation.

monopoly: A firm that has no competitors in its industry; it produces less output, has higher costs, generates a *deadweight loss,* and sells its output for a higher price than it would if constrained by competition; these negative outcomes usually generate government regulation.

myopia: The human tendency to see near-term costs and benefits clearly while giving relatively little thought to costs and benefits that lie in the future. Leads to decisions that favor present options over future options.

natural monopoly: An industry in which one large producer can produce output at a lower cost than many small producers; it undersells its rivals and ends up as the only firm surviving in its industry.

nominal interest rates: Interest rates that measure the returns to a loan in terms of money borrowed and money returned (as opposed to *real interest rates*).

nominal prices: The price as it's actually observed in current dollars; contrasts with *real prices,* which adjust for inflation.

nominal wages: Wages measured in current dollars; contrasts with *real wages,* which adjust for *inflation.*

oligopoly: An industry with only a few firms; if they collude, they form a *cartel* to reduce output and drive up profits the way a *monopoly* does.

opportunity cost: The value of the best forgone alternative option; what you give up in order to pursue a particular option.

perfect competition: A situation in which numerous small firms producing identical products compete against each other in a given industry; perfect competition leads to firms' producing the *socially optimal output level* at the minimum possible cost per unit.

price ceiling: A market intervention in which the government ensures that the price of a good or service stays below the free-market price.

price floor: A market intervention in which the government keeps the price of a good or service above its free-market price.

Prisoner's Dilemma: A situation in which a pair of prisoners (or firms) has to decide whether or not to cooperate; the dilemma is that although the individual incentives favor not cooperating, both players would be better off if they could figure out a way to cooperate.

producer surplus: The gain that producers receive when they can sell their output at a price higher than the minimum amount for which they're willing to make it

production possibilities frontier (PPF): A graph economists use to help them visualize the tradeoffs you make when you efficiently reallocate inputs from producing one thing to producing another; sometimes referred to as the *production possibilities curve.*

productively efficient: Producing a given good or service at the lowest possible cost.

prospect theory: A *behavioral economics* theory of decision-making that has three main features: (1) people evaluate potential outcomes relative to the *status quo* that they're used to; (2) gains are subject to *diminishing marginal utility.* whereas losses are subject to diminishing marginal *disutility;* and (3) people feel losses 2.5 times more intensely than gains.

public goods: Goods or services that can't be profitably produced by private firms because the goods or services are impossible to provide to just one person; if you provide them to one person, you have to provide them to everybody; because all consumers hope somebody else will pay for public goods so they can get them for free, usually nobody ends up paying.

quantity demanded: How much of a good or service a consumer will demand at a specific price, given his or her income and preferences.

quantity theory of money: The theory that the overall level of prices in the economy is proportional to the quantity of money circulating in the economy.

rational expectations: The theory that people will optimally change their behavior in response to policy changes; depending on the situation, their behavioral changes can greatly limit the effectiveness of policy changes.

rationality: Behaviors and decisions that maximize a person's likelihood of achieving his or her goals.

real interest rates: Interest rates that compensate for inflation by measuring the returns to a loan in terms of units of stuff lent and units of stuff returned (as opposed to *nominal interest rates*).

real prices: How much of one kind of thing (such as hours worked) you have to give up to get a good or service, no matter what happens to *nominal prices*.

real wages: Nominal wages adjusted for inflation; wages measured not in terms of current dollars (as *nominal wages* are) but rather in terms of how much output can be purchased with those current dollars.

recession: A period of time during which an economy's total output falls.

recovery: The period after a *recession* ends and during which an economy's total output expands; continues until the next *recession* begins.

scarcity: The fact that people don't have enough resources to satisfy all their wants; the phenomenon that creates the need for *economics*.

short-run shutdown condition: A situation in which a firm's total revenues are less than its *variable costs* and the firm is better off shutting down immediately and losing only its *fixed costs*.

socially optimal output level: The output level that maximizes the benefits that society can get from its limited supply of resources.

status quo: In *prospect theory*, the current situation against which people evaluate potential gains and losses.

status quo bias: The tendency people have to stick with default (status quo) situations rather than make changes. Explained by *prospect theory* and *loss aversion*.

sticky prices: Prices that are slow to adjust to shocks; price stickiness can cause recessions to linger.

supply and demand: An economic model of markets that separates buyers from sellers and then summarizes each group's behavior with a single line on a graph; the buyers' behavior is captured by the *demand curve,* and the sellers' behavior is captured by the *supply curve;* by putting these two curves on the same graph, economists can show how buyers and sellers interact in markets to determine how much of any particular item will be sold, as well as the price at which it will be sold.

supply curve: A line on a graph that represents how much of a good or service sellers will produce at various prices.

systematic errors: Sub-optimal choices that are made again and again as if a person cannot learn from his mistakes.

time inconsistency: The human tendency to systematically misjudge at the present time what the future self will want to do. Caused by *myopia*.

total surplus: The sum of *producer surplus* and *consumer surplus*.

Tragedy of the Commons: The idea that if a resource is open to public use, it typically becomes rapidly exhausted or ruined because each person's personal incentive is to use it up before anyone else can; this problem can be solved by private property rights, which give owners an incentive to conserve the resource and harvest it at sustainable rates.

ultimatum game: A *behavioral economics* game involving two players in which one gets to propose how to split a sum of money and the other gets to accept or reject the proposal. If rejected, neither player gets anything. The game provides evidence that the potential for rejection enhances fair behavior because we observe that the splits offered in the ultimatum game are more generous and more equal than the splits made by dictators in the *dictator game*.

utility: A measure of happiness that economists suppose people use to compare all possible things that they may experience.

variable costs: Costs that vary with the amount of output produced.

wealth: Anything that has value because it produces a flow of desirable goods and services or because it could produce a flow of desirable goods and services.

wages: The prices paid for the use or services of labor per unit of time.

Index

A

absolute advantage, 275, 276, 383
accounting profit, 106–107
actual expenditures, 316–317, 318–320
actual investment, 317
adverse selection, 213–214, 223–226
advertising, 217–218, 245–246
AFC (average fixed costs), 111, 112
aggregate demand (AD)
  asset-price bubble bursting, effect of, 359–360
  defined, 326, 383
  fixed prices in short run, 306
  inflationary expectations, effect on, 348–349
  inventories, changes in caused by shocks, 315
  long-run and short-run responses to shock, 308–309
  in macroeconomy, 302
  shocks to, 304–305
  sticky prices problem, 309–312
  stimulus policies, limitations of, 328–336
  stimulus policies, overview, 326–328
aggregate supply
  defined, 383
  long-run aggregate supply curve, 302, 303–304, 308–309, 327, 329
  short-run aggregate supply curve, 305–306, 308–309, 327, 329–330, 348–349
agricultural price supports, 79, 80–81
Akerlof, George, 207, 208
algebra, in economics, 2
allocation of resources, 37, 38–41, 45–46
allocative efficiency, 12, 34, 42, 44, 383
altruism, relation to happiness, 23–24
American Telephone and Telegraph Corporation (AT&T), 171
amoral nature of economics, 24
anchoring, 246–247, 383
animal extinctions, 203
antirecessionary policies, 15–16. *See also* recessions

antitrust laws, 184, 383
apartments, rent control for, 77–78
area-based property rights, 204
Arrow, Kenneth, 378
asset-price bubbles
  bursting of, 357–360
  defined, 354, 383
  development of, 354–357
  recovery after recessions caused by, 360–362
assets
  in gross domestic product, 261–262
  in international trade, 273–274
  money as, 341
asymmetric information
  in automobile insurance market, 211–214
  as cause of market failure, 13
  defined, 205, 383
  in health insurance market, 224
  as limiting trade, 206–207
  overview, 129, 206
  statistical discrimination, 215
  used car market, 207–211
AT&T, 171
automobile insurance industry, 211–214
autonomous expenditures, 318, 322
availability heuristic, 243
average cost pricing, 169, 170
average costs/benefits, irrational behavior related to, 31–32
average fixed costs (AFC), 111, 112
average total costs (ATC)
  marginal cost equaling average cost, 113–115
  monopolies versus competitive firms, 164
  monopoly output level choices, 158–159
  profits, visualizing, 119
  tracking movement of, 111–112
average variable costs (AVC), 110–111, 112, 113–115

B

balanced budget, 269

banks, 284–285, 358–359, 360–361

bans, government, 48

bartering, 279, 287

Becker, Gary, 380

behavioral economics. *See also* consumer behavior
  brain, research on, 240–243
  brain modularity, 242
  cognitive biases, 242–243
  complementing neo-classical economics with, 239–240
  defined, 383
  fairness and self-interest, gauging, 251–254
  heuristics, 240–241
  microeconomics, 14
  myopia, 248–249
  need for, 238
  nudging people toward better outcomes, 254
  overview, 237
  prospect theory, 244–248
  time inconsistency, 248, 249–250

benefits, irrational behavior related to, 31. *See also* cost-benefit analysis; social benefits of free markets; socially optimal output level

best alternative option, in opportunity cost, 26–27

bias, 242–243, 247–248, 387

Blair, Tony, 232

bonds
  budget deficits and national debt, 338–340
  defined, 344
  interest rates, link between prices and, 345
  open-market operations, 346, 351
  overview, 269, 344–345
  as paying for government spending, 338
  payment types, 344
  rate of return on, 344–345

borrowers, 283–285, 293–294, 295

borrowing, 269, 337–338. *See also* asset-price bubbles

brain, research on, 240–243

breaking even, 106

breaking up monopolies, 171

breaking up oligopolies, 184

broadcast radio, as public good, 217–218

budget, consumer behavior when facing limited, 88–95

budget deficit, 269, 336, 338–340

budget surplus, 269

Bureau of Labor Statistics, 288. *See also* Consumer Price Index

bureaucracies, medical, 231, 232

business cycle, 298–299

businesses, in macroeconomics, 257. *See also* firms; microeconomics

buyers. *See* consumer behavior; demand curve

C

capital
  defined, 383
  human, 35–36, 384
  investment in, 268–269
  as resource, 35

capitalism, 54, 376–377

cardinal utility, 85

Carlyle, Thomas, 237

cartels. *See also* monopolies; oligopolies
  criteria for coordinating, 176
  defined, 383
  incentives to cheat, 176–183
  overview, 175–176

cash holdings, relation to interest rate, 342–344

causation, economic fallacy related to, 366–367

ceilings, price, 77–78, 139–140, 386

centralization, in command economies, 46

choice behavior, individual. *See* consumer behavior; decision-making; economic choice model; microeconomics

circular flow diagram, 259–260, 262–263

cognitive biases, 242–243

coins, 278, 280

collateral, 355–356, 383

collective management of resources, 204

Collegiate Price Index, 288–290

collusion, 175, 184. *See also* cartels

command economy, 45–46, 50, 383

commercial bank collapses, 359

commercials, as paying for public good, 217–218

commonly owned resources, overexploiting, 202–204

communism, 45–46, 53–54, 190

companies. *See* firms; microeconomics

comparative advantage, 274–276, 376, 383

competition. *See also* monopolies; monopolistic competition; perfect competition

  creating, dealing with monopolies by, 171

  firm behavior when facing, 101–102, 103–107

  foreign, protectionism in face of, 367

  in healthcare, 233, 236

  lack of, 12–13

  in market economies, 46–47

  Marxist view of, 377

  in microeconomics, 12–13

  redundant, eliminating, 165–166

  strategic situation, 175

competitive firms, versus monopolies, 161–164

competitive free markets. *See* free markets; social benefits of free markets

complementary goods, 100

composition, fallacy of, 368

confirmation bias, 243

constrained maximization, 379

constrained optimization problems

  choosing by ranking, 84–85

  demand curves, deriving, 95–99

  diminishing marginal utility, 85–88, 95–99

  limited budget, facing, 88–95

  overview, 84

consumer behavior. *See also* behavioral economics; decision-making

  choosing by ranking, 84–85

  complementary and substitute goods, 100

  constraints, 25–27

  cost-benefit analysis, 27–28

  deriving demand curves, 95–99

  diminishing marginal utility, 85–88, 95–99

  economic choice model, 22

  inflation, effect on, 94

  irrationality, 30–32

  limitations of choice model, 29–32

  overview, 21, 83–84

  pursuit of happiness, 23–24

  uninformed decision-making, 29–30

  when facing limited budget, 88–95

Consumer Price Index (CPI), 288, 290–293, 383

consumer surplus

  of continuous good, 135–136

  defined, 383

  of discrete good, 133–134

  overview, 132–133

  in total surplus, 137, 138

consumption

  in gross domestic product, 265, 266–267

  lower interest rates, effect on, 346–347

  in planned expenditures, 316

  relation to happiness, 244

consumption function, 318

continuous good, consumer surplus of, 135–136

contracts, debt, 354

Corn Laws, 274

cost-benefit analysis

  by criminals, 380

  in economic choice model, 27–28

  in families, 380

  by firms regarding production, 116–117

  marginalism, 368

  research on bird behavior, 29

  in Singapore healthcare system, 234

cost-of-living increases, 293

costs. *See also* average total costs; marginal costs; social benefits of free markets; socially optimal output level; total costs

  average fixed, 111, 112

  average variable costs, 110–111, 112, 113–115

  categories of, 107

  diminishing returns, 36–37, 109–110

  economic, 106–107, 384

  increasing returns, 108–109, 110

  irrational behavior related to, 31

  monopoly output level choices, 158–161

costs. *(continued)*
  monopoly profitability, relation to, 160–161
  natural monopolies, effect on, 166
  negative externalities, 197–198, 199
  per unit of output, 108–110
  in perfect competition, 144, 146–150
  production, 66–70, 75–76, 129
  Singapore healthcare system, 233–235
  when calculating profit, 106–107
coupon payments, for bonds, 344
CPI (Consumer Price Index), 288, 290–293, 383
credible threats, resolving Prisoner's Dilemma
    with, 180–183
credit card bills, anchoring on, 246–247
criminals, cost–benefit analysis by, 380
crises, financial. *See* financial crises
Croesus, 280
cross-price effects, 99, 100
currently produced output, in GDP, 263–264

D

dangerous goods, 47, 48
deadweight losses
  caused by monopolies, 163–164
  defined, 383
  overview, 138
  from price ceiling, 139–140
  from taxes, 140–143
dealerships, used car, 210
Debreu, Gerard, 378
debt contracts, 354
debt-driven bubbles. *See* asset-price bubbles
debts
  government, dealing with, 338–340
  increasing money supply to pay, 282–283
decision-making. *See also* consumer behavior;
    economic choice model
  brain modularity, 242
  cognitive biases, 242–243
  heuristics, 240–241
  myopia in, 249, 250
  uninformed, 29–30

deductibles, 214
deferred payment, money as standard of,
    283–284, 286
deficit
  budget, 269, 336, 338–340
  trade, 272–273
deflation, 288, 384
deleveraging, 358
demand. *See also* aggregate demand
  cost-benefit analysis based on, 130–132
  defined, 58, 384
  demand curve, 60–62
  elasticity, 63–65
  elements affecting, 59
  excess, 73–74, 77–78
  inflated, for low-cost healthcare, 228–231
  law of, 17, 228, 385
  market equilibrium, 70–76
  in microeconomics, 12
  for money, 279–282, 288
  opportunity costs, 62–63
  overview, 58
  perfectly elastic, 64–65
  positive externalities, effect on, 200–201
  price controls, 76–81
  in properly functioning market, 129–130
  weak, causing loss for monopoly, 160–161
  when asset-price bubbles burst, 358
demand curve
  cost-benefit analysis based on, 130–132
  defined, 19, 384
  deriving from diminishing marginal utility, 95–99
  drawing, 20
  graphing, 60–62
  market, 104
  market equilibrium, 70–76
  monopolistic competition, 186–189
  monopoly marginal revenues, 154–157
  monopoly pricing, figuring out, 159
  negative externalities, 196–198
  opportunity costs, 62–63
  overview, 17, 57

plotting out data for, 18–19

predictions, making with, 19

in properly functioning market, 129

shifts in, 60–62, 74–75, 188–189

slope of, 62–63

socially optimal output level, 131–132, 194–195

supply and demand, 12

demand elasticity, 63–65

democracy, 9, 53, 372

denial of service, when rationing healthcare, 230

depreciation, 268, 384

depressions, 312. *See also* Great Depression

detailed circular flow diagram, 262–263

developing nations, effect of price controls on, 79

diagnostic tests, in low-cost healthcare systems, 229

dictator game, 253, 384

diminishing marginal utility

  defined, 384

  deriving demand curves from, 95–99

  general discussion, 85–88

  overview, 28

  in prospect theory, 244

  in research on birds, 29

  when facing limited budget, 88–90

diminishing returns

  cause of, determining, 109–110

  defined, 11, 384

  production possibilities frontier, 38–42

  role in production possibilities, 34, 36–37

discrete good, consumer surplus of, 133–134

discrimination, in free markets, 380

disequilibrium, 72

disposable income, 266–267

dominant strategy, Prisoner's Dilemma, 179–180

downward price stickiness, 333

downward wage stickiness, 333

E

Easterlin, Richard, 244

economic choice model

  constraints, 25–27

  cost-benefit analysis, 27–28

irrationality, 30–32

overview, 22

pursuit of happiness, 23–24

uninformed decision-making, 29–30

violations and limitations of, 29–32

economic costs, 106–107, 384

economic growth, 372, 379–380

economic models, 16–20

economic profits, 106–107, 144, 146, 188–189, 384

economic shocks

  causing recessions, 297

  changes in inventories caused by, 315

  combining long-run and short-run responses, 308–309

  fixed prices in short run, 305–307

  price adjustments in long run, 303–304

  responding to, 301–309

  shift in aggregate demand, 304–305

economic systems, versus political systems, 53–54

economics. *See also specific branches of economics; specific economic concepts*

  algebra in, 2

  assumption of rationality, 238

  behavioral economics as complement to, 239

  defined, 7, 384

  history of, 8–10

  jargon in, 2

  models and graphs in, 16–20

  neoclassical, 238, 239, 251

  overview, 1–4

  as science of scarcity, 10–11

economy. *See also specific economy types*

  circular flow diagram, 259–260

  detailed circular flow diagram, 262–263

  government and markets, role of, 43–49

  measuring, in macroeconomics, 14–15

  stimulating with inflation, 285

education, 9, 53, 372

efficiency. *See also* productive efficiency

  allocative, 12, 34, 42, 44, 383

  of free markets, 130–132

  of government intervention, 48, 52

  in low-cost healthcare systems, 228–229, 231

efficiency. *(continued)*
  monopolies as lacking in, 164
  monopolistic competition, 189–190
  of Singapore healthcare system, 232
elasticity
  demand, 63–65
  supply, 69–70
elective surgery, 229
endowment effect, 247, 248, 384
entrepreneur, defined, 384
entrepreneurial ability, 35, 47, 102–103, 384
entry, firm
  graphing profits guiding, 146–150
  monopolistic competition, 188
  perfect competition, 145
environmental problems, 373
equal marginal utility per dollar, 91–95
equality, free markets as working for, 380
equilibrium
  defined, 384
  effect of negative demand shock on, 327–328
  invisible hand, relation to, 377
  in Keynesian model, 314, 317–322
  overview, 70–72
  price controls affecting, 76–81
  stable, 72–74, 320, 344
  supply or demand changes, 74–76
equilibrium (market) price, 71–72, 74–76
equilibrium (market) quantity, 71–72, 74–76
equilibrium interest rate, 343–344, 345
equilibrium level of prices (P*), 303
equity, markets as ignoring, 47
evolution of brain, 240
excess demand, 73–74, 77–78
excess supply, 72–73, 79–81
exchange rates, 370
excludable goods, 374
exit, firm
  graphing profits guiding, 149–150
  monopolistic competition, 188
  in perfect competition, 145
expected rate of inflation, 293–295

expenditures, in GDP
  consumption, 266–267
  government, 269–270
  investment, 268–269
  net exports, 270–271
  overview, 259–260, 265–266
expenditures, in Keynesian model, 316–323
expert opinion, for lemons problem, 211
exports, 266, 270–271, 317
externalities
  defined, 194, 384
  negative, 196–200
  overview, 195–196
  positive, 200–202
extinction, animal, 203

F
face value payments, for bonds, 344
factors of production, 384
fairness
  defined, 251
  dictator game, 252
  experimental evidence for, 251–254
  of health insurance rates, 224–225
  markets as ignoring, 47
  overview, 251
  ultimatum game, 252–253
fallacy of composition, 368
families, as economic units, 380
farmers, price supports for, 80–81
Federal Reserve Bank, 346–349,
    351–352. *See also* monetary policy
fiat system, 281, 342
financial crises
  debt-driven bubbles, 354–360
  defined, 353
  overview, 16, 353–354
  recovery, 360–362
financial markets, 262–263, 384
firms. *See also* microeconomics;
    monopolies; monopolistic competition;
    oligopolies

breaking monopolies into several, 171

circular flow for resources, 259–260, 262–263

competition, facing, 103–107

competitive, versus monopolies, 161–164

cost structure, 107–115

long-run shutdown condition, 125

losses, visualizing, 120–121

loss-making, decision to stay in business, 121–125

marginal revenues and marginal costs, 115–121

overview, 101–102

in perfect competition, 144–145

price takers, 104–105

profits, maximizing, 102–103

profits, visualizing, 118–120

profits guiding entry and exit, graphing, 146–150

short-run shutdown condition, 123–124

fiscal policy. *See also* stimulus policies

after financial crises, 362

as antirecessionary policy, 16

deficits, dealing with, 338–340

defined, 325, 384

increased government spending, 337–338

inflation, generating, 328–336

influence of Keynes on, 378

limitations of, 362

overview, 325–326, 336

real wages, 331–332

Fisher equation, 294–295

fishing, Tragedy of the Commons related to, 203, 204

fixed costs

average, 111, 112

in decision to operate at loss, 122

defined, 107, 384

long-run shutdown condition, 125

in production decisions, 108

short-run shutdown condition, 123–124

fixed prices in short run, 305–307. *See also* Keynesian model

food aid, 79

foreign trade. *See* international trade

foreign wages, economic fallacies related to, 369–370

framing effects, 243, 245–246, 384

Frank, Robert, 244

free healthcare, inflated demand for, 228–231

free market equilibrium. *See* market equilibrium

free markets (market economies). *See also* social benefits of free markets

automatic direction of resources in, 44–45

competition in, 46–47

deadweight losses, 138–143

defined, 49

economic fallacies related to, 369

economist confidence in, 127–128

efficiency of, 130–132

versus government interventions, 43–44

misdeeds of, 47

mixed economies, 49–52

need for government in, 50–51

perfect competition, 143–150

as requiring regulation, 372

traits of properly functioning, 129–130

as working for equality, 380

free online services, in market basket, 293

free trade, 274, 276, 373

freedom, effect on economy, 372

frictional unemployment, 299–300

Friedman, Milton, 232, 378–379

full and complete property rights, 194–195

full employment, 299, 384

full-employment output (Y*). *See also* Keynesian model; recessions

defined, 384

economy's affection for, 328–329

long-run aggregate supply curve, 302

monetary and fiscal policy, effect of, 326–328

overview, 299–300

price adjustments, 300–301

price stickiness, 333–334

real versus nominal wages, 331–332

sticky prices problem, 311–312

trying to increase output beyond, 329–330

G

game theory, 176–177. *See also* Prisoner's Dilemma

Gammon, Max, 232

gateway doctors, 231

gaze heuristic, 241

GDP. *See* gross domestic product

Germany, Weimar hyperinflation in, 283, 284

gold standard, 281, 341–342

Google, advertising on, 218

government expenditures
  in gross domestic product, 266, 269–270
  increasing to end recessions, 337–338
  in planned expenditures, 317

government intervention. *See also* fiscal policy; monetary policy; money supply
  after financial crises, 359, 362
  case against, 48–49
  case for, 47–48
  command economies, 45–46
  deadweight losses from, 138–143
  deciding on amount of, 51–52
  influence of Keynes on, 378
  in Keynesian model, 322–323
  versus market production, 43–44
  in mixed economies, 50–52
  neoclassical synthesis, 379
  political systems versus economic systems, 53–54
  price controls, 76–81
  rational expectations, 380–381
  for sticky prices, 311–312
  support of technology, 52–53

government-run healthcare systems, 231

governments
  adverse selection problem response, 226
  circular flow for resources, 262–263
  inflation, role in, 15
  in macroeconomics, 257
  public goods, providing, 216, 374
  recessions, fighting, 16
  in Singapore healthcare system, 233–234

graphs, in economics, 16–20. *See also* specific graphs

Great Depression, 312, 378, 379

Great Recession, 350–352, 353–354, 361

gross domestic product (GDP)
  actual expenditures, relation to, 317
  assets, 261–262
  consumption, 266–267
  defined, 14, 257, 384
  equation for, 265–271
  government expenditures, 269–270
  healthcare spending as percent of, 227–228
  high, significance of, 258, 264–265
  income streams, 260–261
  information excluded from, 259
  information included in, 259–260
  investment expenditures, 268–269
  Keynesian model, boosting in, 322–323
  markets, 262–263
  net exports, 270–271
  newly produced output, 263–264
  overview, 258
  during recessions and Great Depression, 312–313

group health insurance, 225–226

grouping individuals, 212–215

Gutenberg, Johannes, 219

H

happiness. *See also* constrained optimization problems; utility
  constraints on, 25–27
  consumption, relation to, 244
  deciding what to produce, role in, 42–43
  in economic choice model, 22
  GDP, relation to, 258, 264–265
  individual choice, role in, 84
  pursuit of, 23–24

health economics
  defined, 222
  inflated demand for low-cost care, 228–231
  internationally, 227–228
  limits of health insurance, 222–226

overview, 14, 221–222

in Singapore, 233–236

health finance, 222. *See also* health economics

health insurance

adverse selection, 223–226

group, 225–226

multiple rates for, 224–225

overview, 222–223

health savings accounts, 233

hedonic treadmill, 244

Hershey's, 245

heuristics, 240–241

hindsight bias, 243

household consumption, in GDP, 266–267

households, in circular flow diagram, 259–260

housing market bubbles. *See* asset-price bubbles

human capital, 35–36, 384

hyperinflation

causes of, 282–283

defined, 385

effects of, 283

overview, 277

Weimar, in Germany, 283, 284

I

icons, explained, 3–4

immoral goods, 47, 48

imperfect competition. *See* monopolistic competition

imports, in GDP, 266, 270–271

impulse buying, 239–240

incentives, 239, 253

income

circular flow for resources, 259–260

in gross domestic product, 260–261

inequality, 47, 48

in quantity demanded, 59

increasing returns, 108–109, 110, 385

Indiana, healthcare program in, 235–236

individual choice behavior. *See* consumer behavior; microeconomics

induced expenditures, 318

inequality, 44, 47, 48

inferior goods, 59

inflation

consumer behavior, effect on, 94

defined, 14, 385

effects of, 286–287

employment, impact on, 334

expected rate of, 293–295

explicit target for, 352

gold standard as preventing, 281

hyperinflation, 277, 282–284, 385

measuring, 287–293

monetary policy, 285

money supply and demand, balancing, 279–282

overview, 14–15, 277–278

prevention of, 374

rational expectations regarding, 348–350

when increasing money supply, 282–285, 339–340

when stimulating aggregate demand, 328–336

inflation rate, 289–290, 293–295, 385

inflation tax, 287

information, access to, 129. *See also* asymmetric information

innovation

cost-cutting, in healthcare, 234–235

economic growth as reliant on, 372

government support of, 52–53

intellectual property rights, 373

as propelling economic growth, 379–380

insolvent, 359, 385

insurance market

asymmetric information in, 207, 211–214

health, 222–226

intellectual property rights, 9, 52–53, 373

interest, as income stream, 261

interest rates

in bond markets, 344–345

changing money supply to change, 346

defined, 385

equilibrium, 343–345

inflationary expectations, effect on, 349

investment expenditure, role in, 268–269

lowering, to stimulate economy, 346–348

in monetary policy, 340, 345–348

interest rates *(continued)*
 nominal, 293–294, 343, 386
 real, 293–294, 386
 relation to holding money in cash, 342–344
 when printing money to pay government debts, 340
international trade
 assets, 273–274
 as beneficial, 373
 comparative advantage, 274–276, 376
 foreign wages, fallacies related to, 369–370
 in macroeconomics, 15
 overview, 271
 protectionism, 367
 trade deficit, 272–273
Internet services, in market basket, 293
inventory investment, 317
inventory levels
 adjusting output to, 315–316
 in economic forecasting, 264
 equilibrium, relation to, 320–322
 in Keynesian model, overview, 314
 planned and actual expenditures, 316–317
 target level, 314–315
inventory-management systems, 307
inverse relationship, defined, 17
investment
 defined, 385
 in gross domestic product, 265–266, 268–269
 inventory, 317
 lower interest rates, effect on, 346–347
 in planned expenditures, 316–317
invisible hand
 defined, 12, 385
 fairness, research on, 254
 free market equilibrium, relation to, 377
 overview, 24
 perfect competition, 149
 proof of, 378
 property rights, 193, 194–195
 socially optimal output level, 132
irrational behavior, 30–32. *See also* behavioral economics

K

Kahneman, Daniel, 244
Keynes, John Maynard, 15, 312–314, 378
Keynesian model
 adjusting output to inventory level, 315–316
 boosting GDP, 322–323
 equilibrium, 317–322
 overview, 312–314
 planned and actual expenditures, 316–317
 target level of inventories, 314–315
Keynesianism, 314
King Croesus, 280
Kublai Khan, 280

L

labor. *See also* human capital; wages
 economic fallacies related to, 365–366
 as resource, 35
labor costs per unit, 369–370
laissez faire economies. *See* market economies
land, as resource, 35
law of demand, 17, 228, 385
Law of Unintended Consequences, 370
laws
 antitrust, 184, 383
 negative externalities, dealing with, 199
lemons problem, used car market, 207–211
lenders. *See also* asset-price bubbles
 expected rate of inflation, 293–295
 opposition to inflation by, 284–286
lending standards, relaxing, 356
leveraged position, 358
limited budget, consumer behavior when facing, 88–95
limited liability corporations, 9
limited resources. *See also* scarcity
 production possibilities frontier, 38–42
 role in production possibilities, 34, 35, 37
literacy. *See* education

living standards
  economic fallacies related to, 366
  education, effect on, 372
  future, 10
  history of, 8
  institutions raising, 9
  real, determining, 291–292
  technological innovation, 379–380
lobbying, 48, 49
local collective management of resources, 204
long run
  in microeconomics, 123
  price adjustments in, 303–304
  responses to economic shock in, 301, 307–308
long-run aggregate supply curve (LRAS)
  full-employment output, 329
  long-run and short-run responses to shock, 308–309
  in macroeconomy, 302
  negative demand shocks, 327
  price adjustments in long run, 303–304
long-run shutdown condition, 125, 385
loss aversion
  defined, 385
  endowment effect, 247
  in prospect theory, 244
  shrinking packages to avoid, 245
  status quo bias, 248
losses
  deadweight, 138–143
  defined, 106
  firm exit due to, graphing, 149–150
  framing effects, 245–246
  monopolies running at, 160–161
  monopolistic competition, 188
  perfect competition, 145
  running a loss, 106, 121–125, 160–161
  staying in business despite of, 121–125
  visualizing, 120–121
low-cost healthcare, inflated demand for, 228–231
low-hanging fruit principle, 36
Lucas, Robert, 380–381
Lydia, coins in, 280

M

macroeconomics. *See also* gross domestic product; inflation; Keynesian model; recessions
  defined, 11, 385
  household consumption, 266
  international trade, 15, 271–276
  measuring economy, 14–15
  money in, 279
  natural goals of, 299
  overview, 14, 257–258
mafia, Prisoner's Dilemma resolution by, 180–181
Malthus, Thomas, 366
mandatory health insurance, 226
mandatory health savings, 233, 236
marginal cost curve, 159
marginal cost pricing, 168–170
marginal costs (MC)
  comparing marginal revenues with, 115–121
  defined, 385
  equaling average cost, 113–115
  losses, visualizing, 120–121
  negative externalities, 197
  optimal output level, determining, 116–118
  overview, 112–113
  in perfect competition, 147
  positive externalities, 200–201
  profits, visualizing, 118–120
  setting equal to marginal revenues, 158–159
marginal output (marginal product), 108–109
marginal propensity to consume (MPC), 267
marginal revenues (MR)
  comparing with marginal costs, 115–121
  losses, visualizing, 120–121
  of monopolies, decreasing, 153–157
  monopolies versus competitive firms, 162, 164
  monopolistic competition, 187
  optimal output level, determining, 116–118
  profits, visualizing, 118–120
  setting equal to marginal cost, 158–159
marginal utility. *See also* diminishing marginal utility
  defined, 86, 385
  irrational behavior related to, 31–32

marginal utility. *(continued)*
  negative, 87–88
  overview, 27–28
  price changes and quantities demanded, 96–97
  research on bird behavior, 29
  when facing limited budget, 88–95
marginalism, 368
market (equilibrium) price, 71–72, 74–76
market (equilibrium) quantity, 71–72, 74–76
market basket
  calculating inflation rate, 289–290
  creating, 288–289
  defined, 288, 385
  issues with, 292–293
  price index, setting up, 290–291
market demand curve, 104
market economies. *See also* social benefits of free markets
  automatic direction of resources in, 44–45
  competition in, 46–47
  deadweight losses, 138–143
  defined, 49, 385
  economic fallacies related to, 369
  economist confidence in, 127–128
  efficiency of, 130–132
  versus government interventions, 43–44
  misdeeds of markets, 47
  mixed economies, 49–52
  need for government in, 50–51
  perfect competition, 143–150
  as requiring regulation, 372
  traits of properly functioning, 129–130
  as working for equality, 380
market equilibrium
  defined, 384
  effect of negative demand shock on, 327–328
  invisible hand, relation to, 377
  in Keynesian model, 314, 317–322
  overview, 70–72
  price controls affecting, 76–81
  stable, 72–74, 320, 344
  supply or demand changes, 74–76

market equilibrium quantity, 132, 139
market failures. *See also* asymmetric information; externalities; monopolies; oligopolies; public goods
  defined, 385
  in microeconomics, 13
  overview, 128, 205–206
market price, 186. *See also* prices
market production, 44. *See also* market economies; production
market supply curve, 104
markets. *See also* market economies
  affecting gross domestic product, 262–263
  defined, 57
  financial, 262–263, 384
  missing, 207
Marshall, Alfred, 377
Marx, Karl, 376–377
maximization, constrained, 379
maximum output, 299
MC. *See* marginal costs
medical care economics. *See* health economics
medical procedures, cost-benefit analysis of, 234
MediSave accounts, Singapore, 233
medium of exchange, money as, 279, 286–287
mercantilism, 376
metal monies, invention of, 278
metallic standard, 341–342
microeconomics. *See also* consumer behavior; firms; free markets; *specific aspects of microeconomics*
  areas studied in, 11–14
  defined, 11, 385
  household consumption, 266
  long run, 123
  short run, 122–123
milk, price support system for, 80
minimum output requirements, 167–168
minimum possible cost, 144, 146, 148–149
missing markets, 207
mixed economies
  amount of government intervention, 51–52
  as best option for most societies, 49–50

versus other economy types, 50–51

overview, 44

models, in economics, 16–20

modularity, brain, 242

mohair subsidy, 49

monetary policy. *See also* stimulus policies

after financial crises, 362

as antirecessionary policy, 16

bonds in, 344–345

defined, 325, 340, 385

fiat money versus gold standard, 341–342

during Great Recession, 350–352

inflation, 285, 328–336

interest rates, 342–348

limitations of, 362

overview, 325–326, 340–341

rational expectations, 348–350, 380–381

real wages, 331–332

research on, 378–379

unconventional, 351–352

money

as asset, 341

defined, 279

fiat system, 281, 342

gold standard, 281, 341–342

holding, relation to interest rate, 342–344

inflation, effect on functions ascribed to, 286–287

invention of, 278, 280

as medium of exchange, 279, 286–287

as standard of deferred payment, 283–284, 286

as store of value, 286

as unit of account, 286

value of, relationship with prices, 280–281

money supply. *See also* monetary policy

changing, to change interest rates, 346

gold standard, 281

increases, graphing results of, 348–349

increasing, reasons for, 282–285, 337, 339–340

inflation, relation to, 278

supply and demand, balancing, 279–282

monopolies. *See also* cartels

breaking up into competing firms, 171

versus competitive firms, 161–164

deadweight losses, 163–164

decreasing marginal revenues, 153–157

defined, 12–13, 103, 385

efficiency, lack of, 164

good, 165–166

natural, 166

output level, choice of, 152, 158–161

overview, 151–152

price, ability to control, 153–154

problems caused by, 152–153

profits of, 159–161

regulating, 167–171

monopolistic competition

defined, 103, 385

overview, 174, 185

product differentiation, 185

profit limits, 186–190

moral hazard, in insurance industry, 214

morals, markets as ignoring, 47

MPC (marginal propensity to consume), 267

MR. *See* marginal revenues

multiple-rates solution, adverse selection problem, 224–225

myopia, 248–250, 386

N

national debt, 338–340

National Health Service (NHS), UK, 229–230, 232

National Income and Product Accounts (NIPA), 257–258

National Institute for Health and Clinical Excellence (NICE committee), UK, 230

natural monopoly, 166, 386

natural resources, limited supply of, 25. *See also* resources

negative demand shock

changes in inventories caused by, 315

defined, 327

fixed prices in short run, 305–307

full-employment output, effect on, 327–328

long-run and short-run responses, 308–309

overview, 304–305

sticky prices, 309–312

negative externalities
  accepting positive amounts of, 198–199
  dealing with, 199–200
  defined, 196
  overproduction, 196–198
  overview, 196
  private and social costs, 197
negative marginal utility, 87–88
neoclassical economics. *See also* economics
  assumption of rationality in, 238
  behavioral economics as complementary
    method, 239
  self-interest in, 251
neoclassical synthesis, 379
net exports
  in gross domestic product, 266, 270–271
  in planned expenditures, 317
new technologies
  as public good, 219–220
  shifting PPF outward, 41–42
newly produced output, in GDP, 263–264
newspaper advertising, 218
NHS (National Health Service), UK, 229–230, 232
NICE committee (National Institute for Health and
    Clinical Excellence), UK, 230
NIPA (National Income and Product Accounts),
    257–258
nominal interest rates, 293–294, 343, 386
nominal prices, 291, 386
nominal wages, 331–332, 386
nonexcludable public goods, 215, 374. *See also*
    public goods
nonrival public goods, 215
normal goods, 59

O

oligopolies
  antitrust laws, 184
  breaking up dominant firms, 184
  cartel behavior, 175–176
  criteria for coordinating cartel, 176
  defined, 13, 103, 386

incentives to cheat cartel, 176–183
  overview, 173–174
  regulating, 183–184
  sharing power over prices, 174–175
omerta system, 180–181
online resources, for book, 4
online services, in market basket, 293
OPEC (Organization of Petroleum Exporting
    Countries) oil cartel, 181–183
open-market operations, 346, 351
opportunity costs
  in comparative advantage concept,
    274–276
  defined, 386
  in economic choice model, 26–27
  economic profit, 106
  production possibilities frontier, 40
  slopes of demand curves, 62–63
  total costs, 107
optimal output level, determining, 116–118
optimization problems. *See* constrained
    optimization problems
ordinal utility, 85
Ostrom, Elinor, 204
out-of-pocket costs, in healthcare,
    233–236
output levels. *See* production; socially optimal
    output level
output quotas
  for cartels, 176
  OPEC oil cartel, 182–183
overconfidence effect, 243
overexploitation of commonly owned resources,
    202–204
overfishing, 203, 204
overpopulation, 366
overproduction, 196–198
own-price effects, 99

P

P* (equilibrium level of prices), 303
package sizes, shrinking, 245

paper money, invention of, 280. *See also* money supply
patent rights
  good monopolies, 165
  government protection of, 52–53
  role in raised living standards, 9
  turning public goods into private goods, 219
payments, for bonds, 344
payoff matrix, Prisoner's Dilemma, 177–179
penalties, government, 48
percentages, irrational behavior related to, 31
perfect competition. *See also* monopolies
  causes and consequences of, 144
  defined, 103, 386
  overview, 143–144
  process of, 145–146
  profits guiding firm entry and exit, graphing, 146–150
  requirements for, 103–104
perfectly elastic demand, 64–65
perfectly elastic supply, 69, 70
perfectly inelastic demand, 64
perfectly inelastic supply, 69–70
permits, for Tragedy of the Commons prevention, 204
philanthropy, providing public goods through, 216–217
planned expenditures, 316–317, 318–321, 322–323
planned investment, 316–317
planning fallacy, 243
political systems, 53–54
politics
  behind increased money supply, 283–285
  government interventions as result of, 52
  role in government expenditures, 270
population growth, economic fallacies related to, 366
positive demand shock, 304
positive externalities
  consequences of, 200–201
  defined, 196
  subsidizing things providing, 201–202
post hoc ergo propter hoc, 366–367

PPF. *See* production possibilities frontier
precommitments, 250
preexisting conditions, in health insurance market, 223–226
preferences
  diminishing marginal utility, 88
  role in quantity demanded, 59
price adjustments
  in long run, 303–304
  natural result of, 300–301
price ceilings, 77–78, 139–140, 386
price controls
  overview, 76–77
  price ceilings, 77–78
  price floors, 79–81
  in rich countries, effect on poor countries, 79
price floors, 79–81, 386
price index. *See also* Consumer Price Index
  issues with, 292–293
  real standard of living, determining with, 291–292
  setting up, 290–291
price supports, 79, 80–81
price systems, 45. *See also* market economies
price takers, 104–105, 144
prices. *See also* asset-price bubbles; inflation
  aggregate demand shock, effect on, 304–305
  cross-price effects, 99, 100
  on demand curve, 17–20, 60–62, 96–99
  demand elasticity, 63–65
  diminishing returns, 36–37
  equilibrium level of, 303
  fixed, in short run, 305–307
  hyperinflation, effect of, 283
  long-run and short-run responses to shock, 308–309
  losses, visualizing, 120–121
  in low-cost healthcare systems, 230–231
  in macroeconomy, 301–302
  market, 71–72, 74–76
  market equilibrium, 70–76
  monopolistic competition, 186
  monopoly, regulating, 168–170

prices. *(continued)*

monopoly ability to control, 153–154

monopoly marginal revenues, 153–157

monopoly profitability, relation to, 161

nominal, 291, 386

oligopolies as sharing power over, 174–175

own-price effects, 99

per unit of output, for monopoly, 159

in perfect competition, 103–104

product differentiation, relation to, 185

production cost, relation to, 66–67

profits, visualizing, 120

in properly functioning market, 129–130

quantity demanded, relationship with, 59, 60, 96–97

real, 291, 387

retailer responses to recessions, 307

shrinking packages when raising, 245

slopes of demand curves, 62–63

sticky, 297–298, 309–312, 333, 387

stimulation of aggregate demand, 328–332

stimulus policies, effect on, 334–336

on supply curve, 65–67

supply elasticity, 69–70

in total revenue, 118–119

of utility, determining, 89–90

value of money, inverse relationship with, 280–281

price-taking assumption, 129

printing money. *See* money supply

printing press, as public good, 219

Prisoner's Dilemma

credible threats, resolving with, 180–181

defined, 386

dominant strategy, determining, 179–180

dominant strategy outcome, 180

OPEC oil cartel, 181–183

overview, 177

payoff matrix, 177–179

private demand, 200–201

private goods, selling to provide public goods, 217–218

private marginal cost, 197

producer surplus, 132–133, 136–138, 386

product differentiation, 174, 185, 186, 189–190

production. *See also* gross domestic product; Keynesian model; recessions; socially optimal output level

allocating resources, 37

comparing marginal revenues with marginal costs, 115–121

decision-making behind, overview, 42–43

diminishing returns, 36–37

firm control over, 104–105

government and markets, role of, 43–49

human capital, 35–36

market, 44

mixed economies, 49–52

monopolies versus competitive firms, 162–164

monopolistic competition, 189–190

monopoly marginal revenues, 153–157

monopoly output level choices, 158–161

negative externalities, effects of, 196–198

overview, 33–34

political systems versus economic systems, 53–54

positive externalities, effect on, 200–202

possibilities for, determining, 34–42

production possibilities frontier, 38–42

resources, classifying, 35

subsidies for monopolies to increase, 167

taxes on, as shifting supply curve, 140–141

technology, support of, 52–53

production costs

market equilibrium, 75–76

in properly functioning market, 129

sales price, relation to, 66–67

on supply curve, 67–69

supply elasticity, 69–70

production possibilities frontier (PPF)

defined, 386

efficiency, gauging, 40–41

government intervention, 48

graphing production possibilities, 38–40

interpreting shape of graph, 40

overview, 38

technology, effect of new, 41–42

productive efficiency
  competition, relation to, 46
  defined, 34, 386
  government and markets, role of, 44
  overview, 12
  production possibilities frontier, 40–41
profit-maximizing cartels. *See* cartels
profit-maximizing decisions by firms, 12, 102–103.
    See also firms; microeconomics
profit-maximizing monopolies
  versus competitive firms, 161–164
  deadweight losses, 163–164
  decreasing marginal revenues, 153–157
  efficiency, lack of, 164
  output level, choice of, 152, 158–161
  overview, 152
  price, ability to control, 153–154
  problems caused by, 152–153
  subsidies for, 167
profits
  accounting versus economic, 106–107
  borrowing more in hopes of, 356–357
  economic, 106–107, 144, 146, 188–189, 384
  guiding firm entry and exit, graphing,
      146–150
  as income stream, 261
  of monopolies, 159–161
  monopolies versus competitive firms,
      162–163
  monopolistic competition, 186–190
  in perfect competition, 144–149
  relation to marginal revenues and marginal
      costs, 118
  running a profit, 106
  sharing of, in cartels, 176
  sticky prices problem, 310–311
  total revenues and total costs in, 105
  visualizing, 118–120
property, international transfer of, 273–274
property rights
  environmental problems caused by weak, 373
  externalities overview, 195–196
  in microeconomics, 13

negative externalities, 196–200
  overview, 193–194
  positive externalities, 200–202
  in properly functioning market, 129
  socially optimal output level, 194–195
  Tragedy of the Commons, 202–204
property taxes, justification for, 70
proportions, irrational behavior related to, 31
proposer, in ultimatum game, 253
prospect theory
  anchoring and credit card bills, 246–247
  defined, 386
  endowment effect, 247
  framing effects and advertising, 245–246
  overview, 244
  shrinking packages and loss aversion, 245
  status quo bias, 247–248
protectionism, 367
public goods
  as cause of market failure, 13
  defined, 206, 386
  enlisting philanthropy to provide, 216–217
  government role in providing, 216, 374
  overview, 215–216
  ranking new technology as, 219–220
  selling related private good to provide, 217–218
  taxing to provide, 216
public sector, adverse selection response
    from, 226
purchasing behavior. *See* consumer behavior

Q

quantitative easing (QE), 350–352
quantity demanded. *See also* demand
  defined, 17, 58, 386
  on demand curve, 18–20, 60–62, 97–99
  effect of price on, 96–97
  elements affecting, 59
  inverse relationship with prices, 60
quantity supplied. *See* supply and demand;
    supply curve
quantity theory of money, 281, 376, 378, 386

R

radio, as public good, 217–218

ranking, choosing by, 84–85

rational expectations
  defined, 386
  fiscal policy, relation to, 340
  as limiting monetary policy, 348–350
  overview, 16, 380–381
  stimulus policies, effect on, 334–336

rationality
  defined, 238, 386
  in neoclassical economics, 239

rationing healthcare, 229–231

real estate bubbles. *See* asset-price bubbles

real GDP, during recessions and Great
  Depression, 312–313

real interest rates, 293–294, 386

real prices, 291, 387

real wages, 331–332, 334, 387

recessions. *See also* fiscal policy; Keynesian model;
  monetary policy; stimulus policies
  after financial crises, 353–354
  business cycle, 298–299
  defined, 15, 297, 298, 328, 387
  full-employment output, 299–300
  government intervention, 322–323
  Great Recession, 350–352
  inflation, generating, 328–336
  in macroeconomics, 15–16
  overview, 15–16, 297–298
  post-bubble, overview, 359–360
  post-bubble, recovery from, 360–362
  price adjustments, 300–301
  real GDP during, 312–313
  real wages, 331–332
  responding to economic shocks, 297, 301–309
  sticky prices, 297–298, 309–312

recognition heuristic, 241

recovery
  defined, 298, 387
  from post-bubble recessions, 360–362

redundant competitors, monopolies as
  eliminating, 165–166

regulation
  of free markets, need for, 372
  of monopolies, 167–171
  of oligopolies, 183–184

relative price increase, 288

Remember icon, explained, 3

rent, as income stream, 261

rent control, 77–78

reputation, role in used car market, 210

research
  government funding of, 52
  medical, effect of self-rationing on, 234–235

resources. *See also* property rights
  allocating, 37–41, 45–46
  automatic direction of, in free markets, 44–45
  circular flow for, 259–260, 262–263
  classifying, 35
  competition, relation to use of, 46
  constraints on, in economic choice model, 25
  production possibilities frontier, 38–42
  role in production possibilities, 34, 35, 37
  scarcity of, 10–11, 21, 387

responder, in ultimatum game, 253

retailers, response to recessions, 307

retirement savings, 248

revenues. *See* marginal revenues; total revenue

Ricardo, David, 274–275, 376

rich countries, price controls in, 79

Robinson, Joan, 186, 188, 326

Rockefeller, John D., 184

rolling over the debt, 339

running a loss, 106, 121–125, 160–161

running a profit, 106

S

safety features, marginalism related to, 368

sales price. *See* prices

Samuelson, Paul, 379

Saudi Arabia, capacity to threaten OPEC, 183

savings
  effect of hyperinflation on, 283
  as paying for increased government spending, 338

retirement, effect of status quo bias on, 248

in Singapore healthcare system, 233

scarcity

defined, 387

economics as science of, 10–11, 21

security, collateral as, 355

self-control problems, 250

self-interest

behavioral economic research on, 251–254

in economic choice model, 23–24

as improving society, 371

in neoclassical economics, 251

selfless actions, 23–24

self-rationing, in healthcare, 234–235

self-serving bias, 243

sequence indicates causation fallacy, 366–367

shocks. *See* economic shocks

short run

fixed prices in, 305–307

in microeconomics, 122–123

responses to economic shock in, 301, 307–308

shortages

in low-cost healthcare systems, 230–231

price controls for, 77–78

in stable equilibrium, 73–74

short-run aggregate supply curve (SRAS)

fixed prices in short run, 305–306

full-employment output, 329–330

inflationary expectations, 348–349

long-run and short-run responses to shock, 308–309

negative demand shocks, 327

short-run shutdown condition, 123–124, 387

shrinking package sizes, 245

Singapore, healthcare in, 228, 232–236

Smith, Adam, 12, 24, 132, 193, 251, 375–376

social benefits of free markets. *See also* socially optimal output level

efficiency of free markets, 130–132

overview, 128

total surplus, 132–138

traits of properly functioning market, 129–130

social demand, 201

social marginal cost, 197

socialism, 53–54

socially optimal output level

defined, 387

determining, 131–132

minimum output requirements, 167–168

monopolies as free from pressure of, 152

monopolies versus competitive firms, 163–164

negative externalities, 198

overview, 128

property rights, relation to, 194–195

society, self-interest as improving, 371

Solar City, 250

solar panels, myopic decision-making regarding, 250

Solow, Robert, 379–380

special interests, in government intervention, 48, 49

specialization, in comparative advantage concept, 274–276

SRAS. *See* short-run aggregate supply curve

stable equilibrium, 72–74, 320, 344

stagflation, 350

standard of deferred payment, money as, 283–284, 286

standard of living. *See* living standards

Standard Oil Company, 184

statistical discrimination, 215

status quo

anchoring, 246–247

defined, 387

framing effects, 245–246

in prospect theory, 244

status quo bias, 247–248, 387

steering heuristic, 241

step function, 133

sticky prices. *See also* Keynesian model

defined, 387

overview, 297–298

reasons for, 309–312

role in effect of stimulus policies, 333

stimulus policies
  aggregate demand, increasing, 326–328
  inflation, 285
  limitations of, 328–336, 362
  lowering interest rates, 346–348
  price stickiness, 333–334
  rational expectations, effect on, 333–336, 348–350
  real wages, 331–332
  trying to increase output beyond Y*, 329–330
stocks, assets as, 261
store of value, money as, 286
strategic situation, 175. *See also* cartels; oligopolies
structural mismatches, in recovery process, 360, 361–362
subsidies
  for goods with positive externalities, 201–202
  government intervention through, 48, 49
  for monopolies, 167
  for technologies that can't be patented, 220
substitute goods, 100
sunk costs, irrational behavior related to, 30–31
supply and demand. *See also* aggregate supply; money supply
  cost-benefit analysis based on, 130–132
  defined, 387
  demand, understanding, 58–65
  elasticity, 69–70
  excess supply, 72–73, 79–81
  market equilibrium, 70–76
  in Marshall's research, 377
  in microeconomics, 12
  overview, 57–58
  perfectly elastic supply, 69, 70
  perfectly inelastic supply, 69–70
  price controls, 76–81
  in properly functioning market, 129–130
  supply, understanding, 65–70
  supply curve, graphing, 65–69
  when asset-price bubbles burst, 358
supply curve
  cost changes, 67–69
  cost-benefit analysis based on, 130–132

defined, 387
graphing, 65–69
long-run aggregate, 302–304, 308–309, 327, 329
market, 104
in market equilibrium, 70–76
negative externalities, 196–198
overview, 57
positive externalities, 200–201
price and production cost, 66–67
price changes, 67
in properly functioning market, 129
shifts in, 67–69, 75–76, 140–141
short-run aggregate, 305–306, 308–309, 327, 329–330, 348–349
socially optimal output level, 131–132, 194–195
supply and demand, 12
taxes, effect on, 140–141
supply elasticity, 69–70
surplus. *See also* consumer surplus; total surplus
  budget, 269
  price controls for, 79–81
  producer, 132–133, 136–138, 386
  in stable equilibrium, 72–73
  trade, 272
System 1 decision-making, 242
System 2 decision-making, 242
systematic errors
  brain modularity, 242
  cognitive biases, 242–243
  defined, 238, 387
  offering more options in cases of, 239

T

target level of inventories, 314–315
tastes, role in quantity demanded, 59
taxes
  deadweight losses from, 140–143
  in disposable income calculation, 267
  economic fallacies related to, 370
  government budget, role in, 269
  as government intervention, 48

inflation functioning as, 287

negative externalities, dealing with, 199–200

paying for increased government spending, 337

property, justification for, 70

public goods, providing through, 216

revenues from, as securing government borrowing, 339

TC. *See* average total costs; total costs

Technical Stuff icon, explained, 3

technology

competition as encouraging improvements, 46–47

in economic choice model, 25–26

government support of, 52–53

innovation as propelling economic growth, 379–380

new, as public good, 219–220

new, shifting PPF outward for, 41–42

Third World, effect of price controls on, 79

threats, resolving Prisoner's Dilemma with, 180–183

time constraints, in economic choice model, 26

time inconsistency, 248–250, 387

Tip icon, explained, 3

total consumption, calculating, 318

total costs (TC). *See also* average total costs

defined, 107

long-run shutdown condition, 125

monopoly profits, 159–160

role in profit, 105, 118–120

total revenue (TR)

long-run shutdown condition, 125

monopoly marginal revenues, 153–157

monopoly profits, 159–160

role in profit, 105, 118–120

short-run shutdown condition, 123–124

total surplus

computing, 137, 138

consumer surplus of continuous good, 135–136

consumer surplus of discrete good, 133–134

deadweight losses, 138–143

defined, 387

importance of, 137–138

in Marshall's research, 377

overview, 132–133

producer surplus, 136–137

total utility

diminishing marginal utility, 28

marginal utility, relation to, 86–87

maximizing, when facing limited budget, 91–95

trade, asymmetric information as limiting, 206–207. *See also* international trade

trade balance, 271

trade deficit, 272–273

trade surplus, 272

traditional economy, 50

Tragedy of the Commons, 202–204, 387

trusted third parties, buying information from, 209–210

trusts, 184. *See also* cartels

U

ultimatum game, 252–253, 387

unconventional monetary policy, 351–352

underproduction, 200–202

unemployment. *See also* full-employment output

economic fallacies related to, 365–366

frictional, 299–300

price adjustments in long run, 303

relation to inventory levels, 316

sticky prices problem, 310, 311

uninformed decision-making, 29–30

unintended consequences, 370

unit of account, money as, 286

unit of output, costs per, 108–110

United Kingdom, NHS in, 229–230, 232

United States

Federal Reserve, 346–349, 351–352

foreign property ownership in, 273–274

healthcare in, 227, 228

housing bubble in, 361

medical research in, 235

price controls in, 78–81

upward price stickiness, lack of, 333

used car market, asymmetric information in, 205, 207–211

utility. *See also* consumer behavior; diminishing marginal utility; marginal utility
  cardinal, 85
  defined, 84, 387
  marginal, 27–29
  measuring happiness with, 23
  ordinal, 85
  overview, 12
  total, 28, 86–87, 91–95

V

value, money as store of, 286
variable costs
  average, 110–115
  defined, 107, 387
  role in production decisions, 108
  short-run shutdown condition, 123–124
vehicle history reports, 209–210

W

wages
  defined, 387
  downward stickiness, 333
  foreign, economic fallacies related to, 369–370
  government stimulus policies, relation to, 329–332

  as income stream, 261
  inflation, impact on, 334
  Marxist view of, 376–377
  nominal, 331–332, 386
  real, 331–332, 334, 387
  sticky prices problem, 309–311
  stimulus policies, effect on, 334–336
wait times, when rationing healthcare, 230
Walmart, 307
Wannamaker, John, 246
Warning icon, explained, 4
warranties, in used car market, 210
wealth, defined, 387
wealth inequality, 47, 48
Weimar hyperinflation, Germany, 283, 284
welfare economics, 377
Wendy's, 190

Y

Y*. *See* full-employment output; Keynesian model; recessions

Z

zero economic profits, 144, 146, 188–189
zero-coupon bonds, 344

About the Author

Sean Masaki Flynn, Phd, is an associate professor of economics at Scripps College in Claremont, California.

A recurring commentator on radio and television, Sean holds a BA in economics from the University of Southern California and a PhD in economics from UC Berkeley, where he completed his dissertation under the supervision of Nobel Laureate George Akerlof.

As one of America's leading economic educators, Sean is a coauthor, along with Campbell McConnell and Stanley Brue, of the world's best-selling college economics textbook, *Economics: Principles, Problems, and Policies* (McGraw-Hill). The book's popularity is such that it's also the world's best-selling college textbook on any subject.

Sean's academic research focuses on the often puzzling and seemingly irrational behavior of stock market investors, but he's also investigated topics as wide-ranging as the factors that affect tipping behavior in restaurants and why you see a lot of unionized workers only in certain industries.

His recent focus has been on incorporating proven economic solutions directly into law.

Dedication

To my mother, Lt. Cmdr. Mikiko Flynn, MD, who showed me first-hand just how much is possible for an immigrant if they get to move to a country like ours that embraces education, hard work, and sensible economic policies that lift all boats. I love you, Mom.

Author's Acknowledgments

I'd like to thank the many great economists who managed to get things into my head despite my very thick skull.

Among my teachers, I can't help but thank Caroline Betts, Tim Cason, Richard Ciccetti, Michael DePrano, Richard Easterlin, Robert Kalaba, Timur Kuran, Jeffrey Nugent, and Morton Shapiro for the excellent education I received as an undergraduate at the University of Southern California.

I was equally blessed at UC Berkeley, where I got to complete a doctorate under the tutelage of some true intellectual giants, including George Akerlof, David Card, J. Bradford DeLong, Jan deVries, Barry Eichengreen, Richard Gilbert, Daniel McFadden, Maurey Obstfeld, Matthew Rabin, David Romer, Christina Romer, and Janet Yellen. It was especially fun when Professors McFadden and Akerlof won their respective Nobel Prizes during my last two years at Cal.

However, my fellow economics students often did more than my professors to explain things to me when I wasn't getting them, and they continue to educate me even now. So a very heartfelt thank you to Corinne Alexander, Lorenzo Blanco, Mark Carlson, Carlos Dobkin, Tim Doede, Mike Enriquez, Fabio Ghironi, Petra Geraats, Aaron Green, Galina Hale, Alan Marco, Carolina Marquez, Marcelo Moreira, Petra Moser, Marc Muendler, Stefan Palmqvist, Doug Park, Raj Patel, Steve Puller, Desiree Schaan, Doug Schwalm, Mark Stehr, Sam Thompson, Carla Tully, Jeff Weinstein, and Marta Wosinska.

I've also got to thank my current and former students at Scripps College, Vassar College, and UC Berkeley. Having to answer your many insightful questions made me a much better economist.

A big thank you to my literary agent Linda Roghaar and my old friend Mike Jones for getting me this book deal. They heard *Dummies* and immediately thought of me.

Lindsay Lefevere, Corbin Collins, and the entire production team at Wiley also deserve huge praise. All their edits, suggestions, and formatting have turned out a book that's far better than anything I could have come up with on my own.

I also have to deeply thank Dr. Robert B. Harris, the technical editor of this book. His comments and suggestions have made it far better than it would have been otherwise.

Finally, many thanks to my parents for always making me do my homework.

Publisher's Acknowledgments

Senior Acquisitions Editor: Lindsay Lefevere

Editor: Corbin Collins

Technical Editor: Robert B. Harris, PhD

Production Editor: Magesh Elangovan

Cover Photo: © af_istocker/iStockphoto

Take dummies with you everywhere you go!

Whether you are excited about e-books, want more from the web, must have your mobile apps, or are swept up in social media, dummies makes everything easier.

Find us online!

Leverage the power

Dummies is the global leader in the reference category and one of the most trusted and highly regarded brands in the world. No longer just focused on books, customers now have access to the dummies content they need in the format they want. Together we'll craft a solution that engages your customers, stands out from the competition, and helps you meet your goals.

Advertising & Sponsorships

Connect with an engaged audience on a powerful multimedia site, and position your message alongside expert how-to content. Dummies.com is a one-stop shop for free, online information and know-how curated by a team of experts.

- Targeted ads
- Video
- Email Marketing
- Microsites
- Sweepstakes sponsorship

20 MILLION PAGE VIEWS EVERY SINGLE MONTH

15 MILLION UNIQUE VISITORS PER MONTH

43% OF ALL VISITORS ACCESS THE SITE VIA THEIR MOBILE DEVICES

700,000 NEWSLETTER SUBSCRIPTIONS TO THE INBOXES OF *300,000* UNIQUE INDIVIDUALS EVERY WEEK

# of dummies

Custom Publishing

Reach a global audience in any language by creating a solution that will differentiate you from competitors, amplify your message, and encourage customers to make a buying decision.

- Apps
- Books
- eBooks
- Video
- Audio
- Webinars

Brand Licensing & Content

Leverage the strength of the world's most popular reference brand to reach new audiences and channels of distribution.

For more information, visit dummies.com/biz

Learning Made Easy

ACADEMIC

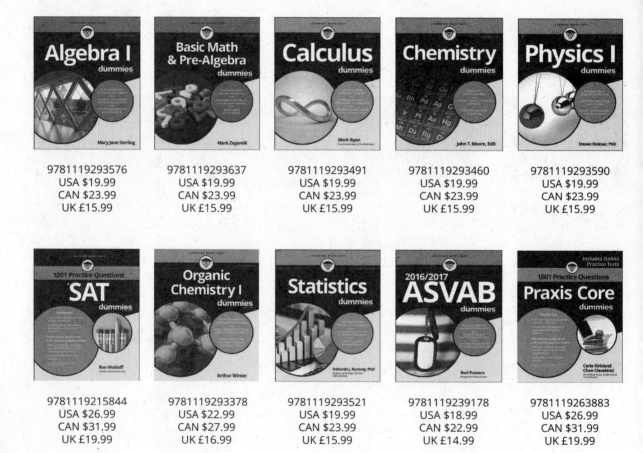

Algebra I dummies
Mary Jane Sterling
9781119293576
USA $19.99
CAN $23.99
UK £15.99

Basic Math & Pre-Algebra dummies
Mark Zegarelli
9781119293637
USA $19.99
CAN $23.99
UK £15.99

Calculus dummies
Mark Ryan
9781119293491
USA $19.99
CAN $23.99
UK £15.99

Chemistry dummies
John T. Moore, EdD
9781119293460
USA $19.99
CAN $23.99
UK £15.99

Physics I dummies
Steven Holzner, PhD
9781119293590
USA $19.99
CAN $23.99
UK £15.99

1,001 Practice Questions SAT dummies
Ron Woldoff
9781119215844
USA $26.99
CAN $31.99
UK £19.99

Organic Chemistry I dummies
Arthur Winter
9781119293378
USA $22.99
CAN $27.99
UK £16.99

Statistics dummies
Deborah J. Rumsey, PhD
9781119293521
USA $19.99
CAN $23.99
UK £15.99

2016/2017 ASVAB dummies
Rod Powers
9781119239178
USA $18.99
CAN $22.99
UK £14.99

1,001 Practice Questions Praxis Core dummies
Carla Kirkland
Chan Cleveland
Includes Online Practice Tests
9781119263883
USA $26.99
CAN $31.99
UK £19.99

Available Everywhere Books Are Sold

dummies.com

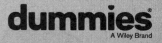

dummies
A Wiley Brand